MESSINES
1917

THE ANZACS IN THE BATTLE OF MESSINES

MESSINES
1917

THE ANZACS IN THE BATTLE OF MESSINES

CRAIG DEAYTON

Pen & Sword
MILITARY
AN IMPRINT OF PEN & SWORD BOOKS LTD.
YORKSHIRE – PHILADELPHIA

First published in Australia in 2017 by Big Sky Publishing Pty Ltd as
At Any Price: The ANZACS in the Battle of Messines 1917

First published in Great Britain in 2018 by
Pen & Sword Military
An imprint of
Pen & Sword Books Ltd
Yorkshire - Philadelphia

ISBN 978 1 52674 014 4

Printed and bound in England
By CPI Group (UK) Ltd, Croydon, CR0 4YY

Pen & Sword Books Ltd incorporates the Imprints of Pen & Sword Books Archaeology, Atlas, Aviation, Battleground, Discovery, Family History, History, Maritime, Military, Naval, Politics, Railways, Select, Transport, True Crime, Fiction, Frontline Books, Leo Cooper, Praetorian Press, Seaforth Publishing, Wharncliffe and White Owl.

For a complete list of Pen & Sword titles please contact

PEN & SWORD BOOKS LIMITED
47 Church Street, Barnsley, South Yorkshire, S70 2AS, England
E-mail: enquiries@pen-and-sword.co.uk
Website: www.pen-and-sword.co.uk

or

PEN AND SWORD BOOKS
1950 Lawrence Rd, Havertown, PA 19083, USA
E-mail: Uspen-and-sword@casematepublishers.com
Website: www.penandswordbooks.com

Contents

List of Maps

GEOGRAPHICAL SYMBOLS

	City area
●	City location
◎	Lake
⎯	Road or track
〰	River
■	Structure
◒	North
	Woods
〰	Railway line
⎯⎯	Canal

MILITARY SYMBOLS

■	British Forces (Second Army)
■	German Forces (Gruppe Wytchaete)
⊠	Infantry
⎐	Headquarters
xxxxx	Army Group
xxxx	Army
xxx	Corps
xx	Division
x	Brigade
III	Regiment
II	Battalion
I	Battery
•••	Detachment
••	Platoon
•	Section
⎯⎯	Boundary
⎯⎯	Reserve line
- - - -	1st stage objective
⎯⎯	1st stage achieved
- - -	2nd stage objective
⎯⎯	2nd stage achieved
▬ ▬	Final objective
▬▬	Front line
⊢⊣	Limit of offensive
··········	Observation line
⇒	Army or Army Group deployment
⟶	Unit deployment
- - -➤	Proposed Unit deployment
⊓⊔⊓⊔	Trench
xxxxxxxx	Wire line
●	Exploded mine
⊗	Unexploded mine
⍐	Machine gun placement

Acknowledgements

If this book adds anything to the historical record of the First World War, it is due in no small way to the wonderful generosity and help of many people and institutions whose contributions have been, in the terminology of the time, 'beyond all praise'. That being true, I will inevitably fall short in adequately thanking first the members of the Australian Army History Unit (AAHU) who supported my first book on the 47th Battalion and also provided further assistance to enable me to complete the research for this book, to visit the many museums and libraries in the United Kingdom, France and Belgium and to complete fieldwork on the battlefield at Messines. The staff of the AAHU have been endlessly helpful and I would like to thank Dr Roger Lee and his team and, in particular, Dr Andrew Richardson for his support, encouragement and advice through the research and writing of this book.

My time in Belgium was hugely profitable thanks largely to Dr Jeroen Huygulier from the Centrum voor Historiche Documentatie vande Belgische Krijgsmacht (Belgian Military Archives). Jeroen not only devoted many days to work as my battlefield guide at Messines, but provided me with copies of his original research and gave me the benefit of his encyclopaedic knowledge of the battle. Having a travel companion who is fluent in six languages also came in very handy when explaining to the Belgian police why my French hire car was not insured. Jeroen's observations and judgements on the battle, together with his extraordinary knowledge of the battlefield were invaluable for this work.

Invaluable also were the helpful people of various institutions in the United Kingdom, at the Imperial War Museum, National Archives at Kew, Liddell-Hart Archive at King's College, National Army Museum, British Library and Bovington Tank Museum who, without exception, went well beyond mere duty to respond to my many and, at times, obscure requests. I need to single out the management of the National Archives for special thanks during my visit for retrieving all of the relevant regimental diaries for the 25th Division for me despite the fact that they had been withdrawn from the borrowing list for digitising. While on that subject, there's no question that the long and difficult work involved in scanning and providing online access to primary sources has been critically important for this book and all the many libraries and museums who are undertaking this work deserve sincere thanks. The National Library of Australia's Trove site is a uniquely valuable resource and in again thanking the hard-working staff of the National Library of Australia, I would urge everyone with an interest in history to be loud in their support for such a far-sighted and valuable project and louder still with petitions to continue the funding that ensures the existence of Trove.

Equally helpful and professional, the staff of the Australian War Memorial (AWM) Research Centre also deserve sincere thanks. Their quiet efficiency in chasing down every request promptly and thoroughly never faltered through my many visits. That support continued long after those visits, and I'd like to again thank the research centre staff for their ever-reliable remote assistance. Likewise, the very accommodating librarians and archivists of the Tasmanian Military Museum and the State Libraries and Archives of Victoria, New South Wales, the Tasmanian Museum and Art Gallery and the people (often volunteers) who manage the many local museums and libraries throughout Australia, Europe and New Zealand that I visited deserve sincere thanks as well.

Professor Peter Stanley's support and advice throughout the writing of this book was also greatly appreciated. I am only one of many researchers who benefit from Peter's willingness to share his time and his expertise as Australia's leading military historian. Thanks to Peter also for passing on the records of Sister Ada Smith on the medical arrangements for Messines. Likewise, I am very grateful to Dr Peter Pederson from the AWM who found time for a long, important and thoroughly interesting discussion on Monash. Despite Peter's assertion that 'no-one under 28 should be allowed to write a biography', his Monash as Military Commander remains by far the best and most authoritative study of Australia's foremost soldier.

It would not be possible to do justice to this story without the efforts of descendants and families who preserved the letters, photos and oral recollections of the men who fought at Messines, the generous researchers who shared their discoveries and the many people who assisted me in countless other ways. Those wonderful people include Judith Anderson, Michael Harman, Carl Johnson, Angus Carver, James Cook, Michael Molkentin, Adrian Howard, Chris Gaskell, Michael Martin from Regimental Books (who issued an appeal for information), Kim Blomfield and the Mather family, Dr Richard Osgood for his generous assistance with details of the investigation and recovery of Private Alan Mather's body, Jacqui Verrall, Richard Henley, Michael Clark, Mark Bainbrigge, Michelle Stolp, Tim Shaw, Judith Andersen, Charles Rowe, Wendy Rowe, Barb Hart, Ron Cody, Nerida Holznagel, Jock O'Keefe, John Wadsley, David Tonna, Mark Latchford, Michael Brereton, Alan Graham, Claude Verhaeghe and Johan Vandervalle. Thanks as well to Les Emery for sharing the letters from Harry O'Toole and Alf Jones of the 40th Battalion AIF and to John Trethewey for passing on the diary of Lieutenant Alan Downie, to Emily Graham for sending me scans of the original diary of Lieutenant George Mitchell, to Captain Nick Bracken for his material on the 43rd Battalion and to Meredith Duncan from the AWM for sharing learned insights on Charles Bean. To those who offered their stories, their help and their memories to this book, but remain, by my omission, unnamed and unthanked, a heartfelt apology.

In the United Kingdom, my sincere thanks to Katie Thompson from the Tank Museum at Bovington for providing a wealth of documents on the tanks at Messines, Philip Mather and the staff at the Fusilier Museum at Bury for searching out and forwarding some very useful material on the 11th Battalion, Lancashire Fusiliers (25th Division), and Andrew Mackay, who wrote the wonderful regimental history of the 11th Fusiliers, for all his help and advice with that battalion's experience at Messines. The research staff at the Cheshire Museum deserve special mention for their help with material on the 13th Battalion, the Cheshire Regiment. I am also very grateful to Richard Pursehouse who generously kept me fully up to date with his team's fascinating archaeological work on the Messines model which was built by the New Zealanders and German prisoners at Cannock Chase. That project opened up a very interesting and unusual window into this story. I am also very grateful to Brian McCleaf who supplied me with a copy of the war diary for the 2nd Battalion, Royal Irish Rifles and to Pamela Langford from the Mercian Regiment Museum for her help with information on the 3rd Battalion, the Worcester Regiment and for sending information from the battalion history and war diary. Thanks must also go to Caroline Mannion from the Cheshire Military Museum for all her help with the three battalions of the Cheshire Regiment which fought with the 25th Division. I'd also like to thank Matt Lund from Cumbria's Museum of Military Life for his very helpful information on the 8th Battalion, the Border Regiment.

Early in the editing process I confided to Catherine McCullagh that any ambition I might have had to take up her profession was dashed by a combination of her outstanding skill as an editor and the tortured, error-ridden prose I sent her to unravel. Cheerfully tolerant of the violence I visited on the English language, wonderfully knowledgeable about the subject, uncannily vigilant about detail and exceptionally gifted as a writer, Catherine's contribution to this book is substantial indeed.

A very big thank-you as well to Denny Neave and his team at Big Sky for all their work on this book. I was very fortunate indeed to have Battle Scarred, my book on the 47th Battalion, produced by Big Sky in 2011 and they have again been a joy to work with.

Five people deserve special mention, and a good deal more than that, having lived with this book's distant and distracted author from start to finish. To Patrick, Dominic, Michael and Annie whose noisy joy and laughter could pull me away from 1917 in an instant, and finally to Tracey, whose love, support and encouragement is indeed beyond all praise and for which I am, and will be forever grateful.

Dedication

On 23 November 1930, Mrs E.J. Clark of Wilcannia wrote to the Army after reading a newspaper report of the discovery of the remains of nine Australian soldiers killed at Pozières 14 years before, only one of whom could be identified. Her son had been reported killed on 7 June 1917.

Dear Sir

I am enclosing a small slip of paper I cut out of the *Broken Hill Barrier Miner* saying that an Australian soldier's body had been found with others. Would you kindly try and find out if my son Pte. Joseph Clark (45 Battalion) was among them? He left Australia in 1916 and was only seven months away when I got a cable to say he was wounded. Later I got another cable to say missing and wounded then later I got a cable to say killed in action.

I could never find out if my little boy's body was ever found. He was not 23 years old. Do please try and find out if his dear body is amongst those found and you will oblige his anxious mother.

Mrs Clark received a reply one week later.

Dear Madam

I have to advise that the remains of your son, the late No. 2876 Private J. Clark, 45th Battalion, are interred in Plot 5, Row "A" Grave 21 of Wytschaete Military Cemetery situated 1 ¾ miles North North-West of Messines, Belgium. Mr. Richard Clark, the deceased's Father, was notified to this effect on 27.4.23.

For all those who died.

For all those who suffered.

Introduction

The enemy must not get Messines Ridge at any price.

The Anzacs of Messines

The ground leapt beneath us again and again … Rockets flared and spread … All the guns opened, stunning comprehension. The greatest artillery fire of all time. Swelling and roaring it climbed up and up to climax beyond incredible climax. Waves of sound beat about us in a madness of vibration, a debauchery of sound. All past standards of measurement were useless.[1]

No battle in history had begun with such spectacular and sudden violence. Lieutenant George Mitchell of the Australian 48th Battalion was one of thousands of witnesses to this stupendous spectacle, very few of whom felt they could do it justice with mere words. At 3.10 am on 7 June 1917, after weeks of relentless shelling and months of preparation in full view of an enemy thoroughly alerted to its imminence, the British Second Army launched its assault on the Messines-Wytschaete Ridge. Almost half a million kilograms of high explosive in 19 giant mines erupted under the forward German lines. One of the few genuine surprises of the war, the mines produced the largest man-made explosion in history, creating an earthquake which shook the surrounding countryside. The British war correspondent Philip Gibbs, watching from Kemmel Hill seven kilometres away, described it as 'a most terribly beautiful thing. The mines spilled lava into fountains of fierce colour, illuminating the countryside with red lights.'[2] Hundreds of Germans died in an instant. While the terrified survivors were bracing themselves against the shaking walls of their dugouts, they were deluged with an artillery bombardment of unprecedented scale from 2226 guns and howitzers along with hundreds of trench mortars firing as fast as they could be loaded. Teams of machine-gunners fired a deadly hail of indirect fire which thrashed the ground as the shells tore it up. This storm of steel and thunder blasted the ground ahead of the British assault troops who rose from their assembly trenches in their thousands along a 14-kilometre front and attacked under its cover. Mitchell and his men watched in awe as the deep crimson glow from the mine explosions grew bright then slowly faded, realising what it meant for their enemy. 'We knew it to be the funeral pyre of complete battalions.'[3]

The Battle of Messines, Charles Wheeler's painting of the 3rd Division commencing its attack at 3.10 am on the morning of 7 June. The mine explosions to the north light up the sky and the shoulder of Messines Ridge with the ruins of the church of St Nicolas silhouetted against the pale glow of dawn (AWM ART03557).

Within two hours the ridge had fallen, its formidable defences overwhelmed by the assault troops of General Herbert Plumer's army. After almost three years of stalemate and bloody failures on the Western Front, the Battle of Messines represented something entirely new, a revolutionary tactical scheme which produced the greatest and swiftest British success of the war. The victory was not due to any lack of resolve by the German command which declared that 'the enemy must not get the Messines Ridge at any price'.[4] The fatal decision to stand and fight magnified the scale of defeat and no price, however high, could buy them victory. The cost of defeat would eventually total some 24,000 German casualties, including over 7000 prisoners. German morale had also been dealt a heavy blow, particularly as the attack was fully expected and its launch date predicted to within a few days. 'Out-planned, out-dug, and out-manoeuvred', the defeat delivered a visceral shock to the German Army, wiping out one of the strongest positions on the Western Front.[5] If Messines could not be defended, no German position was safe.

This is the story of the Anzacs at Messines and their contribution to the first major British victory of the First World War. Principally it is the story of the two Australian divisions of II Anzac Corps, partly because they were the dominating presence in the corps and partly because, for them, the battle raged on long after the opening day when it should have concluded. But this is not solely an

Introduction

Australian story. Though they outnumbered the New Zealanders, Anzac was never exclusively Australian and, in this battle, the name would have an even broader meaning. II Anzac, which included the 3rd and 4th Australian divisions as well as the New Zealanders, also included the British 25th Division. That there were English 'Anzacs' in the battle is an important truth. The British Army that triumphed at Messines was a quintessentially imperial one with English and Irish divisions fighting side by side with the Australians and New Zealanders in a battle launched by the huge mining enterprise in which Canadian and Australian tunnelling companies had assisted. While the Anzacs comprised one third of the attacking force at Messines, in looking at the battle through the lens of II Anzac Corps, this book seeks to place the Australian and New Zealand divisions firmly within their context as part of a larger coalition. This coalition was one that both benefitted and buffeted them, one in which they were both dependent and depended on and, as this narrative will show, one in which the Australians were not 'fully trusted' by any of their partners. At Messines, perhaps more than any other battle in the First World War, the unusual tactical arrangements meant the actions and decisions of each division of II Anzac Corps had a profound impact on the others. Hence, the story of the Anzacs of Messines is, like that of the British Army itself in the First World War, the story of a fraternal and occasionally fractious, but ultimately successful coalition.

The Anzac perspective is important for another reason. For the English and Irish divisions of IX and X Corps attacking in the centre and north of the Second Army's front, the battle, while still very costly, was the closest to a walkover the First World War had produced. For II Anzac Corps however, Messines would be no cheap victory. The Commander-in-Chief, General Sir Douglas Haig, intervened late in the planning to dramatically increase the objectives, changes that would have a profound impact on the Australian divisions. Casualty figures for the Anzacs would be double those of the other two corps in Plumer's army, an aspect which has been largely overlooked in the afterglow of such a resounding victory. The New Zealand Division would suffer needless losses occupying the ridge in unnecessary strength and the 25th Division, kept in the line longest, would suffer similarly. For the Australians, the second phase of the battle, which was supposed to conclude that same afternoon, staggered on for four days and would come perilously close to disaster. Towards its final stages it would begin to resemble the costly battles of the previous summer on the Somme. Given the role of pushing forward from the morning's seizure of the ridge and capturing the final objective, the Australian attack would descend into almost indescribable chaos. Indeed, it is a chaos so impenetrable that it has defied almost all attempts across the years to untangle it. Problems of coordination and communication, particularly with II Anzac's supporting artillery, would produce a crisis on the evening of the battle's first day, one largely unknown to a command group congratulating itself on a great victory.

The presence of an English division in the II Anzac Corps order of battle at Messines reflected the evolution of 'Anzac' itself. In 1915 the Australian and New Zealand Army Corps that landed at Gallipoli was a small, poorly trained force consisting of the 1st and 2nd Australian divisions and the combined Australian and New Zealand Division. By early 1916, thanks to a flood of recruits, there were now two Anzac corps, with the New Zealanders making up a full division and the Australians with four divisions in the field poised to expand to a fifth with the arrival of the 3rd Australian Imperial Force (AIF) Division in France in November of 1916. A sixth AIF division was under formation in England, although that would soon be disbanded to reinforce the existing five. Distinct and individual in 1915, the Australian and New Zealand forces had grown even more so on the Western Front. By the summer of 1917, the New Zealand Division was widely considered one of the finest in the British Army. By contrast, although their bravery was unquestioned (even by their many critics), the Australians were not so admired. Though it must have pained the Australian Official Historian, Charles Bean, to admit it, he conceded that neither the British nor the New Zealanders had much faith in the Australians they would fight alongside at Messines. Pilloried for their poor discipline and leadership, the Australians had, unlike the New Zealanders, suffered a series of defeats and setbacks in 1916 and 1917. In July of 1916, the 5th Division had been virtually destroyed at Fromelles. At Pozières and Mouquet Farm in August and September, the 1st, 2nd and 4th divisions had the misfortune to be thrown into some of the most ill-judged and costly attacks of the drawn-out Battle of the Somme. By the summer of 1917 there were few such disasters among New Zealand's battle honours, but they would come.

That the Australians differed in important ways from the New Zealanders and the English was obvious, but the two Australian divisions at Messines could hardly have been more different. The newly arrived 3rd Division under Major General John Monash was entering its first major battle and fighting alongside the most battle hardened Australian division in the 4th under Major General William Holmes. The 4th not only contained a high proportion of Gallipoli veterans, but had been in France for over a year and had fought in three major battles. They would need all the combat wisdom that such punishing experience had bought them. Remarkably, Holmes' men would enter the battle of Messines just six weeks after the disaster of the First Battle of Bullecourt where they had been sent, in the words of one of their staff officers 'to what was really certain destruction'.[6] Bullecourt was merely the latest in a depressing catalogue of defeats for the AIF in the war thus far. With the catastrophe at Gallipoli in 1915, the unmitigated disaster of Fromelles and the 28,000 casualties it had suffered for paltry results on the Somme in 1916, the wrecking of another entire division at Bullecourt created a crisis of confidence in British leadership in 1917. Fortunately for the Australians, their move to the Second Army for the Messines attack brought them into what would be the most carefully planned major operation of the war. Plumer's army had a strong reputation for staff work thanks to the considerable talents of its Chief of Staff, Major General Charles Harington, who oversaw all the preparations for the battle including the immense engineering and logistic force which had laboured for months under the watchful eyes of the Germans to prepare the attack. Plumer's reputation for caution was also a welcome change for the Australians whose experiences under far less risk-averse British generals had been so ruinous at Fromelles, the Somme and Bullecourt. As well as the massive artillery support for the attack, the British held an ace up their sleeve in the remarkable two-year tunnelling and mining effort for which Messines is perhaps most famous. The story of the mines, how they were placed and defended (and why some are still there) is a fascinating one in itself.[7] Thanks to the prodigious effort of the mining companies (including the 1st Australian Tunnelling Company) and the vision of the eccentric British mining engineer, Lieutenant Colonel John Norton Griffiths, the British achieved a degree of surprise previously regarded as impossible. Although the Germans knew they were being undermined at Messines, they understandably failed to appreciate the fantastic ambition of Norton Griffiths. Luck played its part and, while such an enormous gamble would never again be attempted, its success, though not central to the outcome, was a significant factor.

Equally remarkable is why a battle of such major significance — the first clear British victory of the war — should be so little known today. This may be partly due to the idea, lingering still, that military success was defined by sweeping advances and the seizure of enemy territory. Soon after the battle, the opposing trenches re-formed some three kilometres east of where they had been, the ridge had been won and lost and the fighting returned to the more usual routine of small attacks, artillery exchanges and sniping that characterised daily life on the front line. Seen in isolation and measured by major battles of previous wars, the results seem inconsequential. No major city was captured, the German Army was not put to flight and the Germans remained in possession of most of Belgium. Vital weeks would pass before the British attacked again and, when they did, a combination of rain and poor planning resulted in what Bean described as 'the tragedy of August'.[8] In September the British regained their momentum with a series of successful attacks with limited objectives based on the Messines model, but progress was slow and costly. A.J.P. Taylor in his 1963 history of the First World War devoted one error-riddled paragraph to the battle which concluded: 'Two years of preparation and a million pounds of explosive had advanced the British front at most two miles. How long would it take at this rate to get to Berlin?'[9]

Second Army commander General Herbert Plumer (left) with Generals Edmund Allenby (Third Army) and Henry Horne (First Army) (AWM H08558).

And yet, both sides knew at the time that the importance of Messines was not measured by the yard. As Sir Basil Liddell Hart wrote in 1924, 'The peculiar glory of the Messines attack is that, whereas in 1918 the decline in the German power of resistance brought the conditions to meet the methods almost as much as the methods were developed to meet the conditions, on June 7th, 1917, the methods were perfectly attuned to a resisting power then at its height.'[10] The British *Official History* would hail it as a 'great victory', while the German army group commander responsible believed it 'one of the worst tragedies of the war'.[11]

For both, it represented a major turning point, although like most such moments in war, this was not obvious at the time. Messines, and the battles for the ridges to follow, exposed the fatal vulnerability of the German defensive strategy and did much to shape the ultimately disastrous decisions of the German High Command in the spring of 1918. Although Berlin would not fall through losing one ridge in Flanders, German defeat was a mere 17 months away.

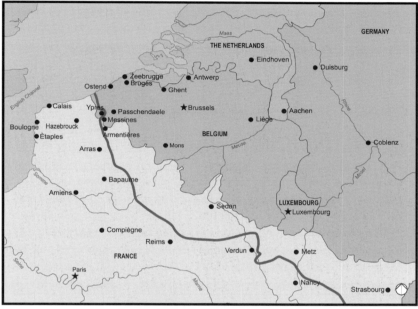

Map 1. The Western Front in northern Europe, May 1917

What was perhaps more alarming for the Germans was the relative ease with which the British were able to sweep aside their defences at a point which should have been impregnable and which they themselves had decided to hold 'at any price'. This was due in no small way to the adoption by the British of the developing philosophy of the all-arms battle, something that would be justifiably termed a revolution in tactics and would shape conventional war to the present day. For the first time in any truly coordinated sense, artillery and armour were present alongside the assaulting infantry, assisted by an air force which (in the first stages of the battle) dominated the skies and performed the vital task of intelligence gathering and even ground attack. Coordination of firepower at Messines using armour, aircraft and indirect fire was designed to deliver infantry to a position they could occupy rather than have to fight for. The adoption of the new platoon formations with specialist roles and weapons was another innovation successfully employed at Messines. The fact that the battle was effectively concluded across most of the front in a day, with the majority of objectives achieved and with the casualty toll, although still heavy, far lower than in previous major battles, was an unprecedented and very welcome outcome for the British. The only failure was in the Anzac sector and that was but temporary. This was a far greater shock than the mine explosions and, more importantly, it drove home the unpleasant truth that the strategy of static defence — in which the Germans had invested heavily — was ultimately and fatally vulnerable. It was this, more than any other factor, which would move the land war towards its climax with inexorable certainty.

Another reason Messines slipped into the background of history is undoubtedly the bloody failure of the Flanders campaign for which the battle was the opening act. Although initially and stunningly successful, Haig's 1917 campaign in Flanders has earned a reputation as one of the most disastrous (if not *the* most disastrous) in British military history. The memory of the battles which followed the victory at Messines and the optimism they provoked, would eventually sink without trace in the dreadful mud of Passchendaele in October. Into that swamp also sank the prospect of victory in 1917 and, along with it, Haig's reputation, something to be argued over ever since. The ponderous and costly Flanders campaign ground on for five months and cost over 300,000 British casualties, petering out a mere eight kilometres from its launching point at Messines, its major objective unachieved and its meagre gains swept away within days by the German spring offensive of 1918. Against such a backdrop of catastrophe, the success at Messines indeed seems worthless. Lloyd George weighed in with his memoirs in 1931 and dismissed the battle with withering sarcasm as 'a useful little preliminary to the real campaign, an *aperitif* provided by General Plumer to stimulate the public appetite for the great carousel of victory to be provided for us by G.H.Q.' Although conceding it was 'a perfect attack in its way', Lloyd George had little interest in doling out praise to the army. His chief object in his narrative of the fighting in 1917 was to distance himself from the bloodshed and pen a jeremiad against Haig and the High Command on whom he heaped scorn, describing the Flanders campaign as an 'insane enterprise'. This was one of his milder criticisms.[12]

However, while the significance of Messines may have been forgotten, its myths are remembered all too well. It is passed over as merely a 'transitional' battle whose success was supposedly unrepeatable due to the novelty of the mines. Herbert Plumer is transformed from a relatively unimportant army commander on the verge of dismissal into a kind of benevolent military mastermind and eventually 'everybody's favourite British General of the First World War', a view which conveniently forgets his role at Passchendaele.[13] Messines is trumpeted as a clear-cut 'clockwork' victory, where the casualty toll for the German defenders was significantly higher than the British, something which ignores both mathematics and the chaotic second phase of the battle. The figure for German deaths due to the mine explosions is routinely put at 10,000 — men who were 'vaporised' by the massive explosions. None of this is true. Nor is Messines' most enduring and harmless myth — that Lloyd George heard the sound of the mine explosions from this '*aperitif*' at his country retreat in Surrey some 130 miles away (or occasionally in his rooms at 10 Downing Street), an impossibility recorded in the newspapers of the time and repeated unchallenged ever since. The truth about Messines, from its spectacular opening to its many moments of drama and crisis, is a great deal more interesting than its myths.

The village of Messines before the war showing the rue d'Eglise with the church of St Nicolas in the background. Badly damaged by the fighting in 1915 and 1916, Messines was almost completely destroyed by the preliminary British bombardment. The village was captured by the New Zealand Division and Lance Corporal Samuel Frickleton of the New Zealand Rifle Brigade would win the first Victoria Cross of the battle at the end of this street (AWM C03120).

In Australia and New Zealand, where the battle should be very well known indeed, the chimeras of the First World War, particularly the inordinate focus on Gallipoli in the Anzac story, have undoubtedly overshadowed the wider history of the war. That the first major victory of the First World War in which the Anzac divisions played a pivotal role should be so little known today is partly due to our enduring fascination with Gallipoli. To even the most casual observer, Bean's observation that 'the influence of the Gallipoli campaign upon the national life of Australia and New Zealand had been far too deep to fade' is obvious indeed, something reflected in the Australian national school curriculum which mandates that all Year 9 students will cover the battle of Gallipoli in depth while no such requirement extends to teaching about the Western Front.[14] That such a concentration is disproportionate to its importance to the war's outcome is equally obvious, but Bean was right in predicting that Gallipoli would come to mean much more than the heroic failure it was. His statement at the end of Volume II that 'Anzac now belonged to the past' however, was far less prescient and, if the proliferation of books, articles and films on Gallipoli is any indication, he might, if anything, have more correctly claimed that the future now belonged to Anzac.[15]

In one sense however, the battle of Gallipoli was very firmly consigned to the past by Messines and the battles which followed. By 1917 the war had changed utterly. The weapons, tactics and systems of command and control bore little similarity to those existing in 1914 and 1915. The vast and complex planning required to mount an infantry attack of 12 divisions, the enormous effort involved in the preparatory work, the arrangements for artillery, tank and air support required hundreds of separate units to communicate and coordinate their efforts. Mundane though it might seem, the 'paper war' as its opponents derisively termed it, was critical to the success of such a giant effort. Likewise, its failures could invite disaster. The voluminous and highly prescriptive orders for the 3rd Division, reaching down to the minutiae of sections, would be scoffed at by the Second Army's Chief of Staff as micro-management, but the stark difference with the 4th Division's staff work is one of the most interesting and important aspects of Messines. While the sparseness of the 4th Division's orders, along with their ambiguities and omissions, can be partly explained by the lack of time available (and their losses at Bullecourt), there is little doubt about their influence on the battle. The fatal mistakes of the Australian 52nd Battalion on the afternoon of 7 June, deftly airbrushed by Bean in the *Official History*, were the direct result of poor staff work. The fact that such failures were not subject to inquiry after the battle merely underlined the problems in the 4th Division, and the contrast with the 3rd Division's methods point to what would arguably be the turning point for Australian effectiveness in the war. Despite the problems however, the victory at Messines was a much longed for and very important one.

Introduction

It was particularly important for the Australian divisions to experience success and put an end to their procession of disasters on the Western Front. For the New Zealanders, it was their greatest achievement of the war to that point.

Any new work on the First World War has a responsibility to contribute something new and the story of II Anzac Corps in this battle presents such an opportunity. Nowhere else on the Second Army's front would the brilliantly successful elements of the battle be so sharply juxtaposed with its worrying failures. Although Messines is a famous early example of the tactical scheme which would bring victory in 1918, II Anzac's experience in the battle also sounded a series of warnings for the British Army which were tragically overlooked in the aftermath of so complete a victory. Four months later, the failure to fully absorb the lessons of such a rapidly evolving tactical landscape would partially contribute to catastrophe at Passchendaele. Another reason that new perspectives on Messines are possible is the astonishing richness and unprecedented availability of its records thanks to the efforts of libraries and archives across the world to digitise their records and make them available online. Hundreds of eyewitness accounts of the battle, particularly its spectacular opening, survive in letters and diaries. The papers of senior commanders such as Monash of the 3rd Australian Division and II Anzac's commander, Lieutenant General Alexander Godley, add a vivid dimension to the narrative of command. An army is the military equivalent of a medium-sized city and the administrative paperwork for this battle, so complex in conception and lengthy in preparation, is enormous. Much of this relates to the unspectacular areas of logistics, communication and transport, but these contributed overwhelmingly to its success. II Anzac Corps itself produced a library-sized collection, including the detailed action reports from its composite units. While the focus of this work is largely on the Australian divisions, it draws heavily on the English and New Zealand records to explain the many complexities of the Anzac story of Messines and provides a fascinating glimpse into how these units fought together.

That we know more about the Australian story of Messines than we do of almost any other aspect of the battle is due in large part to the work of Charles Bean and the uniquely detailed *Official History* he would author. Neither the New Zealand nor British official histories would approach the quality and depth of the Australian history and, although he focussed on the Australian divisions, Bean included a wealth of additional detail from the German histories, a comprehensive narrative of the mining efforts at Hill 60 as an appendix to Volume IV and a thorough analysis of the strategic build-up to the battle as well as a summary of its outcomes and an appreciation of its importance. History's debt to Bean doesn't end there. As a witness to the battle, his notebooks, which include not only his own observations at the time but also those of key actors, are among the most important of primary sources. In the years following the war, he corresponded with hundreds of officers and enlisted men concerning key details, often astonishingly minor points which, although at times contradictory or confused, helped to build the most complete picture of the battle possible. We owe much to Bean also for the clarity and completeness of the Australian records of the battle (and the war) and his foresight in collecting and preserving the records of Allied units. The trove of detail in private correspondence that he amassed, far more than he could ever use, was preserved for future researchers. He sent his draft chapters to the British Official Historian, Sir James Edmonds, for comment and further inquiry and the unguarded comments of both historians provide fascinating insights. Such a wide-ranging and determined search was bound to unearth some treasure and he found it in the memoirs of a humble private from the 4th Division who left the most complete, lengthy and startlingly honest account of any participant in the battle. To Bean's credit, he did not hesitate to use Private Denver Gallwey's lengthy narrative alongside the records of generals to construct his history although, as will become evident, some of it was far too troubling to reveal. The result of all those endeavours is a master class for would-be historians, and his chapters on the 3rd and 4th Australian divisions' attack at Messines are among his finest.

But they are also among his most problematic. Both of his major conclusions about the battle are highly contestable. Likewise, just why the Australian attack on 7 June fell apart so completely when across the rest of the Second Army front it was described as 'unstained by any form of failure' is a question the *Official History* only partially answers.[16] Perhaps most important, his analysis of command, where it does occur, is largely uncritical (with one famous exception), a conclusion the uncomfortable facts about the Australian attack make difficult to justify. That Bean faced many challenges in writing the true and complete story of the battle is beyond doubt. He was certainly conflicted by his often well-justified admiration for some Australian officers and nowhere is this more apparent than at Messines. He had to cope with a British Official Historian reluctant to the point of dishonesty to admit British failings in the battle. He had to confront direct evidence of the brutality of Australian soldiers in the killing of surrendering Germans. All of this had to be dealt with at a time when most of the main actors were still alive and in the sober, measured and truthful history he had committed to write. In Bean's defence, it would be manifestly unjust to condemn him for a largely uncritical account of a dearly won victory

Introduction

in which Australians had played a crucial role and where it was also impossible (and remains so) to tell the whole story in any case. However, much of interest and importance was either left unsaid or was hidden between the lines in his work. The failures and mistakes of the 4th Division's attack, the searing criticism of the Australians by the British, the terrible sacrifice of the 45th Battalion in hopeless attacks in the Blauwepoortbeek Valley, the fatal blunders of the artillery in the second phase and Godley's ineptitude in dealing with the battle's many confusing twists and turns would all receive scant attention in the *Official History*. Discovering just how and why those problems arose and their sleeping influence on later battles is one of the aims of this book. It is a fascinating story, but it is also much more than that.

The Western Front is Australia and New Zealand's largest war cemetery. In the peaceful fields and quiet villages of France and Flanders lie over 60,000 men from both countries who paid with their lives to end what was then the world's most bitter and bloodiest war. Others paid dearly as well. Over 300,000 returned wounded, many forever traumatised. Thousands of bereaved lived out their lives in sorrow, their only comfort a photograph of a faraway grave and for some, not even that. The legacy of tragedy and loss is with us still in the silence of family attics and the faded sepia portraits of proud young men in uniform who never returned. The price of ending the war was heavy indeed. But it was ended through victory and defeat, by battles in which the Anzacs played an important and sometimes central role. As we move beyond the centenary of the First World War, it is now more important than ever that we revisit and consider anew the battles of the Western Front, and equally important that we understand their full significance in Australian, New Zealand and world history. The story of many of the great battles of 1918, the defence of Amiens, the offensives of August, the breaking of the Hindenburg Line, among others, are still to be critically re-examined in the modern era, as is the first real victory of the Great War in which the Australians and New Zealanders in a British army played a pivotal role — Messines.

1

... one great and striking success ...
will have far-reaching results.

The Flanders Plan

1

... one great and striking success ...
will have far-reaching results.

The Flanders Plan

Captain Oliver Woodward of the 1st Australian Tunnelling Company spent the night before the Battle of Messines with 'nerves stretched to the breaking point', checking and re-checking the cables and circuits connecting the mines at Hill 60 to the firing switches.[1] Similar preparations were under way across the battle front at the 18 other workings in what was the First World War's most ambitious and remarkable feat of engineering. Woodward was one of the few below the very senior levels of command aware of both the existence of the mines and the timing of the attack. Beneath Hill 60, and the nearby high point known as the Caterpillar, among the most hotly contested positions on the Western Front, the 3rd Canadian Tunnelling Company had placed 55,000 kilograms of high explosive in two giant mines. The Australians, having taken over from the Canadians in November of 1916, were responsible for ensuring that all the work and sacrifice invested in constructing and defending the mines would not be in vain. Woodward was right to be nervous. The mines, along with their detonators and the network of electrical cables to fire them, had been in place 30 metres below the damp Flanders clay for almost a year.[2] The thought that some minor fault in the equipment, a break in a cable, or circuit failure would, at the eleventh hour, undo all the effort that had been invested, drove his relentless cycle of checks. 'I approached the final testing' wrote Woodward, 'with a feeling of intense excitement.'[3]

For two years an unseen but immensely important battle had been fought underground at Messines as the British undermined the ridge and the Germans counter-mined to block them.[4] It was a battle very few knew about and fewer still could face. By June 1917 the ground under Hill 60 was honeycombed with tunnels dug by both sides, the Germans searching for the galleries which led to the mines and the Australians digging to divert, deceive and block them. The suffocating darkness of the deep tunnels was the province of the brave. 'Generally men are not afraid of death, but only of the manner of dying' wrote Bernard Newman, companion writer to Captain Walter Grieve in his 1936 book on the tunnellers of the First World War. 'No one envied the Tunneller his comparative security from enemy bombardment, deep in his burrow, usually far out in front of our front line. Everyone could easily visualise the special terrors which awaited him at every second of his duty – the collapse of a gallery, due to the wrath of Nature or enemy, and the subsequent waiting for death in its most horrible form, gasping for air until death came as a relief.'[5] The tunnellers of Messines, most of them miners in civilian life, were fully aware of the dangers they faced, but those 'special terrors' did little to slow the incessant digging. Messines and Wytschaete today sit above an underground network of shafts, dugouts and tunnels so extensive that the ground above is still unstable in places. At the widest point of no man's land, the tunnel entrances were over 600 metres from their mine chambers and, because the miners needed to penetrate the deep layer of water-bearing 'Kemmel' sands, a soggy glutinous soil which could not support tunnels, they were up to 40 metres deep. The deep vertical shafts through the Kemmel sands were created by 'tubbing', successively adding cylindrical segments of steel which bolted together creating a solid and watertight vertical shaft down to the layer of blue clay which was ideal for tunnelling. At Hill 60, the vertical shaft was 28 metres deep before it hit the clay layer and the two branches were eventually driven under the German lines. 'Clay-kickers', lying on wooden supports, used their feet to drive spades into the clay, the spoil bagged by an assistant and wheeled out along rails on small trolleys. The distinctive blue clay from the lower strata was then carefully hidden from airborne German cameras to disguise the fact that the British had driven shafts so deep below the surface. The tunnel was progressively boarded as the kickers drove forward at an impressive rate of up to eight metres a day. Although men could stand upright in the entrance galleries and ante-chambers, the narrow tunnels which ran for hundreds of metres to the working face were just over a metre high by half a metre wide. The claustrophobic narrowness was important for economy, but also because the tunnel had to be 'tamped' (sealed) for much of its length to concentrate the explosive force upward instead of back along the tunnel. With the two giant mines at Hill 60 and the Caterpillar placed and tamped in July and October 1916, the Australians defended them by creating 'dummy' tunnels, drawing the German miners away from the actual mine chambers by digging shallower works. Such back-breaking labour in the narrow, deep confines with the danger of death by carbon monoxide poisoning, a sudden crushing enemy explosion, slow suffocation or being trapped by a tunnel collapse required a nerve few possessed.

Dead beat, the tunnel, Hill 60, Will Dyson's drawing of an exhausted Australian soldier sleeping in the tunnel at Hill 60. The sketch poignantly captures the impact of the difficult and dangerous work of the tunnellers. Dyson set out to show the true impact of the fighting, at one point noting, 'I never drew a single line except to show war as the filthy business that it was.' (AWM ART 02210).

After two and a half years of digging, the British had successfully placed 25 mines under the ridge and zero hour was fixed for 3.10 am on 7 June.[6] Most of the works had been silent for months. The lack of activity led the Germans to the mistaken conclusion that the British had abandoned most of their tunnels, and active counter-mining threatened few of the established mines. At Hill 60 however, fierce mining and counter-mining continued until the eve of detonation. Several times the Germans came close to breaking into the main galleries and, as the final hours approached, the galleries at Hill 60 were still guarded by listeners. As they maintained their lonely vigils on the night of 6 June, the men of IX, X and II Anzac Corps left their barracks and staging areas to begin their long, circuitous and intricately planned marches to arrive ready for the launch of the attack. Crawling towards the front lines in the dark at six kilometres per hour were 72 tanks which would support the infantry attack. Since coordination with the infantry was vital for the attack, the timetables and routes for the tanks were also carefully prepared to position them just in time for the assault. In the skies above the ridge, scores of British aircraft circled, occasionally diving to strafe the German trenches and masking the noise of the tanks. Nothing on this scale and with such grand ambition had been attempted by the British so far. At a press conference that night Harington would famously quip, 'Gentlemen, I don't know whether we are going to make history tomorrow, but at any rate we shall change geography.'[7] By 2.00 am most of the nine divisions of assault troops were in their assembly trenches and the gunners stood silent and ready beside the huge dumps of shells waiting for the orders to unleash the heaviest bombardment of the war. In his memoirs, Oliver Woodward described the agonising anxiety of waiting as Brigadier John Lambert of the British 23rd Division, whose men were to capture Hill 60, stood beside him in the firing dugout, watch in hand, ready to count down the minutes to firing. As Lambert began the countdown from 10 seconds, Woodward grasped the handle of the firing switch.[8]

• • •

The chain of events that laid Woodward's hand at the ready can be traced back to 1914 and the bloody deadlock which descended on the Western Front when the invading German divisions slowed and stalled in Flanders. Fighting around the medieval market city of Ypres began in October 1914 when the British commander, General Sir John French, fell back on the city, determined to hold his line with the small British Expeditionary Force of seven divisions. For centuries the Flemish who farmed the land around Ypres have known it as *Heuvelland* (Ridgeland) for the modest heights that gently undulate across the otherwise pancake-flat farmlands of Flanders. The low ridges radiating out from Ypres formed natural defensive lines and, with the French under General Ferdinand Foch defending the southern flank, the defenders of Ypres held back German attacks throughout October. The opposing lines began to take the shape which would become so familiar to the British defenders over the next three years, bulging out around Ypres with the city at the centre of a dangerous salient, an intrusion into the enemy lines. The southern quadrant of the salient was dominated by the Messines-Wytschaete Ridge which rises to just over 65 metres above the surrounding countryside commanding a view which sweeps to the far horizon.[9] Woodward wrote that:

> On leaving Ypres by the Lille Gate there is seen about two miles distant a low range of hills, the highest point of which is slightly over 100 feet above the level of the city. This ridge forms the northern section of what is known as 'The Messines Ridge'. Virtually due east of Lille Gate, the Ypres-Menin railway runs through this ridge just to the north of the cutting here is the highest point 'Hill 60'.[10]

On 31 October, German cavalry captured Messines and the heights to the south of Ypres and, two weeks later, French's battered divisions held back an offensive aimed at capturing Hooge, just four kilometres to the north of the city. The fighting continued until 22 November when winter closed down the battle. The wreckage of the Schlieffen Plan had left the Germans in command of the ridges ringing the Ypres salient and both sides planning offensives for the spring. South of the city, the Germans began to dig in on their high tide mark on the Messines-Wytschaete Ridge. The villages on the crest of the ridge were slowly pulverised by regular shelling, the houses and public buildings systematically destroyed. Driven below the surface, the Germans began to fortify the villages. Cellars were strengthened and converted to dugouts, farms were turned to concrete fortresses and everywhere the crenelated trench lines meandered across the contours of the ridge. Linked by communication and supply trenches, they formed what became effectively a subterranean street network. The Church of St Nicolas in Messines, with its foundation stone laid in 1057 by Countess Adela of

France, mother of an English queen, was gradually reduced to rubble. Her crypt now served as a German first aid and command post.[11] Messines' grandest and largest building was the Institute Royale de Messines, a school and orphanage for the daughters of Belgium's war dead. In one of the Great War's many cruel ironies, the orphans of Messines were put to flight by the invaders of 1914 and the Institute Royale, along with the sanctuary and comfort it offered to some of the most defenceless victims of war, was eventually obliterated by the fighting.

The Ypres salient would acquire an odious reputation in the First World War. The crescent of German lines around Ypres allowed the German artillery to target the British positions from three sides and nowhere within the salient was safe. For the Germans, their occupation of the Messines Ridge also produced a salient, although they held the high ground and, unlike the British, were not so easily observed and targeted. However, such broad intrusions into the enemy's territory were obvious targets for attack at the curves' extremities which could 'pinch off' the salient, surrounding and trapping an enemy in the line's forward positions. Even to an untrained eye glancing at a map of the ridge, the key points for any British attack on the Messines-Wytschaete Ridge are so obviously the positions between Hill 60 in the north and St Yves in the south that no-one on either side was unaware of their importance. Thanks to the deadly equilibrium of the salient, and the spoil from the railway cutting that raised it slightly above the surrounding heights, the unimpressive Hill 60 became one of the most important positions on the Western Front and, by 1917, it had changed hands several times since the outbreak of war.

Plumer's plan to attack the ridge and wipe out the threat to his southern flank was patiently developed over 1915 and 1916. While the British intention to capture the ridge was certainly no secret, the hugely ambitious mining program which began in 1915 certainly was. Although the mining at Hill 60 and other highly prized positions was a constant threat, at no stage did the Germans fully appreciate the massive scale of the mining effort nor the very real threat that it posed to their positions. Nevertheless, an attack on the Messines-Wytschaete Ridge in 1916, although it would have been an important tactical victory and removed a major threat to the Ypres salient, would still have been only of local importance. By May of 1917 however, a shift in the Allied grand strategy would bring an entirely different and far more significant purpose to the capture of Messines Ridge as the first important step towards a war-winning offensive.

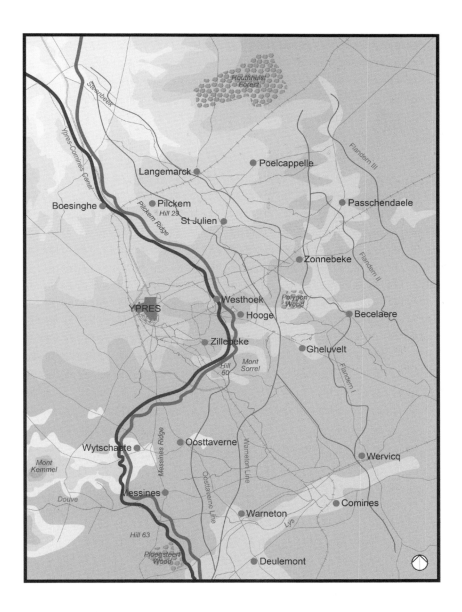

Map 2. The Ypres salient. The German offensive of 1914 stalled in Flanders and their armies occupied the ridge tops ringing the Belgian city of Ypres. The resulting salient with Ypres at the centre could be fired on from three directions and was a costly and dangerous position for the British to hold.

• • •

As the winter of 1916–17 closed in, fighting on the Western Front wound down. Major offensive operations were impossible during winter and this one would prove exceptionally severe. The opposing armies were occupied with the mundane but crucial business of preparing their winter quarters, strengthening defences and supply. All the while, shelling, sniping and raiding as well as illness produced the 'wastage' that so concerned the commanders of both sides. The winter itself took men from the firing line through trench foot, hypothermia and influenza, and an army confined to trenches in the winter of northern Europe, as both sides knew, was an army slowly yet surely wasting away. With the stalemate on the Western Front showing no signs of breaking, the Allies met at Chantilly in November of 1916 to plan for the coming campaigning season. They quickly agreed on a strategy of exerting maximum pressure on the Central Powers through coordinated offensives which would involve major attacks by the French and British north and south of the Somme, coordinated with offensives by the Russians, Italians and the minor powers on their own fronts. Such cascading hammer blows would, it was believed, rob the Central Powers of any opportunity to shift reserves to counter each individually. The advantages of an offensive strategy lay also in seizing the initiative, keeping the enemy off balance and forestalling any assault on their own lines. It was also a strategy which played to the Allies' strength, for 1917 was judged to be the year in which the power balance in guns and men would be at its optimum in their favour. The awful casualties of Verdun and the Somme were weighed against what were believed to be even greater German losses and the mathematics of attrition promised to force a result even if the enemy's lines remained unbroken.

The plan for 1917 which emerged from the conference committed Haig's First, Third, Fourth and Fifth armies to attack again on the Somme in February, in conjunction with four French armies, the whole attack on a front of 62 miles stretching from Vimy Ridge, north of Arras, south to the River Oise. Following that, Haig would attack in Flanders, pushing the enemy from the Belgian coast and liberating the Channel ports of Ostend and Zeebrugge. This latter ambition was Haig's chief urging at the Chantilly conference. It was 'the expressed desire of the British Admiralty and War Committee, and to which [Haig], as trustee of Great Britain's interests, attached great importance.'[12] In its broad thrust, the Chantilly plan was a doubling down on the attrition strategy of 1916. No alternative plan was offered, much to the frustration of British Prime Minister

David Lloyd George who, contemplating the disasters of 1916, feared more of the same. Attack was not only the default strategy of the British High Command; no other course of action was remotely politically acceptable to the French. Lloyd George, doubting both the judgement and competence of Haig and his command group, searched for and suggested alternatives in vain. Boxed in to a strategy he loathed and distrusted, Lloyd George seized on a rare French success for a way out.

General Robert Nivelle was elevated to Commander-in-Chief of the French armies on the Western Front following his successes at the head of the Second Army at Verdun. The apparent fresh genius of his methods, epitomised in his catchcry of 'No more Sommes', captured the enthusiasm of both political and military leaders — with the exception of a sceptical British General Headquarters (GHQ) — who believed that, in him was to be found the alternative to the ponderous and costly failures of 1916. Nivelle proposed a massive surprise attack in the spring of 1917 using over a million men in a large-scale encore of his victories at Verdun to shatter the German lines in the Chemin des Dames. The plan required the British to come under French command, take over some 22 kilometres of the line and attack in the north to draw in German reserves. Nivelle promised to win within 24 hours (48 at the outside) or close his offensive down. In effect, Nivelle guaranteed 'no more Sommes' by deluding himself (and the French government) that his strategy was certain to deliver success and, in the unlikely event of a reverse, promising to withdraw from the battle rather than throw good after bad by investing in a lost cause. Of course, if gamblers were really able to keep their promises to walk away, there would be no casinos.

Nivelle's plan backfired spectacularly. The French ran into a German Army fully prepared and well aware of Allied intentions. Forty-eight hours later, Nivelle was no closer to putting the German Army to flight and winning and he continued hammering away until his army's death ride finally ground to a halt on 9 May with the loss of 187,000 men and the French Army seriously damaged physically and psychologically. Having backed a loser, Lloyd George now found himself manacled to GHQ's plan in Flanders. Adding to the grim outlook for the Allies, the March revolution in Russia threatened the Eastern Front. Despite assurances from the provisional Russian government on April 9, Haig seriously doubted that the Russians would be able to fulfil their commitment to the Chantilly agreement. Russia was not alone in its domestic troubles which, in October of 1917, would ultimately prove fatal.

Each of the Allied powers had its own vulnerabilities and, for the British, it was the Channel ports and the sanctuary they provided to the marauding, and increasingly successful German submarine fleet. Admiral Jellicoe's memorandum of October of 1916 to the First Lord of the Admiralty (and former Prime Minister) Arthur Balfour made the dramatic claim that the submarine menace 'may by the early summer of 1917 have such a serious effect upon the import of food and other necessaries into the allied countries as to force us into accepting peace terms. Such a situation would', he added with truly English understatement, 'fall far short of our desires.'[13] Discussed at the War Committee meeting at the end of October, Jellicoe's alarming estimation had the effect of bolstering the Navy's long-held desire for the British Army to capture the Channel ports (thereby denying them to the German submarines) as well as providing the compelling case for an offensive in Flanders, plans for which had been drawn up in 1916. If England could be starved out of the war by the summer of 1917, the land operations planned at Chantilly would be pointless.[14] Following its meeting on 21 November, the Committee was moved to write that 'there is no operation of war to which the War Committee would attach greater importance than the successful occupation, or at least the deprivation to the enemy, of Ostend and especially Zeebrugge.'[15] By April of 1917, with the Somme fighting at its height and Nivelle's catastrophe about to unfold, Sir William Robertson wrote to Haig warning that '[T]he situation at sea is very bad indeed. It has never been so bad as at present.'[16] Meeting this crisis in the way favoured by the Navy however, had its obvious difficulties. As the submarine bases were well behind German lines, a hitherto unprecedented advance by Haig's armies would be necessary to capture them.

It would have surprised the miners at Messines, toiling away underground for months, that their ultimate objective was to defeat the enemy's submarines. Finding and sinking them at sea was very much a hit and miss affair which, for the British Navy, was very much the latter. To capture the bases on the Channel coast however, required a land advance of over 24 kilometres. As the opposing lines had swayed back and forth by a mere handful of kilometres over a period of two years, this presented a monumental challenge. The new Flanders Plan also proposed the landing of a seaborne invasion force on the Belgian coast as a subsidiary operation, a scaled-down version of a far more ambitious earlier proposal by Winston Churchill for a full-scale combined assault by the British Army and the Royal Navy to sweep the Germans from the coast. Admiral Sir Reginald Bacon, who had specific responsibility for denying the Channel to U-boats, produced a paper for GHQ outlining the pros and cons of the amphibious landing. He proposed the use of monitors to batter the shore defences, a smokescreen to hide the surface vessels, and landing ships and tanks to deal with shore entrenchments and machine-guns. Testing with tanks proved they were capable of driving over the shore defences then in place, although tank tactics were still in their infancy.

The Flanders Plan

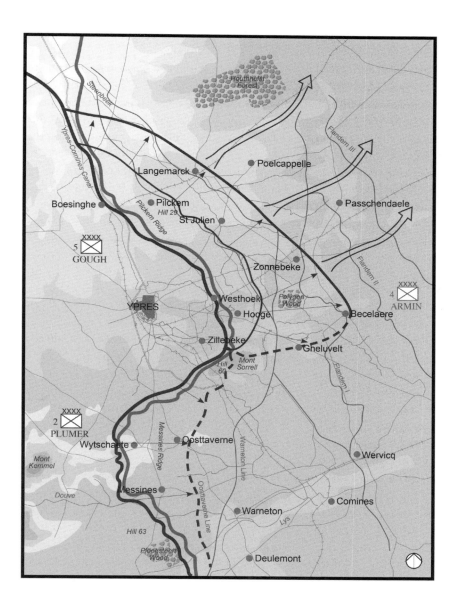

Map 3. The Flanders Plan. Haig needed to capture the Messines-Wytschaete Ridge to secure his right flank for the drive north-east towards the Channel ports of Ostend and Zeebrugge.

Bacon's confidence was undiminished by the risks, although he conceded that 'nothing in war is a certainty'.[17] The Admiral believed (in a reprisal of the Dardanelles strategy) that the loss of some or even all of the monitors to shore batteries was worth the gamble given the prize on offer.[18] 'We must expect losses' he wrote, 'but we have a big object in view ... there is a good prima facie reason to suppose not only that it will be successful, but that it may be a very great success.'[19] Bacon posed a number of questions in his plan, the first and most important of which was 'Is the scheme impracticable?' which he immediately batted away. 'There is no inherent impracticability in the scheme, no flaw which condemns it and no gambling on the enemy doing the wrong thing at a critical moment.'[20] Fortunately for the British, Bacon's plan, fraught with risk and riddled with improbabilities, was never tested. Before it could be seriously considered however, Haig's even more ambitious and challenging assault from the salient would need to succeed.

Barbed wire was deployed in thick belts in front of trenches as a barrier to infantry assaults and had to be heavily shelled to create paths for the attacking infantry. Artillery in 1914–16 was only partially successful in cutting wire. The invention of the 106 fuze in late 1916, an instantaneous percussion fuze which exploded the shell on contact, was a revolutionary advance in wire cutting (Wikipedia Commons Barbed Wire).

Haig was grappling with the unpalatable truth, as was every First World War general, that a war of manoeuvre, breakthrough and encirclement was, for now at least, an impossibility. The failure of the Nivelle offensive ended all hope of rapid and sweeping advances that year. The tactical orthodoxy of piercing the enemy's line, flanking and encircling his disorganised forces and pursuing the fleeing remnants with cavalry was consigned to the Edwardian past by the advent of automatic weapons, successive lines of defence, and even by the simple massing of wire in front of trenches. The chaotic battles of 1915 had proven that artillery would be the decisive weapon, but even a seismic shift in the science of gunnery and a dramatic increase in gun and shell production had not brought the hoped-for breakthroughs on the Somme in 1916. Even where tactical genius, surprise and local superiority in guns and men delivered successes, such as at Vimy Ridge, the attempt to exploit it often descended into overreach and, at times, disaster. As soon as infantry outran the protection of the guns, the advantage swung decisively back to the defender. The German response, to launch counter-attacks against exhausted assault divisions, often threw back attacking forces with heavy losses and regained lost ground. Moreover, the problems of supplying a truly mobile offensive would not be solved until the Germans almost managed it in their offensive of March and April of 1918. 'All were agreed', wrote Bean in the wake of Nivelle's failure, 'that grandiose enterprises aimed at "immediately breaking through the enemy's front and ... at distant objectives" were now out of the question.'[21]

The only tactical scheme which offered any hope of success against the German defensive strategy would become known as 'bite and hold', a process succinctly described by Bean as consisting 'of minutely-prepared offensives with limited objectives ... Accordingly, advances were now to be limited to the ground that could be enclosed within an overwhelming artillery-barrage.'[22] The logic of artillery superiority transformed the battle into something close to mathematical certainty. If sufficient guns could be massed to batter down the enemy's trenches, kill and demoralise their occupants, suppress his own guns and provide protective creeping barrages for the attacking infantry, then the Germans could be methodically pushed back. By continuing to oust the Germans from one prepared defensive position after another, prising his fingers one by one from his grip on France and Belgium, victory (albeit local) would surely follow. '[W]ith the artillery now available to the Allies', Bean continued,

> successes of that sort should be attainable almost whenever desired. If economy of life was carefully planned for, these attacks should furnish what those on the Somme had never furnished - a practical method of

wearing-down the enemy. No opponent could indefinitely endure shocks like that of the first Arras-Vimy attack. If they could be repeated often and quickly, the enemy's power of resistance must become more and more exhausted and more extensive thrusts might then become possible.[23]

Defence in depth. These two ruined pillboxes were part of the strong German third line behind Fromelles which the 5th Division failed to reach in that battle on 19 July 1916. They were not captured until 1918 (AWM E04034).

The coming summer campaigning season would indeed bear this out, but as events in the latter stages of Haig's offensive from Ypres would show, all hinged on the two 'ifs' in Bean's paragraph. A slight shift in the balance of advantage, shortcomings in planning and supply or adverse weather conditions could undo such tactics with disastrous consequences.

The Third Battle of Ypres, as the British offensive in Flanders would come to be known was, despite its ultimate failure, based on these sound strategic foundations. Flanders was one of the few places where such methods promised decisive results. For most of the Western Front, the only concern raised by the loss of a few miles of territory, as Bean pointed out, was a moral one:

But northeast of Ypres a British advance of twelve or fifteen miles would so endanger the German garrisons on the Belgian coast that the enemy must either withdraw them or run the grave risk of seeing them cut off; and it was certain that the German leaders would not willingly give up the enormous moral and physical advantages of close access to the English Channel ... They must hold the Ypres front at all costs.[24]

Haig believed that, with the enemy compelled to stand and fight, the tactics of the successive hammer blows in Flanders 'would render the position of the Germans precarious even if their power of resistance had not then been broken down.' Moreover, what was effectively inching forward in its initial phases might well translate into a breakthrough if the demoralisation that Haig believed was near were to set in. It was the critical meeting of 4 May in Paris where Lloyd George and the British High Command met with the French Premier and Minister for War along with the chiefs of the British Army and Royal Navy, that launched the British offensive in Flanders and the Battle of Messines that opened it. In the shadows cast by the Nivelle disaster, the main objective of the British representatives was to ensure the French remained in the fight with all the vigour agreed to at Chantilly. There was obvious self-interest in their actions given that one of the main objectives of the Flanders Plan was to defeat the submarine menace. Happily for the British, self-interest aligned with previously agreed policy and they succeeded in securing the French commitment to large-scale attacks in support. Lloyd George gave his cautious support to the Flanders Plan on the proviso that the French did their utmost to support the offensive in accordance with the Chantilly strategy of concerted action.

• • •

Messines then would be the first of these hammer blows, as no thrust to the north-east would be safe from enfilading artillery unless the ridge was in British hands. Bean described the salient as resembling a sickle with the blade sweeping around Ypres and the handle formed by the Messines-Wytschaete Ridge. 'No British commander could attempt to capture the blade of the sickle leaving the Germans in possession of the handle (Messines-Wytschaete) behind his southern flank.'[25] With that flank secure, Haig could begin his drive over the ridge tops of Flanders and across the plains beyond. Although blizzards had blanketed the Western Front with snow in mid-April, Haig was eager to use every day of the spring and summer to push the Germans back. There was little time to spare.

The man entrusted with command of the Second Army's attack at Messines had not been short of time to draft and redraft his plans to capture the ridge. Despite the fact that he would face exceptionally strong and well-prepared positions, and the Germans fully anticipated his attack, Plumer held advantages that no other British general had previously enjoyed, nor would again in the First World War. The first of these was that his tunnelling companies had decisively defeated the Germans underground and planted over a million pounds of explosives directly beneath the German lines, a fatal danger of which they were largely unaware. The second was that during May, with the Flanders Plan now the main British effort, Haig had provided the Second Army an artillery force of such overwhelming power that it almost guaranteed the success of Plumer's attack. Finally, despite a vigorous debate within Crown Prince Rupprecht's command group, the German decision to stand and fight on the ridge rather than withdraw so that the massive British punch would simply swing through thin air, would turn a potential setback into a true disaster.[26]

Haig met with his army commanders on 7 May and revealed his plan for the Flanders offensive and its importance to the grand strategy. Plumer's Second Army, consisting of IX Corps, X Corps and II Anzac Corps, had the job of capturing the Messines-Wytschaete Ridge and, with that secure, either Rawlinson or Gough would then push on to the north-east with a larger force of 16 divisions. Plumer's plans to capture the ridge were discussed at that meeting. Bean claimed in his *Official History* that Plumer and Harington's scheme involved an advance up the ridge in stages over three days, which he wrote 'undoubtedly erred on the side of over-caution' and which Haig overruled, insisting the ridge be captured in one day. Harington, in his post-war correspondence with Edmonds, strongly refuted this. 'I have no recollection whatsoever of any idea of the Messines attack being spread over several days and Plumer never had any doubts. I was with him on May the 7th when Haig decided on Messines & asked Plumer when he cd do it. "Today month" was the reply & we did.'[27] Despite being aware of Harington's statement, Bean left his version of this important point unchanged.[28] What is certain is that Haig considered the original plan too modest, believing also that it made no provision for exploiting a panicked German retreat should this occur. Haig saw far more clearly the opportunities in the hand that Plumer held and consequently staked far more on these, insisting that the capture of the ridge be achieved in one day in order to exploit any advantage that might present itself, particularly to threaten the German gun line. Even if the Germans pulled their guns out of danger (which was likely), the proposed finish line would provide Haig's right flank with considerably more safety as he pushed north-east from the Ypres salient.

The impact of Haig's intervention was summarised by Harington in the Second Army's war diary on 10 May: '... the Army Commander wishes every effort be made to reach the final objectives allotted to Corps in one day ... A matter which emphasises the importance of the attack being pushed on as rapidly as possible in the possibility of capturing some of the enemy guns on the east side of the ridge.'[29] The objectives were then circulated to corps commanders by Harington that same day:

> With a view to enforcing the enemy to withdraw reserves from the main battle front (VIMY-ARRAS) the Second Army will capture the Messines-Wytschaete Ridge on a date (Zero) to be fixed later.
>
> 3. The objects of the operations are:
>
> (a) To capture the enemy position from St. Yves to Observatory Ridge
>
> (b) To capture as many as possible of the enemy guns in the vicinity of Oosttaverne and N.E. of Messines.
>
> (c) To consolidate a position to secure our possession of the Messines-Wytschaete Ridge and establish a series of posts in advance.
>
> 4. The final objective of each Corps – Black Line ... It is imperative, in order to effect surprise and to capture enemy guns that the attack should be pushed through without delay in one day.[30]

What had not even been included in the Second Army's plan on 7 May had become 'imperative' just three days later. Haig's changes would be enormously significant. Rather than an overly cautious set-piece attack to claw up the ridge over three days, the Second Army's main attack would now be pushed forward to capture the ridge in one day and Plumer was to take every opportunity to capture the enemy's guns. What was left unsaid was just how that was to be achieved given that the German artillery line ranged back 1000 yards (and beyond to over 10,000 yards) from the top of the ridge. Haig's changes also had the effect of putting in place a contradiction which would lie at the heart of many of the problems encountered in the battle, with Plumer holding fast to his prime objective of securing the ridge and now required to risk that prize by pushing on to a much deeper stop line and making an opportunistic grab for the enemy's guns. Like the dog with the bone in Aesop's fable which sees its reflection in the water, he would risk dropping the bone he already held in his mouth by snapping at its reflection. In the forefront of Haig's mind was also the possibility, fed by overly optimistic intelligence reports, of the enemy's collapse.

In an indication of the rapidly inflating optimism in Haig's headquarters, Lieutenant-General Sir Launcelot Kiggell (Chief of the General Staff for the British armies in France), in his summary of the conference of 24 May, which included the main points from the earlier conference of army commanders on 7 May, saw even greater possibilities than a raid on the enemy's gun line:

> G.O.C. Second Army must be prepared to exploit his success if the situation becomes favourable, seeing that the capture of the Messines-Wytschaete Ridge might be the beginning of the capture of the Passchendaele-Staden Ridge.
>
> The responsibility for exploiting success on the present Second Army Front rests with the G.O.C., Second Army, and he should issue suitable instructions for this purpose to the II and VIII Corps for taking advantage of such opportunities as may arise according to the situation. In the event of the situation developing greatly in our favour, reserves will be placed at the disposal of the G.O.C., Fifth Army in order to enable him to co-operate in an effort to gain the PASSCHENDAELE-STADEN Ridge.[31]

The problem for Plumer was that Haig's revision came barely one month before the projected attack and now the Second Army would need to dramatically recast its plans to include this enlarged objective. The bulk of the operational planning now fell to the three corps commanders, their staffs and, most importantly, each division's staff. On 15 May, Harington wrote to the corps commanders informing them that Plumer had decided to broaden the scope of the operation. While the prime objective would remain the capture and retention of the ridge 'at all costs', the capture of the enemy guns would be 'a serious blow to the enemy' and that 'provided … the ridge is made secure, the situation is such that risks may and should be taken to secure the guns.'[32] Harington then described the new final objective which lay just short of the German support line.[33]

On 18 May Harington asked all corps commanders to submit revised and extended plans of attack. By then it was quite obvious that IX and X Corps, with greater distance to travel than II Anzac Corps, could not simply push on with sufficient strength and speed to the new and distant objective. There would have to be a pause so that attack coordination could be maintained. 'A premature advance by II Anzac Corps without the co-operation of the other two Corps' wrote Harington, 'would be obviously unsound.' The attack on the Green Line would take place five hours after the ridge (the Black Line) was secured, 10 hours from the launch of the attack and included an ominous but necessary escalation.

'It is to be distinctly understood' continued Harington, 'that this further advance is to be carried out by fresh troops.'[34] The initial attack was now to be delivered by nine divisions grouped in three corps (IX, X and II Anzac) while the reserve division for each corps was to move through the assault divisions to 'capture … the Oosttaverne line by deliberate attack.'[35] This was the important extension in the orders which changed the nature of the afternoon attack from one of probing forward opportunistically to capture guns to a full-scale assault on the German reserve line. So it was on 18 May, barely three weeks from its launch, that the order came which committed the 4th Australian Division, along with the reserve divisions of IX and X Corps, to battle on the afternoon of 7 June.

• • •

With the go-ahead for Messines for early June, the Second Army began to prepare for a major battle. There was no hope that such a vast undertaking could be hidden from the Germans or disguised as a feint. Preparations included the construction of railways, light rail tracks, roads, bridges and paths, storehouses, wells, communication centres, pipelines and workshops as well as enormous shell dumps that would feed the huge artillery force being diverted to the Second Army. The Royal Flying Corps (RFC) was over the battlefield in ever-increasing numbers, building to a maximum strength of 300 aircraft and doing its utmost to prevent German observation, a sure sign the attack was imminent if any more were needed. Further back, the preparations were even more obvious with dressing stations and hospitals, headquarters and barracks for assaulting infantry as well as the enormous storage sheds and dumps that would feed both troops and the machines necessary to wage modern war. Thousands of men were engaged in construction and supply for the great offensive and the planning was every bit as detailed as that required for a vast engineering project. Indeed, what was being constructed along the 17-mile front was something akin to a medium-sized city. The Second Army intelligence summary following the battle admitted that 'He [the Germans] was able to overlook all of our preparations and it is evident from documents found that he had full knowledge that an attack was impending.'[36] The build-up to major battles was immense and included, as at Messines, 'tremendous preparatory bombardments, which entailed months of preliminary railway and road construction [with the result] that G.H.Q. had been forced to give up the notion of keeping an attack secret until it was delivered.'[37] The intense artillery bombardment planned for the final days would signal that a major attack was just days away.

The impossibility of surprise attack on any large scale was a troubling reality of the First World War. Bean touched on the anxiety of the infantry in his chapter on the Battle of Messines in the Australian *Official History* by tracing their journey from billets, into wheeled transport, before they wound their way across open ground into communication trenches and silently into position in jumping-off trenches or lying prone behind the white tape which marked the start line. 'One thought' Bean wrote, 'was usually uppermost in the men's minds: does the enemy know?'[38] Of course, as he conceded, such a great undertaking could not be kept secret. 'But' he added hopefully, 'the enemy would not know the date and hour unless he actually detected the troops concentrating or captured some well-informed soldier who was so imprudent or unfaithful as to speak of these matters.'[39] As the many captured documents would show, the Germans had pinned the attack to within a few days. The withdrawal of German heavy artillery had started and, in a further ominous sign, concentrations of German guns were observed gathering on the flanks, dispositions which almost exactly predicted the length of front of the coming British attack.

On 5 June, two days before the battle, Haig gave his army commanders a glimpse of his thinking in a secret communiqué which included a further startlingly optimistic assessment. 'After careful consideration of all the available information' wrote Haig, 'I feel justified in stating that the power of endurance of the German people is being strained to such a degree as to make it possible that the breaking point may be reached this year.'[40] The 'available information' he spoke of was a mixture of accurate intelligence, gossip and grumbling picked up by lowly placed spies in Germany, defeatist reports from prisoners and some optimistic forecasting from his Chief of Intelligence, Brigadier General John Charteris. He noted that it was the German intention 'to hold on in the hope of outlasting the determination of the Allies'. Haig listed the dubious successes of the Somme and the battles of the Ancre and Arras as the 'great efforts already made' which had, in his mind, brought 'final victory so near that it may be attained [this year]'. On the eve of the battle for Messines Ridge, Haig wrote that 'one great and striking success, combined with general activity and steady progress on the whole front, and a secure hold of all that has already been won, will have far-reaching results.'[41]

Haig's desire for the Second Army to prepare to take advantage of a battered and perhaps broken German line, rather than content itself with possession of the ridge, was perfectly sound strategy. Indeed, many of those who fought and later wrote about the battle wondered why, in its immediate aftermath, the British did not drive on even further. Its result, however, was to create two separate battles. The first, meticulously planned over months, overwhelmingly supported by artillery, machine-gun barrages and mines, and timed to take place in the pre-dawn darkness, would be to capture the ridge. The second, planned much more quickly over the final days of May, had to be supported by the same artillery, much of which would need to fire on the more distant lines beyond the Black Line with little opportunity to register, and would be launched down an open slope in broad daylight for 1000 metres in full view of the German artillery and machine-guns.[42] The risks which 'may and should be taken' were many indeed.

The late changes to the battle plan meant major changes to the Second Army's order of battle, with the reserve divisions for each corps now required to spearhead the second phase. For X Corps [23rd, 47th (London) and 41st Divisions], the 24th Division was now committed to the battle. In IX Corps [19th (Western), 16th (Irish) and 36th (Ulster)], it would be the 11th (Northern) Division and for II Anzac (25th, New Zealand and 3rd Australian) the 4th Australian Division. All three reserve divisions were battle tested but also had a history of severe losses. The 11th was one of the 1914 divisions that had experienced much hard fighting at Gallipoli and on the Western Front. The 24th was one of Kitchener's New Army divisions pushed prematurely into the fighting at Loos in 1915 where it had suffered over 4000 casualties. In 1916 the division had experienced the German gas attack at Wulverghem and gone on to suffer crippling losses at Delville Wood and Guillemont on the Somme. Most recently, the 24th had a major success to its credit at Vimy Ridge in April. The 4th Australian Division had also suffered heavy losses on the Somme in 1916 and, just six weeks before, a catastrophic defeat at Bullecourt.

II Anzac's order of battle was finalised on 18 May with the 3rd Australian Division on the right flank to capture the Black Line and then push fresh troops forward in the afternoon to capture the Green Line. To its left, the New Zealand Division would have the daunting task of capturing Messines itself, pushing on beyond the village to the Black Line and the crest of the ridge. On the left flank, the 25th Division would have the furthest to travel to capture the ridge to the north of the village and dig in on the Black Line alongside the New Zealanders. Both divisions would then establish an advanced line of posts to serve as the jumping-off point for the next phase. In the afternoon, II Anzac's two Australian divisions would push on and capture the German reserve line, seizing what opportunities might arise from the expected disruption and chaos in the German defences.

Of the four divisions Godley commanded, the New Zealanders had the most accomplished record. The division had arrived in France in April of 1916 to the relatively quiet 'nursery' sector of Armentières on the River Lys. There it completed vigorous raiding and defence improvements, suffering over 2000 casualties during its four-month stay until entering the Somme battle at Flers-Courcelette on 15 September as part of XV Corps. This was the division's first major attack and, despite heavy casualties, it was remarkably successful.[43] Further success at Morval on 25 September and again on 1 October spelled the end of the division's baptism of fire and marked it as singularly fine. Rawlinson, commanding the Fourth Army, was generous in his praise. 'The endurance and fine fighting spirit of the Division have been beyond praise, and their successes in the Flers neighbourhood will rank high amongst the best achievements of the British Army.'[44] Rawlinson's accolades were well deserved. The division had captured over five miles of German front line and advanced over two miles. It had taken and held every objective, often fighting unsupported on both flanks. It had also captured a great deal of materiel including large numbers of machine-guns and over 1000 prisoners while losing just 20 of its own. Importantly also, the division had an early and successful experience of cooperation with tanks.

The New Zealanders were fortunate in one respect — their entry into the Somme battle was relatively late. The experience of the four Australian divisions from July to October of 1916 was very different. On 19 July the 5th Division had been thrown into an ill-considered and ultimately disastrous attack on German trenches at Fromelles, resulting in a casualty toll of over 5000. The grim struggle for Pozières in July and August had consumed the 1st and 2nd Division (costing 5283 and 6846 casualties respectively). The 4th Division entered the battle on 5 August and lost over 4000 men. The next weeks saw all three divisions again engaged in the battle for Mouquet Farm with the final casualty toll for the Somme battle over 28,000 in six weeks of fighting. The 5th Division was too badly damaged to participate in any further major action until the summer of 1917. A comparison of casualty figures reveals a roughly equivalent experience for the four Australian divisions and the New Zealand Division on the Somme. But where the Australians had been employed in the tragic and badly planned assaults on the Somme (and in the case of Fromelles and Bullecourt, complete disasters), the New Zealand Division had the distinction of a remarkable and rare success.

The shifting circumstances of the Western Front brought the 25th Division into II Anzac Corps in place of the 34th Division when the latter moved to XVII Corps for the Arras offensive. The 25th was formed in September of 1914 with all the shortcomings of rapid mobilisation — green volunteers, a shortage of trained non-commissioned officers (NCOs) and officers and a good measure of chaos around equipping, housing and training. They were sent to France in September of 1915, defending the southern part of the Ypres salient, and first saw action in May of 1916 when the Germans attacked Vimy Ridge, in which the division won its first Victoria Cross (VC). Entering the Somme battle on 3 July, the 75th Brigade attacked Thiepval Spur and suffered, according to the history of the division, 'very heavy casualties, and were met by heavy flanking fire and never reached their objectives'.[45] By the end of the first week of the Somme, the division had been badly mauled, something it shared with much of the British Army in July of 1916. The history of the division was written hastily during the war and closely followed the war diary, which may explain why its author, with an air of desperation, lapsed into present tense while describing the bloody chaos of the Somme. 'With its units working under a strange staff, divisional cohesion becomes seriously impaired; all mutual understanding and confidence which is so vitally necessary for the efficient and energetic execution of an offensive operation, will soon cease to exist.'[46] In mid-July the 25th was again severely battered in the Battle of Bazentin and then rotated in and out of the line at Pozières and Mouquet Farm in support of Australian attacks. In September, the division won a notable, if pyrrhic success capturing the northern face of Stuff Redoubt in the battle for the Ancre Heights. In many ways the ordeals of the 25th Division are typical of those of the New Army on the Somme in 1916.

The Australians were another matter. The novice 3rd Australian Division was an unknown quantity. Impressive enough on the parade ground and successful in the raids it had conducted since moving to France in November of 1916, the 3rd was yet to experience the extreme pressure of a major battle on the Western Front. The best trained of the Australian divisions, it was hoped that what the 3rd lacked in combat wisdom would be offset by thorough preparation and the most careful and exhaustive staff work. The contrast with the 4th Division could hardly have been more stark. Created from a mixture of newly arrived recruits and Gallipoli veterans in Egypt when the AIF doubled in size in March of 1916, the 4th had endured terrible casualties in the Somme battles of the previous summer. The division's discipline record, already poor in Egypt and exacerbated by the absorption of some 1000 'undesirables' who had been abandoned in Egypt by the 1st and 2nd divisions when they left for France, had deteriorated even further following the dreadful trials of Pozières and Mouquet Farm. Dealt a further crushing blow at Bullecourt in April of 1917, the battle-scarred division arrived in Flanders on 16 May hoping for a period of rest to recoup its numbers and rebuild morale. Unfortunately for the hapless Australians, they were in for what the *Official History* would describe as 'an unpleasant shock'.[47]

2

The Anzacs are very brave men,
but they are simply a mob in uniform.

The Australians

2

*The Anzacs are very brave men,
but they are simply a mob in uniform.*

The Australians

Even in a war notorious for ill-considered attacks and the bloody fiascos that resulted, the disastrous First Battle of Bullecourt still has few parallels. In the spring of 1917 the 4th Australian Division was under command of General Hubert Gough's Fifth Army as part of I Anzac Corps. On 11 April Gough attempted to exploit what he believed were the opportunities provided by General Henry Horne's successful assault on Vimy Ridge by attacking the Hindenburg Line near the villages of Bullecourt and Riencourt. Gough's aim was to break through the German line and join up with Horne's supposedly advancing First Army. Driven by an extravagant optimism which the tragedies of 1916 had failed to dim, Gough's plan ignored almost every one of the war's hard-learned lessons. Bean lapsed into sarcasm to describe it in the *Official History*, comparing the chances of success with 'a plan to capture the moon'.[1] Attacking on a narrow front during a snowstorm without a preliminary artillery barrage, and gambling on the success of a tiny force of tanks (which failed utterly), Gough sent the unfortunate infantry of the 4th Division to their doom. Having fought their way into the Hindenburg Line, the Australians were denied artillery support in another of the errors which characterised this battle. Surrounded, trapped and decimated, the two attacking brigades of the 4th Division were cut to pieces. The division suffered over 3000 casualties in a few short hours on the morning of 11 April with the 4th Brigade virtually destroyed, suffering an astonishing casualty rate of 78%. A total of 1142 Australians were captured, by far the most of any engagement in the First World War. 'Everyone was aware' wrote Bean, 'that the 4th Division had been employed in an experiment of extreme rashness.'[2]

In their bitter depression and anger following the battle, the 4th Division's shattered battalions were visited by the corps commander, General William Birdwood, who didn't help by quietly congratulating them on a 'victory' and claiming that, although they had suffered heavy losses, their sacrifice had drawn in German reserves which had been annihilated by British artillery. The men of the 4th were used to Birdwood's post-battle speeches. Bean described their mood after a similar occasion at Pozières: 'Some caught his spirit; many more listened grimly to his praises and called them by a harsh Australian name for idle flattery.'[3] Private Denver Gallwey of the 47th Battalion was less reluctant than Bean to give such nonsense its vivid Australian name. 'Some were commenting on the General's remarks and said it was all bullshit … Our men will not tolerate anything like that.'[4] The 12th Brigade's command group had been particularly savage in its criticism. Lieutenant Colonel Raymond Leane of the 48th Battalion had lost his brother at Bullecourt and would neither forgive nor forget Gough's blunders, nor the disastrous showing of the tanks, whose crews he accused of incompetence and outright cowardice.

Now, with Haig's change to the plan for Messines, the reserve divisions of Plumer's three corps were to be committed to the battle, driving forward from the original stop line to capture the German reserve trenches and, hopefully, their guns. The transfer of the 4th Division to II Anzac Corps as reserve in May, which would have provided the hard-pressed division a period of rest, thus dealt the 4th another desperately unlucky hand. Not only was it now certain to be thrown into yet another major battle, it was to be given perhaps the most complex and difficult task of pushing down an open slope in broad daylight for almost 1000 metres to capture the German reserve line. The men of the 4th Division could also expect to be the first to meet any counter-attacks, while the artillery that supported them with a creeping barrage would need to accurately hit the advanced lines following the morning attack despite firing blind over the ridge. The heavy artillery would need to lift its barrels and fire on previously unregistered lines. As if their mission was not sufficiently difficult, they were given the least time to prepare their part in an already hastily conceived second phase plan. Worse still, the 4th Division would again be expected to cooperate with tanks, a prospect which filled the survivors of Bullecourt with a mixture of fury and dread. Seldom in the war was a division so recently mauled sent back into a major battle with so little time to recover and with such a difficult and important role.

Someone on the Second Army's staff may have recognised that the 'most rugged and recently-battered' Australian division, as Bean described it, was being pushed very hard.[5] Buried in the mass of orders and administrative arrangements for the coming battle was an item which clearly suggested some concern over the Australian divisions of II Anzac Corps. The number of men assigned to the role of apprehending 'stragglers' in II Anzac was over three times that employed in X and IX Corps.[6] There are no comments on the perceived fighting qualities or 'steadiness' of the divisions to be employed, but such a precaution is clear evidence that Plumer's staff expected problems. It is very unlikely that the highly regarded New Zealand Division or the veteran British 25th Division would have merited such measures. But, with the 3rd Division entering its first battle and with more expected of it in an enlarged assault, and the ravaged 4th Division drafted in despite its poor discipline record and high desertion rate, such precautions were considered necessary.

The 4th Division held a sports carnival at Bresle in May 1917 as the men recovered from the disaster at Bullecourt. In a few short weeks they would be in Flanders preparing for another major battle at Messines. Identified, from left to right: (arms folded) Lieutenant Colonel Sydney Herring (45th Battalion commander) and Lieutenant Dudley Salmon, 47th Battalion (on Herring's left). In the foreground are Major General William Holmes (Commander 4th Division) and, to his immediate left, Brigadier General James Robertson (12th Brigade commander) and Captain Edward Salier (AWM E00595).

Bean would reluctantly concede that the staff of the 25th Division, alongside which the AIF would fight at Messines, 'knew little of the Australians, and did not fully trust their battle discipline'.[7] Evidently the little they knew was enough to make that adverse judgement. One of the 25th's staff officers, Major Walter Guinness of the 74th Brigade, had fought alongside the Anzacs at Gallipoli and considered the Australians 'an infernal nuisance'. He described having to post guards at a British dugout, not so much to prevent them pilfering from it as undertaking its wholesale removal. When caught, they claimed to be New Zealanders. 'They say here that an Australian would steal your toe nail' wrote

Guinness, 'and attribute it to the convict origin. It is among them a case of every man for himself and there is no thought of consideration for anyone else.'[8] He later praised Birdwood for his 'extraordinary tact' in handling the Australians 'who' he said, 'are a most difficult and undisciplined though very brave rabble.'[9] He didn't find the New Zealanders any easier to work with, including a long anecdote in his memoirs describing their intransigence and incompetence.[10]

Bean also admitted that the New Zealanders 'had less faith in the Australians than in their own troops' and this opinion could hardly be said to be due to having little knowledge.[11] It was certainly true that adverse opinions of the Australians existed at the highest levels of British command.[12] Most of this was due to the Australians' often spectacularly ill-disciplined behaviour away from the firing line. The British Assistant Provost Marshal for Ypres, Brigadier General Walter Ludlow, had more than just his frequent police reports to confirm this. He had personally stared down an angry mob of drunken Australian troops, pistol in hand, from behind the bar of an estaminet they had besieged in Bailleul in 1917, threatening to shoot the first man who came through the door. 'They howled and swore and refused to "clear out". It took half an hour of intense excitement to clear the place … The Anzacs are very brave men' he concluded, 'but they are simply a mob in uniform.'[13] Such scenes were not unknown in any army of course, but by 1917 it was clear that, among the Australians, they were far too common. On average, the AIF's crime rate was nine times higher than other forces in the British Army and even that alarming figure almost certainly understated the problem given the acknowledged reluctance of Australian officers to report and prosecute military offences.[14] In the British Army, the connection between battle performance and basic discipline was considered axiomatic. If the Australians couldn't be trusted — or handled — behind the lines, what reason was there to expect anything different under fire? The concerns over discipline extended well beyond the atrocious crime rate of the AIF. Timely and reliable adherence to orders and efficient and dependable systems of authority affected everything. Communication, supply, transport and other everyday but crucial components of military organisation could all be crippled by the corrosive impact of poor discipline. Furthermore, if officers needed to 'earn' the respect of their men or rely on persuasion and personality to command effectively, this added a further complication to an already lonely and difficult job.

The English were astonished by the easy familiarity of the Australian officers with their men. Guinness wrote that '[t]hey all seem to address their officers as Bill or Dick and though wonderfully brave, they have no discipline.'[15] Some saw different qualities. One of the tank commanders who would support the

4th Division wrote that 'the troops we are with are the magnificent colonials. The finest body of men I ever saw. Determined, thoughtful, brooding, dignified faces.'[16] Lieutenant George Mitchell of the 4th Division's 48th Battalion found the English habits just as foreign. Invited to dine with some officers of the 25th Division in the days before Messines, Mitchell found himself the object of curiosity. 'Gently and obliquely they probed for information as to the ways of Australians. The clipped, concise English was a delight to hear. But even in my enjoyment, I had a sneaking suspicion that my hair was fuzzy and my loin-cloth somewhat frayed.' He reflected on the gulf between his own experience of command and that of his dining companions:

> *Journeys End*, with its five officers sitting together in a front line dugout, could never have been written of an Australian company. Rather would you have seen each platoon officer glumly feeding from his mess tin among his men, the company commander sitting in solitary glory. I have often had my rum issue swiped by some dissolute private when my back was turned. And cigarettes – blazes! While I had one left, the platoon considered they had an option on it.[17]

Such stark differences in basic military culture were jarringly obvious to the English.

Australian indiscipline was a key concern for the British from the earliest days. Following the Anzac withdrawal from Gallipoli and as they were preparing to leave for France in 1916, the newly appointed commander of the Mediterranean Expeditionary Force, Sir Archibald Murray, wrote to the Chief of the Imperial General Staff, Sir William Robertson, claiming that 'I have never seen a body of men in uniform with less idea of discipline … The streets of Cairo, Ismailia and Port Said are difficult to keep clear of drunken Australians.' Warming to his theme, he complained that 'many of the men seem to have no idea of ordinary decency or self-control.' Murray had statistics to support his case. 'Of a total of 8858 Venereal Disease cases treated in Egypt since the beginning of military operations, 5924 were Australians, 955 New Zealanders and 1979 British troops. On the 21st of February there were 1286 Australians being treated for Venereal Disease at the Dermatological hospital. 1344 soldiers have been returned to Australia suffering from the disease.'[18] Murray lamented that these 'magnificent men … the finest by far that I have ever seen … have been nearly spoilt by the neglect on the part of their commanders to instil into them even the rudiments of soldierly instinct.' He praised their 'magnificent bravery' while damning the inefficiency of their officers and mentioning their 'enormous conceit in themselves' thanks to a fawning press whose custom it was 'to laud the Australians "as the finest soldiers in existence".'

Murray's fear was that the combination of reckless bravery, overconfidence, indiscipline and ineffectual leadership would lead to 'unnecessarily heavy losses' in France. Later events were to prove his warning singularly prescient.

Murray's letter, the responses to it from Godley and Birdwood and Bean's later judgements in the *Official History* provide not only a fascinating insight into the difficulties of command in the AIF, but also the British Army's responses to the issue. Murray's views have largely been dismissed in Australian history for a number of reasons, the foremost of which was his incapacity as a general.[19] He sent a draft of his letter to Birdwood and Godley prior to sending it to London. Godley's single page response was in broad agreement, although mentioning that Murray was seeing the Australians 'at their very worst, just at a time when they are back from an arduous campaign' and that they were improving daily. He had 'written and talked forcibly to Divisional Commanders' and believed this was producing results. Godley ended his letter with the observation that he had less experience of the Australians than the New Zealanders but 'from what I now know of the former, I do not by any means despair of them.'[20] Birdwood's response ran to eight pages and is illuminating for many reasons. In no sense did he disagree with Murray's observations. He had, he said, discussed the matter often with the late General Bridges 'a regular Australian officer of very high principles and with a great sense of discipline, and very jealous of the good reputation of Australian soldiers.' Bridges reminded Birdwood that many of the Australians 'belonged to the strongest of socialistic communities in the world – men, who a few weeks before had looked upon it as an absolute degradation to humanity that they should salute any other man or call any man "sir".'[21] Bringing such men into the normal orbit of military discipline would, he believed 'be a very lengthy matter indeed'. He pointed to problems with Australian officers who 'in the vast majority of cases came from exactly the same class as the men, and it was therefore very difficult for them to exercise proper command, or to command respect from their men until perhaps they have the opportunity of proving their superiority in the field.'[22]

Birdwood went on to add some minor mitigations around irrelevant details — that the officers' uniforms resembled closely the men's, that most Australian soldiers could not recognise an officer's badges of rank and so on — before turning to a much more important point: their battle discipline. He noted the absolute silence maintained by the men at the landing and the evacuation of Gallipoli, and their perfect order during the latter as well as their attention to sanitation in the trenches. Birdwood then politely but pointedly reminded Murray of his distance from the fighting, informing him that in battle the Australians showed 'a resourcefulness and determination to pull themselves together and prove that they can show discipline, when called upon to do so, in a way which cannot be realised by one who has not actually seen it.' Birdwood cautioned Murray about making comparisons with the New Zealanders saying he was not personally prepared to say decisively what advantages one possessed over the other. Russell, who commanded both the 4th AIF Brigade (which Birdwood considered the worst he had seen) and the New Zealand Infantry Brigade, assured Birdwood that the latter were the least disciplined of the Anzacs.[23]

There were two important differences between the New Zealand Division and the Australians which influenced the character of the two Anzac forces in France. The first was the New Zealand government's adoption of conscription in 1916, a move almost unanimously supported in that country's parliament and which took effect in November of 1916. Two tortuous conscription campaigns in Australia, in 1916 and 1917, would fall short of providing forced enlistment in Australia. Controversial and unpopular though it was, the issue of conscription never assumed the divisive proportions it did in Australia and the New Zealand Expeditionary Force (NZEF) and the New Zealand government were thus spared the anxiety (and at times desperation) in Australia over whether the force could be maintained. The second and highly significant point of difference was the New Zealand government's subvention of its forces under the British Army Act through the New Zealand Defence Act of 1909. For New Zealand's volunteers and later conscripts (although few would have known it when they enlisted), this meant that the King's Regulations allowed the death penalty to be imposed for a range of military offences. For Australians, although nominally subject to the same regulations (and sanctions), any death penalty had to be approved by the Governor-General — in effect by the government. Given the tensions surrounding conscription in Australia, any enacted death sentence on a volunteer would not only have seriously damaged the case for compulsion, it would have further diminished the already rapidly dwindling supply of voluntary enlistments. It is very likely also that, rather than improving discipline in the Australian divisions, it would have produced a backlash as the British custom of announcing the imposition of capital sentences to their armies produced a mixture of resentment and pride in Australian units where they knew themselves beyond the reach of such awful justice. The fact that throughout the war most senior British commanders, including the Australians themselves, believed that applying the death penalty was a necessary step to take, speaks of their concern over the discipline of the Australians. It would never be imposed in the AIF. The recruitment crisis, the failure of the conscription referenda and the wild independence of the Australians meant that the imposition of the death penalty in the AIF was, as Dr Christopher Pugsley points out, 'politically impossible'.[24]

Dwindling Australian enlistments made it more likely that lies about age would not be questioned by recruiting officers. Private George Forrest of the 34th Battalion enlisted in January 1916. A veteran of the Boer War, he understated his age by some 15 years. He was 60 when he was killed by a shell during the 34th Battalion's advance on 7 June (AWM P08568.001).

Bean downplayed the discipline issue in the *Official History*. In dealing with Murray's letter he acknowledged problems with the minor matters of saluting and uniform, neither of which Murray raised with Robertson. [25] These were issues raised by Birdwood with his generals in response to Murray's letter as ways of visibly tightening discipline and encouraging subordination to military authority. Bean described Murray as 'cold, scholarly and somewhat exclusive', a man who considered 'the smart appearance of troops, neatness of uniform, and punctilious ceremonial both on parade and in the streets, weighed most heavily as signs of their military worth.'[26] This was unfair as Murray's chief worries were the venereal disease rates and drunkenness, both matters important to fighting quality and both clearly proven by statistics. Bean suggested that Murray's opinions were the unfortunate product of the proximity of his headquarters to the teeming attractions of Cairo and the curious, naïve, shabbily dressed and occasionally rowdy Australians who frequented them. This brought them into jostling contact with the supposedly desk-bound and intolerant Murray who, according to Bean, had come 'fresh from the hushed corridors of the War Office into surroundings which perceptibly shocked him'.[27]

Bean went on to describe the Australian attitude to military discipline rather romantically, as akin to 'a colt from a large paddock' which 'at first resented all restraint.'[28] It underplayed what would eventually become an issue of persistent frustration and difficulty for the Australian divisions and one which was more than borne out statistically. Privately, Bean admitted that Murray was right, writing in his diary that:

> … the streets of Cairo were anything but pleasant for an Australian who had any regard to the good name of Australia. There was a great deal of drunkenness and I could not help noticing that what people in Cairo said was true – the Australians were responsible for most of it … I think we have to admit that our force contains more bad hats than the others, and I think also that the average Australian is certainly a harder liver. He does do bad things – at least things that the rest of the world considers as really bad.[29]

Murray and others in senior command were, of course, right to be concerned about the men taken from the firing line by venereal diseases, by the poor quality of the officers and the general indiscipline. But Birdwood pointed to a critical factor. Desertions aside, the battle discipline of the Australians seemed unaffected by the many other problems evident away from the firing line. This pattern would continue throughout the war and, as the Australian contribution to victory in 1918 would show, they remained a highly effective fighting force despite the very high crime and desertion rates, despite the lack of a death penalty and despite the heavy casualties they suffered. Bean, although despairing at times of his countrymen's habit of finding trouble, their often crude insubordination and contempt for the norms of military behaviour, believed they would not fail in the area that really mattered. 'I think the sum will come out on the right side when all is totted up. That is my great comfort when I wonder how I shall ever manage to write up an honest history of this campaign. I fully expect the men of this force will do things when the real day comes which will make the true history of this war possible to be written.'[30] Ultimately, he would be proven right.

• • •

When the 4th Division arrived to join the 3rd in Flanders in mid-May, the two presented 'an interesting contrast'. The division with the worst discipline record in the AIF was now quartered alongside the division which could lay claim to the best. This was due largely to the determination of Monash to rehabilitate the reputation of Australians, in his division at least. Bean devoted a long passage in Volume IV to the qualities of the new division, to its military efficiency and freedom from crime. He also praised Monash for the care and concern he showed for his new command and for the efforts he devoted to building unit pride.[31] While Monash's qualities as a fighting general were soon to become very apparent indeed to his critics and the enemy alike, what could be fairly said was that he could, at times, display a curious ineptitude in dealing with men. As a brigadier he was more than once 'counted out' by his men and his ham-fisted attempt to rally the 4th Brigade suffering through the rigours of the infamous desert march in Egypt was shown up for the foolishness it was by the 14th Battalion historian.[32] Minor missteps followed his promotion to divisional command. Seeking to make the 3rd even more distinctive than it already was in the AIF as the only division trained in England and the only one still yet to fight, Monash insisted that his men wear their broad-brimmed hats, the prime and cherished symbol of their identity as Australians, with the brims flat rather than looped up.[33] Writing to Lieutenant Colonel Malcolm Lamb in London, he described his regulations covering the wearing of the hat, which were very specific: 'with brim turned down, sun badge in front and just overlapping the hat band and with the hat slightly canted over the right eye-brow.'[34] This regulation provided the clear signal that Monash wanted his men to be, or at least appear to be, separate and distinct from the rest of the AIF given the appalling crime rate in the other Australian divisions, a fact he confirmed in his letter:

My reason for insisting so strongly on the above matters is that it has become more than ever necessary to be able to distinguish not merely between units, but also between men of the 3rd and other divisions. We have, now, in this district, a very large number of Australians belonging to other units [referring to the 4th Division]. I am sorry to say their behaviour and deportment is very bad, and I am most anxious that it should be impossible to mistake any 3rd Division men for any of them.[35]

Many of 'them' did not appreciate Monash's motives. This was so obviously akin to the petty thinking of an image-conscious headmaster that Bean used exactly that metaphor to describe its effect on the men of the 4th Division who looked on the 3rd 'much as the rougher boys at a state school might look upon an immaculate, tenderly brought-up little cousin at a neighbouring dame's school.'[36] The message behind Monash's order was obvious both to the 'rougher boys' in the other divisions and the men of the 3rd 'whose most cherished desire', according to Bean, 'was to be just one of the five, and, if General Monash had known how his order as to hat-brims burned in the men's hearts, the brims would possibly have been looped up that same hour.'[37] But Monash did not know. Fawning press reports describing their training in England and parades before the King also did not go unnoticed by the rest of the AIF who, fighting and suffering in France, dubbed the 3rd Division the 'Lark Hill Lancers' and 'the neutrals' and put up posters in the trenches offering rewards for finding the 'lost' division.

The 3rd's oval colour patch gave it the most enduring nickname of 'eggs-a-cook' — yet another backhanded insult. Referring to the cry of Arab street vendors, this was a reminder to the men of the 3rd that there had already been much fighting in Gallipoli and Egypt and none of it by them. 'Eggs-a-cook' was an insider's joke, an age-old barb that used the language of the old hand to exclude the uncomprehending newcomer.[38] While 'half humorous', Bean described the grievances nurtured against the 3rd Division as 'very definite' and almost every battalion history in that division makes reference to the jibes, brawls and volleys of insults that occasional contact with the other divisions would bring. Most of the 3rd Division's battalion histories recalled the needling that their division suffered prior to Messines. The 42nd Battalion historian wrote that:

> When the 3rd Division troops appeared with their turned down hats and their oval, or egg shaped colour patches, members of the other four "Fighting Divisions" as they called themselves immediately yelled out: "Here they are. Eggs-a-cook. Verra nice, verra sweet, verra clean. Two for one." It may have started as a joke, but it unfortunately developed into a term of derision.[39]

The much criticised casual and self-confident attitude of the Australians is perhaps apparent in this photo of men of the 4th Division's 14th Battalion at the Romarin terrain model on the eve of the battle. In the background, men of the 13th Brigade (who would attack the next day) depart in fighting order while two impeccably turned out New Zealanders approach. The 14th Battalion was a reserve unit for the battle, and the unkempt uniforms, scattered gas masks and rifles and relaxed demeanour of its troops could hardly escape the notice of the many critics of Australian discipline (AWM E00607).

Insults were also put to music such as the following ditty sung to the tune of *The Girl I Left Behind Me*:

> Oh the First and Second are in the line,
> And the Fourth and Fifth are behind them.
> But when you look for the Eggs-a-cook,
> I'm d_____d if you can find them.

As the 42nd Battalion historian commented, 'This when sung in the hearing of men of the Third Division was usually the signal for a box-on or a brawl.'[40] George Mitchell of the 4th Division's 48th Battalion described how his men maintained a silent respect for the New Zealanders they met in the back areas at Messines, 'but no inhibitions were there when we encountered the outliers of the 3rd Division with their oval colour patches.' Mitchell described just such an outburst from one of his men, along with its ridiculous postscript:

"You eggs-a-cook _____s have been malingering down here while we have been doing all the fighting. Wait till we get going, we'll show you what war is! Write home and tell your mothers you have seen some real soldiers, you lead-swinging _____s." I turned to look at the speaker. He had joined us fresh from Australia, two weeks before.[41]

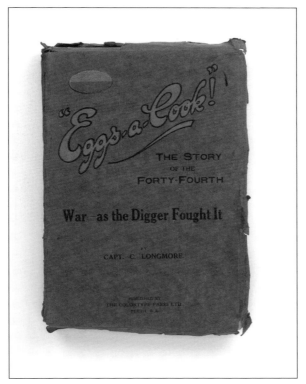

The 3rd Division would prove itself at Messines, ending the taunts and jibes that had been directed at its men by the other divisions. The author of the 44th Battalion's unit history chose 'Eggs-a-Cook' for its title, turning the insult into a badge of honour (author photo).

Such treatment produced a cold determination at every level of the 3rd Australian Division to prove itself worthy in the coming battle and, although the chaffing and catcalls from men of the battle-tested divisions provoked frustration, there is also no doubt that these added to their resolve.[42] By May of 1917 the 3rd Division had hardly been idle, even though it had taken part in no major operations. Arriving in France in November 1917, it had been stationed in the quiet sector of Armentières where it had raided the enemy's trenches and, in turn, defended its own lines from raiding by the enemy. Through December, January and February, the 3rd Division maintained an active program of raiding, providing vital experience for all infantry battalions and testing the staff work which, thanks to Monash's exacting standards and intimate involvement, was of the highest order.[43] As May turned to June, the men of the 3rd Division recognised from the immense preparations around them that the time was drawing near. Private George Davies of the 36th Battalion, a former missionary, wrote: 'I am looking forward to this push to bring me a happy release from further military life which I hate, and I hope to be wounded and sent home, or else to be killed, either is preferable to this hell upon earth.'[44]

· · ·

Success or failure in the coming battle would hinge on the quality of the commanders and their decisions. General Sir Alexander Godley, in command of II Anzac Corps was well known to the Australians and New Zealanders, first as the person chiefly responsible for the formation and training of the fledgling New Zealand force, and later as the commander of the Australian and New Zealand Division at Gallipoli. He was an unhappy choice for command of II Anzac which he had held since its creation in March of 1916. Godley had joined the British Army as an 18-year-old and graduated from Sandhurst in 1886. His biography noted that '[a]s a young and impecunious subaltern he trained polo ponies for an income and spent much of his regimental life, whether in Ireland or England, riding with the hounds. Along with other junior officers of the time he seems not to have received training relevant to the battlefield apart from annual manoeuvres.'[45] In fairness, the same could be said of much of the officer class of Britain's Edwardian army. He first saw action in 1896 in the Mashonaland rebellion before service in the Boer War where he eventually became Plumer's Chief of Staff.[46]

During his visit to New Zealand in 1910, Field Marshal Lord Kitchener advised the government on the development of the nation's military forces and recommended the establishment of a staff college. Asked to further recommend a commandant, Kitchener proposed Godley, who had some New Zealand connections. Godley's understanding of the British Army and his own organisational ability were chiefly responsible for the creation and modernisation of the fledgling New Zealand Division and he must take some credit for its subsequent successes in the First World War. Command of the New Zealand and Australian Division at Gallipoli was among the severest tests of combat leadership and one that exposed his limitations. A stern disciplinarian, Godley had a poor grasp of the battlefield and did little to make himself better informed. Profligate in attacks at Gallipoli, he was also, with Bridges, a key member of the panicky counsel of war that urged Birdwood to request re-embarkation on the night of 25 April. He was also deeply unpopular with his men, the Australians christening The Nek 'Godley's abattoir'.[47] During the Gallipoli campaign he lost the confidence of the New Zealand Prime Minister, James Allen, who was keen to appoint a New Zealander at the first opportunity and later regretted Godley's appointment to operational command.

'It makes me wonder how on earth we are going to win this war when men like Godley can remain where he is, and dispose of men's lives in such an easy fashion.' Lieutenant General Sir Alexander Godley, General Officer Commanding (GOC) II Anzac Corps at Messines. A competent peacetime administrator, Godley was completely out of his depth in operational command and his many flaws were plainly exposed at Messines (AWM P03717.003).

Perhaps his greatest failure as a field commander was his inability to properly coordinate operations. 'Out of touch with front line realities ... aloof and tactless', Godley was recommended over Birdwood by Murray for the Anzac Corps command although this may have had more to do with Murray's distrust and evident dislike of the latter.[48] The expansion of the AIF and the NZEF which led to the creation of two corps meant that both generals were appointed to corps command. Godley's rise to command II Anzac Corps thus had little to do with ability and much to do with the politics of command of the newly created New Zealand Division, his seniority and his field experience. The fact that his battle experience was far from exceptional did not disqualify him as such failures hardly stood out as especially unusual at Gallipoli. Guinness of the 25th Division remarked that Godley 'was considered quite useless as a Corps commander'.[49]

Godley was, however, fortunate in the quality of his generals and the divisions they commanded. Major General Sir Andrew Hamilton Russell was a professional soldier with an impeccable imperial pedigree. Educated at Harrow, he graduated from the Royal Military College, Sandhurst, in 1887 with the Sword of Honour as the year's top graduate. He led the New Zealand Mounted Rifles Brigade to Gallipoli and cemented an outstanding reputation despite the cascading disasters of that campaign. He gave his name to the plateau on the northern end of Anzac, establishing his headquarters on what would become Russell's Top, and planned the immensely difficult assault on the approach to Chunuk Bair in the August offensive. His men seized the heights on 8 August in a tenacious feat of skill and bravery, the closest thing to a decisive success that could be claimed in the entire campaign. With Godley's elevation to corps command in 1915, Russell was the obvious choice to succeed him in command of the Australian and New Zealand Division and later (having been knighted for his feats at Gallipoli) to lead the newly formed New Zealand Division in March 1916. Haig recognised Russell as 'a most capable soldier with considerable strength of character'.[50] Indeed, as a general there were few qualities Russell lacked. Utterly fearless (some subordinates believed him too careless of his own safety), he was a highly active front-line commander, equally adept at hands-on leadership of men as he was in the demands of staff work. He was a meticulous planner and felt keenly the responsibility of bearing his country's flag in the war where he agonised over the plans that, however careful, would cost hundreds of his men their lives. Yet he could also be ruthless when required, strongly advocating — and imposing — the death penalty for desertion in his division. Above all, he was a superb tactical thinker and an inspirational leader of men. Few generals in the First World War matched him. Very few, if any, surpassed him.

Major General Sir Andrew Russell who commanded the New Zealand Division at Messines and throughout the First World War. An outstanding battlefield commander and inspirational leader, Russell was widely admired (AWM E04712).

The 25th Division was commanded by Major General Guy Bainbridge, a regular officer of considerable experience. He had served in the Egyptian and Boer wars where he proved himself a more than capable leader. A cavalryman, he was selected for staff appointments in the Boer War (Deputy Assistant Adjutant General and General Staff Officer Grade 2). At the outbreak of the First World War he was given the 110th (Leinster) Brigade of the 37th Division. In June of 1916 he was appointed to command of the 25th Division in time for its severest test in the Battle of the Somme. His contemporaries regarded him as a dour and unspectacular but competent general. Guinness, the Brigade Major of the 74th Brigade, described him as 'a horrible man who only thinks of his own advancement'. Following the fighting on the Somme, Guinness was equally scathing. 'It is generally hoped that Bainbridge may lose his job for having thrown away so many lives by asking exhausted troops to perform an impossibility.'[51] If such an offence was deserving of a general's dismissal in the First World War, it was a sanction rarely applied. The few observations of Bainbridge that survive suggest a rather gloomy and forbidding personality. Even Haig, famously taciturn and devoid of personal charisma himself, described Bainbridge as 'not a popular or tactful officer'.[52]

Dour, tactless and utterly untroubled by casualties, Major General Guy Bainbridge, commander of the 25th Division, was a competent but deeply unpopular figure. One of his staff described him as 'A horrible man who only thinks of his own advancement.' (Image by Walter Stoneman, courtesy of the National Portrait Gallery, United Kingdom).

The 4th Australian Division shared with the 25th Division the experience of heavy loss on the Somme. In those battles the division was commanded by Major General Herbert Cox, a British regular officer. Bean makes the claim that pressure from the Australian government for Australians to command their divisions led to the change of command in the 4th Division, although the severe winter of 1915–16, his Gallipoli wounding and the enormous stresses of Pozières and Mouquet Farm also took a toll on Cox. He was promoted lieutenant general and quietly moved aside to the position of Military Secretary to the India Office.[53] The Australian chosen to replace him in command of the 4th Division was the citizen-soldier, Secretary of the New South Wales Water and Sewage Board and former militia officer, William Holmes, then brigadier general commanding the 5th Brigade. Holmes had commenced his military career as a part-time soldier at age 10, serving as a bugler for the colonial New South Wales forces in 1872 and commissioned in 1886. He won the Distinguished Service Order (DSO) in South Africa with the New South Wales contingent and, when the First World War broke out, he was given command of the Australian Naval and Military Expeditionary Force which occupied German New Guinea. He was, according to Bean, 'hearty and cheerful', although Haig was unimpressed. Touring II Anzac after the battle, he confided to his diary that Holmes 'does not seem to have the same qualities of character as Russell and others'.[54] Personally courageous, he would make a point of visiting the most dangerous sectors of his line and ensuring strict adherence to his high standards. His habit of visiting those posts while wearing a red-ribboned staff cap, disregarding his own orders on the wearing of helmets, meant his appearances 'which must have been only too visible to the enemy, were not always welcome to garrisons of outposts who sometimes suffered the shellfire induced by them.'[55] Like Bridges before him, he 'drew the crabs' — hostile fire which continued long after he had left the line — and, like Bridges, he would die at the battle front.

Major General William Holmes, GOC 4th Australian Division. A career soldier, Holmes had the toughest assignment at Messines, one that would test his battered and poorly disciplined division to the limits of its endurance. Messines would be his final battle (AWM 133440).

Commanding the 3rd Division in its first battle, Monash was an experienced and accomplished officer. Unlike Russell however, his command at Gallipoli had resulted in a surprising number of adverse judgements for a man who would later be acclaimed as Australia's greatest soldier. The difficult to please Guinness knew of him from Gallipoli where 'he was not much thought of as a Brigadier … and was given a Division because Australians don't like being commanded by British professional soldiers.'[56] The landing had unstrung many commanders and Monash seemed, according to Bean, 'badly shaken' and 'talking of disaster' at the end of the first week as his men hung on to the ridge above what would become Monash Valley.[57] In September Bean, after savaging him in his diary for what he (unjustly) perceived as his failures in the August offensive — a view he would correct in the *Official History* — described him as 'an able C.O. but never knows the facts about his command'.[58] Monash's failure to move his 4th Brigade through the broken and poorly mapped Aghyl Dere for its assault (which as a result could not be delivered) during Gallipoli's August offensive was well known. Though he could hardly be blamed for not achieving the impossible, Bean's estimation at the time that Monash was 'not a fighting commander like Walker, M'Cay or Chauvel' was no doubt shared by others in the ranks of senior command.[59] Worse still, according to Guinness, he was 'a typical old Jew'.[60]

Monash was highly educated with degrees in Engineering, Law and Arts and was a successful civil engineer in civilian life. A very gifted man with a formidable intellect, he had the misfortune to show his flaws easily, perhaps the source of some of those adverse opinions. 'His ingratiating and yet combative manner, his craving to be the centre of attention, his sensitivity to slights, his vanity were all obvious but his intellect and achievements won respect and friendships.'[61] His experience as an engineer honed a clarity of thought and action which became his trademark. His papers reveal a meticulous attention to detail in both his professional and personal life which bordered on the obsessive. His planning for the Messines attack is astonishing in its preciseness and length as well as the depth to which his guiding hand descended. Mistakes and muddles at Gallipoli which cost lives made a lasting impression and clearly influenced his planning. He would later write of his aims in penning orders of such unusual detail and clarity: 'What I am so anxious to achieve is complete uniformity of thought, policy and attitude throughout the whole Division.'[62]

Major General John Monash, GOC 3rd Australian Division. Messines would be Monash's debut in senior operational command, revealing his emerging greatness as clearly as his flaws (AWM A02691).

With the late change to the plans for Messines, Monash's scheme would need to be re-cast to take in the extended objective. The 3rd Division, like the New Zealanders and the 25th Division, had reaped the benefit of the quiet months leading up to June to deal with the many complications and problems that beset the plans to capture the ridge. Although the New Zealand and 25th divisions were not unduly affected by the changes (apart from arrangements for cooperation with the 4th Australian Division and the new artillery plans), Monash's staff had to cope with major revisions to push on further to the new finish line. While inexperienced, they were well suited to the challenge. Much more complex was the role of the 4th Division and it was to Holmes' overburdened staff that the bulk of the work fell.

The combination of circumstances that committed an Australian division to a major attack while it was still recovering a mere six weeks after decimation at Bullecourt also placed enormous pressure on the divisional staff least equipped to deal with it. Although not to blame for the disaster, the 4th Division's staff work at Bullecourt had been poor.[63] Plummeting morale, desertion and chronic discipline problems added to Holmes' headaches. Success in the coming battle would depend on many elements, but among the most crucial was the leadership and staff work of II Anzac Corps. All of its divisions, but particularly the 4th Australian, would have to rely not only on their own hard-pressed staff, but on the work of the II Anzac staff and, crucially, the leadership of Godley. For the Gallipoli veterans of the 4th Division, with bitter memories of 'Godley's abattoir' still fresh, the prospect of again serving under him was an unwelcome one. It was even more unwelcome for the New Zealanders. Brigadier General George Johnston, Commander Royal Artillery (CRA) of the New Zealand Division, left little doubt about his feelings when he wrote:

> It makes me wonder how on earth we are going to win this war when men like Godley can remain where he is, and dispose of men's lives in such an easy fashion. One unscrupulous man without a conscience.[64]

3

*Tomorrow many men must go to their God ...
If I die, I die.*

The Brink of Eternity

3

Tomorrow many men must go to their God …
If I die, I die.

The Brink of Eternity

By May 1917 Messines Ridge was a hellish place. For the Germans, it was unpleasant at the best of times, but as the British shelling of late April grew heavier by the day, the once orderly trenches with their distinctive thatched walls and wooden floors were systematically smashed to pieces, the wreckage re-pulverised each day by the endless procession of British shells. Captured German letters would reveal the mood of impending defeat. 'Our position looks as if 10,000 mad shells had ravaged there. On the other hand, the English one is quite smooth. Our artillery does not fire at all. If ours fire one shot, the English return 100 … I think that if the end doesn't come soon, he'll beat us.'[1] From the middle of May the shelling stepped up again as the Second Army's full artillery complement of guns and howitzers, one for every six yards of front, arrived and joined the battering in preparation for the battle. Even the usual comforts of regular food and water deliveries began to fail. Reliefs were delayed when the shelling was at its worst or when it targeted the communication trenches in the rear. A soldier from the *44th Infantry Regiment* wrote: 'I cannot describe what it is like here, soon there will be no hope for us. We have a frightful lot of casualties here, drum fire night and day, 14 days of it already. So we can't compete with the English.'[2] The shelling drove the front-line defenders into their concrete shelters and deep dugouts and trapped them there for hours on end. As the shells rained down on the German positions, one witness from the German *40th Division*, stationed in the northern part of Messines, recalled the devastating pounding his unit received:

> Gradually the lighter rounds gave way to 280 mm shells, which crashed down with massive detonations, sending up huge pillars of earth and dust … Our concrete pillbox heaved and swayed with each close impact of the shells. Thick powder smoke filled the room whenever a shell exploded really close … There was not much left of Messines. What had once been an attractive village was reduced to a heap of ruins.[3]

Camouflage was an essential precaution given the increasing sophistication of aerial photography. The Second Army's Intelligence officers also discovered that the tank tracks were clearly visible from 3000 feet and had teams of men sweep behind the tanks as they moved to their parks (AWM A01734).

With the attack now fixed for the first week of June, the Second Army's preparations gathered pace and Godley's staff and those of his divisions plunged into the planning for what would be a much larger, more ambitious and far quicker battle than Plumer had originally presented at the conference of army commanders on 7 May. The glorious weather of the previous weeks persisted through May and the Second Army's infantry continued their training, unaware of the exact date of the attack but certain that it would be soon.[4] The commander of the German *Fourth Army*, General Sixt von Armin, was determined to deny the ridge to the British. A captured German corps order dated 1 June stated that:

> ... the absolute retention of the natural strong points Wijtschate [Wytschaete] and Meesen [Messines] becomes of greater importance for the whole Wijtschate Salient. These strong points must not fall even temporarily

into the enemy's hands … both these strong points must be defended to the utmost and held to the last man, even if the enemy has cut the connections on both sides and threatens the strong points from the rear.[5]

German observation of the British preparations had at least two important results. The first was a clear indication of the timing of the assault and the Germans pinned it to a week. The second was the fact that such a concentration of men and materiel offered unmissable targets for the German artillery. No-one doubted that it was simply a matter of time before the British attack commenced. The long siege of Messines Ridge was, like most sieges, uncomfortable for both sides, but it also produced benefits for each. The Germans had time to construct defences of enormous strength and complexity and could easily observe the British preparations below. The British had time to prepare their assault in unhurried detail and choose exactly which point on the long front it would fall. They also had time to undermine the ridge to unheard-of depths and prepare the greatest mining attack in the history of warfare. Though most of the tell-tale British preparations were made in plain view, the crucially important undermining was not and would prove one of the few genuine surprises of the war. One advantage belonged solely to the besieger. Though the British could not hope for surprise in the all too obvious fact of their coming attack, they could, like a boxer repeatedly testing an opponent's defences with jabs and feints, choose the exact moment for the knockout blow.

The preparatory work for the coming battle intensified in May. In the 25th Division's sector, the work of the 105th, 106th and 130th field companies of the Royal Engineers was lavishly praised and exhaustively described:

> … road making, water supply storage, trench tramways, and sidings, Divisional Reserve and Advanced Magazine, advanced dressing station, two regimental aid post shelters for walking wounded, two protected cable crossings over River Douve, five bombproof telephone exchanges … dumps for R.E. stores, dumps for rations, one tunnelled dugout for Brigade Headquarters, 12 Battalion Headquarters, three concrete report centres, two communication trenches repaired and made good, six new communication trenches revetted and boarded the whole way, five artillery Group Headquarters, Command Posts and shelters for gun crews of 25 batteries, three heavy trench mortar emplacements, six complete lines of assembly trenches within 500 yards of German front line.[6]

However the 25th Division's preparations for battle were not all-consuming. On 13 May, in a very low scoring affair, A Company of the 8th Battalion, the

Border Regiment, lost its cricket match against B Company, 28 runs to 36. Such diversions proved an interesting sideline for the Adjutant of the 8th Battalion whose very sparse diary entries on the build-up to the battle were regularly interspersed with sporting updates. He noted the battalion's disappointment that Lance Corporal Shields, the 8th's boxing champion, lost the brigade championship in the tenth round to Private Newbiggin of the 11th Cheshires.[7] The Borders hoped it wasn't an ill omen for the coming battle.

Men of the 4th Australian Machine Gun Company training with Vickers machine-guns in old trenches near Estaires in preparation for Messines (AWM P02670.007).

The same careful planning was evident in the medical arrangements. Sister Ada Smith arrived at of the 2nd Australian Casualty Clearing Station at Trois Arbres on 4 January. Even then, the coming attack was a topic of conversation.

'The patients in the wards often told us what was going to happen "when we take Messines Ridge." We had heard of that ridge so often, and the time it was going to be taken, that we only laughed when they spoke of it. However, when the Ridge was really to be taken, we heard very little about it.'[8] The II Anzac Corps main dressing station was located at Pont d'Achelles. The bitter experience of previous battles had produced a quiet revolution in medical care. The arrangements for evacuating the wounded from the front line to Regimental Aid Posts and forward dressing stations were based on triage principles which aimed to ensure the swift evacuation of wounded men to care which would save their lives, ease their pain, comfort their shock and, in specially designed 'moribund' wards, allow them to die in peace and, if possible, without pain. The moribund wards 'well fitted with beds, saline apparatus, stimulants, hot water bottles etc.' gave the dying a peaceful, if falsely hopeful death.[9]

The miners were also pressed hard. The 1st Australian Tunnelling Company not only had the job of defending the Hill 60 mines, but also of excavating the famous underground barracks known as 'the Catacombs', deep inside Hill 63 at the southern end of the battlefield. Named 'Wallangarra' by the Queenslanders among the tunnellers after the small southern town of their home state, the dugout's extensive network of chambers and galleries could house over 2000 men. Although it was deep enough to provide absolute security from shells, the atmosphere inside when fully occupied drove some to consider taking their chances with the German artillery. Dank and reeking it may have been, but it was a safe haven in a dangerous place and its construction was another major achievement of the Second Army's engineers, recognised in a formal opening ceremony performed by the army commander himself:[10]

> If the striped awning and carpet, which provide the hall-mark of dignity at functions in this country, were missing, at least they were represented in principle by the archway of tree branches erected over the entrance, and the liberal application of sawdust underfoot. Little bunches of gaily coloured bunting relieved the sombre green in the triumphal arch ... A band helped to enliven the proceedings, and with the presence of no less than twenty generals and their staffs ensured the function was not lacking in dignity. If not quite a red-letter day, this was indeed a "Red Hat" day ... Fortunately, the ceremony passed off without any molestation from the enemy. Had a searching gun got busy, then promotion would have been accelerated.[11]

'The Catacombs' constructed by the 1st Australian Tunnelling Company, the kangaroo cut-out proudly marking the entrance to 'Plumer Road' and the underground barracks which could accommodate almost an entire brigade (AWM E04486).

Extensive though they were, the Catacombs could only shelter a tiny proportion of the force needed to attack the ridge. As Plumer was cutting the ribbon to open the tunnels at Hill 63, his staff officers were hard at work finalising the intricate and complex movement plans that would deliver the assault divisions from their staging areas to the battle front, timed to arrive just prior to the mine explosions. While tunnelling was an ancient art for the engineers, by 1917 they were learning an entirely new field of operations — one that would become routine in the years to come. Bridges had to be strengthened, roads repaired and tramway crossings, communication cables and water pipes protected to cope with the weight and the tearing tracks of the 29-ton British battle tanks. The rapid growth of the 'Heavy Machine Gun Branch', as the Tank Corps was then known, coined the new word 'tankodrome' for the tank parks that served as marshalling areas for the Second Army's armour. New also were the Mark IV tanks, a slightly improved version of the Mark I and II tanks that had failed the Australians so dismally at Bullecourt. Arriving by rail and motoring to their parks, the Mark IVs had entered service just a month earlier. Getting them battle ready was a remarkable achievement, as was the Second Army's administrative effort to deploy them ready for action in June. Orders for infantry cooperation with the tanks had also evolved since Bullecourt, reflecting a far more cautious and less ambitious appreciation of their capability. At Messines, no aspect of the operation was to be dependent on the success of the tanks and they would play a purely subsidiary infantry support role. Every effort was made to keep their presence hidden from the Germans. The 2nd Tank Brigade's summary of operations at Messines records that the specially prepared ramps and unloading arrangements allowed one company to detrain its 12 tanks in 23 minutes, an effort that compares favourably with the present day. An aircraft was sent up to photograph the tanks' tracks as they motored away from the trains, revealing that the tracks, barely noticeable at ground level, carved out trails which were clearly visible at 3000 feet. Pioneers were subsequently sent to scrub them out. Moving at six kilometres per hour meant a long, noisy approach to the ridge and plans were put in place for the RFC to increase its patrols over the British lines on the morning of the battle to drown the noise of the tanks. Such evidence of Harington's exacting standards in staff work permeates the entire record of Messines.

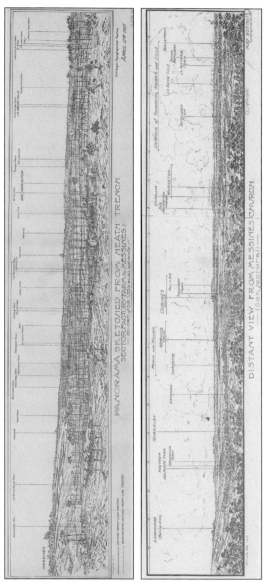

Map 4. Topographic drawing of the 3rd Division front, April 1917. A remarkably detailed sketch of the 3rd Division's attack frontage from Factory Farm to Messines. Sketched prior to the preliminary bombardment, the village of Messines can be seen on the ridge, heavily damaged but with many buildings still standing. Known strongpoints are marked. The village is shown prior to the massive artillery bombardment of May which flattened the ruins.

II Anzac's headquarters was no less focussed on thorough preparation, its engineers constructing railways and trench tramways, ammunition dumps, sidings and stations. 'A complicated system of cable had to be buried for communications. Water supply had to be organised. The roads … needed urgent repair. An infinite number of gun positions had to be constructed.[12] 'Infinite' in this case was roughly one third of the Second Army's arsenal of guns and howitzers and the enormous dumps of shells required to feed them. The dramatic build-up of artillery from the start of May became apparent to the Germans as the newly arrived units began to register their guns. Although counter-battery work and harassing fire was almost constant from April, II Anzac's headquarters charted the systematic smashing of German front-line trenches and roads, destruction of known strongpoints, increased counter-battery fire, wire-cutting and, with unceasing night fire, wearing down the German morale and driving them into the safety of dugouts and reinforced concrete pillboxes. As May ended, the artillery duel was rapidly becoming one-sided. 'It is mad work here as the English blow a few batteries to bits every day, it is no laughing matter here for the Artillery in the West. He has not yet found the exact position of our battery but when he has once got us there will be proper firing, he has already shot a few away.'[13]

Gunners from the New Zealand Division remove a camouflaged screen to reveal a howitzer (AWM E03865).

While the pillboxes provided some protection from the storm of fire and flying steel outside, they did nothing to save men from the psychological trauma of the interminable shelling. If anything, confinement made it worse and some took their chances outside in shell holes.[14] Of all First World War writers, Charles Bean came closest to describing what he called 'the acute mental torture' of artillery, with 'each shrieking tearing crash bringing a promise to each man – instantaneous – I will tear you into ghastly wounds – I will rend your flesh and pulp an arm or a leg – fling you, half a gaping quivering man like these you see smashed around you one by one, to lie there rotting and blackening like all the things you saw by the awful roadside or in that sickening dusty crater.'[15] Such was the ordeal of the unfortunate Germans who, day after day, were crowded together underground or under the low concrete roofs of the pillboxes, breathing stale and fetid air and unable to communicate with their units for long periods. The screaming shells and relentless concussions shredded nerves already raw from waiting for the attack they knew was coming. Every soldier knew the deep dugouts were death-traps if the British broke through before their defenders had the chance to emerge. The first they might know of the attack could be grenades and phosphorous bombs tumbling down the stairs, a horrible prospect in the crowded darkness. Surrender, always a very dangerous business in the frenzied midst of an attack, was often impossible from their deep holes underground. Clearing dugouts was 'ratting' to the Australians, a term that described both the method of driving out the frightened inhabitants and their attitude towards them. Little mercy could be expected. For now, such rat holes were the only hope of safety for many.

In the eight days leading up to the launch of the battle, the British fired some 3,258,000 shells at the Messines-Wytschaete Ridge across its 14-kilometre front, a weight of fire unimaginable at the beginning of the war. Those statistics are almost as stupefying as the bombardment itself. Captain Ernest Boon of the 306th Siege Battery thought it 'a sheer waste of ammunition as the Jerries simply withdrew to their deep dugouts at the commencement of a definite bombardment until the action ceased and then came up again and rebuilt their trenches.'[16] As the artillery duel entered its second week, the Germans forced to endure it were beaten down, their morale crippled as, deafened and numbed, they waited for the inevitable:

It went on like this day after day. By then we were worn down so much that, finally, careful watchfulness in the face of danger gave way to complete indifference. None of us believed any longer that we should escape the witch's cauldron in one piece, so it was all the same to us if we met our fate a few days earlier than we otherwise might have done. Our situation was desperate, but it did draw us together. We went into our letter cases and drew out letters and photographs of our relatives to show to one another, [but] our conversation tended to be confined to speculation about when we should be hit.[17]

For those doling out the punishment, the emotions were entirely different. Gunner William Lyall of the 8th Battery (3rd Australian Field Artillery Brigade) wrote home enthusiastically about the work of his battery on 2 June in the midst of the Second Army's withering artillery attack, describing it as:

> … just wonderful and Fritz never has a ghost of a chance against it – prisoners say it is pure murder to face it … The infantry swear by the artillery and never cease praising their magnificent work. You see whenever we make an advance, the artillery puts up a barrage and paves the way for the infantry who follow behind this curtain of shells. After we've blown old Fritz's front line to atoms, we lift our fire further ahead and so we go on advancing until our objective has been taken and consolidated.[18]

Forward German trenches at Messines showing the scale of destruction wrought by the Second Army's artillery bombardment in the weeks leading up to 7 June (AWM E00554).

Though gradually worn down, the German artillery was still dangerous. Private Alexander MacIntosh of the 7th Australian Field Artillery Brigade wrote of the perils faced by the gunners. 'Worst of all is when they [shells] are falling round the guns and we have to go and get ready for action, and do some firing. I am not at all brave under such circumstances. Shells bursting give one a very funny feeling.'[19] Unlike many of his German counterparts, MacIntosh and his gun survived the duel unscathed.

The effectiveness of Plumer's counter-battery fire was significantly increased by RFC aircraft which brought back hundreds of photographs of the rearmost German lines for intelligence officers to pore over with magnifying glasses searching for the camouflaged gun pits. RFC observers spotted for the flashes of German guns and plotted their locations on the horizon, radioing back reference points. The rapidly improving British techniques of sound ranging could, when triangulated with the visual reference of flash spotting, plot the distance and direction (and therefore the location) of a German gun with unprecedented accuracy. The Second Army's gunners would then rain shells into the chosen 50-yard map square in the hope of blowing another German gun to smithereens. The German response grew weaker as zero day approached, but their long-range guns remained a threat and, on 6 June, they hit the 42nd Battalion at Pont de Nieppe, over 10 kilometres from the front. Lieutenant William Fisher recalled the terror: 'Then a shell came shrieking over and landed some 30 yards away, knocking 16 men of No. 8 platoon. Pandemonium broke loose. Shells rained upon the town – the civilians shrieked and ran all over the place. The groans of the wounded, the crash of falling masonry and the tinkle of glass from hundreds of windows – and the wailing of the poor little children, some of whom were hit – all combined to make one realise how hideous war can be.'[20]

As zero hour on 7 June approached, the mathematics of destruction weighed heavily in Plumer's favour. The Second Army's intelligence summaries record the degradation of the German artillery. On 3 June they described direct hits on 32 gun pits, eight of these detonating nearby dumps of shells. The next day, 42 gun pits were hit, resulting in 20 explosions. 'Enemy batteries' the summary continued, 'were neutralised on 263 occasions.' In response, the Germans managed to hit only 17 British guns, causing three explosions.[21] Practice barrages designed to mimic the launch of the expected attack revealed that the German artillery response was weakening by the day. However, in a sign that the Germans had closely pinpointed the time of the attack, a captured German artillery observer revealed that heavy artillery (four 15-centimetre Russian naval guns) had been moved back from 2200 metres to 4100 metres on the night of

6/7 June to avoid capture. 'This partly accounts for the weakness of the hostile fire', the Second Army's intelligence concluded. 'This fact was carefully concealed from the [German] infantry and F.O.O.'s [forward observation officers] were sent forward to delude the infantry into belief that the artillery would give them ample support; the prisoner was on a mission to the Infantry for this purpose when he was captured.'[22]

As effective as it would prove to be in breaking the resistance of the defenders however, such immense preliminary bombardments also created problems for the assault troops. Weeks of shelling the same targets turned the dry soil to powder and what was once firm ground took on the consistency of beach sand. Rain could then make it impassable. 'This drumfire thoroughly wrecked the entire landscape, ruined the natural drainage and turned the battlefield into a moonscape of mud and craters over which assaulting infantry had to walk as best they could and through which, as events proved, the supporting artillery could not keep pace with the infantry.'[23] The Tank Corps records also point to the problems such immense poundings created for heavy armour, noting at Messines that the tanks averaged 30 yards a minute on the good going of the approach to the British front line but only a perilous 10 yards a minute in the most heavily shelled zone between the German front line and the first objective or 'Blue Line', picking up speed again when they moved on beyond the ridge towards the Oosttaverne Line at 20 yards a minute.[24]

• • •

While the crawling rhomboid British tanks were the slowest engines of war on the battlefield, even outpaced by the horse-drawn artillery, the fastest roared through the air above at over 100 miles per hour. From his vantage point high above the battlefield, Lieutenant Thomas McKenny Hughes of 53 Squadron, RFC, was engaged in gathering that most vital of military commodities, intelligence. As complex as the job of collecting intelligence was, the equation for the opposing air forces was a simple one. Mastery of the skies conferred an enormous intelligence advantage on the winner and, in the summer skies above Messines, the British were winning. The RFC had deployed 18 squadrons and more than 300 aircraft over Messines in the weeks leading up to the battle. One third of those were fighters whose task it was to clear the skies of German aircraft and limit as much as possible the photography which was crucial for identifying the rapidly growing threat. The Germans on the ground observed the worrying build-up of British air power, recognising it as a sure prelude to attack. The

British could not hope to hide the vast preparations which were clearly visible to the German observers on the ridge and their flyers who managed to pierce the screen the RFC had thrown over the entire battlefront, an area stretching back 10,000 yards from the German balloon line. The dogfights were a riveting spectacle for the troops of both sides who, hemmed in by trench walls, enjoyed rare moments of interest above, and who noticed the growing British confidence and daring as their numbers increased:

> The daily air battles were most interesting. It was far from rare to see the enemy flying in battle formations of sixty to seventy aircraft. We were not in a position to put up so many sorties but when we did, the British tended to stay away … The aircraft made a special effort to destroy balloons. If one of the latter was shot down the observers used to jump and descend to earth by parachute … Those of us on the ground were frequently the targets of enemy aircraft; the boldest of these came down to twenty metres to fire at us.[25]

Ground strafing was another innovation. First introduced on a wide scale at Messines, strafing had been made possible by the faster, more manoeuvrable aircraft of 1917. It would also add a new threat to the unfortunate infantry trapped in trenches far below:

> Yes, the Flying Corps … Up all the time, night and day, swooping and bombing behind enemy lines, smashing his hangars and aerodromes, pulling down his flyers, putting out his eyes, you might say, and then spotting his batteries for our artillery … They've got a new wheeze … flying low down, some of 'em, just in front of our advancing line, putting machine guns into action against the enemy infantry. It's terrific![26]

However death in the air could be awful to watch as men from the AIF's 33rd Battalion recorded. 'At 4.00 a.m. 12 of our planes flew over Messines' recorded the observers. 'Enemy crashed one of these in flames. Both occupants jumped out when 1000 ft from ground.'[27] Despite their losses, the RFC maintained the upper hand throughout May. For the German soldiers who manned the forward trenches, such overwhelming air power sapped morale as surely as the relentless shelling. On 1 May, II Anzac reported that a German pigeon had arrived in its loft with a message which spoke volumes both about British air superiority and deteriorating German morale. 'Hostile machine has been directing fire of batteries since 7.00 a.m. this morning. In spite of repeated requests for aircraft protection, not one German aeroplane has been seen over our sector.'[28]

While the dogfights and strafing may have been lethal and presented a terrifying spectacle to those on the ground, the most important weapons the aircraft carried were their cameras. The aerial photographs they took were used to update maps (daily if necessary), to plot trenches and strongpoints and to discover and help destroy the all-important German artillery. The photographs, along with sketches made by the artists in the topographical companies and the intelligence gathered from raids, produced the most comprehensive picture of German defensive positions ever achieved in the First World War. Aerial photographs at the end of May showed that the Germans had made no attempt to repair their shattered front-line trenches, the artillery so heavy that there was probably no chance of doing so. Prisoners reported that they expected the attack at the end of May and that, although there were plenty of machine-gun emplacements (one regiment reported that there were 44 machine-guns to protect its front lines), the unceasing British artillery and daily air attacks gradually but effectively degraded every aspect of defence from the destruction of guns and gun pits to the erosion of morale:[29]

> Swarms of enemy aircraft enhanced the efficiency of the artillery. They interdicted the rear areas by day and night, attacking all manner of live targets with bombs and machine gun fire. It was clear to us all what lay before us and everyone held his breath, waiting for the infantry assault which just had to come.[30]

• • •

But, as clear and detailed as aerial photographs had become, they could only ever be part of the intelligence picture. A greater portion of the German defensive scheme was either underground, too small, or too well hidden to be discovered from the air. All across the front, the Second Army's divisions conducted nightly raids to test the enemy's readiness, chart his trenches and, most importantly, bring back prisoners. The 3rd Division's extraordinarily detailed intelligence summaries for May reveal just how valuable that information could be. On 6 May, the war diary records the capture of Johann Hektor, 'an educated man' of the *5th Bavarian Reserve Infantry Regiment* who, although 'unwilling to give any information about his comrades', was somehow persuaded to provide the German order of battle in his sector, their method of holding the line, details of reliefs as well as their counter-measures against gas attack. He also informed his captors that the Germans fully expected an attack on Messines. Hektor had mistakenly bolted into the arms of the Australians after a Lewis gun had been turned on his fossicking party.[31] Frequent raids launched all across the Second Army's front yielded more invaluable intelligence. A captured briefing note to the *40th (Saxon) Division* read: 'Intended enemy attack can be reckoned on any day now … According to experiences up to date, big English attacks have usually taken place in the early hours of the morning. Infantry and artillery must therefore be particularly on watch at these times.'[32]

The raids could be very substantial indeed. The 3rd Division's assault east of Houplines on 27 February, launched by the 37th and 38th battalions, involved 800 men and pushed through into the German third line, remaining in the enemy system for 50 minutes and bringing back 17 prisoners.[33] Raiding often resulted in sudden and desperate hand-to-hand fighting in the dark as the intruders surprised a garrison and attempted to snatch prisoners to interrogate. The account of the 33rd Battalion's raid on the German trenches at Point Ballot on the night of 24 February provides some insight into the mayhem and horror of a raid: '30, probably more Germans were killed and an officer and three other ranks taken prisoner, none of whom were brought in alive. In the German trench 5 Germans were found chained to a wire stretched between two posts in a fire bay.'[34] Three of those were dead and the remaining two were understandably 'quite willing to surrender'. Lieutenant Donald McKenzie of the 33rd cut one free but, 'as he dropped his knife in some water he had to shoot the other.' The 33rd had captured four prisoners including one officer, but in shepherding them across no man's land, a shell killed the officer and wounded McKenzie. Private George Seagrott went back to look for McKenzie and found him 'in a dazed condition, and with the mangled body of the officer prisoner he was escorting lying beside him.'[35] The slightly built Seagrott picked up McKenzie and carried him back. Of the other prisoners, one 'became fractious' and had to be shot, the second dropped to his knees and begged for his life but as he wouldn't (or, more likely, couldn't) move, was also shot. 'The fourth prisoner' the narrative continued, 'was also killed. The three men escorting him had two wounded men to bring in and as the going in no man's land was very bad, they shot him and used his body as a bridge to get over the enemy wire.'[36]

Raids, by their nature, also turned up surprises. On 24 May, as Haig was meeting with Godley to tour all four divisions of II Anzac, two men of the 25th Division, who had been missing since a raid on 22 May, walked back into the British lines after lying low in the German trench system. They reported that the trenches were unmanned during the day and, by night, only a few patrols came through. This news confirmed the shadowy intelligence picture built up from aerial photographs and distant observation that the enemy were not garrisoning their front lines strongly. As May drew to a close, raiding took place almost every night. A silent raid by men of the 3rd Division on 31 May turned back when they found the trenches in the Douve Valley 'strongly manned', the wire badly knocked about in places, strong in others. A raid the next night again tested the enemy's reaction:

> The ... patrol ... entered the trench, shot a sentry on the parapet, and came upon 2 or 3 of the enemy descending into a dugout ... As they refused to surrender the dugout was bombed and screams indicated the enemy suffered casualties.[37]

On 28 May the 3rd Division captured an officer of the *5th Bavarian Reserve Infantry Regiment*. His interrogation again yielded a wealth of information — three full pages including the locations of battalion headquarters, routes used and not used by reinforcements and very detailed descriptions of the German defences including locations of hidden machine-guns and dugouts. Although he talked freely, he remained confident that the British attack would be resisted. 'Prisoner states that his officers are confident that Petit Douve Farm locality will hold up our attack, and that in any case we shall not get past Messines. He says Messines is full of machine guns and that there are 120 Batteries behind Messines which have only fired one gun each. Prisoner appeared to have great confidence in his officers statements on these points.'[38]

Saxon prisoners of the *40th Division*, which held the line to the north of Messines, captured on 3 June reported the devastation wrought on their trenches and dugouts, many of the latter now uninhabitable, that communication trenches were cut off every few yards and that there had been no effort to organise any defence of the front-line system. In fact, this system had been all but abandoned, only lightly held 'to avoid unnecessary casualties'. Defensive plans to cope with tanks were in similar disarray, with some units supplied with 'K' (armour-piercing) ammunition and expecting tanks, and others not expecting tanks at all or completely unprepared. II Anzac's interrogators assessed their prisoners' morale as poor, commenting that they 'seemed to have been resigned to their fate'. Prisoners of the *4th Bavarian Division* reported on 4 June that the British attack was expected any minute and the Germans were practically on 24-hour stand-to. They added that, although morale in the division was good, 'their officers dread the coming attack greatly'.[39]

The intelligence summary of the 33rd Battalion for 25 May recorded the increasing intensity of the artillery bombarding the enemy trenches with shells of all calibres and targeting a working party at Factory Farm. Trench mortars also contributed to the wrecking of German trenches and snipers regularly targeted periscopes. The 33rd noted the build-up of British air supremacy which kept the German photographers at bay. This was a critical success. If guns and dumps were located, the German gunners could accurately target them. If they could map the roads, trenches and railways under construction, they could also plot the course of the coming attack and disrupt it. Most dangerous of all, should they spot the assault divisions on the move, they could annihilate entire battalions.

Major attacks placed an often overwhelming pressure on army communication systems. Battle by its nature was confusing and chaotic and the chaos of the fighting was reflected in the message slips that flooded in from battalions and brigades, hastily scrawled under fire by candlelight and thrust in the hands of runners. Telephone lines in armoured cable buried two metres down might survive the shelling, but often didn't. Most ominous of all was the silence that told of units disintegrating somewhere ahead, unseen and unheard until runners arrived with their fragments of news on which commanders had to make harried life and death decisions. The most urgent need in battle was for that information to find its way to headquarters as quickly as possible and for that information to be accurate, or as close as possible to it. Plumer's Chief of Staff applied his considerable intellect to this problem and designed a new system at army level. Too often, battles had fallen apart while the highest level of command sat ignorant and paralysed, cut off by poor communication or hopelessly confused by scraps of news, hours old and sometimes contradictory. Harington's design of the 'Army Centre' was a revolution in the organisation of communication, forming a nexus of command and control, collecting information from forward observers, battalion, brigade and divisional headquarters, from runners, pigeons, balloon, drops by aircraft and power buzzers, radio and telephones — literally and metaphorically at the centre of the complex network of every communication on, under and above the battlefield. The Second Army Centre was located at Locre Château and connected to similar organisations created for the three army corps (II Anzac Centre was located at Bailleul). Harington designed the system to operate without interfering with the normal work of corps or army staffs. With typical attention to detail he outlined the optimum working climate within this vital nerve centre, a polar opposite to the chaos of battle:

> The successful working of the Centre largely depends on everyone keeping their temper, not getting flustered, having a reasonable amount of sleep (proper reliefs) and being well fed and comfortable. No visitors during the battle should be allowed. If the Centre gets shelled it upsets everyone, so if

possible it should be put in as quiet a place as possible. If the floor is boarded, it is worthwhile getting canvas shoes for clerks as it is difficult to hear over the telephone when heavy footsteps are added to the other noises.[40]

Australian troops of the 4th Division studying the terrain model of the Messines battlefield constructed at Romarin. Descriptions of the model and the careful planning that it represented was the subject of much comment in letters and diaries (AWM E00648).

• • •

During April and May, the specialist draftsmen, builders and artists who staffed the dedicated modelling units produced three large-scale models of the ground to be attacked by each of the corps, a skill present from the earliest days of war and one still practised today. The terrain models created for Messines were unique — superbly detailed and large enough for entire battalions to surround and view. Platoon commanders were able to clearly run through the coming battle with their men, adding a vital mental picture to help guide them through the twisting maze of trenches and blasted landscape they would cross. Viewing the models supplemented the regular training exercises conducted for each of the assault battalions. Lieutenant Alan Downie of the 3rd Division's 40th Battalion described II Anzac's model at Romarin, behind Hill 63:

> I come now to explain how it was that we all had such a good knowledge of the ground we are destined to attack and pass over. Some distance from our present camp, and tucked away on a nice secluded spot, is an absolute work of art in the form of a model and exact replica of the trenches and country which our particular Brigade has for its attention on the day of the attack. Done by the pioneers in sand, brick, tiles and concrete and covering in all nearly forty square yards, this excellent model is doing a great deal to make our task a far easier one in the way of knowledge of some of that which is before us. Standing on the raised platform we are able to look down on the enemy positions, the whole thing being done to scale we are able to follow it with our maps, and winding away from us, on the right of what remains of the village of Messines, we can see the whole of the Douve Valley … this model was kept up to date by aeroplane photographs etc. which revealed the destruction caused by our artillery from day to day.[41]

While the continual probing of the German defences by raids produced intelligence of enormous value, it could not answer one burning question. Would the Germans, realising a major attack was imminent, pull back from the ridge and allow the massive British effort to swipe harmlessly through thin air? Haig grew increasingly nervous about this possibility, suggesting that perhaps the mines should be exploded early, falsely announcing the start of the great offensive and triggering an inevitable all-out effort by the German artillery which would disclose any guns the Germans had successfully kept hidden from the airborne cameras. Plumer put this suggestion to his corps commanders who all rejected it in favour of two practice barrages which closely resembled that planned for the actual attack. Plumer's monstrous collection of guns fired full battle rehearsals on 3 and 5 June, the second rehearsal accompanied by machine-guns and a smokescreen to hide the phantom infantry. RFC observer Thomas McKenny Hughes was flash spotting for the first of the barrages: 'At 6 p.m. our artillery put up a practice barrage (a) to see how well they did it and (b) to make the Germans think 'der tag' had come and start firing with their reserve guns to show where they were … We had six machines up simply for spotting flashes … and saw innumerable flashes, quite a number being very far back.'[42] Nevertheless, on both occasions, the response from the Germans was weak. Either the British counter-battery work had succeeded beyond all hope or the Germans had not been fooled.

However the Germans had certainly been fooled underground. Although they were fully aware that the ridge was being undermined, they had little idea of the vast scale of the mining or the whereabouts of the mines. Oliver Woodward's men of the 1st Australian Tunnelling Company engaged in a long and bitter battle with their German counterparts under the vital ground at Hill 60. In the narrow galleries deep underground, the listeners crouched, silent and lonely, beside the low, damp walls monitoring the sounds of the enemy's hunt. Woodward described the listener's lot:

> The standard mine gallery is only 4ft. 3in. high and 2ft. 3in. wide. It is not exactly pleasant to realise that if the sides are squeezed in only a few inches one is successfully entombed. In addition to this the galleries, especially in the clay areas, are saturated with water. The anxious time for a listener is when silence follows a period of previous activity on the part of the enemy … It is rather thrilling when one is stalking, but decidedly nerve-wracking when one is being stalked … I have listened in the "D" Right Gallery as immovable as piece of statuary and have been equally cold, from fear.[43]

In most of the mine galleries at Messines, offensive tunnelling had ceased. Not so at Hill 60 however, where the underground fighting reached a level 'which was not surpassed anywhere on the British front' as the Australians tried to blunt and deceive the many German tunnelling attempts to locate the two enormous mines.[44] In the depths of winter came the first major crisis at Hill 60. The Germans began sinking a vertical shaft which threatened to meet the main gallery. Aerial photographs confirmed the threat and the 1st Australian Tunnelling Company began digging a tunnel from the main Caterpillar gallery towards the German shaft. It was an audacious and skilful move. Two tons of ammonal were placed in a chamber beneath the enemy's works on 14 December as the German miners burrowed unwittingly towards it. So close to the Hill 60 mine was this charge that its explosion threatened to set off the main mine and arrangements were made for the infantry to storm Hill 60 if it went up. Such an eventuality would, of course, deal a huge blow to the coordination of the main attack, then some six months in the future, and it was decided to delay the firing of the counter-mine as long as possible.

Officers of the 1st Australian Tunnelling Company at a rest camp two weeks after the successful detonation of the Hill 60 mines. The officers are (left to right, back row): Lieutenants John Royle, James Bowry and Hubert Carroll. Front row: Captain Oliver Woodward, Major James Henry and Captain Robert Clinton (AWM P02333.002).

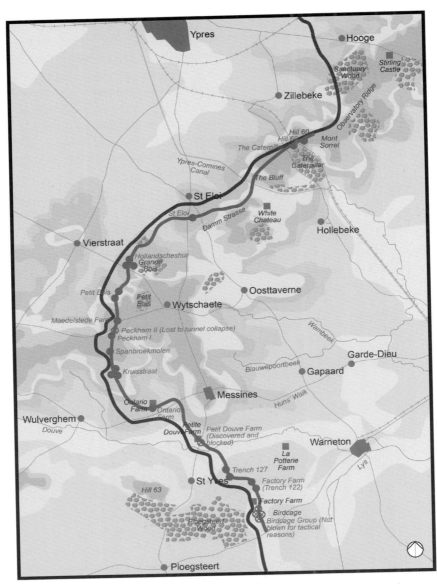

Map 5. The Messines mines. In the largest and most successful mining attack in the history of war, 25 mines were placed under the German front lines targeting key strongpoints (19 were detonated on 7 June). While the Germans, aware of the danger, withdrew most of their men behind the blast zone, they suffered devastating losses at Hill 60 and at several other sites. The moral effect of what was the largest man-made explosion in history was profound.

As the Germans dug ever deeper towards the Hill 60 mine, it became obvious that, if they continued digging, they were only days away from breaking into the main gallery and neutralising the mine. At 2.00 am on 19 December the Australians blew the counter-mine. To Oliver Woodward's intense relief, the Hill 60 mine did not go with it. A 'huge tongue of flame' leapt up from the head of the German shaft, killing and entombing an unknown number of miners. The Australian counter-mining not only wrecked the German deep works at Hill 60, it sowed confusion in their ranks. Despite this dramatic message from the 1st Australian Tunnelling Company, the German mining engineer at Hill 60, Lieutenant Colonel Otto Füsslein was, according to Bean, 'satisfied that the British had been outwitted and outworked'.[45] The German infantry of the *204th Division*, sitting atop the Hill 60 mine, were evidently told that the explosion was an accidental German firing despite the fact that their staff were fully aware that it was the result of enemy action. Füsslein's wishful thinking was not shared by the infantry who viewed the incident with foreboding and suspicion.[46] Ominously, the only person with the means and responsibility to keep them safe from the British tunnellers was fatally convinced they already were.

Four British soldiers attached to the 1st Australian Tunnelling Company construct a dugout beneath an artillery observation post on Hill 63. The cramped conditions and slimy mud provide some indication of the slow, back-breaking work required. The candle was used to detect the presence of gas. If the candle burned brighter, methane was present, if the flame was low it indicated a lack of oxygen (AWM E01513).

On 28 April, when the issue of withdrawing their lines from the ridge was actively under discussion by Crown Prince Rupprecht and his commanders, they were assured by Füsslein that a mine attack 'was no longer possible'.[47] By 10 May, after some weeks of obvious activity at Hill 60 with both sides blowing camouflets (the Australians on 18 April and the Germans on 19 and 20 April) and indications in other systems, Füsslein had changed his mind. He now believed, and reported to the *Fourth Army* that the British had probably planted deep mines not only at Hill 60 and the Caterpillar, but at St Eloi, Spanbroekmolen and Kruisstraat as well and that these represented a real threat. Füsslein's miners too were feeling the strain, particularly given British air superiority. 'Penal servitude would be better' one wrote. 'There one sits from 6.00 a.m. till 11.00 p.m., as wet as a cat, and there is no air as no ventilators are working; one has to go up to get a breath … but the aviators won't have this as they hover over us at a height of 20 m.'[48]

Sapper Eugene Kelly of the 3rd Australian Tunnelling Company at a Mine Rescue Station wearing the proto apparatus used for mine rescue operations (and fighting) in the presence of poisonous gas. Kelly is carrying a cage with either canaries or mice ('the miner's friends') to indicate the presence of gas (AWM E01683).

On 25 May the Germans struck back, blowing a charge which collapsed one of the Hill 60 galleries, trapping two listeners, Sappers Edward Earl and George Simpson. Despite the awful fate that awaited him, Earl somehow continued his duty, listening for the enemy activity which might discover the mine. The Adjutant recorded his remarkable heroism in the war diary:

Extraordinarily cool report from an entombed miner Spr Earl 1st A.T. Coy. He was listening in one of the long deep galleries at Hill 60 when Germans on May 25th exploded a mine, breaking down the gallery behind him. He was believed to be dead but was heard signalling 17 hours later and was rescued on May 27th. Meanwhile he continued to listen to the enemy at work in a neighbouring shaft & gallery which were dangerously near our main gallery under Hill 60; he made his will, wrote to his mother, heard a neighbouring listener rescued from another gallery & when his signals were answered - lay down & slept on and off till he was rescued.[49]

The two men were eventually rescued, Earl not until two days later and too late to prevent his eventual death three months on from the effects of his ordeal.

By the end of May, Füsslein had again changed his mind, reporting to *Fourth Army* headquarters that the mine danger, although not defeated, had been contained. The thinning-out of the German front lines was an added insurance and the *Gruppe Wijtschate*'s commander, General Maximilian von Laffert, believed that, given this precaution, any mines would have only local and limited effect. Others did not share his confidence.[50] Füsslein's wholly misplaced optimism over his battle with the British miners, combined with a dangerous complacency in *Gruppe Wijtschate*'s command group, now set the scene for what Crown Prince Rupprecht's Chief of Staff, General Herman von Kuhl, would describe as 'a great tragedy'.

• • •

While Haig's optimism on the eve of Messines that the end was in sight would prove extravagant, it was certainly not baseless. Victory at Messines would be a very serious shock to the Germans and a once powerful army's collapse and headlong flight is, by its nature, sudden and unpredictable. The Germans had conducted a major withdrawal only weeks before. But tempering the enthusiasm at Messines were some worrying signs, particularly for the Anzacs. Three days before the attack, Bean spoke to Lieutenant Colonel John Hurst (36th Heavy Artillery) who told him he thought that the Germans had taken most of their guns out of harm's way behind Messines, 'not leaving their guns to be captured' and relying on long-range guns on both flanks. Although no such frank assessment was made by the Second Army, its intelligence maps confirmed this.[51] Bean confided his fears to his notebook: 'The majority of their howitzers are back out of range of our heavies, and our infantry will not come within range of them until actual advance.'[52] This was yet another indication that the Germans fully anticipated the direction and correctly estimated the frontage of the British attack. The positioning of the artillery on both flanks of the predicted attack front meant that the Second Army, should it actually succeed in breaking through the German lines around Warneton, would advance into devastating enfilade artillery fire. More worrying still for II Anzac was the concentration of German guns on its southern flank on the far bank of the River Lys. These guns could fire in enfilade along the exposed southern slope of Messines Ridge.

Worrying as well was the pressure on the staff of II Anzac to draft the altered artillery arrangements to support the afternoon attack and attend to the thousand other administrative details of logistics, movement, supply and communications. Bean was scathing in his criticism of Godley's staff, describing them as 'rotten'. He had similar concerns about the 4th Division staff which he expressed obliquely, comparing the voluminous and highly detailed orders of the 3rd Division with the 4th Division's which 'were as short as those of the 3rd Division were long'.[53] While the 4th could point to its combat wisdom to account for some of the shorthand in the orders, it was still an ominous sign; but the late decision to commit the division to the battle was the prime factor. Holmes' staff had blundered badly in April at Bullecourt, admittedly under the pressure of a rushed and misconceived operation. Now, just three weeks on from that disaster, they were again under intense pressure to plan a major attack in haste.

That same pressure fell on Plumer's staff. Perhaps the most critical task was the production of accurate maps for the second phase of the attack which would guide the infantry and the artillery that would protect them. This was an issue vital to the success of the second phase of the infantry attack in the afternoon. Overwhelmed with new intelligence, the Second Army's cartographers struggled under the weight of work. Even where the maps were accurate, many other factors could undo coordination with the artillery or affect the accuracy of artillery fire. Wind strength and direction, air temperature and density, and the varying weight of shells could all have an effect on the fall of shot.[54] Add to this the stability of the gun platform, small movements caused by recoil, the increasing wear and temperature of the barrel, and the difficulty of achieving highly accurate fire can be imagined. Poor visibility, mistakes by the forward observation officers, breaks in communication and errors in watch synchronisation added to what was often a dangerous degree of inaccuracy. On 5 June Bean recorded watching the Australian artillery destroy a New Zealand raiding party near Petit Douve Farm which was later reported to have failed 'owing to strong opposition'. This was the first recorded incident of the much larger scale problems that would plague II Anzac in the days ahead.[55] As every passing day brought the great offensive closer, the likely time and date became clearer to the German defenders and, as the end of the first week in June approached, the moonless early mornings of 5 to 8 June pointed to these dates with near certainty.

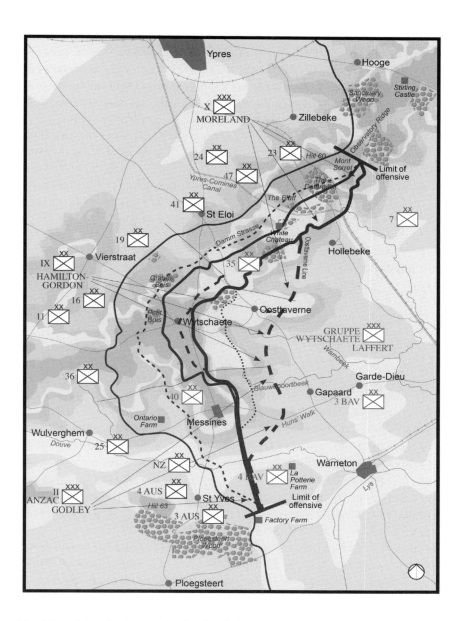

Map 6. Second Army battle map and order of battle showing the 14-kilometre front of the Second Army's attack on 7 June with X Corps in the north, IX Corps in the centre and II Anzac Corps in the south. The crest of the ridge was the first objective (the Black Line) and the final objective was the Oosttaverne (Green) Line.

Bean dined with Godley on the night of 5 June and with Monash on the eve of the battle. He did not, for obvious reasons, record the substance of those conversations in his notebooks, but there's little doubt that the plans and hopes for the coming battle dominated proceedings. As the sun set behind the British lines beneath Messines Ridge late on the evening of 6 June, the familiar, brooding heights ahead darkened slowly in the gloomy fog of dust which hung permanently in the air, stirred and thickened by the British shells which fell in a slow incessant drumbeat as the hours counted down to battle. The air was still thick from the heat of the day and, as darkness finally fell, the assault divisions prepared to set off on the carefully planned journeys that would bring them to their start lines. Charles Bean made his way forward to watch the battle's opening. Clasping his notebook and winding his way past hundreds of New Zealanders moving up to the line, he donned his gas mask and settled into his pre-selected viewing spot on the opposing heights of Hill 63, a few thousand yards from the German lines on the ridge. In a darkness deepened by the glass eyepieces of his mask, he began to make notes describing all he saw and heard. Bean's eyes were smarting and the familiar stench of gas was everywhere. Someone in command of the German artillery group on the southern bank of the River Lys had a very strong suspicion that the British would use the cover of Ploegsteert Wood to assemble opposite the Douve Valley for any attack. A heavy gas bombardment had fallen on the night of 3 June which disrupted the preparatory work of the signallers and pioneers preparing the jumping-off trenches. On the night of 6 June, whether by blind hunch or educated guess, the German artillery opened again, this time in strength and, just after 11.00 pm, with the 3rd Australian Division on the move in the darkness towards Ploegsteert, gas shells began to fall 'like the scattered heavy drops before a thunder-shower'.[56]

The men of the 4th Division, who would not move from their camps until the morning, at least had the opportunity to sleep, even if it was to prove impossible for many. For four young officers of the 47th Battalion, the reprieve allowed a final visit to the village estaminets. Lieutenants William Dixon, George Goode, Dudley Salmon and Captain John Millar returned to their barracks, Millar still clutching a half-empty bottle of wine. Someone caught that moment on camera and the photograph of their final night together would survive to be passed down, preserving forever a moment of happiness amid war's brutality. Lieutenant George Mitchell of the 48th Battalion was also one of the sleepless. As was his nightly habit, he picked up his pencil to record his thoughts and, on 6 June, they were deep:

The Brink of Eternity

Again we stand on the brink of eternity. Who can see the other side? And who would dare if he could? For the great advance commences tomorrow. Tomorrow many men must go to their God. For it is Zero Day.

If I die, I die.[57]

4

*We are now in this hell. One might believe
God would not allow it to go on any longer.*

Cataclysm

*We are now in this hell. One might believe
God would not allow it to go on any longer.*

Cataclysm

As the warm summer evening of 6 June slowly faded to dusk, the men of the all-Tasmanian 40th Battalion gathered in full fighting kit outside their huts at Regina Camp, located between Romarin and Point Nieppe, and waited for their orders to move off. The tension was palpable. '[M]en betrayed their nervousness by fumbling with their equipment, making sure their gas gadget was easily accessible (a timely precaution), and here and there men were giving a final "pull-through" to their rifles. It was something to do for the temporary idleness was mentally stifling.'[1] Captain Frank Green, author of the 40th's history, took a swipe at the war correspondents who, keen to support government recruiting efforts, wrote that soldiers were often eager to get into battle. 'A man who says he went into battle with a light heart is either a liar or a mental pervert.'[2] Silent and tense though they were, the men of the 40th felt well prepared. They had been garrisoned at Regina Camp since 27 May and, like all the battalions of II Anzac, had visited the model of Messines Ridge constructed at Romarin to familiarise themselves with the approach march and their objectives for the attack. All across the rear areas of the British front the assault divisions were on the move, timing their march to assemble in the jumping-off trenches just prior to zero. For the 3rd Division, the approach march from Regina Camp would start at 11.00 pm and proceed through Ploegsteert Wood via four separate routes, adhering to a meticulous timetable.[3]

The objectives of the morning attack were to seize the ridge, capture the villages of Messines and Wytschaete and establish a line just over the crest, the 'Black' Line, which had been the final objective prior to Haig's extension. For the first phase each of the nine divisions had a series of subsidiary objective lines to capture on the way forward for which the 'lifts' of its supporting artillery were precisely timed. It was vital that the infantry arrive at their start lines before zero as any delay could have fatal consequences. The attack plans varied considerably across the front. The 25th Division, for example, had nine subsidiary lines to capture, each identified by a different colour. Once the Black Line had been seized, there would be a pause in the attack to allow the artillery to reorganise for the afternoon assault, while the reserve divisions moved up and through the main force to capture the Green Line a further thousand metres down the slope. For II Anzac, the Green Line rested on the trench system known as the Oosttaverne Line and both names were used to describe it. The reserve divisions preparing for the afternoon advance were warned that the 'new zero' hour, the moment they would cross their start tapes on the Black Line, might be pushed out, depending on the progress of the morning's attack.

As the advance guards of the 3rd Division approached Ploegsteert Wood in the darkness, they could hear the ominous sounds of gas shells falling among the trees and noticed the distinctive odour, faint at first, of tear gas mixed with chlorine. The artillery batteries and their dumps around Romarin were frequently targeted by the German guns and the sheer weight of concentration of materiel for the offensive meant that dumps and guns were hit regularly. On 4 June the battalion had its first experience of gas when the surrounding artillery was drenched in toxic vapour forcing the 40th Battalion to move to Brune Gaye and bivouac in the open. Despite the move, 36 men had been gassed.[4] Their first experience of gas shelling, unpleasant though it had been, was nothing compared with what was to come.

Widespread use of poison gas began in January 1915 and the first counter-measures were primitive. The PH (phenate-hexamine) hood, though much less effective than the SBR (small box respirator) was still in use at Messines (image courtesy of Len Thurecht).

Gas instructors in the First World War were fond of reminding their students that, during a gas attack, there were two classes of soldiers, 'the quick and the dead'.[5] Poison gas made its first significant appearance in the war in April 1915 at Ypres where the Germans used it with fearsome effect, tearing a four-mile gap in the Allied defences which, underestimating its success, they failed to exploit. Like all weapons in World War I, poison gas and, more significantly, its delivery systems, underwent rapid development and refinement as the war progressed. Although chemical weapons have been a feature of war since prehistory and gas was widely used by both sides from 1915, it never lost its odious reputation.[6] A later American study claimed that no other weapon in World War I 'stimulated public revulsion more than poison gas'.[7] This was partly due to the deadly and debilitating effects of the various gases used, but also the moral effect that they produced. While tear gas (lachrymatory) and various sneezing and vomiting agents were used to harass troops, lethal gases such as chlorine and phosgene resulted in a terrible, lingering death or a lifetime of constricted breathing. Later, blistering agents (mustard gas) added to the tortuous nature of gas warfare. Gas training was thus an essential aspect of preparation for battle on the Western Front and the 3rd Division undertook extensive gas training in England. This involved entering a specially sealed gas hut or trench wearing the British small box respirator (SBR) while cylinders of suffocating gas were discharged inside. As Henry Oxley, a civilian gas instructor remembered, the training was designed to 'give confidence that you were in a gas cloud and wouldn't [panic] and to give you an idea of what it was like.'[8] Although poison gas killed very few in the First World War, it was the ultimate terror weapon. Edgar Rule described it as 'the best thing in the world to put the wind up men who have not implicit faith in their respirators, and it is only through constant training that they acquire confidence.'[9] Private Alan Mather of the 33rd Battalion, like many, carried not only his SBR, but a spare PH (phenate hexamine) hood as well as extra gas goggles. Since he also took with him his most prized souvenir, a German *pickelhaube* helmet, Mather's pack was very full.

The men of the 3rd Division, Mather among them, donned their gas masks for the long, dark approach march to Ploegsteert Wood. The instructions for wearing the SBR in battle were carefully outlined as a series of steps:

In step one, the [soldier] had to hold his breath, knock off his [helmet], grip his rifle between his legs and reach into the case on his chest to grasp the mask by its "breathing joint" and nose clip. At step two, the soldier thrust his chin out, held the mask in front of his face with both thumbs inside and under the elastic headband. In step three, the chin was placed into the facepiece while the headband was pulled over the head to secure the mask. Next, at step four, the soldier grasped the mouthpiece with his teeth. The last step, five required the soldier to reach through the facepiece to secure the nose clip and then run his hands around the mask to ensure a snug fit.[10]

Any delay in putting on a gas mask could be fatal. Troops were ordered to have their gas masks worn 'at the ready' (across the chest) when there was a threat of gas. This sign dates from the Somme battles of 1916 (RELAWM00757).

This series of actions often had to be performed in the midst of battle, in the dark and within six seconds. The SBR mask was, according to the American study, 'extremely uncomfortable', and the commander of the United States (US) Second Army, General Robert Lee Bullard, claimed that he 'could not wear the mask for more than three minutes without feeling smothered'.[11] In fact, on top of gas 'panic', the smothering effect of wearing a gas mask could itself produce panic even in the absence of gas.[12]

So began what was, according to Lance Corporal Reginald Biggs of the 40th Battalion, 'a long harrowing ordeal', an introduction to battle as desperate as it was unexpected.[13] Loaded up with almost 30 kilograms of kit, half-blind in the dark and wearing gas masks that reduced visibility even further, Biggs records that 'The mouth to mouth order was passed along to begin the approach march. The column headed into the now visible cloud of gas towards the Ploegsteert-Messines road ... we were to ... maintain our position between the men in front and behind (whose identity we were to keep constantly in mind) and were to reach our part of a certain trench before Zero Hour (3.10 a.m.).'[14] Bean records that the eight attack battalions of the 3rd Division were met with 'steady gas shelling' which had drenched Ploegsteert Wood south of Hill 63 throughout the night.[15] He speculated, as no doubt all of the men about to cross no man's land did, that the shelling 'might indicate that the enemy knew the date of the attack, or it might signify merely an attempt to harass the general preparations.'[16] As the 40th Battalion approached Ploegsteert, the gas cloud grew denser:

> As we moved forward the "fiffle-fiffle" and accompanying noises of the gas shell barrage were continuous. Occasionally a man would stop a gas shell or a nosecap, and several were thus killed. There were groans or cries of pain followed by calls for stretcher bearers. In the darkness men were cursing as they tripped or received a painful bump from a neighbour's rifle or shovel. The sweat streamed out of us, our muscles ached and our limbs chafed. Violent movement caused gas to leak in under our gasmasks and we felt the agonising smarting in our weeping eyes as both tear and gas shells were sent. Our eyeballs were scalded, sending a flood of tears down our nostrils and faces and into our mouths. Our vision, already limited by darkness, was further affected, inducing a feeling of helplessness which in an unsteady man leads to bewilderment and panic.[17]

There were many unsteady men that night. High explosive and incendiary shells were raining into the wood among the silent gas shells. 'The actual wearing of a small box-respirator is a physical discomfort at any time' wrote Green, 'but on a hot, dark night for men loaded with ammunition, arms, equipment, it is a severe strain. Wounded and gassed men were falling out, and officers and non-commissioned officers were continually removing their respirators to give orders.' He described the approach march as 'like a nightmare … The columns of goggle eyed [men] moved forward among the trees, and on both sides was the glare from burning dumps lit up by incendiary shells.' By 2.00 am the 3rd Division's tortuous approach march was nearing its end, but the delays, occasional wrong turns and the inevitable confusion caused by the shelling meant that they were over an hour late entering their jumping-off point, with some platoons very seriously depleted. On the southern edge of the wood, the 33rd was losing the race to the start line with the men double blind in the dark and fogged goggles of their gas masks. Private Dick Blomfield recalled that 'One could … only feel one's way along the side of the trench', adding that they were blocked by a panicked carrying party which would not move.[18]

Australian infantry training in the use of the SBR in England in May 1917. Such training was vital to overcome 'gas panic' (AWM C01320).

Lieutenant Alan Downie of the 40th knew there was no option but to push on. 'I knew, and most men with us that night had realized, that to drop out meant death, slowly and horribly, from the deadly gas, which was now ever increasing, and our only chance was to strain every nerve and muscle and grit our teeth and literally force our minds to dominate our aching and suffering bodies.'[19] The 40th Battalion was to take the most northerly track of the 3rd Division's battalions. As the men moved out of Ploegsteert Wood to the north, onto the forward slopes of Hill 63 and Prowse Point, they reached clearer air, fell to the ground and pulled their respirators off. For those unaffected, the fresh air was 'as refreshing as cool beer on a hot Australian summer day'.[20] However, the gassed lay all around, 'retching and collapsed'.[21] Biggs estimated that almost a third of the 40th Battalion were gas casualties while, with 20 minutes to go, only 120 men of the 39th were in position on their start lines at Anton's Farm. The 39th's leading groups at Ploegsteert Corner, suffering under shellfire for almost the entire journey, were now hit by a volley of gas shells which burst among them, killing and wounding many. This was followed by a further heavy shower of gas shells which created havoc in the column now halted due to the carnage at its head. 'It was almost impossible for Officers and some of the N.C.Os. to wear their masks properly owing to the necessity for directing the men. As a result, Officers and N.C.Os. were among the first casualties,, and their track up through Bunhill Row and Mud Lane was strewn with men overcome by the gas. The Battalion leader was one of the casualties. A senior Company Commander reached the R.A.P. [Regimental Aid Post] in Anscroft Avenue at about 2.20 a.m. with only 12 men, though stragglers, much dazed, gradually dribbled in afterwards.'[22]

Even those unaffected by gas had suffered throughout the gruelling approach. 'For troops in masks the mere effort of marching under load of rifle, ammunition, tools and rations and the excitement of the occasion, caused heavy breathing and consequent distress.'[23] It says much for the 3rd Division's training, and for Monash's attention to this, that his men were largely able to survive the ordeal of a sustained and saturating gas attack in the midst of their already arduous approach march and as they prepared to launch their first ever assault. The 3rd Division had experienced its first run of luck in the battle and it had all been bad.

• • •

As the gas shells rained down on Ploegsteert and its approaches to the south, the New Zealanders were also moving into their jumping-off positions. To them fell the task of taking the fortress of Messines itself. The Germans had burrowed deep into the village's ancient foundations, fortified its cellars, dotted its crest with reinforced concrete bunkers and criss-crossed its former streets with a maze of trenches, wire and hidden redoubts. Despite the intense shelling of the previous two weeks, which had degraded those defences and battered their occupants, there was no exaggeration in naming this place one of the strongest positions on the Western Front. Moreover, there would be no mines to carve a pathway for the New Zealanders, the Petit Douve mine having been lost to counter-mining and Ontario Farm just beyond their left flank. On an attack frontage of some 1400 metres, the New Zealand 2nd Brigade would attack with the 3rd (Rifle) Brigade on its right to capture the front trench system, move on to take the reserve trenches and, finally, the village itself. The 1st Brigade would then move through the 2nd to take the Black Line on the eastern crest of the ridge just beyond the village.[24]

One glance at the trench maps for Messines with their tangled, spidery mess of front and support lines, communication trenches linking and bisecting, bunkers, machine-gun nests, belts of wire, and the use of natural features, should dispel the myth that the red-tabbed staff officers who planned attacks were callous, slow-witted fools. This would be no orderly advance against neat lines of regular trenches, with troops walking forward protected by a creeping barrage and then rushing and overcoming a battered and demoralised enemy. The logic that produced the crazy haywire of a trench map was that imposed by the combination of high velocity weapons and the contours and elevation of the ground. After two years of sniping, shelling and seeking every small advantage the ground offered, the British and German lines settled like opposing magnets into their own unique pattern of equilibrium. And it was far from regular.

So it was that the men of the New Zealand Division's 2nd Brigade, attacking on the immediate left of the Rifle Brigade, confronted a tangled skein of difficulties caused by the meandering front line which followed the contours of the ridge and which produced a pronounced salient on their left flank protruding well into the 25th Division's line. The German line, which ran north-south along the ridge's forward slope, turned a right angle around Ontario Farm opposite the left boundary of the New Zealand Division and ran east-west for some 800 metres before turning north-south again to face the British lines. This created two major problems for Russell. First, there would be a considerable time lapse before the 25th Division, with a greater distance to travel, would be level with the New Zealand flank. Second, Russell's men would have to attack with their left exposed to the long German trench, perhaps exposed to deadly enfilade fire. When Haig visited Russell's headquarters on 24 May, he expressed his concern over the difficulties the New Zealanders faced and argued that Russell's plan resulted 'in an awkward salient prematurely!' He suggested instead that Messines 'should be taken in three "jumps" so as to give artillery a greater chance of producing its effect.'[25] In essence, Haig was proposing that the New Zealanders pause (between the 'jumps') to allow time for the 25th Division to come up on their left flank and the artillery time to batter down the opposition. It took considerable courage and self-belief for Russell to disagree with his Commander-in-Chief and argue the case for his original plan (something Haig would later note with approval in his diary), but he was correct to reject Haig's suggestion.[26] Speed was of the essence and Russell's complex and intricate artillery and machine-gun arrangements were designed, through a combination of standing and creeping barrages, to deluge the long, open flank with a withering hail of fire to keep the Germans under cover and provide a screen for his rapidly moving left. If all went according to plan and the standing barrage of 18-pounders suppressed the German fire from the left, the 2nd New Zealand Brigade could be beyond danger in under 15 minutes and storming the deadly strongpoints that lay directly in their path on the crest of the ridge. However, given the extra distance the 25th Division needed to travel, it was expected that it would be fully 45 minutes before the 25th would arrive at a point level with the New Zealand Division on its right. This was a dangerously long time to advance with a flank 'in the air' as the 2nd Brigade's would be, and much would depend on the skill of Russell's gunners.

But that was not the only problem for the 2nd Brigade. Not only did the re-entrant at the foot of the ridge bend the line almost at right angles, the contour winding along the course of the River Steenbeek on the brigade's frontage widened no man's land to a depth of some 600 yards, a highly dangerous and perhaps even impossible distance. On the night of 13 April, 400 men of the 1st Otago had toiled through the darkness, protected by a covering party from the 2nd Wellington, to dig a safe and deep communication trench, reducing the width of no man's land to a more manageable 370 metres. It was an exhausting and unglamorous but lifesaving job. However, despite those efforts, despite Russell's careful artillery plan and despite the proven quality of the New Zealanders who would storm the ridge, the serious danger posed by the German front line that ran alongside and above the 2nd Brigade's line of attack for over 600 metres still caused, according to the Canterbury Regiment's history, 'a great deal of anxiety'.[27]

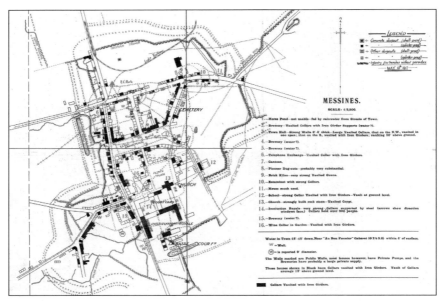

Map 7. The fortress of Messines — a map drafted from aerial photos showing the immensely strong defensive system the Germans created in and around the village of Messines. As well as the trenches and wire which ringed the village, numerous shell-proof and splinter-proof concrete dugouts are shown along with other shell-proof dugouts and cellars vaulted with iron girders. The diagram perhaps explains the confidence of the German divisional commanders that they could hold the village despite von Kuhl's urgings that they withdraw. On 7 June the New Zealand Division captured the village within an hour of crossing its start lines.

The 1st Canterbury had spent the evening of 5 June and most of the next day in the Catacombs on Hill 63, emerging at 9.30 pm for its journey across the rear of the hill via Plum Duff and Calgary avenues. The battalion had a disastrous start to its approach march when searching German shells had landed among men dividing rations at the entrance to the tunnels, killing and wounding 30. The New Zealanders were also caught in the gas attack which drenched Ploegsteert Wood and Hill 63 and were forced, like the 3rd Division, to march in gas masks. Unlike the 3rd Division however, the men of the Canterbury Regiment were marching away from the gas cloud and, although their brigade reported the effect of the gas shells as 'most demoralising and depressing', they arrived in their assembly trenches at midnight with morale restored by the clear air.[28] The 2nd Battalion, around 700 strong, was formed up in its assembly trenches by 1.30 pm. The gas was far less intense along 'Y' route as the 2nd Canterbury advanced, silent and smokeless, towards battle.

The 1st Canterbury Battalion spent the night of 6 June in the Catacombs under Hill 63. Excavated by the 1st Australian Tunnelling Company, the Catacombs could accommodate over 2000 men. Oppressive at the best of times, the atmosphere inside when the entrances were sealed during gas attacks was unpleasant to say the least. This photo shows officers of the AIF's 6th Infantry Brigade in the Catacombs in January 1918 (AWM E01509).

Although the gas deluging the Australians' approaches merely brushed the extreme right of the 2nd New Zealand Brigade's approach and the men arrived in their jumping-off trenches with over an hour to spare, this was to prove a mixed blessing. 'There is a touch of unreality in this waiting for the appointed hour', wrote the New Zealand Division historian. 'All is so quiet. Everything seems to be so safe … men are intensely alive. Yet a dozen men standing in a bay know that in an hour two of them will probably be dead, and three or more lying wounded.'[29] In silence the men, loaded with weapons, kit and ammunition, counted down the minutes. At 3.00 am there came 'some relief' as the brigade historian wrote 'when bayonets … were quietly drawn from their scabbards and fixed. Now only ten minutes remained.'[30]

Alongside and to the north of the New Zealanders, similar preparations were under way in the 25th Division and, still further north, the assault divisions of IX and X Corps were also moving to the carefully prepared timetables which would concentrate their forces at the jumping-off tapes shortly before they were due to be launched at 3.10 am. The most dangerous and critical phase of the final preparations for the English and New Zealand divisions was now almost complete and the movement of the assault columns and their placement at the foot of the ridge had gone unnoticed. Of the massive infantry force gathered against them, the Germans had managed to disrupt only Monash's 3rd Australian Division, which had been subjected to the heavy gas shelling. The high pitch of tension felt in every battalion gathered and waiting in the darkness was matched in equal measure in the firing dugouts as the miners and engineers, after two years of patient and prodigious effort, made final preparations to unleash the gigantic explosive forces that that lay beneath the German lines.

Just after 2.00 am, a very nervous Captain Oliver Woodward was again testing the leads for the Hill 60 and Caterpillar mines, a ritual repeated across the base of the ridge for the other 18 mine systems. 'I set out to check the leads and as each one in turn proved correct I felt greatly relieved. At 2.25 a.m. I made the last resistance test and then made the final connection test before firing the mines. This was rather a nerve wracking task as one began to feel the strain and wonder whether the leads were correctly joined up.'[31] That so much depended on the successful detonation of the mines and that so many lives had been spent in their placement and defence nagged at Woodward's nerves in those final minutes. Woodward and Lambert, the commander of the 69th Brigade (British 23rd Division) and the other members of the 1st Australian Tunnelling Company's firing party waited in silence in the Hill 60 dugout for the countdown to begin.[32]

As the minutes ticked down to zero, the incessant British shelling eased into the desultory pattern of early mornings of the past weeks which was itself part of the ruse to conceal the actual moment of the battle's opening. A German soldier somewhere in the pulverised village of Messines was part way through a despairing letter home. 'We are now in this hell. One might believe God would not allow it to go on any longer.'[33] The darkness over the ridge was deepened by moonset and, for the thousands of troops gathering to assault the ridge, and the gunners, now still amid their silent guns and huge dumps of shells, the tension was as intense as the blackness around them.

Leaving the New Zealand Division's headquarters at midnight, Bean, the New Zealand war correspondent, Malcolm Ross and the New Zealand official photographer, Henry Sanders, motored towards Hill 63, noting that the roads were clear of infantry, indeed traffic of any kind, a sure sign that the final and most critical aspect of the preparation, the movement of thousands of assault troops, had gone almost without a hitch. Approaching Hill 63 they ran into the gas which was deluging the 3rd Division's approach march and donned their gas masks. Bean spent the final minutes before the battle with the New Zealand Division, as close as practicable to the front line. At 2.10 am he recorded that the Germans fired a white flare high in the sky towards the 3rd Division's front, but saw no movement. Aircraft flew a circuit overhead, the noise of their engines filling the sound gaps between the artillery fire which had maintained its normal nightly pattern. The engine noise of the British aircraft helped mask the sound of the approaching tanks which lumbered slowly towards their start lines. Of all the dramatic records of this unforgettable day, perhaps the most compelling is contained in Charles Bean's notebook in which he recorded, in a rushed and scrawly hand, the sights and sounds of the final moments:

> 2.52 Two green and two yellow flares (first time any coloured flare has come up)

> 2.53 Red flare other side of ridge. This is off Ypres (that the flares are going up)

> 3 to 3 Has he seen the 10 Corps or is this a stunt – some raid of ours further up?

> 2 to 3 Gas again on … Men have had their breakfast. Pat, pat of gas … still undiscovered.

> 3.1 Red of dawn over Messines last 5 minutes (things must be all right now). One feels as if it were a won battle. N.Z. asks "Where's these bloody bombs?"

The silence imposed on the thousands of waiting troops would be broken four minutes before zero by a section of New Zealand machine-gunners whose commander's watch was well ahead of the synchronised time:

> 3.6 Double green in front of Messines. M[achine] G[uns]. 2 or 3 [machine-guns]

> 3.7 One big shell near. One flash of rifle

> 3.8 One g[reen] flare, m.g. silent

> 3.9 Our bom[bardment] begins.

In the dugout, Woodward gripped the firing handle as Lambert counted down the seconds. Just before he reached zero, Woodward began to feel the earth quake as the other mines exploded. With the earth heaving, Lambert completed his countdown and yelled 'Fire!' Woodward threw the switch, his hand contacting the terminals as he did, throwing him backwards. 'For a fraction of a second I failed to realise what had happened, but there was soon joy in the knowledge that the Hill 60 mines had done their work.'[34] Bean's hand was shaking as he wrote the next two lines, scrawling erratically:

3 mines up by Messines.

Mine after mine.[35]

The war correspondents braced themselves against the walls of their trench as the mines produced 'considerable earth movement' which shook the ground violently for six seconds.[36] An RFC radio operator, fighting a rising panic after two hours in his gas mask, 'thought Earth had come to end'.[37] As the earthquake rumbled, the Second Army's massed artillery, firing as fast as each gun could be fed, merged thousands of thunderclaps into one incredible roar. Hundreds of machine-guns poured a continuous fire overhead and, on the ridge, scores of flares shot into the air as the German defenders, calling for help, also signalled the start of the great battle. Bean watched in awe as the ridge erupted in smoke and fire and the assault troops surged forward. The 3rd Battalion of the New Zealand Rifle Brigade described the explosions 'Ontario Farm and Petit Douve [sic] and one in the direction of Ontario Farm (3 times as great as other two). In appearance jagged flames – crimson red accompanied by severe tremors.'[38] The mine '3 times as great' was the giant Spanbroekmolen mine, 41,000 kilograms of explosive buried 29 metres under the German lines. It would be eight long minutes before Bean could put pencil to paper again to scribble the moment-by-moment history as it unfolded before him.

The mines had erupted at 19 separate points along the ridge, swelling the earth upward from deep below like giant mushrooms until they finally burst through the darkness in deep red hues, 'the most diabolical splendour I have ever seen' wrote war correspondent Philip Gibbs watching from Mount Kemmel.[39] Exploding over a period of 21 seconds, the shock waves collided as they radiated through the substrata, setting off the earthquake.[40] The tremor was a profound shock to both German and British troops, neither of whom had any warning of the mines. The instances of panic, recorded as far away as

Lille, some 15 miles behind the German lines, were also evident among the waiting British troops, some of whom thought it was the Germans who had exploded mines *behind* them, given the curve of the British front line, which gave the appearance of explosions to their rear. Private Lancelot Smith of the 10th Field Ambulance was on Hill 63 opposite the Ontario Farm mine. '[B]y Jove if it didn't make our old dugout roll. For about five minutes we thought the jolly thing might cave right in.'[41] The closest surviving witnesses were German. Leutnant Meinke of the *176th Infantry Regiment* was, like his colleagues, taken completely by surprise. 'Suddenly, what is it? The earth roared, trembled, rocked – this was followed by an utterly amazing crash and there, before us in a huge arc, kilometres long, was raised a curtain of fire about one hundred metres high. The scene was quite extraordinary; almost beyond description. It was like a thunderstorm magnified one thousand times! ... The wall of fire hung in the air for several seconds, then subsided to be replaced by the flashes of artillery muzzles, which were clearly visible in the half light.'[42] The German *Official History* would record the most lyrical of descriptions:

> The trenches shook and rocked like a ship in a heavy sea, and in some places fell in, and at the same moment a mass of earth, thrown hundreds of feet high, was seen in front against the sky, like a black column capped with a dull red flame. The infantry climbed the parapet and walked quickly towards the enemy. The battle of Messines had begun.[43]

Lance Corporal Harris Fuljames of the 3rd New Zealand Machine Gun Company 'but a true Australian', struggled to find the words to describe the scene. 'I have never experienced anything like it and I hope I never do again ... at the tick of three these [mines] started going off as well as the artillery which was wheel to wheel, the earth quaked and trembled, if any-one had been there that didn't know anything about it, they would have thought the world was coming to an end, behind us was a sheet of flame from our artillery and in front the mines roared and blazed like great furnaces at white heat which made me shiver when I thought of the poor beggars that were going up in there.'[44] His commanding officer, Lieutenant Colonel John Parks, recorded the scene in his diary. '[N]ow she goes – the place sways – again – again and oh what has happened. The guns ... are creating an inferno. Machine guns are rattling away and still there is this seeking gas. Hell cannot be worse than this.'[45]

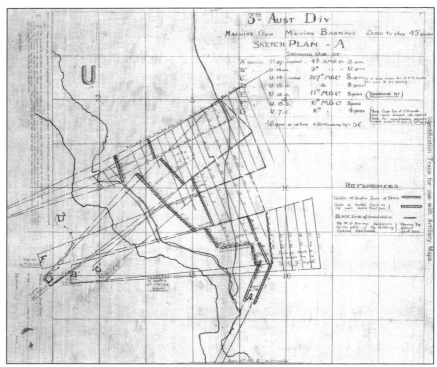

Map 8. The 3rd Division machine-gun barrage. Creeping barrages of indirect fire from batteries of Vickers machine-guns were as critical to the success of Messines as those of the artillery. Shown here is the scheme for the 3rd Division's machine-gun barrages for the first 45 minutes of the battle. With 48 guns in action (and eight in reserve), the machine-guns fired 450 rounds a minute, thrashing the ground ahead of the assault divisions and effectively keeping the defenders under shelter in dugouts until the troops overran them. The Vickers' reliability made it an ideal weapon for this purpose, as it was able to fire for hours on end with regular replacement of barrels.

British Prime Minister David Lloyd George, staying at his country house at Walton Heath in Surrey, asked to be woken at 3.00 am for the start of the battle. Famously he would claim that he heard the explosion of the mines that heralded the assault, a detail reported in newspapers across the world at the time and repeated unquestioned ever since.[46] In fact, this was impossible given the depth of the mines, which absorbed most of the sound, something on which those closest to the explosions remarked. Far noisier and more prolonged was the massive British artillery barrage, joined shortly after by German retaliation which, although much weaker, added to the tremendous din that may possibly have been audible at such great distance. Lieutenant Percy Dobson, serving with the Siege Artillery Brigade, knew the report to be untrue:

There was a lot of rot in the English papers about Lloyd George being called in London to hear the mines go up. I was asleep at the Rest Billet about four miles from Hill 60 and they didn't even wake me up. One paper said that Hill 60 was flattened and another that Messines Ridge had disappeared – the papers always talked a lot of tosh.[47]

Officers of the 12th Machine Gun Company with their Vickers guns. The creeping machine-gun barrages were a vital factor in the success of the attack on 7 June. Each assault division was screened by over 50 machine-guns firing 450 rounds a minute for the first hours which directed a hail of indirect fire on the German trenches (AWM H00177).

Major Ronald Schweder of the Royal Artillery was another of the many to cast doubt on Lloyd George's unlikely claim, describing the sight of the mine explosions as 'like hell opening. The nearest description is the pantomime scene of the devil's grotto. A great flare of red; the craters were huge .... The whole earth quaked. It was a wonderful sight, one I shall never forget.'[48]

Despite having no warning of the mines, there was no panic in the New Zealand Rifle Brigade. 'Most of us thought when the first went up that Fritz had got one on to us, but we soon saw from the position of the explosions that they were our own.'[49] The giant mines at Kruisstraat, Petit Bois and Spanbroekmolen on the New Zealanders' left were the largest and most spectacular. Lieutenant Edward Winchester of the Rifle Brigade recalled seeing 'at least six tremendous shafts of fire mottled with dark patches of earth ... shoot hundreds of feet into the air ... the whole earth heaved up and down like a rough sea ... we had to clamber out of our trenches in case they fell in.' He described the massive thunder of the artillery 'as if all our guns were operated by a single button'.[50] Private George Davies of the Australian 36th Battalion found time to scratch a few words in his diary before going 'over the top'. 'Men who have been in other pushes say there has never been such a bombardment as this one, they once smiled at our division but they now say the lads are grand. I am not sorry I have to be amongst those who will fight in such a terrible battle. Bullecourt was terrible, Verdun was awful, Pozières was villainous, but this will soon be hell on earth.'[51]

One of the flooded Hill 60 mine craters in the winter of 1918 showing the scale of the destruction (AWM A02326).

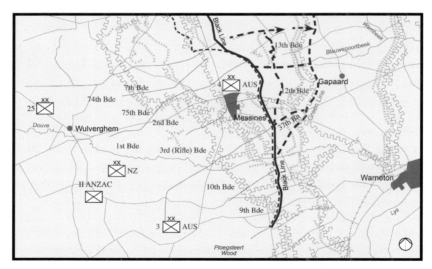

Map 9. Map showing II Anzac's plan for the attack on 7 June. Taken from an early version of the original, this map does not show the 4th Division's intended boundaries and positions for the attack on the Green Line. The boundaries shown here would later be amended..

Cataclysm

• • •

'Under cover of the greatest weight of artillery ever employed in battle' wrote the diarist of the 3rd Battalion, the Worcestershire Regiment, with a sense of history, 'the Battalion moved forward to the assault.'[52] There was some initial panic among the Worcestershires, the war diary recording that the shock of the mines and the resulting earthquake 'had momentarily a bad effect on them'.[53] The regimental history confirmed that the 'awful and unexpected explosion paralysed the troops in the British front line. Even the war-hardened veterans of the 3rd Worcestershire were for a moment unnerved.' This was understandable since Ontario Farm went up just 600 yards away on their right flank, followed by Kruisstraat some 900 yards on the left and the huge Spanbroekmolen mine a further 400 yards beyond that.[54] Lieutenant Arthur White of the 1st Battalion, the Wiltshire Regiment, remembered that 'their effect was appalling, the whole ground under us seemed to be giving way'.[55] Officers and NCOs quickly smothered the panic and, shouting orders, roused the men from the trenches and led them into a chaotic, deafening darkness, lit up by the flares and lingering glow from the mines.

The 25th Division's diary described the difficulties the men faced once they crossed the Steenbeek under the heading 'Description of the Objective'. '[F] rom this point the ground rises steeply, flanked on either side by Hell Farm and Sloping Roof Farm, with 4 Huns Farm, Chest Farm, Middle Farm on the crest of the Ridge and Lumm Farm a little further on to our left front. These farms, both naturally and tactically strong points, had been converted by military science into positions of immense strength and importance, impregnable to all else than overwhelming heavy artillery.'[56] Thanks to the thoroughness of the Second Army's planning, the 25th Division had just such artillery. On a front of a mere 1000 metres, nine separate artillery units disposed of 262 guns of various calibres ranging from 18-pounders through to the super-heavy 15-inch howitzers.[57] Back on Hill 63, the 42nd Australian Battalion was in reserve. Lieutenant William Fisher had felt the mines go up and then climbed Hill 63 to watch the attack. 'Their concussion shook the earth for miles around ... nothing could have existed in that hell. No wire was left - and before the bombardment it had been a model of defensive wiring ... But all was shellhole – lip on lip – up and down, up and down all the time ... At the moment of writing our guns are pouring in a hurricane of drum-fire, so that one cannot hear one's neighbour even at a distance of a few feet.'[58]

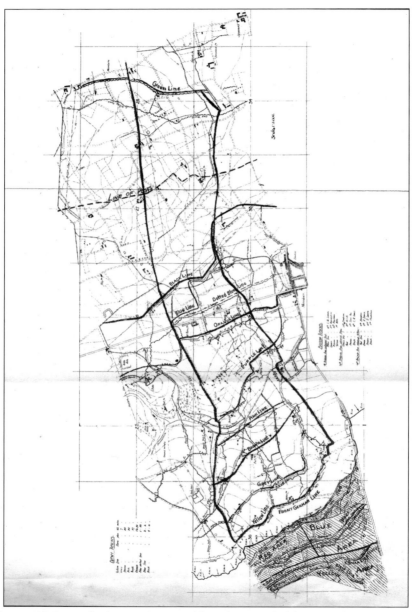

Map 10. 25th Division battle map, 7 June 1917. The 25th Division had the greatest distance to travel on II Anzac's front and nine separate objective lines to capture. Numerous fortified farms, strongpoints and pillboxes lay in its path.

In addition to their overwhelming artillery advantage, the attackers were assisted by the concentrated machine-gun barrage. On the 25th Division's front, the Ontario Farm mine wiped out a strong German defensive position along with its garrison. Even with those considerable advantages, the men of the 25th were under no illusions about the difficulties they faced. The forward slope they climbed was dotted with pillboxes and fortified farms. As with all battles however, that morning blind luck would deliver a huge and unexpected advantage to one side and a savage blow to the other. Just as the attack was launched, the exhausted *40th (Saxon) Division*, defending Messines itself, was in the final stages of its relief by the *3rd Bavarian Division*, the shattering artillery barrage catching both units moving, unprepared and fatally vulnerable, and set to be overrun.

The 25th attacked with its 74th and 7th brigades leading with the 75th Brigade to follow on and assault the further objectives. Two battalions in each brigade led the assault with the remaining two following up to consolidate and leapfrog. While each battalion frontage was only 300 metres, even in this carefully rehearsed attack the complexity of the ground, and the darkness and dust from the artillery and mine explosions meant that the men experienced 'great difficulty' in keeping direction, identifying the enemy trenches and maintaining cohesion. The 74th Brigade diary recorded that the disadvantage of the poor visibility was counterbalanced 'by the immunity it afforded from aimed machine gun fire'.[59] One British artillery observer 'almost suffocated by smoke' likened it to 'a November fog in London'.[60] The blinded German gunners were unable to see the dense ranks of the British as they surged up the rising ground beyond the Steenbeek. Fortunately, there was little resistance. 'Very few of the enemy remained in the front line and those survivors, utterly bewildered and unnerved, at once surrendered.'[61] The men of the 3rd Battalion pushed past Nutmeg Trench to take the ominously named Hell Farm just 20 minutes after emerging shaken from their own front lines. The concrete dugouts they encountered in the line at Hell Farm were full of sheltering Germans, too terrified to move from their last refuge of safety towards the incomprehensible shouting from outside. 'They would not come to until bombs had been hurled inside', the bombs bursting in the thickened darkness, killing and wounding the nearest and driving out their comrades, mad with fright. Some enemy soldiers were killed in this fighting, while the remainder were taken prisoner.[62] The vividly written summary in the 25th Division war diary included a description of the impact of the weeks of shelling on the German defenders:

The sight of the battlefield with its utter and universal desolation stretching interminably on all sides, its trenches often battered out of all recognition, its wilderness of shell holes, debris, tangled wire, broken rifles and abandoned equipment confirms the opinion that no troops whatever their morale and training, can withstand the fire of such overwhelming and concentrated masses of artillery. With a definite and limited objective and with sufficient artillery support complete success may be reasonably guaranteed.[63]

All of the battalion diaries record that resistance in the first German lines was negligible and, even in positions that were still eminently defendable, the garrisons were too shaken to put up a fight. Nevertheless the divisional diary disagreed, recording that, despite the enormous weight of artillery, the Germans 'though dazed and shaken were able to put up a good resistance for an appreciable period'.[64] The speed with which the various objectives were taken and the light casualties suggest otherwise. That rapid movement in the darkness and dust storms from the mines and artillery, combined with the twists and turns of the winding, ruined trenches in the enemy's front lines, inevitably caused confusion. 'From the beginning of the assault owing to the darkness at the time of launching the attack, and the almost unrecognisable state of the ground, direction was lost by most units in the proximity and early in the advance regiments became very mixed.'[65] Given the walkover these first hours produced, the disarray was of no consequence.

On the right, the Royal Irish Rifles left their trenches as Ontario Farm mine, directly in front, went up and 'effectively shattered the enemy [stationed] there'. They followed a barrage 'as perfect as could be', meeting little opposition, although the Royal Irish war diary commented that '[a] few small isolated resistances made the advance a little interesting'.[66] The 9th Loyal North Lancashire Regiment, on the left of the Irish, was held up by 'stubborn resistance' at Middle Farm. This was overcome, as it would be in many parts of the German line that morning, by a neighbouring battalion pushing past the flanks of these isolated pillboxes. B Company of the Irish Rifles worked around Middle Farm and attacked from the rear, an operation which, 'owing to the gallantry of OC 'B' Co[mpan]y, was entirely successful and the enemy resistance at the Farm completely broken.'[67] The Royal Irish captured 200 prisoners, five machine-guns, two trench mortars and a quantity of ammunition.

The four leading battalions of the 25th followed the barrage produced by sixty 18-pounders — one for every 20 yards of front. On the far left, the 75th Brigade's 8th Battalion, Loyal North Lancashire, had the 3rd

Battalion, Worcestershire Regiment, on its right flank. To the right of the Worcestershires, the 7th Brigade's two leading battalions were the 2nd Battalion, Royal Irish Rifles, and the 13th Battalion, the Cheshire Regiment. The battalions covered the 130 yards over no man's land, across the Steenbeek and into the German front line (the Yellow Line) unopposed. While their creeping barrage drew them forward, a standing rain of shells from twenty-four 18-pounders and thirty-six 4.5-inch howitzers descended on the second objective, the Nutmeg Reserve Line (the Grey Line) and a further 36 guns pounded the spur defended by Occur Trench and bounded by Hell Farm and Sloping Roof Farm. The latter strongpoints with their concealed machine-guns were hit with shells from twenty 6-inch howitzers while a battery of 8-inch howitzers pounded 4 Huns Farm and Middle Farm in October Trench a further 500 metres beyond.

The few Germans who managed to mount machine-guns and who were not obliterated by the shells and the hailstorm of indirect machine-gun fire were overrun and surrounded by the assaulting infantry. Many others remained sheltering in what they believed to be the comparative safety of their dugouts, unaware that the British were swarming over their lines above them. Their first warnings were shouts in English followed by bombs. The Grey Line fell a mere seven minutes after the 25th left its front trench and the men of the leading battalions swept on to the Brown Line where the Loyal North Lancashires and the Worcestershires captured a handful of prisoners while the Cheshires and Irish Rifles seized six machine-guns in the trenches known as Nutmeg Lane, Ugly Reserve and Ozone Alley. The combination of withering artillery fire, superbly coordinated with the movement of the advancing infantry, completely overwhelmed resistance. The German artillery, despite replying with a barrage on the British front line within an impressive four minutes after the attack began, was weak and ineffective.[68] The weeks of counter-battery fire saved many lives in the 25th Division, men who now fought their way through no fewer than nine lines of German trenches, captured a series of heavily fortified farms and established themselves on the Black Line almost 3000 metres from their start line, something which had not been achieved in three years of war. Much depended on the New Zealand Division on their right which, while their battalions had a much more modest distance to travel, confronted the immensely strong subterranean fortress that was the former village of Messines. Failure by the New Zealanders amid the cellars, tunnels and pillboxes of Messines would doom the 25th to lethal enfilade fire from its right flank.

The 13th Battalion of the Cheshire Regiment was in the vanguard on the left of the 74th Brigade's advance and its progress was similarly straightforward, as the men overran October Trench and the support line beyond it. 'Very little opposition was encountered except in the few cases when m[achine] guns opened fire from a flank. These were swiftly dealt with.'[69] The 13th Cheshires lost 31 killed and around 150 wounded on 7 June, taking 160 prisoners and four machine-guns. The war diary noted the enemy's disarray, describing him 'being so disorganised that his shelling was wild and ineffective. No counter attack launched.'[70] For a major battle, Messines would stand out as a remarkable and welcome contrast to the Cheshires' grim and bloody history in the Great War. Brigade headquarters however, knew little of the progress of its battalions. 'All we knew was that the Brigade had advanced into the black fog; our cable line operators in our front could see nothing else.'

Brigadier General Keppel Bethell, the eccentric and volatile commander of the 74th Brigade, remained in his deep dugout reading Shakespeare and barking demands at his staff for information which couldn't be answered. Fearing the attack might have stalled, Bethell sent his Brigade Major, Walter Guinness, forward to find out what was happening. Guinness emerged into an eerie, hellish world as he passed over the old British front line and scaled the ridge. '[A]s soon as I was over the parapet, the whole ground was changed. Trees and hedges, reduced to poles and sticks before, had now nearly disappeared, and the ground was like a giant pumice stone, huge pits and craters up to ten feet deep. Streams of wounded walking back and a certain number of bewildered men wandering about not knowing where they were.'[71] Reaching the top of the ridge, Guinness discovered his battalions on the final objective but, while there had been little hostile fire on the way up, the shelling and machine-gun fire was heavy on the crest of the ridge. While Guinness was taking a bearing with his compass, his companion was shot through the head by a sniper.

The battalions of the 75th Brigade moved through their comrades in the 74th and 7th brigades to consolidate on the narrowed front on the far side of the ridge and their final objective on the Black Line. The 8th Battalion, the Border Regiment, left its assembly trench 'Newcastle' at 7.00 am with the morning sun lighting up a battlefield shrouded in dust and smoke. It took the 8th Borders some 90 minutes to move up and over the ridge, picking their way past some isolated parties of Germans still bravely holding out despite having been bypassed by the assaulting waves of British.[72] Likewise, the 11th Cheshires, who had been in the rear assembly trench (Durham Trench) since 1.00 am on the night before the battle, finally moved off at 6.45 am. In the dull morning light, they moved quickly through the old German lines captured by the battalions of the 7th Brigade and passed through the 8th South Lancashire which held the trenches around Lumm Farm on the Black Line. Machine-gun fire from isolated parties of Germans around Lumm Farm caused some losses before the Cheshires moved to establish their posts at around 9.00 am on the Black Dotted Line south from Despagne Farm to the small creek known as the Blauwepoortbeek. The problems at Lumm Farm were caused by the late arrival of the 36th Division on the 25th Division's left flank. The left company of the 8th South Lancashire was unable to deal with Lumm Farm on its own and the 11th Cheshires pushed north on the left to help silence the farm, capturing four field guns, a handful of machine-guns and many German prisoners in the process. The non-arrival of the 36th Division recorded in the battalion diaries was the first hint that something had gone wrong in an otherwise flawlessly executed plan. It would also herald the major problems the Australians of the 4th Division would face in the afternoon.

• • •

Some 20 minutes after zero, Malcolm Ross, watching the attack with Bean on Hill 63, worried that the assault troops would find it difficult to follow the barrage in the darkness and fog of dust. The red German SOS flares lit up the clouds with a dull, deep crimson glow, adding to a world made even more hellish by the terrible roar of the Second Army's artillery. But the battle was fearfully one-sided. McKenny Hughes, flying above the battlefield in his SE4, could spot only 10 flashes from the German guns. He also noted that none of the flashes was forward of the O35 square on the map, meaning that Haig's drive for the guns would be entirely fruitless as the Germans had pulled them out of the expected forward extent of the British attack.[73] At 4.00 am Bean recorded that visibility was less than 100 yards and that, from his vantage point on Hill 63, he couldn't see the Douve Valley. Thirty minutes later, he could just make out the trees on the crest of Messines Ridge, while the chatter of enemy machine-guns marked the progress of the New Zealanders in and through the village. The same anxieties pervaded the New Zealand headquarters as the men of the 2nd and 3rd brigades launched their attack.

Russell's stationary barrage of 18-pounders rained shells along the German trench on the 2nd Brigade's left, protecting the 1st Otago Battalion from enfilade fire as it advanced. The Otagos moved forward on the left of the 1st Canterbury, both battalions moving rapidly in extended order. The Canterburys' war diary charted the rapid success of the advance, crossing no man's land in under 10 minutes, moving on past the captured front line, taking the reserve (Blue) line five minutes later and the Brown Line at 3.50 am.[74] Standing barrages also protected the Rifle Brigade's flank as it moved forward with its 3rd Battalion on the left and the 1st Battalion on the right, ready to rush the German front lines. To its rear, the Rifle Brigade's 4th and 2nd battalions followed on to consolidate and clear the positions their comrades had overrun. The 1st Battalion raced through Petit Douve Farm, clearing isolated pockets of resistance, bombers dealing swiftly with machine-guns in the darkness, now even more dense from the dust and smoke of the mines and bursting shells. Individual feats of valour dealt with what resistance remained among the defenders who were now rapidly being overrun. The 3rd and 1st battalions raced over the Blue Line in far less than the 16 minutes allotted for the capture of the front and support lines and pushed on to the Brown Line, collecting prisoners and quickly overcoming the weak and isolated resistance. The posts between these objectives were captured 'with ease ... our men made the final dash and reached their goal before the Germans could raise their heads.'[75]

However the tanks supporting the New Zealanders made an inauspicious start. At 3.20 am, to everyone's surprise, a tank had appeared, heading directly for the 1st Canterbury Battalion headquarters, stopping just 10 metres short before turning to the right and tracking behind the British front line for a short distance, then crossing into a deluge of high explosive shells which fortunately missed. 'Then', reported the 1st Canterbury diarist, '[it] moved across our front line and stuck in a shell hole ... till 4.00 p.m. on June 9th when it was dug out and taken home.'[76] Attitudes among the infantry commanders towards the tanks ranged from occasional enthusiasm to suspicion, mistrust and even derision. Reports of their failure would be a common theme in the infantry accounts following the battle. The 74th Brigade (25th Division) reported under 'lessons learned' with a mixture of condescension and thinly veiled contempt that 'All units were amused and interested by the tanks but it will not be necessary in future to warn them against placing any reliance on these engines of war.'[77]

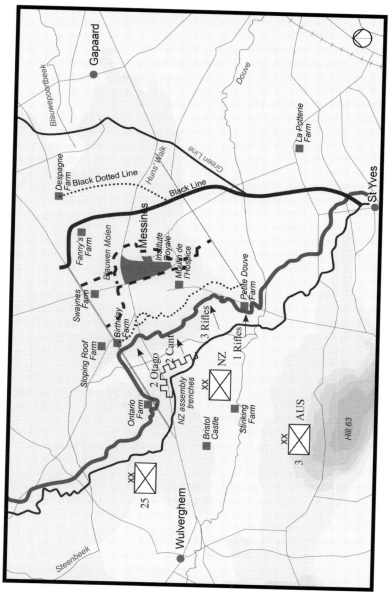

Map 11. The New Zealand Division plan of attack, 7 June 1917. Speed was key to Russell's plans to capture the village. His long, open left flank was a major danger neutralised by a standing barrage from his 18-pounders. Pre-dug assembly trenches shortened no man's land for the New Zealanders and Russell estimated that it would take almost 45 minutes after zero hour for the 25th Division to arrive and cover his left flank.

By 4.00 am the 2nd Canterbury had captured all its objectives and, by 4.25 am, battalion headquarters had moved into a pillbox on the forward slope of the ridge.[78] The 2nd Battalion had captured 20 machine-guns, only five of which had been brought into action and these were rushed before they could do any serious harm. It was a stunning success across broken, angular trenches in darkness thickened by dust from the mines and artillery. This action demonstrated the enormous benefit of the extraordinary degree of planning and preparation that characterised Messines, with the 2nd Brigade conducting no fewer than six rehearsals in the Quelmes region where the trenches had been replicated.[79] Private Jim Blakemore of the Rifle Brigade commented in 1988, 'I reckon we could have taken Messines with a wet sack … not that much opposition.'[80]

One of the pillboxes in Uhlan Trench captured by the New Zealand Division. Note the low profile of the strongpoint, making it very difficult to spot (AWM E00555).

Lieutenant Edward Winchester of the Rifle Brigade wrote a detailed account of the 4th Battalion's attack. Quickly following on behind the 3rd Battalion towards its objective, the southern half of the village, the men moved *en masse*, scattered and stumbling, through the 3rd which had captured the German front lines. Just as they cleared no man's land, the enemy barrage descended, fractionally too late, on the ground they had just crossed safely and they began to reorganise in the cloudy gloom before racing up the slope.

'I don't think I ever swore so much in my life as I did climbing up there' wrote Winchester, 'I blackguarded every N.C.O. I could see for not keeping his men together, but they seldom heard me for the noise.'[81] The 4th Battalion fought its way through isolated pockets of resistance, silencing machine-guns with rifle fire until the men found themselves outside the crumbling walls of the Institute Royale. With the barrage moving forward, Winchester was separated from most of his platoon and lost touch with the rest of his company. The small party that remained clambered through a gap in the wall and dashed into a courtyard they knew was 'full of huns'. Running along the inside of the Institute's wall, Winchester and his men found themselves trapped. 'I thought it was goodnight nurse then, for we ran into uncut wire, and machine guns opened up on us from the front, while we were fired on from the right flank.'[82] Rescue came from Winchester's lost platoon which started bombing towards them from the right, silencing the machine-guns and clearing the courtyard. Winchester sent men forward to clear the church, tasking the remainder with bombing dugouts and cellars.

The 3rd Battalion was held up by machine-guns firing from bunkers near the ruined church. Although he was wounded, Lance Corporal Samuel Frickleton dashed through the barrage and bombed one of the guns into silence before rushing the other gun and killing its entire crew. Frickleton's actions virtually ended German resistance in that area and, as his VC citation would record, 'undoubtedly saved his own and other units from very severe casualties'.[83] Frickleton was later wounded more severely as the Rifle Brigade dug in on the Black Line. Winchester wrote of the disintegrating resistance following Frickleton's heroic charges: 'At the Church a party of Germans threw some bombs, then went inside: some of our men immediately dashed round the back and prevented them getting out: then we put in some smoke bombs and seventeen of them came out crying like kids.'[84] The four battalions of the Rifle Brigade had effectively secured the village within the hour and the 1st Brigade of the New Zealand Division passed through the village and on towards the Black Line which it had secured by 5.20 am, just three hours later. With its artillery reorganised and a protective barrage established ahead, the 1st Brigade consolidated on the Black Dotted Line. For the New Zealanders, apart from some mixing up of units in the half-light of the dusty dawn, the attack had gone precisely to plan. The history of the Canterbury Regiment records the men's belief that the 3rd Australian Division on their right would have 'a comparatively easy task'.[85] For Monash's men however, the battle was far from straightforward.

The ruins of the tenth-century Church of St Nicolas in Messines, captured by the New Zealand Rifle Brigade on 7 June and the scene of Lance Corporal Frickleton's heroic action. It was the only structure still partly standing in the village after the battle (AWM E01484).

• • •

The gas attack at Ploegsteert Wood had seriously disrupted the 3rd Division. The 9th Australian Brigade was late arriving at the start line as the mines went up. The 36th Battalion (commanded by Lieutenant Colonel John Milne), providing the carrying parties at the head of the columns, did not reach the start line in time for zero, while Lieutenant Colonel Leslie Morshead's 33rd Battalion arrived with just minutes to spare.[86] Despite the ordeal of the approach march and the delays in the attack coordination, the 33rd Battalion diary recorded that the men went forward 'without hesitation', noting that 'our men had been so well organised, trained and informed by their Company Officers that each individual man knew his task and was not effected [sic] by the lack of organisation in the assembly trenches and the consequent rush.'[87] Morshead's report to 3rd Division Headquarters however, would admit that 'the assault went over in some confusion' before the companies organised themselves on reaching the enemy front line.[88]

Map 12. The 3rd Division plan of attack, 7 June 1917. Monash's division, with the shortest distance to travel, had a relatively straightforward task in the Douve Valley compared with the difficulties faced by the 25th Division and the New Zealanders. However the German gas attack threatened to completely disrupt the 3rd Division's meticulously drafted plans (AWM LIB100001710).

On the left, the 35th Battalion arrived in time for zero, but was somewhat disorganised. Lance Corporal Charles Akers waited as the seconds ticked down to zero '… and then – talk about earthquakes, up went our mine under Fritz's dugout about 60 yards ahead of us. Our sandbag parapets fell in, and over the bags we went and waited in no man's land for the barrage to lift and then forward after it.'[89] In the confusion, the planned scheme of attack in two waves merged to one, the men of the left company still wearing their gas masks. With the artillery creeping at 100 yards over three minutes, some of the 35th rushed ahead and into their own barrage. As would happen across most of the

Second Army's attack frontage, the German barrage descended, weak and late, on the now vacant British front lines. German defenders trapped or sheltering in dugouts were helpless as the Australians bombed them from above. The 35th reported no serious resistance but remarked on the heavy casualties caused by the bombing of dugouts. Akers commented that:

> A captured German captain said there were 300 men in the large dugout originally meant for 500 or 750, waiting for us to come over, but this mine settled that lot ... I helped to take lots of prisoners, but can safely say that I did not kill anybody, as I never saw an armed man for they all put up their hands when they saw us, and I do not wonder after the shelling our men had given them ... We had the 9ᵗʰ Bavarians against us, and they were a miserable lot of men to look at; some were mere boys.[90]

As with the 9th Brigade, the 10th Brigade's assault battalions also arrived at the start line with only minutes to spare. Lieutenant Norman Meagher of the 40th Battalion described the spectacular opening of the battle:

> The sight was magnificent, huge sheets of yellow flame bursting and thrusting their way to the sky. The ground beneath us quaked and trembled. We grasped revolvers and rifles more tightly, and in the pale moonlight I could see the faces of men, wild with the look of eagerness for the fray. Another half minute of awful suspense, and then the heavens were rent with a tornado of sound. First came the rattle of hundreds of machine guns, behind us opening with wonderful unanimity. What a feeling of confidence they inspired ... And then – just one 18-pounder fired, just one gun – another moment and thousands of guns of every calibre opened up behind us. The sky behind Hill 63 was as light as day, the noise was hellish but the guns were ours![91]

Given the weakened state of the 3rd Division, it was indeed fortunate that the morale of the defenders was so low. Two weeks of incessant and heavy bombardment, the shock of the giant mine explosions and the intense artillery and machine-gun barrages that preceded the depleted attack waves of the infantry had so degraded the German defences that resistance was almost entirely absent. The German response to the artillery — thinning out their front lines, occupying shell holes in no man's land and sheltering in deep dugouts — merely accelerated their collapse. The speed with which Monash's well-trained battalions moved behind the barrages in the pre-dawn simply overwhelmed them. The 40th Battalion diarist described 'the enemy making no resistance at all and appearing utterly demoralised'.[92] Bean described these first minutes of securing the German front and forward support lines as 'child's play compared with the nightmare of the approach march'.[93] The 40th Battalion however, had been seriously weakened by the gas shelling. Its report to division at the end of the battle indicated that the five platoons on the northern side of the Douve River totalled just 50 men and the five platoons on the southern side around 100. Effectively unopposed, the 40th secured all its objectives by 3.30 am. The Tasmanians had carried specially constructed bridges to cross the Douve River (in reality a stream little more than two metres at its widest point) and these were laid for both the men of the 40th and the 38th Battalion who would follow through, leapfrogging to the final objective on the Green Line. German aircraft appeared at around 10.00 am and accurate hostile shelling began once their position was relayed back to the German gunners on the far bank of the Lys.

The 38th followed up through the pathway created by the 40th Battalion's advance. For many of the men, the assault was chaotic. Private Ernest Popping wrote that 'We tripped in our own barbed wire, lost our parties and there was a great mixup.'[94] The battalion diary gave the impression that all went according to plan, the only mention of any problem the 'crowding' with the 40th at the start line and the late arrival.[95] The 38th moved on to Ulcer Reserve and further to Ungodly Trench meeting no resistance and taking few casualties. Leaving half of one company in Ulcer Reserve Trench, the men of the 38th arrived at the Black Line with 12 platoons and 12 Lewis guns and dug in. With their position indicated to both sides' artillery by the firing of flares to alert their observation planes, the German artillery hit both Ulcer Reserve Trench in the rear and the Black Line 'and never lifted off the vicinity'.[96] On the right of the 40th Battalion, the 39th Battalion moved forward along the Green Route via Ploegsteert Corner and Ashcroft Avenue Trench. As the leading platoon reached Ploegsteert Corner a heavy German shell burst among them. 'This', according to the 39th's narrative, 'with a heavy bombardment of gas shelling in the vicinity, disorganised the Battalion.'[97] Given that the 39th had suffered over 60% casualties on the approach, this was something of an understatement.[98] The 39th, despite its ordeal, arrived with some 20 minutes to spare and moved forward in one wave, as had the northern remnants of the 40th. No mention was made of the mine explosions in the 39th's report.[99] The weak enemy barrage which descended on the German front lines fell in a zigzag pattern through which (again fortunately, given their depleted numbers) the men of the 39th were able to negotiate gaps and to penetrate without serious loss. They were also fortunate that the Germans shelled their own front line, trapping the defenders below ground and making the task of suppressing any resistance more straightforward still. The 3rd Division's creeping barrage lifted to beyond the strongpoint of Grey Farm, leaving two machine-guns in action on the roof of one of the blockhouses on the northern edge of the farm which pinned down the advance until they were silenced by Captain Alexander Paterson. With resistance crushed around Grey Farm by the 34th and 39th, the two battalions linked up and began to dig in on the Black Line.

On the extreme right, news from the assaulting companies of the 33rd and 35th battalions charted the rapid success of the 3rd Division, reporting that the right company of the 33rd on the extreme flank (and with the shortest distance to advance) was digging in on the Black Line 10 minutes after zero with the whole of the German front line taken some 40 minutes after zero. There had been considerable dash shown by the novices of the 3rd Division. Lance Corporal John Carroll rushed a trench, bayoneting four Germans and clearing the way for his platoon. He would later rush another German position and silence a machine-gun. Nicknamed 'the wild Irishman', Carroll's actions over the three days the 33rd was in the line, which included rescuing three men buried by a shell, would earn him the VC. Thanks to their determined advance, the 9th Brigade battalions were safely on the Black Line and digging in by 6.35 am.[100] The 33rd then had to occupy and defend the 35-metre-wide Ultimo crater, the southernmost of the mines, and dig an outlying defensive trench ahead of the Black Line known as the Black Dotted Line.[101] Rushing and securing Ultimo mine crater was critical to the 9th Brigade's success. It had been recognised since the American Civil War that mine craters in modern warfare presented both an opportunity and a threat. Occupied by a quick-thinking enemy, the rim created a new and dominating defensive position from which to pour fire into the advancing troops. Quickly rushed by the attackers, the crater provided a springboard for further advance. On the left of the 9th Brigade, the 34th Battalion had first to leapfrog through the 35th and push on to the final objective on the Green Line. Since the 3rd Division's intended line ran on a north-east axis to conform with the southern slope of the ridge, the 34th was to advance in two stages, capturing the Black Line in the first rush, establishing a series of posts on the Black Dotted Line and then joining up with the 10th Brigade's push on to the final objective in the afternoon. As with the other battalions, the 34th reported virtually no resistance, adding that 'all enemy dugouts were bombed, their occupants killed or wounded'.[102]

One of the bridges placed by the 40th Battalion over the Douve River on the morning of 7 June (AWM E01286).

It was only on the far right flank, where the 33rd encountered snipers and machine-guns firing from the trench known as Ultimo Avenue, that there was any serious resistance. Pushing forward, the advanced Lewis gun teams of the 33rd came under sporadic machine-gun fire and had to withdraw to the safety of some shell holes around midday. Private William 'Paddy' Bacon was hit in the back as he retreated. Private Owen Thorogood recalled that Bacon 'said he was hit and I saw blood coming from his back below the shoulders. He told me to go on and catch the others up ... About 2.00 p.m. we went forward again and I came to Bacon in the same shell hole. He wasn't dead, but he could not speak or move and his lips were black. I left my water bottle with him and went on as we had been ordered to do. This is the last I saw of him.'[103]

Private Alan Mather was probably killed near Ultimo crater although, in the confusion of the battle, the details were sketchy. Privates Alfred Pitkin and Herbert Taylor and several other comrades from the 33rd reported seeing Mather hit by a shell and lying dead in 'Plug St Wood', the anglicised version of Ploegsteert. Corporal William Hadkins believed he'd been buried at 'Dead Horse Corner' on the edge of the wood and St Yves Avenue Trench. 'Pte Mather was a particular friend of mine and as to him being one of the unfortunate to fall there is no doubt.'[104] Like so many others that day, his body disappeared in the chaos of the battlefield.

The 3rd Division had been desperately unlucky in one sense. While the Germans had pinned down the likely attack date to within three or four days of 7 June, the gas shelling on the night of 6/7 June was a gamble which paid off. The assault battalions, particularly those of the 10th Brigade, had been seriously depleted both in numbers and in fighting condition. In another sense however, Monash was extremely fortunate that the Germans were incapable of mounting any serious resistance as the weakened 3rd Division advanced across their lines. A determined defence might well have broken the attack on the southern flank with serious consequences for the New Zealanders on the left and the subsequent arrangements for the second phase of the battle. Fortunately for the attackers, however, there was almost no serious fighting in the first rush and most had little more to do than clear dugouts and coax the demoralised German defenders from what for many became their last refuge.

At the 2nd Australian Casualty Clearing Station at Trois Arbres, some 13 kilometres back from the ridge, the nurses had been woken by the earthquake and the enormous artillery barrage and couldn't get back to sleep. Ada Smith was 'wondering how the Australians and other troops were faring. Wondering if they had won the hill, or were being slaughtered.'[105] The medical staff knew that, whichever way it went, they were bound to have streams of wounded arriving shortly, although it would be some time before they reached Trois Arbres. By 7.00 am word had reached the hospital that the ridge had been taken with light casualties. But that was not what Ada Smith saw 'as all those strong healthy men came in dead, dying, unconscious and moaning' to be examined and then stripped of their 'bloodstained dusty khaki' to be treated. Many bore horrific wounds, with limbs blown off, torn by high velocity projectiles, shrieking in pain or quietly dying on stretchers. The medical staff worked through the day and night to treat the wounded and comfort the dying.

Although sporadic fighting across II Anzac's front continued as pockets of resistance were cleared, the three divisions were on top of the ridge and digging in on the Black Line by 7.30 am in preparation for the afternoon attack. The same story of rapid and overwhelming success was repeated along the entire Second Army front. Had the battle ended there, it would have been the most spectacular *coup de main* of the war and by far the most economical in lives. But the alluring prospect of a German collapse and the possibility of an advance extensive enough to threaten the German gun line were too tempting for Haig and, on his urging, Plumer's army was now poised to charge forward from the crest of the ridge. While, to this point, this had been a singularly flawless battle, its flaws would now begin to emerge.

5

… push on as quickly as possible without any regard for the distress of the troops.

To the Green Line

... push on as quickly as possible without any regard for the distress of the troops.

To the Green Line

The Australians of the 12th Brigade were asleep in their barracks at Bulford Camp in the Belgian hamlet of Korte Pijp, some five kilometres behind the British lines, when the mines exploded at 3.10 am. Private Denver Gallwey woke to a surreal sensation. 'The hut rocked as the earth trembled and I felt a sensation such as one would on a sinking ship ... and as the rocking effect continued I instinctively grasped my covering to try and save myself from a fall.'[1] He recalled that most of the men in his hut, though shaken awake by the earthquake, soon drifted back to sleep to the rolling thunder of the artillery. Of the thousands of men preparing for battle on the morning of 7 June, one would have an influence on the narrative of Messines far beyond his role as a humble private in the 47th Battalion. Gallwey was a 19-year-old recruit from Rockhampton in Queensland and Messines would be his first experience of battle. Such would be its impact on him that, after the war, he would produce a fascinating and prodigiously lengthy account of his war experiences in three volumes, a task which took him 10 years to complete. Gallwey's memoirs represent one of the most remarkable collections in the Australian War Memorial's archives. Volume II of Gallwey's magnum opus, 'The Silver King', contains 136 pages of close typescript describing, with near photographic recall, almost everything he witnessed during the 47th Battalion's attack at Messines.[2] Though never published and rarely read, it remains one of the most powerful, honest and confronting accounts of battle ever written. Bean, fully aware of its historical value, would mine Gallwey's account extensively to describe the afternoon attack.

As the 12th Brigade prepared to set off from Bulford camp, the men loading up their kit and checking their rifles, they watched a crowd of prisoners shambling past, escorted by two New Zealanders. Lieutenant Colonel Alex Imlay, in command of the 47th, was 'gladdened by the sight of a group of 100 most miserable looking and cowed huns passing as prisoners. Nothing more propitious for us.'[3] Buoyed by news of the morning's success, the 45th and 47th battalions moved off at 7.40 am with a comfortable margin of four hours to reach their jumping-off points at the top of the ridge. The second phase of the battle, the scheme for capturing the Green Line, had been hastily drafted in late May, and subjected to many amendments as zero day approached, the most important of which was the timing for the second phase. The 4th Australian Division, according to orders issued on 30 May, was to set off from the old British front line just under nine hours after zero (at 11.55 am) to join the other reserve divisions in place ready to move forward from the Black Line without pause, at zero plus 10 hours (1.10 pm). On 3 June Bean noted the uncertain provision of a 'new zero', writing 'I don't think the program is yet fixed. Everything seems liable to change.'[4]

Private Denver Gallwey of the 47th Battalion. His highly detailed and vivid memoirs would contain a uniquely valuable and starkly honest account of his battalion's actions at Messines and would be used extensively by Bean in his narrative for the *Official History*. (Photo courtesy Val Gallwey).

German prisoners acting as stretcher-bearers on the morning of 7 June. In the background, three British Mark IV tanks are moving up to the ridge to support the 4th Division's attack in the afternoon while a large calibre shell can be seen bursting on the ridge (AWM E01414).

The Australian order of battle for the assault on the Green Line would see the 4th Division's 13th Brigade (52nd and 49th battalions) on the left of its front alongside the 12th Brigade (45th and 47th battalions) on its right with the 4th Brigade in reserve. The 3rd Division, which formed the Second Army's right flank, would push on to the Green Line on its front — its final objective line — winding back to meet the Black Line on the right extremity of the line and giving the 3rd a shorter distance to advance. Given the narrower and shallower front, the 3rd Division required just one battalion (the 37th) with one attached company of the 40th to reach its final objective. However the timing was critical. What Godley had feared most in the morning's assault was German discovery of the troops concentrating for the attack on the ridge and a consequent 'annihilating barrage' on their formations.[5] In the clear daylight of the afternoon the troops of the reserve divisions advancing over the ridge to attack the Green Line would be plainly visible to what remained of the German artillery and, while they would have a creeping barrage for protection, it was essential they move through the Black Line and on to their final objective without delay.

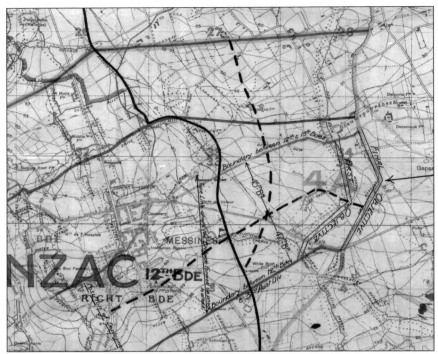

Map 13. The 4th Australian Division plan of attack, 7 June 1917. The 4th Division was given the least time to prepare the most difficult attack on the ridge, assaulting down an open slope for almost 1000 metres in broad daylight. Numerous pillboxes, some housing field guns, and uncut wire and hidden machine-guns decimated the 12th and 13th brigades (AWM LIB100001710).

Haig's late change to the main plan created tension between two competing objectives which, despite the talents of Plumer's staff, they failed to reconcile, a failure which would profoundly influence the battle. The Second Army's planners remained focussed on what they regarded as the main objective — the capture and retention of the ridge. Bean reflected this in his account, adding that the afternoon attack was 'purely subsidiary' and that the capture and consolidation of the Black Line was the main objective.[6] To hold the Black Line, Plumer believed he would have to defeat strong German counter-attacks which had become the standard response to local successes. The counter-attack had been a successful (though costly) tactic for Germans. Once an enemy advance reached high tide and the momentum of the attack slowed through casualties and fatigue, they were hit with fresh troops, the specially trained *eingreif* (counter-attack) *divisions*. Just six weeks prior to Messines, a counter-attack at Bullecourt had dealt a devastating blow to the 4th Division. Bean knew what to expect at Messines:

The thing that we are all very anxious about was the German counter-attack. The system had been immensely successful and was regarded as having a mysterious, rather awe-inspiring force which attaches to things overly heard of – until familiarity destroyed the illusion.[7]

Haig was confident that Plumer had sufficient infantry, guns and momentum to defeat any attempt to retake the ridge and believed that the Second Army could push on beyond the Black Line to capture and hold the German reserve line (the Green Line) and leave open the possibility of exploitation. As suggested by their plans, Plumer and Harington were never fully committed to the latter two ambitions and the difficulty of planning for both 'bite and hold' and 'exploitation' would be a key contributing factor to the problems that dogged II Anzac Corps at Messines. A sign of the Second Army's uneasiness with the plan for exploitation was apparent in the orders for 30 May. 'Under cover of the … barrage, patrols from Corps Cavalry and from Infantry of the attacking Divisions, will be pushed out to clear the ground, to capture the enemy's guns and to establish a line of strong posts close to the barrage.'[8] The assaulting divisions were then to follow and capture the final objective.

The idea that men on horses could not just survive on the battlefield, but perform a useful task, was a matter of blind faith rather than reason. After 1914, cavalry had succeeded nowhere on the Western Front, let alone captured guns. The cavalry orders were not amended until 6 June by which time they read that mounted troops were to merely 'assist in establishing a line of posts' once the Black Line was captured. Added to this was the very optimistic role of reconnaissance east of the Green Line.[9] The main role of attacking and capturing the Green Line was, however, now the responsibility of the infantry of the reserve divisions who were to commit two brigades each to this role, a far more realistic proposition. As for the imagined role of cavalry, Bean (and many others) at the time considered this laughably impractical.

Another problem created by the extension of the objective, and one that would have serious consequences for the Australians, was the lack of detail in some of the maps covering the areas to be assaulted beyond the Black Line. The quality of the Second Army's maps for Messines varied considerably. At their best, they are remarkably complete and accurate, a tribute to the work of the intelligence officers and cartographers and to the courage and skill of the airmen who captured the high resolution aerial photographs on which this work relied. The topographic units produced superb drawings of enemy positions and the mapmakers at every level added vital detail as it was gained from trench raids, from prisoners and from infiltrating scouts. The large battle maps which can still be found in the British National Archives at Kew (and reproduced in unit diaries) bear witness to this vital work. But the rich detail to be found in the maps for the morning attack on the ridge is conspicuously absent in those for the assault on the Green Line. Some confusion was also caused (and remains) due to the different subsidiary objectives allotted to different divisions and different nomenclature of lines across the Second Army front. Although the 'Black' and 'Green' lines were common across all maps in referring to the Messines-Wytschaete Ridge (Black Line) and the final objective of the German support trenches on the Oosttaverne Line (Green Line), the advanced line of posts 130 metres ahead of the Black Line was known as both the Red Dotted Line and the Black Dotted Line in II Anzac and became the Mauve Line in IX Corps. It was marked simply as 'line of Posts' on the 25th Division's maps. The careful planning for the morning attack is abundantly clear in the 25th Division's maps which had a succession of objective lines (Yellow, Grey, Brown, Pink, Purple, Orange, Dotted Blue, Blue) before reaching the Black Line. This stands in sharp contrast to the maps for the afternoon attack which simply show the bare expanse of the afternoon's advance to the Green Line with no intermediate objectives whatsoever.

Where mapping failed, it cost dearly in lives. McKenny Hughes of the RFC confided to his diary on 5 June: 'I am trying to get a decent map made for our observers as the one produced by the Second Army is an outrage. To begin with, it is not even the latest edition. It has no railways marked on it nor the military roads which were made 18 months ago, and the method of putting hostile batteries with rows of black blobs 1/8" in diameter practically obliterates what there is on the map, and the two main lines of defence through Oosttaverne and Kortewilde are not shown.'[10] Even when all the information was to hand, human factors could intervene to degrade the accuracy of maps. On the night before the battle, McKenny Hughes wrote that he had been 'trying to get some decent maps made for counter battery work but found at 9 p.m. that Martin had got the whole lot about 1/16" out. One does meet a frantic pack of fools.' In another exchange which may have had unfortunate consequences for the hapless men of the 19th Division, McKenny Hughes rang them 'to tell them of a new dug-out which had appeared but got on to an old and typical Colonel who was so uncivil that I just rang him off.'[11]

• • •

As the sun climbed higher that morning, the troops on the Black Line across 14 kilometres of the captured ridge laboured to dig themselves to safety. According to the Australian *Official History*, the Maori Pioneer Battalion 'in less than an hour's vehement effort dug themselves out of sight below the surface'.[12] By 10.00 am the German guns were beginning to find their targets and hostile aircraft appeared over the ridge to spot for their artillery. The reserve divisions were also on the move, the X Corps' 24th Division, the IX Corps' 11th Division and II Anzac's 4th Australian Division, which would carry most of the Green Line, with the 3rd Division's 10th Brigade to push the attack through on the much shorter distance on the far right flank. For the 4th Division's 13th Brigade, quartered at Nieuwkerke, and the 12th Brigade close by at Korte Pijp, this meant a march of almost five kilometres before they arrived at their jumping-off point. The 11th Division, which would protect the Australians' left flank, had a far longer route to its jumping-off line due to the contour of the ridge and the distance from its barracks. The narrow front of the 25th Division meant that the 11th would need to move past and ahead on the 25th's left to join up with the 13th Australian Brigade, rather than leapfrog through as the 4th Division did. II Anzac's arrangements for capturing the Green Line and coordination with the neighbouring IX Corps on its left flank were indeed complex.

The orders for the 4th Division continued to evolve over the final days. By 5 June the provisions covering cavalry and infantry patrols moving out to capture guns which had existed on 30 May had disappeared. Now, once the Green Line was captured by the infantry, the barrage was then to rest ahead of the Green Line for a further 30 minutes and then lift to allow cavalry patrols from the Otago Mounted Rifle Squadron to move forward beyond the Green Line for reconnaissance, an order which once again imagined an almost complete absence of resistance. The time for the attack on the Green Line remained unchanged, its start time zero plus 10 hours (1.10 pm), with the attack across the whole front of the Second Army to be protected by a creeping barrage which would lift in 100-metre increments every three minutes to arrive on the Green Line 20 minutes after the troops had left their trenches. As the barrage was due to come down 130 metres ahead of the line of posts in front of the Black Line, this meant the distance was, on average, around 900 metres (although much shorter on the right of the 3rd Division, the 'corner' where the Green and Black lines met). The orders concerning the tanks, with the recent catastrophe at Bullecourt firmly in mind, made it clear that, although they would cooperate in the attack, 'plans will be made out as if no co-operation from tanks is to be forthcoming'.[13]

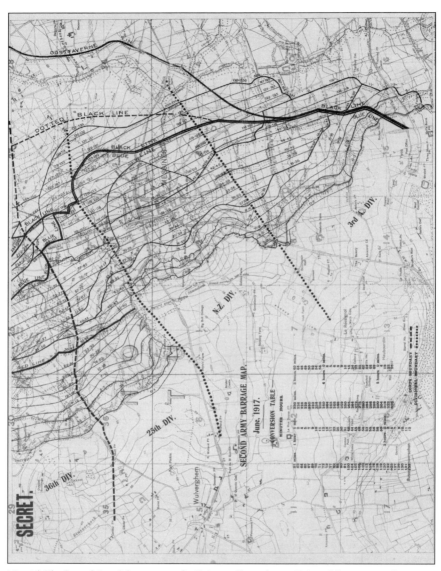

Map 14. The Second Army's barrage map for II Anzac. Shown here is II Anzac's barrage map for the attack on 7 June. The Second Army's creeping barrage of 18-pounders advanced 100 yards every three minutes and provided a screen for the advancing infantry. The map shows signs of the careful preparation and intricate planning which characterised the first phase of the Messines battle. Dating from 30 May, it also reveals that plans for the creeping barrage to protect the attack on the Green Line in the afternoon were still being drafted with just over a week until zero.

Gunners from the 14th Battery of the Australian Field Artillery and their 18-pounders. These guns were critical in providing the creeping barrages that covered the advance to the Green Line (AWM E00920).

Once again, the extension of the objective to the Green (Oosttaverne) Line meant that the assault battalions for the afternoon attack faced a far more formidable prospect than those that launched the morning's attack. Not only would they need to move down an open slope in daylight, clearly visible to the German artillery, the cloudless day then dawning meant the attack would be delivered in the midday heat by men laden with 30 kilos of gear, in thick woollen battle dress with only two water bottles which they were ordered not to touch until they had taken their objective. The complication for the artillery was that the heavy guns would need to accurately elevate to bombard the Green Line without the same degree of observation and correction they had been provided in the past weeks. The 18-pounders would need to fire on lengthened ranges to provide the creeping barrages. Barrage maps for the afternoon attack showed the straight lines across the maps for 'lifts' working forward from 150 metres in front of each start line for the assault battalions. Although the barrage lines were drawn straight and evenly spaced on the map, neither the 'line of posts' nor the Green Line itself was a simple straight line, both meandering irregularly. To conform to their shape would require individual guns to fire accurately at differing ranges for their shot to fall over both the Red (Black) Dotted Line and the Green Line. The 12th Brigade's line of attack, for example, lay diagonally across the Red Dotted Line, with the right of the 47th Battalion some 50 yards in advance of it, and the left of the 45th Battalion some 100 yards to its rear.

The arrangements for the launch of the second phase attack were also amended in the final days. That this was worrying the Second Army staff a good deal was underscored by the appearance in the orders as the final days approached of the term 'new zero' to mark the time of the attack on the Green Line. The 'new zero' outlined in a memo produced by the 3rd Division involved no new plans. The change was that 'new zero' would not necessarily be at zero plus 10 hours (1.10 pm), but would not be before that time. 'It is practically certain that we shall know the "New Zero" hour by Zero plus six [9.10 am]. Everyone will work towards the "New Zero" being Zero plus 10, but as stated above, it may be later.'[14] Plumer and his staff were not confident that all the units would arrive in time, particularly given the different distances they would need to travel to reach their afternoon start lines, the broken country they would have to traverse and the many other reasons a unit might be delayed.

The option to delay the launch of the afternoon attack was a critical provision. It was important because, in the event of the late arrival of a unit on the start line, it would be advancing without the cover of a barrage since the artillery had to fire according to a strict timetable in order for the creeping barrage to be effective. This risk had to be weighed against the risks of a delay which might allow a shaken enemy time to recover and bring forward reinforcements. Even the most carefully planned battles have their moments of uncertainty and every great commander has faced the need to take calculated risks at critical moments. The greatest have the boldness and wisdom and sometimes the luck to make the right call. Plumer now faced such a moment with the timing of the second phase of the attack. Three factors should have led him to proceed with zero hour as planned at 1.10 pm. The first was that there was every reason to expect that most, if not all units, would be on time and that missing the barrage would be a potential problem (rather than an actual one) for just a small number of units. The second was that some level of disarray in the German defences should have been expected and thus speed was of the essence. This was the point Haig urged on him in suggesting he try to capture the German guns. The third was that a late change to the timing risked 'order, counter order, disorder'. Plumer, cautious by nature, opted to delay.

Profoundly important though this decision was, a simple administrative error in the 13th Brigade would prove far more important still. The 4th Division's orders anticipated the possible late arrival of the 16th Division's 33rd Brigade (IX Corps) alongside Glasgow's brigade, directing that the 'GOC 13th Brigade will be prepared to refuse his left flank in the event of the Brigade on his left being held up', an order which Glasgow duly passed to the 52nd Battalion.[15] 'Refusing' the flank meant bending it back at right angles to the line of attack so that, in this case, the 52nd Battalion's left flank would be protected.[16] This was obviously not ideal as it meant lining men across the left flank, perhaps even digging trenches which might become useless in a matter of hours when the late unit arrived. However, this was tactical orthodoxy, an essential measure to safeguard an open flank, providing defence against an enemy attack from that direction, and the risks of not doing this were far greater than the risks of weakening the front line.

In command of the 52nd Battalion at Messines was the 44-year-old Lieutenant Colonel Harold Pope, the man whose gallant defence of a vital gap in the Anzac line at Gallipoli on the night of 25 April made 'Pope's Hill' a place famous in Australian history. In 1916 he had the misfortune to be in command of the 14th Brigade at the battle of Fromelles, losing 2000 men in one disastrous night. The following afternoon his divisional commander, Major General James McCay, unable to wake him from an exhausted sleep, concluded he was drunk and sacked him. Pope vehemently protested his innocence, but faced with compelling evidence and anxious to avoid scandal, Birdwood refused to grant a court martial.[17] Pope returned to Australia in disgrace. Determined to clear his name, he fought his way back to the war in Europe by taking command of troops (as an unpaid continuous service officer) on the transport *Hororata*. Back in England, Pope argued his case with such vigour that Birdwood relented, giving him command of the 52nd Battalion in February 1917.

Lieutenant Colonel Harold Pope who commanded the 52nd Battalion at Messines. Returning to senior command in 1917 after being sacked in disgrace the previous year, his orders for the 52nd's attack would omit vital instructions from Holmes and Glasgow about safeguarding his left flank which would result in a disastrous loss of direction (IWM HU 109298).

Pope received his orders from Glasgow on 6 June. In addition to the order to be ready to refuse his flank, he was given six guns from the 13th Machine Gun Company with orders to use these to further strengthen his left should the 33rd arrive late. Glasgow's orders were copied to the 33rd Brigade so that, should they be delayed, they would be expecting the 52nd to refuse its flank and the English would subsequently encounter the Australians on their right in that deployment as they advanced. Crucially, the 52nd Battalion orders make no mention of the order to prepare to refuse the battalion's flank should the 33rd Brigade arrive late, Pope interpreting Glasgow's order as simply requiring deployment of machine-guns to guard his flank. This was a critical mistake. It left unanswered the question of what his officers on the left should do if they did not join up with the English, a question that would somehow have to be answered if this occurred. The 33rd Brigade would indeed be delayed and, as events will show, the failure by Pope to include this provision in the 52nd Battalion's orders would have disastrous consequences.

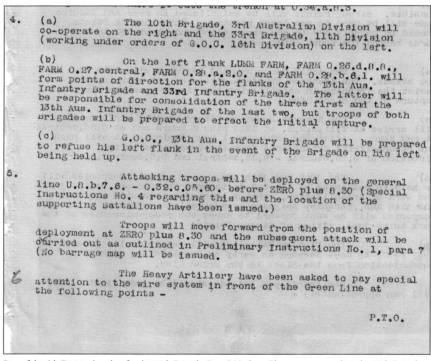

Part of the 4th Division's orders for the 13th Brigade. Part 4 (c) alerts Glasgow, commanding the 13th Brigade, to be prepared to refuse his left flank if the 33rd Brigade were late (AWM4 1/48/15, 4th Division War Diary).

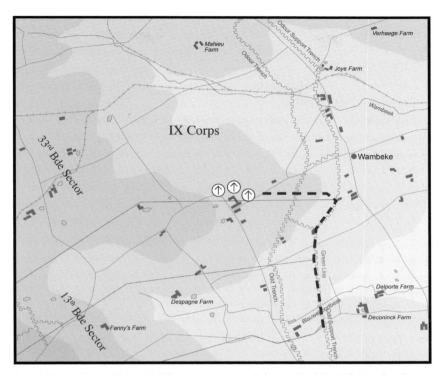

Map 15. The 13th Brigade's intended dispositions, 7 June. Holmes ordered the 13th Brigade to be prepared to refuse its left flank in the event of the late arrival of the 33rd Brigade. Further orders indicated where the 12th Machine Gun Company should deploy its guns should this occur. This map illustrated the defensive scheme designed to protect the 13th Brigade's flank.

Allowing sufficient time for the units to reorganise following their march, and scale the ridge was all important, as the problems encountered by the 33rd Brigade would illustrate. The troops for the afternoon attack would be in columns until they reached the foot of the ridge and then move into the wide-spaced 'artillery formation' to climb it. The 4th Division was to leapfrog through the troops of the 25th and New Zealand divisions before digging in on the Black Line. The orders for the 12th Brigade (which was on the right of the 4th Division's line) stated that the brigade would 'shake out into lines so that the Right rests about Bethleem Farm and the Left on Blauwen Molen.'[18] Both brigades made good time to the foot of the ridge, although the 13th Brigade reached its position of deployment behind the New Zealanders, almost an hour later than the 12th Brigade on its right. The 13th had the 49th Battalion on its right (alongside the 12th Brigade's 45th Battalion) and the 52nd Battalion on its left. The 52nd was due to link up with the 33rd Brigade (from the British 11th Division, but attached to the 16th Division for this attack) on its left. The 50th and 51st battalions remained in reserve in the old British front line at the foot of the ridge. While preparing to move over the Black Line to the start tapes, Glasgow received word that Plumer had delayed the attack by two hours. 'New zero' would now be 3.10 pm.

Although the 13th Brigade reported after the battle that it had suffered few casualties as the men waited the extra two hours, one significant casualty was Lieutenant Colonel Pope, who was wounded by the steadily increasing German artillery. Tasmanian Captain Claude Stubbings assumed command of the 52nd and it fell to him to guide his battalion through its perilous advance. If Pope was planning to issue verbal orders for the left flank to be refused if the English brigade was late, that chance was now lost as he was stretchered away in agony with a shattered thigh. With the minutes ticking down to the start time, Stubbings' men moved forward to the start line with the reassuring presence of the 49th Battalion on their right. On their left, however, and despite the two-hour wait, the 33rd Brigade was nowhere to be seen. The 52nd advanced with its left flank 'in the air' — unprotected.

To the south, the 12th Brigade had made excellent progress to the foot of the ridge and, as the men climbed, they had to pass through a barrage from the enemy artillery which was just beginning to recover some cohesion following the shock of the morning and the weeks of counter-battery fire which preceded it. Denver Gallwey waited with his D Company, 47th Battalion, as a curtain of fire threw up wood and stones which pinged off his steel helmet accompanied by the sound of shrapnel whipping through the air above. Privately doubting they would be sent through, Gallwey and the rest of the 47th Battalion were given the order to move forward in artillery formation and passed through, fortunately with few losses. Less fortunately for Brigadier General James Robertson's men of the 12th Brigade, they were late receiving the news that the attack had been delayed. The order was received at division at 10.30 am but, according to the 12th Brigade's post-battle report, 'did not reach their company commanders until after both Battalions had reached the Red Dotted Line East of Messines where they formed up under the protective barrage ready to attack the final objective.'[19] While no explanation is given for the late receipt of this crucial message, it is possible that the ferocity of the barrage encountered by the 12th Brigade was to blame. Having not received their orders to wait, they moved forward from the deployment position, passed the New Zealanders on the Black Line, who greeted them with a cheer as they moved through, and forward to their start tapes where they were informed of the change. There was nothing to be done other than wait and the men sought shelter in shell holes behind the start tapes, many already taxed by the morning's exertions. 'It seems incredible that any one could sleep in a shell hole packed in like sardines knowing that any minute death might enter. Such it was however', wrote Gallwey.[20] At 2.10 pm, one hour before the scheduled attack, the men of the 12th noted ominously the Germans 'advancing to counter attack in considerable strength'.[21] The Green Line, which had been open for the taking had the attack proceeded when originally planned, could now be seen rapidly filling with fresh troops. In the full sunlight of that brilliant day and down an open slope, the 12th Brigade would attack a line dotted with concrete pillboxes, hidden machine-gun nests and strongly held trenches.

Further to the right, Monash's 10th Brigade had the task of taking the Green Line on the southern end of the line. Despite having a shorter distance to travel, the 3rd Division had to move across the southern slope of Messines Ridge, into the Douve Valley, again in view of the largely unsuppressed German artillery, and also, although they were as yet unaware, on a collision course with fresh German troops moving up to counter-attack. The shape of the line on the southern shoulder of the ridge and the complexity and strength of the defensive trench systems around Grey Farm and La Potterie made this a very difficult task indeed, particularly for an inexperienced division. The assault on the Green Line was entrusted to three companies of the 37th Battalion with one company of the 40th Battalion attached, the remaining company of the 37th in reserve and two companies of the 40th Battalion as carriers. The 10th Brigade received news of the two-hour delay in good time but, as with the 12th Brigade, was in full view of the German artillery, and the men took cover where they could in the vicinity of the Black Line once they had passed Schnitzel Farm. Having already suffered casualties, the men 'lay down in open order about 150 yards behind the Black Line for a little over two hours'.[22]

• • •

On the heights beyond the village, the Australians were experiencing their first glimpse of the other side of the fearsome Messines Ridge. The scene was remarkable: 'In front was a green countryside, with woods of leaf covered trees and the gentle sloping grassland was intersected by tree-lined hedgerows.'[23] With many of the German troops on the reverse slope having fled their defences, their artillery incapable of responding effectively following the shock of the attack, and swarming British aircraft preventing observation from the air, the ground ahead seemed open for the taking. On the far left of the Australian line, a taping party from the 49th Battalion wandered freely about, surprised to find four abandoned field guns near their battalion's jumping-off point and, encouraged by the lull in the fighting, wandered some 250 yards further, claiming another 5.9-inch howitzer as a war prize for their battalion and penetrating almost as far as Despagne Farm. Haig had been proven right. The enormous shock of the attack had thrown the Germans completely off balance. But as Lieutenant Hallam and his taping party of 14 men from the 49th Battalion would discover, the risks of pushing on were not confined to German resistance. Their own protective barrage which had searched ahead, now fell back and hit them in their advanced position. Four of Hallam's party were killed and five wounded by their own artillery.

Captured German trenches on the Green Line (AWM H08723).

The infantry and gun crews who had abandoned the guns claimed by the 49th Battalion had withdrawn to the Green Line in disorder. There the harried officers did their best to rally them to counter-attack in line with the German defensive scheme. Promised that the counter-attack divisions would arrive soon, they sat under the British barrage then searching ahead, some launching the minor counter-attacks that were reported by a few of the more advanced troops of the New Zealand and 25th divisions who were then engaged in digging the line of posts in advance of the Black Line. Despite a determination to retake the ridge 'at all costs', the forces which eventually arrived to accomplish this were late, weak and observed as soon as they came into sight from the south-west, moving along the Messines-Koretje road which was known as 'Huns' Walk'. The SOS signal of single red flares was fired by men in the line of posts on the Black Dotted Line at 2.10 pm and the British artillery responded with full force, crushing quickly and with ease what would turn out to be the main German attempt to retake the ridge.[24] All the available machine-guns of the New Zealanders and the 25th Division on the Black Line joined in, firing at 700 metres. 'By 2.30' recorded Bean in the *Official History*, 'the effort was completely spent. Whatever Germans had passed the Oosttaverne Line fell back upon it.'[25]

As the minutes ticked down to 3.10 pm, the 3rd and 4th divisions readied for the advance to the final objective. However the arrangements for the 11th Division (IX Corps), which was to deliver the attack in the centre and protect the left flank of the 4th Division, were in disarray, although II Anzac headquarters was unaware of this at the time. But, for the assault troops of X and IX Corps, opposite whose lines the full force of the mines had been felt and where the counter-battery work had been considerably more effective, the prospect of the afternoon advance was less ominous. German shelling, though scattered and weak across most of the front, was heaviest in the south, affecting the 3rd Division, the New Zealanders, who were furiously digging the trenches on the Black Line, and the 4th Division, all of whom were within reach of those German guns which had survived the massive artillery duel of the previous weeks.[26]

On the extreme left of the Australian line, Captain Stubbings, now in command of the 52nd Battalion in place of the wounded Pope, watched his flank anxiously for any sign of the 6th Lincolns, the right battalion of the 33rd Brigade.[27] Patrols sent out to find them returned with no news. The 33rd Brigade had marched through the night to reach its jumping-off points. As the men moved into the IX Corps sector, they came under the control of the 16th Division. Although the official histories don't identify who was to blame for the muddling in IX Corps, the troops of the 33rd, 'through no fault of the Brigade', had not received their orders to advance until 10.45 am (more than three hours later than the Australians).[28] This was but one of the errors which contributed to the delay and confusion. They were also not informed until 12.30 pm that the new zero was now 3.10 pm, as the 33rd Brigade War Diary recorded:

12.30 Information received from 16th Division that new zero would be at 3.15 p.m. [sic] and that our objective had been slightly altered. GOCs IX Corps and 16 Division conferring re the situation: 19th Division doubtful as to whether they could reach the position of deployment in time for the new barrage and we were warned to watch our left flank.[29]

At 1.15 pm, less than two hours before the attack was due to be launched, the 33rd recorded that verbal orders had been received from 16th Division Headquarters altering the objective (which was now to exclude Oosttaverne village), informing the 33rd that the 57th Brigade from the 19th Division would assault and capture that part of the Green Line and that the 33rd was to proceed 'at once' to its jumping-off trench. 'As the enemy was demoralized and surrendering freely every effort was to be made to push on as quickly as possible without any regard for the distress of the troops.'[30] However, by that time the distress of the troops was considerable. In an additional blunder, they were then sent by a circuitous route which further delayed and exhausted them.[31] At 1.05 pm they reached Chinese Wall Trench below the Hollandscheschur mine crater, where the message from brigade headquarters concerning the change in time for 'new zero' was passed to the battalions.[32] The forced march in the heat and needless detours had disrupted the brigade and the attack was hastily reorganised on the spot. The hurried orders in the 7th South Staffordshire's diary chart the mounting confusion:

> … as 6 Bord. R [6th Border Regiment] and 9 Sher. For. [9th Battalion Sherwood Foresters Regiment] might be unable to arrive in time for the attack, 2 companies of the 7th South Staffordshire would advance in the first wave with 6th Lincoln Regiment on the right and 2 Companies 7th South Staffordshire in close support. The frontage of the Brigade was also shortened as a Battalion of the 19th Division would co-operate on the left. Our left was now to rest on Polka Estaminet (inclusive to us). Information was given that this battalion (of the 19th Division) too might be late for new zero.

> 1.50 p.m. Only one company of 6 Linc. R. [6th Lincolnshire Regiment] was in readiness to move, and was followed immediately by [7th South Staffordshire] … There was intermittent shelling from the enemy during the advance, which gradually increased in intensity.[33]

The South Staffordshires and one company of the 6th Lincolns set off from Chinese Wall at 2.00 pm. The other three companies of the 6th Lincolns were lost and had not even arrived at Chinese Wall. Once glance at the map reveals the difficulty they now faced in reaching the position on time. The 33rd Brigade report summarises the confusion succinctly: 'Owing to the shortness of time, all orders from the Division downwards had to be transmitted verbally and no check of their being understood was possible before they were put into execution.'[34] The first tired and disorganised companies of the 33rd Brigade did not reach the foot of the ridge below Wytschaete, still well to the north of their jumping-off point, until 2.45 pm. At that point the diary of the 7th Battalion, South Staffordshire Regiment, recorded that, 'Owing to the great heat and the unexpectedly hasty move from Vierstraat Switch, the men were very exhausted, having been marching almost continuously for four hours already.'[35]

The commanders of the 16th and 19th divisions met under intense pressure to try to save the 33rd Brigade's scheduled attack, a prospect now rapidly diminishing. Major General Shute of the 19th Division suggested that his 57th Brigade take over part of the assault (600 yards) and relieve some of the pressure on the 16th Division. It was only through good fortune that the 57th Brigade's battalions had not been needed and thus not employed in the walkover that the morning attack had become. Nevertheless, the 57th Brigade had been given less than three hours' notice that it would deliver an attack which was then hastily planned, the brigade left with no opportunity to brief its officers who would assault an unknown (to them) section of the line in daylight and, once again, down an open slope in full view of the enemy. This was the antithesis of the morning's attack, with its weeks of planning, training, practice attacks and briefings, its careful and precise artillery arrangements, its visits to models of the ground and rigorous drilling of participants. Here was the worst of prospects, pregnant with all the risks and follies that had been so bloodily punished in 1916. Ultimately however, despite the best efforts of the British to cobble together an attack on the 4th Division's left, the men of the 52nd Battalion moved forward alone and unsupported on their flank.

When the protective barrage opened at zero on the ground 130 metres ahead of his line, Stubbings, then unable to wait any longer, gave the order for his battalion to advance. The brigade machine-gun section was sent out on the left to create a strongpoint and one platoon was pushed out before the advance on the left in the hope that it could provide some protection to the open flank. The 52nd's diary records that the right of the battalion was in touch with the 49th Battalion.[36] The two battalions began their advance with two companies in front and two in the rear. Captain Arthur Maxwell, commanding the left rear company (D) of the 52nd, aware of the yawning gap on the left, swung his men around to the left and into the gap (alongside B company which was front left) to the north to try to link up with the 33rd Brigade. Unaware that the 33rd was not to be found (the men of the 33rd were still climbing the ridge, strung out and exhausted), Maxwell led his company ever further to the left in a fruitless search.[37] While the 49th Battalion had managed to reach its deployment positions without loss, the men were shelled heavily during the half hour it took to move over the ridge to their start tapes. As they set off, they had the misfortune to suffer not only shellfire from the enemy's guns but their own artillery firing short on their right flank. The barrage was lagging behind time and, still resting on its first objective, prevented the 49th entering the trench. The luckless 49th then ran head on into a concentration of pillboxes in the Blauwepoortbeek Valley where it quickly suffered heavy casualties.

Maxwell's decision to lead his men to the left in search of the English was to have a series of consequences, few of them good. The company on Maxwell's right, with orders to keep touch with its flanks, was pulled to the left, which had the effect of dragging the whole battalion away from its axis and well north of its intended final objective. The 49th Battalion's left companies were dragged north also and, in trying to maintain touch with both the 52nd and its own right companies, the 49th was eventually pulled apart at the head of the Blauwepoortbeek Valley. The 4th Division's front line was stretched by Maxwell's northward move until it broke apart as units tried to maintain contact with one another. The 49th Battalion lost touch with the 52nd and its two right companies lost touch with the two on its left. The two right companies of the 49th, dragged north also, lost touch with the left of the 45th and this separated the two brigades. The result was a calamitous fracturing and, instead of the one open flank (the 52nd's left) which had been anticipated and a contingency plan put in place, there were now five and the whole front of the 4th Division was fatally fragmented.[38] This was the potential disaster that Holmes' order of 5 June, that the 52nd should refuse its left flank if the 33rd Brigade were late, had been intended to prevent.[39] Bean referred to this as an 'accident' which clearly it was not.[40] It was a failure of command, either by Pope whose omission of the vital order left his men to make the decision on the spot, or by Glasgow who had failed to impress its importance. Those failures aside, tactical orthodoxy still dictated that Stubbings or Maxwell should have refused the flank when faced with a gap on the left. Instead Maxwell took his men across to the 33rd Brigade's position. Given that every order about this issue from division down to battalion mentioned the possibility that the 33rd Brigade might arrive late, Maxwell's 'searching' across his front to link up was another error since the most likely explanation was that the brigade was late rather than out of position away to the north. The one positive result for the 52nd was that it avoided the deadly fire from the Blauwepoortbeek pillboxes. The same could not be said of the unfortunate 49th Battalion which had suffered severely and, while the Green Line in the 33rd Brigade's area was now occupied by the 52nd Battalion, there was a large gap of over 1000 metres across the Blauwepoortbeek in the middle of the 4th Division's line.

• • •

For the 12th Brigade, which had not received the message about the delay to the attack until after it had moved over the ridge, the enforced wait was more than simply inconvenient. The men had been spotted by German gunners waiting in shell holes and had the misfortune to appear over the ridge just as the main German counter-attack was developing soon after 2.00 pm. Although the feeble German effort had managed to get no further than just beyond the Oosttaverne Line, their supporting artillery shelled the ridge heavily and the men of the 12th Brigade, now immobilised by Plumer's change of time, were forced to wait beneath it. At 1.00 pm a forward artillery observer reported back that the 4th Division was 'being knocked about'.[41] Captain Frank Davy, in command of D Company, was killed by the steadily increasing shellfire. The 45th Battalion records that, following receipt of the order for the delay, 'a large amount of enfilade shrapnel was sent over amongst the troops coming from the direction of Warneton and Deulemont … hostile Artillery and Machine Gun fire was very fierce and our losses were heavy.'[42] The 47th Battalion also recorded that 'He poured MG's at us … and kept up an incessant fire.' The enemy fire was not the only problem, however. 'Our artillery about this time became very erratic in their shooting and accounted for quite a number of our own men. It continued this uncertain way for the rest of the afternoon and by that means prevented us taking advantage of it that we otherwise would.'[43] After suffering under the shellfire for two hours, the 45th and 47th finally moved off. The New Zealand 1st Brigade diary recorded the start of the attack: 'A little after 3.10 p.m. troops of the 12th Australian Brigade advanced through Black Dotted line for attack on Green Line. They did not seem certain of their task.'[44]

The 45th Battalion on the left had also suffered as the men waited ahead of the Black Line for the postponed new zero hour. Heavy machine-gun fire from their left just before their jumping-off time was accompanied by a German artillery barrage and, as the 45th's diary reported, 'our losses were very heavy'.[45] The left two companies of the 45th ran straight into heavy opposition as they moved down the slope, the battalion split in two with the two right companies clinging to the left of the 47th Battalion.[46] With the failure of the 49th on its left and separated from the rest of its battalion on the right, the left of the 45th found itself isolated, alone and pinned down well short of its objective and with impenetrable defences in front. 'These two companies suffered very heavily' the diary of the 45th records, 'and a great number of their officers became casualties.'[47] The attack by the left companies of the 45th suffered the same fate as the shattered 49th in the Blauwepoortbeek. Indeed, this part of the Australian line effectively disintegrated. The withering fire pouring from the pillboxes split the 45th Battalion in two, the right companies maintaining touch with the 47th Battalion and the two left companies trying vainly to push forward to maintain contact with the 49th Battalion which was itself cleaved in two by the leftward movement of its two companies trying to keep touch with the 52nd Battalion. Although the right of the 45th and the 47th reached the Green Line, capturing prisoners and machine-guns as they went, the 45th's left companies were cut to pieces. The 45th Battalion diary records that a counter-attack at 5.00 pm was driven off, but this was probably just another localised action by a small party of German troops who were themselves cut off and isolated. Unable to link up with the 49th Battalion, hit by their own artillery as well as German guns, the 45th's diary reported that its left companies 'having both flanks in the air and being greatly reduced in strength and the troops on the left having already retired, began to fall back on the Red Dotted Line.'[48]

With officer casualties heavy, Captain Arthur Allen took charge of the 45th's right companies and led them forward, capturing prisoners in the outlying Oxygen Trench, fighting their way into Owl Trench some 60 metres further on and leading them into their final objective in Owl Support Trench. He also led an attack on a pillbox which was well protected with wire and directing withering fire on his men. Allen and his men captured more prisoners and two machine-guns in Owl Support. Awarded the DSO for his gallantry, his citation hinted at the devastation wrought on the rest of his battalion, noting that 'from the afternoon of the 7/6 to the morning of 11/6, Allen had charge of the whole battalion front with only two officers to assist him.'[49]

The 12th Brigade made much faster progress on the right. Sapper Edward Hughes of the New Zealand Engineers, digging the line of posts in front of the Black Line, described the 47th Battalion's advance towards Oxygen and Owl trenches:

> The Australians launched another attack about 3.00 p.m. It was a magnificent though dreadful sight to witness. Firstly up came the lumbering tanks, then the infantry in artillery formation and again more tanks ... As the 'Ossies' advanced, they were literally smothered with shells. At times one felt that a whole section of men was blown out, but when the dust settled, there they were still wandering in their leisurely way, with rifles slung, and whilst going through the 'Hun' barrage not a man was scratched ... As usual the 'Ossies' made a clean sweep ... to watch the 'Huns' run out of the trenches toward us - and to see the way the 'Ossies' harpooned them one after another, it was a sight I will always recall.[50]

Rear view of a German pillbox on Huns' Walk. The camouflage which hid it from aerial observation has been blasted away and the roof heavily damaged but still intact. The entrances show just above ground level, the cavities above them designed to store ammunition (AWM E00552).

While the 47th Battalion attack had proceeded quickly down the slope, the well-ordered lines soon fractured as they clambered into enemy trenches for cover and proceeded to clear them. A and C companies raced on through the maze of trenches on the left of the battalion's frontage, Lieutenant Dudley Salmon, commanding A Company, guiding one of the four tanks that supported the 12th Brigade's attack onto the enemy machine-gun nests. On the right, B Company's commander, Captain John Millar, described by one of his men as 'brave beyond reason' was killed leading the charge into Unbearable Trench and the company lost direction and contact with D Company which was supposed to move through it.[51] 'One big trouble we knew we would have to contend against was loss of direction', wrote Lieutenant Clifford Mendoza, who had taken command of B Company after Millar's death, 'and because of the lay of the trenches and the slope of the ground we knew we would work too much to the right unless we were awfully careful. That is just what happened and it was intensified by the fact that most of the enemy who surrendered were on our right flank and immediately the men saw them there was on each occasion a move in that direction, which had to be stopped.' Unfortunately for the 47th, it wasn't stopped, and the remnants of Captain Frank Davy's D Company, who followed on expecting to move through B Company, missed it completely, kept going and moved past their objective and on into clear country ahead, unsupported on either side.

In the Douve Valley, the 3rd Division also ran into trouble. The 37th Battalion (together with a company of the 40th Battalion) reported only hearing of the postponement of new zero 45 minutes after leaving their assembly trenches. When they set off at 3.10 pm they were almost immediately hit by heavy machine-gun fire from undiscovered positions. 'Heavy casualties were suffered during the capture of Uncanny Trench and Uncanny Support, the enemy having many machine guns in well-established positions … They were posted in small wooded areas which were not shown on issue maps or on aeroplane photos.'[52] Snipers and incessant enemy artillery fire took a further heavy toll on the 40th Battalion. Captain Robert Grieve, commanding the 37th's A Company, led his men forward through the intense machine-gun fire to Ulna Trench where, although the wire was largely intact, they were able to find enough gaps to slip through. 'Here we suffered many casualties', wrote Grieve. 'The whole of our Stokes and Vickers gun crews were knocked out and at this stage, Lieut. Fraser did wonderful work. He brought the gun into action himself – located hostile guns and brought continuous and accurate fire to bear on them. In this way, he saved the lives of many men in my Company.'[53]

At 4.15 pm the British barrage slackened to allow mounted patrols to go forward, as the Second Army planners had imagined. The impossibility of men on horseback moving on a battlefield where sweeping machine-gun fire often made it fatal to raise the top of one's head above cover and where artillery was falling like hail, was obvious to everyone within range of either, and the orders drafted by the Second Army were plainly hopeful to the point of fantasy.

'The task allotted to them will be that of: (a) reconnaissance. (b) occupation and consolidation of posts on the Black Dotted Line. (c) Capture of guns. (d) harassing of the enemy. (e) Working parties.'[54] It was abundantly clear to the men of II Anzac Corps Mounted Regiment that the orders were not just impossible, but also patently absurd, as the Mounted Regiment's Major Dunlop recounted:

> At 3.00 p.m. just as Wood and I were going up to Mid Farm to watch the second attack, we got a message from Hindhaugh telling us to come back to Boyle's Farm for a Conference … Talked over the whole show & I put the question to the meeting "Have we done anything the Infantry could not have done?" The general answer was an undoubted "No".[55]

Fortunately for both men and horses, the mission was cancelled.

• • •

In the heat of the afternoon sun, both Australian divisions were locked in a desperate struggle as they fought their way towards the Green Line. The character of the battle had changed dramatically. The fighting of the morning had been sudden and savage, but it had ended quickly. The ridge had been wrenched from German hands almost within an hour and lost beyond hope of recapture. In the afternoon, some measure of equilibrium in the German lines returned as the shock of the overwhelming firepower diminished. The German defences along their lines stretching back from the ridge were still formidable. Dotted throughout were mutually supporting concrete pillboxes which contained machine-guns (and even field guns in some), ample ammunition and garrisons of men holding on in the belief that every minute they could delay the English was a minute closer to relief by the counter-attacks they had been promised. German orders captured by the Second Army on 31 May directed that 'Every man is to be notified that he must resist to the utmost in the front line. He must know that support will always be available to help him. Company leaders are reminded that immediate counter-attack will always be effective.'[56] This empty promise doomed many of the unfortunate Germans now trapped in their concrete prisons unable to surrender, their only option to kill or be killed. The very strong defences behind Messines would now put the two opposing tactical schemes to a bloody test.

The new British platoon tactics outlined in the pamphlet SS143 *Training of Platoons for Offensive Action*, published in February 1917, represented a quiet revolution in the way infantry fought the war.[57] Partly a response to the development of specialist weapons such as the Lewis light machine-gun and rifle grenades, and partly influenced by learning from other armies (particularly the French), SS143 was a model of clarity and helpful instruction. The platoon was to be divided into four mutually supporting specialist sections — riflemen with bayonet, a Lewis gun team, bombers and rifle grenadiers. It emphasised the advantages in firepower that the new specialist sections provided. The Lewis gun section carried 30 drums of ammunition, the bomb-throwers five bombs each, while the remainder in the bomb section carried 10. Each man in the rifle grenade section carried six bombs and everyone except bombers, runners, scouts and the Lewis gunner carried a rifle with bayonet, bombs and 120 rounds of ammunition. Each 'mopper up' carried two P (phosphorous) bombs for clearing dugouts. The tactical advice stressed the need to close with the enemy quickly, each man trained in the use of all weapons and flexibility in both attack and defence. Platoons pinned down could rely on neighbouring platoons to work around a flank while they found cover. Confronted with pillboxes, the platoon would use Lewis gunners from the flanks, rifle bombs, small arms fire and bombs fanning out to take advantage of the limited traverse of the German machine-guns inside. Once a pillbox fell, it weakened support for neighbouring pillboxes and the scheme, along with the defence line, would begin to crumble. Intelligence appraisals following Messines concluded that '[t]he suitability of the recently introduced organisation of Platoons for dealing with the situation indicated has been demonstrated, and successful results in recent fighting from the tactics mentioned above have been frequently reported.'[58]

Notes on Dealing with Hostile Machine Guns in an Advance (SS155) was published in April 1917 and dealt directly with the new German defensive scheme. '[O]n being compelled to fall back from any organised position of defence, the enemy usually does so covered by small infantry rear guards which hold tactical points (armed with machine guns). To continue a general advance in these conditions in attack formation is therefore usually inadvisable. Small tactical advance guards should be pushed well forward, charged among other duties with locating and, if possible, dealing with hostile machine guns.'[59] Certainly the desperate, close-quarter fighting that pillboxes provoked was marked, as Bean would write with studied understatement, 'by a ferocity that renders the reading of any true narrative particularly unpleasant.'[60] The vast majority of surviving accounts of the fighting at Messines spare readers the terrible details that inevitably accompanied it. The 37th Battalion's Captain Robert Grieve's brief description of the capture of a pillbox, for example, which remarks that its guns were 'put out of action by the aid of Mills Bombs', hid what were no doubt gruesome details. However it also hid the fact that the guns' fire had killed many of his men and that he personally had stormed it, dodging fire and running under a cover of grenade blasts until, flat against its wall, he was able to drop bombs through the gun port. Grieve, seriously wounded shortly after, was awarded the VC for his actions.[61]

Septieme Barn Pillbox on Huns' Walk behind Messines, captured by the 47th Battalion and the scene of savage fighting on 7 June (AWM E01295).

The 47th Battalion was also held up by pillboxes. Gallwey's description of the capture of a pillbox near Huns' Walk was included in his lengthy diary which the Official Historian would justly describe as 'exceedingly vivid and detailed'. Unlike Grieve however, Gallwey did not hide the full truth of what he encountered:

> Taking refuge in shell holes while our machine guns concentrated on the fort. Peeping out occasionally I could see the concrete being chipped away by this fusillade of bullets. Two machine guns were firing 800 rounds a minute each on to a particular spot on this block house ... soon a large hole was being bored into the thick concrete wall and eventually the two feet thickness with steel rails was perforated ... All during this time, from the loophole in the wall, spurted a fire that was as intense as ours.[62]

Captain Robert Grieve of the 37th Battalion was awarded the VC for his actions on 7 June in silencing a pillbox at Messines which had decimated his company. Remarkably, Grieve's recommendation for the VC was forwarded by his men as there were no surviving officers in his company (AWM H00038).

Gallwey was mistaken on one point. The 47th's Lewis gunners were not boring a hole in the near metre-thick reinforced walls. They were exploiting one of the pillboxes' weaknesses and directing a hail of bullets at the firing slit, forcing a blizzard of bullet fragments and stone chips inside, suppressing fire and wounding its occupants. Gallwey described in horrifying detail what occurred when the fire from the pillbox was silenced:

> ... a couple of men went to the entrance where the gun crew was found all huddled up inside. They had evidently been wounded and killed by our fire. No time was lost here however and these men fired point blank into the group. There was a noise as though pigs were being killed. They squealed and made guttural noises which gave place to groans after which all was silent. The bodies were all thrown in a heap outside the blockhouse to make sure they were all dead ... nearly all were young men.[63]

Bean chose to lift the veil on the true nature of war for his readers by including a version of Gallwey's account which he only mildly sanitised. While shocking, it served to portray the reality of war and the awful nature of the fight in which the Australians were engaged. However it prompted from the Official Historian that rarest of occurrences in his writing, his own voice. The 'tension' of pillbox fighting, as Bean described it, characterised by 'murderous fire from a sheltered position followed by the sudden giving in' meant that it was often a fight to the death where the unimaginable impulsions of survival in battle could not simply be turned off like a tap:

> Where such tension exists in battle, the rules of "civilised" war are powerless. Most men are temporarily half mad, their pulses pounding at their ears, their mouths dry. The noblest among them are straining their wills to keep cool heads and even voices; the less self-controlled are for the time being governed by reckless, primitive impulse. With death singing about their ears, they will kill until they grow tired of killing. When they have been wracked with machine gun fire, the routing out of enemy groups from behind several feet of concrete is almost inevitably the signal for a butchery at least of the first few who emerge, and sometimes even the helpless will not be spared. It is idle for the reader to cry shame upon such incidents, unless he cries out upon the whole system of war ...[64]

German dead outside a pillbox at Messines. German troops found it impossible to surrender once their position became hopeless and Australian troops were often unwilling to accept their attempts. Charles Bean warned his readers that a true narrative of pillbox fighting was 'particularly unpleasant' (AWM A00791).

Having read and used Gallwey's diary extensively however, Bean was fully aware that some of the butchery that day could not be excused by the fragile justification of 'reckless, primitive impulse'. As Gallwey's company of the 47th Battalion advanced at Messines, a group of Germans emerged from some bushes to surrender:

> … about a dozen men rushed out all unarmed, holding up a white shirt on a stick and shouting 'mercy Kamarad'. Some held out watches, field glasses and all kinds of curios in lieu of the proverbial Olive branch. With these gifts they tried to barter for their lives. This was our opportunity and we fired point blank as fast as we could, dropping them wholesale. The majority had fallen and the remainder consisting of three or four had got so close that it was impossible to shoot them. They grovelled at our feet like whining dogs asking for mercy. We had made the most of our time and now we were too tired to finish these off. Such specimens of humanity I have never seen. Like mangy dogs, their clothes in tatters, filthy, dirty faces drawn like skeletons and eyes staring out of their heads, these were the men we beheld now. We did not want their peace offering and spurned their salaaming at our feet. As they wiped the dust from our boots, we thought how degraded and low these human beings had become. Like snakes they crawled on their bellies crying 'Kamarad,

Kamarad' and as treacherous too. Calling them to their feet, we drove them before our bayonets [as] a screen for ourselves.[65]

Although Bean was careful to warn against the unreliability of private soldiers' diaries and recollections which were often 'improved' and expanded with time, he was certainly aware of the verifiable authenticity of Gallwey's account which was, after all, why he used it so extensively. Mendoza's account of Messines also appears to confirm Gallwey's description:

Nevertheless the advance was not held up for more than five minutes at any time by them [machine-guns] before the miserable Huns came trooping out of their very strong positions with their hands up and with very scared expressions on their faces, asking for mercy and grovelling in the ground at our feet, until the lads found an effectual method of making their progress much more rapid.[66]

Even the Commander-in-Chief confided to his diary after Messines that '[t]he Australians took very few prisoners, being enraged at the suffering inflicted on the Australian prisoners at Bullecourt.'[67] Despite being the source of a pamphlet that urged his men in the coming battle to remember the treatment meted out to Australian prisoners at Bullecourt, Monash was quite explicit in the 3rd Division's orders that German wounded were to be treated 'in every way similar to our wounded' and that in the case of the death of prisoners 'through other than natural causes, a full report will be rendered to the Divisional Headquarters'.[68] No such orders existed in the 4th Division. Gallwey considered it impossible to leave wounded Germans behind as they advanced. 'They all have to be killed', he noted simply.[69]

While the attacks by IX and X Corps in the north met with near total success, the desperate fighting in the II Anzac zone continued. In the late afternoon the assault battalions of the 3rd and 4th divisions, having fought their way to the Green Line, were locked in a titanic struggle for its possession. The ground behind them was strewn with dead and wounded. Wide gaps existed between battalions and brigades, and some had gone to ground well short of their objective in the face of intense and well-protected machine-gun fire. Most were uncertain of the security of their flanks; some were sure they were alone. The 45th Battalion in particular had suffered heavy losses — almost 100 killed and three times that number wounded, most of those from the two left companies. The 13th Brigade, dragged across to the north by the 52nd Battalion's futile attempt to link up with the missing British 33rd Brigade, had split in two, a wide gap opening between its two wounded battalions. Likewise, the 12th Brigade, with its left badly cut up in the Blauwepoortbeek Valley, had ruptured into two uncertain and fragile fronts. Some companies were lost, others so depleted that they were reduced to platoon strength. Sapper Thomas Linney, one of the 4th Division's signallers, had the unenviable task of keeping the vital channels of communication open and functioning:

> At about 2.30 pm our Brigade [12th] went through the NZ line and advanced about 800 yards. They had a terrible hard time gaining their objectives. Two of us were on forward comms and had a very rough go. The artillery was terrible. Messines was absolutely blown to atoms … I did not think it possible for a man to get out of it … Our Brigade is now 1300 strong out of 4500. There was dead lying everywhere, NZ's Aust & Fritz. This was much hotter than Bullecourt.[70]

The toll in officers who, in many cases had bravely stormed ahead of their men, was very high, depriving platoons and companies of leadership at a vital moment and consigning the survivors to trust their luck and initiative. Even the glorious summer weather conspired to worsen their ordeal, quickening their thirst and wearying bodies laden with the weight of full fighting kit and heavy woollen uniforms. The light of that long day showed every movement above ground to snipers and machine-gunners. Many were trapped in front of pillboxes unable to move back or forward. And always there was the fear of the counter-attack they were drilled and drilled to expect and to defeat. Their one saviour was their artillery which might defeat the onrushing waves of enemy they expected to see at any moment.

The wounded suffered untended on the battlefield. Mendoza, shot through the back and leg and with a machine-gun searching for him, crawled into a small depression in front of Owl Trench, about halfway to the Green Line:

> … for about two hours the guns kept up an incessant fire above me. My haversack was riddled with bullets and several glanced off my helmet. I knew it would be suicide to move so I decided to wait there for darkness – a matter of five hours. It was a real hell lying in the sun, without being able to move a finger; without a drink and with no dressing on my leg or back. I moved my arm a couple of hours later and this drew fire again, so I pretended to be dead. The sun was playing the devil with me and I was longing for darkness.[71]

The Germans also suffered fearfully. The chaotic morning had destroyed a formerly impregnable front and almost 4000 prisoners had passed through British hands to the cages well behind the enemy lines. Everywhere their friends and comrades lay dead, many missing. The promises of salvation from the counter-attack divisions had blown away like the dust which drifted across the battlefield. The incessant British shelling of the past weeks had shredded nerves as well as flesh. A note found on the body of a soldier of *No. 2 Company, 2nd Guards Reserve Regiment*, recorded the onset of the creeping barrage falling in front of the attacking Australians:

> … 2.00 p.m. a terrible firing has driven us under cover. To the right and left of me my friends are all drenched with blood. A drum fire which no one could ever describe. I pray the Lord will get me out of this sap. I swear to it I will be the next … While I am writing he still gives us power and loves us. My trousers and tunic are drenched with blood all from my poor mates. I have prayed to God he might save me, not for my sake, but for my poor parents. I feel as if I could cry out, my thoughts are all the time with them. The slaughtering takes place behind Messines which place the English have taken. I have already twelve months on the Western Front have been through hard fighting, but never such a slaughter.[72]

Despite the fierce resistance in the Douve Valley, the 37th and an ever-dwindling company of the 40th Battalion reached the Green Line and began to dig in, all the while under fire. They linked up with the remainder of Mendoza's leaderless men of the 47th Battalion's B Company (who were well to the right of their objective) near Huns' Walk. D Company of the 47th, which should have had Mendoza's company on its left and the 37th Battalion on its right, had stumbled on beyond the Green Line, having missed passing through B Company as planned and believing the company still ahead. Unwittingly, the much-reduced D Company of the 47th Battalion became the spearhead of the Second Army thanks to its failed rendezvous with B Company. As the afternoon faded, this small band of Australians was alone, isolated and well ahead of the final objective.

While the men of the 47th Battalion were fighting their way along Huns' Walk, the left battalion of the 13th Brigade was searching ever further on its flank for the English. It was sometime after 4.00 pm that the advanced patrols of the 52nd Battalion finally met some English troops of the 33rd Brigade behind Odonto Trench, still short of the Green Line. Beyond that, they reported that the front line was empty for at least 450 metres. Maxwell had led his company across until they occupied practically all of the 33rd Brigade's position. Gradually the exhausted Englishmen were dribbling in from their forced march and Maxwell sent two companies of the 6th Border Regiment across to the right to plug gaps in the line at the junction of the 49th and 52nd battalions. The diary of the 7th Battalion, South Staffordshire Regiment, records that the confusion had seen troops crowding into the area under fire and now occupied by the right of the 52nd Battalion and the task of sorting them out was proving difficult:

> B and C Coys having lost touch Bn H.Q. waited at Rommens Farm which was not reached by these companies until 3.50 p.m. The whole at once moved forward towards Mahieu Farm to regain touch with the leading companies, who had advanced through the hostile barrage on to the objective. Owing to the barrage, the fatigue of the men, the large frontage being covered, and the lack of all landmarks owing to our shell fire, D Coy on reaching the Mauve Line [the Black Dotted Line in II Anzac Corps] found itself practically isolated. Realising that our barrage would soon lift off the objective, O.C. D Coy pressed on and at 0.21.D. found the 13th Bde A.I.F. converging on his right and a Bn 57th Brigade on his left. Gaining touch and filling up the gap, he advanced on Odour Trench in 0.22.c. which he cleared of the enemy taking 15 prisoners. He then proceeded to clear the houses and dug-outs in 0.22.d which were held by the enemy. Several prisoners were taken here and were handed over to the Australians for escort to the rear. The 13th Bde A.I.F. and the 9th Gloucestershire Regt., now arrived in greater force, so O.C. D Coy being weak, withdrew to Mahieu Farm in close support.[73]

Maxwell arranged for a platoon from the 9th Gloucestershire to attack Van Hove Farm from which harassing machine-gun fire was threatening the left of the 52nd. The Gloucestershires took the opportunity to work with three of IX Corps' tanks which had topped the ridge past Wytschaete and moved straight on to silence the fire from the farm and capture its garrison. With the Green Line in the 33rd Brigade's front secured by Maxwell's men and the 'sixes and sevens' of the English battalions who were still dribbling in and sent off to plug gaps, the patchwork force prepared to defend its lines:

> When we arrived at the Odonto trench we found we had got the Australians with us. We prepared to dig ourselves in for the night ... When we had settled down, the Germans put a barrage on our new line. At the same time some of our own men who were in rear of our line got shaky and sent up the S.O.S. signal to our own artillery who then proceeded to shell the line we were holding. You can just guess our position, being shelled from the front by the Hun, also being shelled from the rear by our own artillery.[74]

The shelling drove the 52nd and the fragments of battalions from the 33rd Brigade back from the Green Line. Further south, the 49th was also forced back and the gap which had opened between the 12th and 13th brigades in the Blauwepoortbeek was now almost 1000 metres wide. The relentless German fire pouring from a strong belt of pillboxes threatened the flanks of both Australian brigades. The heavy machine-guns employed by the German gunners had an effective range of almost 1800 metres and the field guns which were also concealed in the pillboxes made close approach completely impossible. In the noisy pandemonium of the battle, the arc of machine-gun bullets travelled silently and unseen from the distance ahead and the only warning the men of the 45th received was the sight of their comrades falling around them. Against such a lethal screen, the only option for the Australians was to seek what cover they could in shell holes and the remains of German trenches.

According to the battalion diary, the two left companies of the 45th Battalion had 'suffered very heavily and a great number of their officers became casualties'. The 45th also had both flanks in the air, 'the 49th Battalion having failed to connect up'.[75] Whether this was due to the late start of the 49th, the weight of fire from the enemy pillboxes or the movement across to the left caused by the 52nd Battalion's deviation (Bean concluded it was the latter) is difficult to determine with any certainty. The 49th blamed the 45th, convinced that it had gone to ground some 250 metres to the 49th's rear, describing in some detail the measures taken by the officer charged with keeping the connection with the 45th to secure the right flank of the 49th. With its flank battalion pinned to the ground in the face of the murderous fire in the Blauwepoortbeek, the 49th then (at 5.00 pm) reported its own artillery firing on its lines and that the 52nd had withdrawn, although the 49th remained in its trenches. The diary of the 52nd records this barrage somewhat later (at around 8.00 pm):

> The shelling of our artillery had become so severe that on the centre and left sector the posts were withdrawn to Odious and Odour Trenches, about 9.15 p.m. On the right the posts were withdrawn to the Support Line, and all troops except sentries were kept absolutely down under cover, all work ceasing.[76]

The 33rd Brigade reported that, at 8.30 pm, following an SOS signal (more likely a red German flare) on the left flank, 'our artillery opened in response, some of our heavies firing very short. This caused several casualties to the Australians.'[77] Although the 13th Brigade diary does not mention the 52nd's withdrawal, the 13th's after-action report notes the 'many complaints ... that both Field Guns and Howitzers were firing short.'[78] To add to the confusion, the two battalions of the 12th Brigade reported beating back an attempted German counter-attack at 5.00 pm.

Under Allen's leadership, the 45th Battalion's two right companies had reached the Green Line, capturing 120 prisoners and two machine-guns on the way. Allen reported the British barrage (at 7.30 pm) falling in front of this line and cutting off the two right companies of the 45th in their advanced positions. 'This was most unfortunate as it inflicted a number of casualties on our own men. After "sticking" it for another hour these two companies together with the 47th Battalion had to retire to the Red Dotted Line.'[79] They then joined the remnants of their left companies who had retired earlier due to similar 'friendly' fire. There are no reports in any of the 4th Division's war diaries of SOS rockets fired or of requests for artillery fire to be lengthened as the artillery was under the command of the New Zealand and 25th divisions. Mendoza wrote that he fired off some flares, which no doubt added to the confusion. The narrative of the battle in the 4th Division's diary records the impotence of a headquarters blind and deaf to the mayhem of the afternoon. 'Shortly after the attack commenced forward communications from Brigade were constantly interrupted and considerable difficulty was experienced in getting information back.'[80]

Lieutenant Colonel Alex Imlay of the 47th, perhaps alone among the 4th Division's battalion commanders, had a reasonably clear grasp of events for the first two hours thanks to reports from his forward scout, Lieutenant Charles Scott, an effective group of runners and his forward position in a pillbox close behind the Black Line. When Scott was killed at around 5.00 pm, Imlay's grip on the battle slipped and, unaware that one of his right companies was lost and the other had overrun the objective, he sent his adjutant, Lieutenant Norman Bremner, to reconnoitre and report. The Second Army had arranged for the infantry on the Green Line to fire signal flares to contact aircraft flying above so that their positions across the ridge and the progress of the attack could be followed. Nowhere does the system appear to have worked. McKenny Hughes, flying above the battlefield, wrote that 'at 3.15 the hate started again and we tried to take the Oosttaverne Line. Very conflicting reports have come in, as the infantry have refused to light flares, the official way of indicating their position.'[81] The men of the 47th noticed their own contact aeroplanes overhead, recognisable by the two black streamers fluttering from their wing tips and the sound of the klaxon horn from above. D Company of the 47th, watching the signs of a German counter-attack gathering in the distance ahead, decided not to fire the flares for fear that they would identify the position. 'This seemed to me to be absurd' wrote Gallwey, 'because the enemy already knew we were here, whereas our own people did not know where we were.'[82]

Thanks to its advanced position, the 47th was the first to spot the Germans moving towards the Green Line and, thanks also to the extraordinary bravery and initiative of one of its signallers, Private Caleb Shang, the battalion was able to get a message back to the Black Line asking for an artillery barrage. The men of D Company, ahead and alone beyond the Green Line, used Lewis gun and rifle fire to fight off two attempts by the Germans to push them back from the Green Line. According to Gallwey, just after 8.00 pm, and while the daylight of the high summer lingered, the promised artillery barrage commenced.[83] To the dismay of the men it was meant to protect however, it crashed to earth behind them and began to creep towards their position. 'On it came like the wind. Portions of the hedge went high in the air and pieces of wood fell on us.'[84] The barrage also fell on C Company (with Lieutenant Joshua Allen's right company of the 45th Battalion) in its final objective in Owl Support Trench. With their ammunition running low and the Germans advancing, the 47th and 45th broke and ran all the way back to the New Zealand position on the newly dug Black Line. Many were hit by the barrage and scattered small arms fire. Bean would famously quote Captain Edward Williams of the 47th describing the shelling: 'They would stand all the enemy fire you were likely to give them, but they would not put up with being shelled by their own guns.'[85] According to Bean's notes, Williams later told Captain Dewas Cumming of the 48th that 'he could do nothing with the men in this retreat – he couldn't manage them – they were very shaken and scattered'.[86] Gallwey wrote of the 47th, 'It seems to me we have no battalion now. All I can locate are stragglers who have attached themselves to other units.'[87]

• • •

Three minutes before launching his own attack on the Green Line, Monash sent a message to his brigadiers that he was 'not satisfied with present arrangements at B.HQ. [Brigade Headquarters] for answering urgent operational telephone calls. It takes far too long to get an officer to the telephone who is in touch with the situation.' This would be the first of a series of frustrated messages Monash would send over the following crucial hours seeking information on the position of his line. He received a prompt and disturbing message in response that the 33rd was being heavily shelled and counter-attacked and that there were 'very few left'. The report of the counter-attack was incorrect as would be so many alarmist reports of the same that day, but the estimate of the 33rd's strength was disturbingly accurate. The available men of the 36th (about 100) were put on standby to go in. The 37th however, had fought its way into the Green Line and 'precisely carried out their duty of forming the flank of the Green Line'. With its one attached company from the 40th Battalion, and after much hard fighting, the 37th Battalion 'began to dig – as air photographs afterwards showed – exactly on the line intended.'[88] The 37th had suffered heavily from the fire of concealed machine-guns while fighting its way through the German trench lines and, as the men now began to dig in on the Green Line, constant sniping and bursts from hidden machine-guns killed and wounded more of their dwindling number. Patrols crept out to silence the machine-guns which threatened this work while 'the enemy artillery fire continued without abatement'.[89] Monash reported his Green Line secure at 4.00 pm.

At around 7.30 pm, the first reports of shelling to their rear came from the 3rd Division. Lance Corporal Reginald Biggs of the 40th Battalion recalled the widespread fear that this shelling might herald the expected German counter-attack:

> At 7.30 the enemy started heavy shelling, well behind us. We recognised it as a cut-off from our rear and a prelude to the expected counter-attack. This was nearly our undoing, as a direct result of the silly bragging we had heard from the seasoned troops of the 4th Division, who had more than their share of fighting on the Somme and wanted to show superiority over us "raw new chums". They skited in this strain: "You mugs will wonder what you've struck when you fly the bags in your first hop-over, but that's nothing to the awful ordeal you will cop from Fritz's TERRIBLE counter-attack. You'll never face that!" We were therefore in a general funk when we realised the imminence of the dreaded counter-attack. I for one was "dead scared".[90]

The 37th reported to its forward commander, Major Story at Bethleem Farm, that British artillery was firing on its positions in the Green Line. Although it is difficult to piece together the exact sequence of events, it is most likely that this barrage, falling also on the 47th Battalion on its left, followed the one requested by D Company of the 47th to defeat the feared counter-attack the company beat off in the late afternoon and which was reported by Lieutenant Colonel Imlay as falling at 5.00 pm. The retirement of the 47th was clearly not the orderly withdrawal reported by Imlay, who wrote that 'it was deemed desirable to fall back a little to clear the barrage and endeavour to gain touch with the right flank', but rather a rout of most of the forward garrison who sprinted back through the fire to the Black Line.[91] Some private records revealed the panicked retreat that occurred across much of the Australian line. Gibbs of the

40th Battalion described it as a 'harrier race'. Private Bob Summers of the 50th Battalion likened it to the Spring Handicap: 'I don't like my chances ... there are too many starters.'[92]

The New Zealanders, observing the retreat of the 12th Brigade, called for a barrage to protect the Black Line. The barrage that then descended around 7.30 pm fell on the ground between the Green Line and Black Line, driving out most of the men of the 47th and 45th who had remained in their posts during the first retreat. Lieutenant Roadknight's message to Major Story indicated his bewilderment: 'D Company on right, 47th Battalion on left have gone and our own shells landing behind us on left and right. What shall we do?' This was supplemented by Lieutenant Murdoch: 'Do you know what this barrage is for? Our men were driven out, as far as I can see, by our own artillery fire.'[93] Story, in defiance of Monash's orders that the Green Line was to be held at all costs and that there was to be no retirement, bowed to the inevitable. 'This fire became so distressing that it eventually became necessary in the judgement of [Story] to withdraw the Battalion to the Black Line in order to avoid serious loss and as his left flank was quite exposed owing to the direction of his front and the withdrawal of the 47th Battalion.'[94] Monash, acting in the mistaken belief that the 37th had already fallen back, ordered his barrage shortened, and this fell on part of that garrison as it was withdrawing at 9.00 pm. To complete the confusion in the 3rd Division's forward line, Story's order was not communicated to the 40th Battalion, which remained in the Green Line, and the men watched, mystified, as the 37th on their left pulled out. Captain Cecil McVilly of the 40th, then back on the Black Line, heard that the barrage was to be shortened and raised the alarm, reporting that his battalion was still out in the Green Line.[95]

Biggs, a signaller with the 40th Battalion, recorded the moment the 37th withdrew. '[W]e saw 37th Battalion men slipping out of their Front Line and making for the rear, which meant that our left flank was in the air. Maybe they had their colonel's order to retire, even to dribble out a few at a time; if so, he hadn't bothered to give us that order though we were under his command. Barney Balmforth ... saw the 37th men getting away. He ran out to stop them even with his fists, and then threw a bomb or two after them.'[96] McVilly managed to get a message to the sole surviving officer of the 40th Battalion in the Green Line, Lieutenant Richard Loane, to withdraw. With the artillery from both sides raining down on the beleaguered company of Tasmanians, the order resulted in a panicked flight back to the Black Line:

> During the preparations for this battle we had been told repeatedly that during a battle we must always WALK, never RUN, when moving to

the rear. This applied even to 'runners' when carrying messages, because of the psychological effect causing a stampede rearward. Now Loane did a mad thing. As soon as he got that order to withdraw us, instead of passing the word to us to dribble out a few at a time, he screamed out "RETIRE!" and took to his heels ... For some reason never explained, our SOS barrage had lowered its range, which dropped a curtain of fire between the Green and Black Lines. Simultaneously a Hun barrage as thick as hailstorm came down along the same stretch of ground. We had to run through this double curtain of fire. It was terrifying. I feared that, if I didn't collide with one of our own shells, I would stop a hun shell in the broad of my back. We simply ran, chancing our luck. At last I tumbled breathless into the Black Line trench. Both strafes soon died down.[97]

With the withdrawal of the remnants of the 40th Battalion sometime after 8.00 pm, the failure of II Anzac Corps was almost complete. Apart from the extreme left flank and a few isolated parties from the various assault battalions who remained in their posts in or near the advanced sections of the Green Line, either determined to stay regardless or unaware that the rest of their unit had gone, the Green Line was abandoned. Some of the troops found what shelter they could on the Dotted Line of posts ahead of the Black Line, some were in the Black Line itself. Others, Gallwey among them, had travelled even further back to the old British front line. In the 3rd Division's area, the Black Line was so crowded that the men of the 37th and 40th who had returned from the Green Line had to be stationed even further back.

While messages of congratulation were flowing to and from Second Army Headquarters celebrating the success of the offensive, the afternoon assault by II Anzac was in tatters. Bean summarised the disaster of the Australians' attack:

Thus, owing to the action of its own artillery – for which defects in the maps, over-eagerness of the infantry, over anxiety of some of the staff and commanders and a dangerous degree of inaccuracy in the barrage were responsible – the whole of the final objective between the Blauwepoortbeek and the Douve had by 9.00 p.m. been left open to the enemy.[98]

The 'defects in the maps' were all too apparent to McKenny Hughes, who 'rang up intelligence to ask for some more Wytschaete maps and was told that 2nd Army had run right out of them. Really someone ought to tell 2nd Army when a "Push" is coming off, so that they might be in some small degree prepared for it.'[99] Bean left unstated perhaps the most important factor contributing to the confusion in II Anzac on the afternoon and evening of 7 June. The late changes to the plans for Messines and the subsequent decision to drive on to the Green Line had taxed the Second Army's staff and planning to the limit. The failures in communication and artillery arrangements, the lack of oversight in divisional planning and the slowness to respond to the changing nature and crises of the battle were the responsibility of corps and army headquarters. The clumsy independent command arrangements, with the New Zealanders and the 25th Division still in charge of their own artillery and ordering a shortening of their barrage, represented a fatal error still unaddressed by corps. It was fortunate for Plumer that the only semblance of effective resistance from the Germans had occurred in II Anzac's zone. Had the Germans not made crucial mistakes in the deployment of their counter-attack divisions and had the shock of the morning been more effectively reversed, the outcome of the second phase across the Second Army's entire frontage may well have been very different indeed.

Private Marcus Brown of Cape Barren Island. A Tasmanian aboriginal man who had successfully enlisted despite the 1909 Defence Act which required all recruits to be 'substantially of European descent', Brown was wounded the day after he carried his friend's body back to the Black Line and died on 11 June (photo courtesy of the Brown family).

The fierce shelling which had cleared the Green line on the 3rd Division's front died down as the long daylight of high summer began to fade. A patrol from the 40th Battalion kept its abandoned position under observation, noting that the Germans had not occupied it and small groups crept forward to gather the wounded. The 40th Battalion's 'Private Ashmead', Lance Corporal Biggs, recalled one tragic scene:

'Billy' [Marcus] Brown, a fine type of man, quarter or half caste Tasmanian aboriginal, was seeking his bosom pal Dave Marriott ... Dave had been killed in the harrier race, and his body lay in the bottom of a shellhole. Billy wept aloud. Several of us offered to help getting his body up, but Billy said, "No, he's mine!" Refusing aid, he got down in the shell hole, picked up the massive corpse and carried it balanced over one shoulder back into the darkness. There is much poignant pathos in a battle, for those with seeing hearts![100]

6

... all was confusion and mix up ...

Crisis

6

… all was confusion and mix up …

Crisis

Realisation of an unfolding disaster dawned slowly at II Anzac Corps Headquarters. At 8.30 pm, some three hours after their own artillery began falling on the Australians on the Green Line, the corps diary reported that the 'situation on both Divisional fronts became very obscure' — always an ominous phrase.[1] In stark contrast to the regular and detailed messages from the morning's attack, there were only four brief messages in II Anzac's war diary for the entire second phase attack between 3.10 pm and 8.30 pm. The news that 'portions' of the 4th Division had been driven back was received at 8.30 pm and, 40 minutes later, Monash messaged Godley that the 3rd Division had also retreated 'in consequence' he said 'of withdrawal of 4th Division'.[2] Considering the withering barrage also falling on the 37th's position, this was only partly true. It was, however, more accurate than the entry in II Anzac's diary that 'the enemy put down a heavy barrage and followed it up with a series of local counter-attacks, of a very determined nature and well driven home.' While the German artillery had certainly been troublesome, the shelling from British guns had been far more lethal and there had been no German counter-attacks.[3] It was not until the final line of the 8.30 pm entry that II Anzac staff touched on the main problem. 'The situation became more complicated by the fact that various subordinate Commanders, fearful of the safety of the Black Dotted and Black Lines shortened their artillery barrages.'[4]

The was certainly the case in the 12th Brigade and Brigadier General Robertson, after piecing together the events of that afternoon from the reports of survivors, would have reason to be bitter. After noting at 6.00 pm that he had been uncertain of the position of his brigade for some hours, Robertson wrote that 'a verbal message, apparently sent from one of the Battalion Commanders of the 1st New Zealand Brigade stated that our troops were retiring to the Black Line and he had asked for our Artillery barrage to be brought down in front of the Red Dotted Line. This was done without consulting me and it caused a considerable number of casualties among my officers and men and forced them to temporarily evacuate their positions gained and fall back on a line near the

Red Dotted Line in front of the Black Line.'[5] The men of the 12th Brigade had been victims of error piled upon error. Shelled out of the Green Line by their own guns, their attempts to escape this were interpreted as a prelude to a German counter-attack by the New Zealanders who shortened their barrage further, shelling them a second time and driving them all the way back to their starting tapes. Short shelling had affected, to varying degrees, the entire front of II Anzac Corps, pushing not only the 13th Brigade back, but the entire 3rd Division. Although after-action reports by battalion and brigade commanders would paint these movements as unavoidable and generally orderly, the truth was that the withdrawal was, in many places, chaotic and panicked. As one of the officers of the 47th Battalion would describe it, 'all was confusion and mix up'.[6]

There were many contributing factors, as Bean would point out in his summary of the battle in the *Official History*, but one of the most important was an overburdened and unreliable communication system. Fatigue was also a factor. Bean himself was flagging as he tried to gather as much information as possible for his notes. 'There has been a noise of very heavy firing for an hour now, since 10 p.m. or there-about. More c-attacks I'm afraid. Too dead sleepy, what with gas and fatigue of this morning's work, I can scarcely write sense – keep on dropping to sleep.'[7] Despite the best attempts by Harington at Second Army Headquarters and the corps and divisional signallers to maintain touch with their forward units, the systems frequently broke down. Messages from the hard-pressed 12th Brigade battalions to 4th Division Headquarters had to pass through the New Zealand Division on the Black Line, a further complication. The inevitable time lag between despatch and receipt of messages, which sometimes stretched to several hours, added to the difficulty of divisional commanders in reacting effectively to problems during the course of the battle. The 47th Battalion, for example, sent a message at around 4.00 pm by pigeon (relayed to II Anzac Corps) which was logged at 5.25 pm, 'to the effect that a company [of the 47th] was held up at Owl Trench by heavy machine gun fire, could not advance and asked for artillery support.' A second message, from the two left companies just east of Oxygen Trench and timed at 5.12 pm, but not received at divisional headquarters until three hours later, told of the first counter-attack at 5.00 pm, warned that another was under way and requested a barrage on Owl Support Trench. A third message, timed at 7.25 pm, asked for artillery to be directed against Steignast Farm. Given that each much-delayed message requested urgent action, at different times and on three separate frontages varying in depth, any effective and timely response was simply impossible.

The surest and quickest method of requesting artillery support was the SOS system of firing flares. However, this could and did go wrong. The artillery could not be completely sure of the exact position of the forward infantry, particularly as the careful arrangements with the RFC contact planes spotting for the artillery required the men in the forward positions to fire flares. There was an understandable reluctance by men under fire to so clearly reveal their positions. The system also broke down because the Australian infantry were at times themselves unsure of their exact position, as was the case with the forward elements of the 47th Battalion along Huns' Walk. Plain bad luck contributed too, as the Germans had chosen a similar red signal flare for their SOS and this brought wildly inaccurate artillery fire down on both sides as Allied and German artillery responded to what they imagined to be their own troops asking for barrages. Runners risked a dangerous, time-consuming journey back through shellfire to deliver messages which were often delayed or overtaken by events. Telephone lines were frequently severed and even less reliable. The fog of war has rarely been thicker than at Messines on the evening of 7 June. At 9.00 pm the divisional war diary recorded that the situation was 'very obscure and complicated by forward communications from Brigades being continually interrupted'.[8]

Artillery falling on the Green Line near Fanny's Farm at 6.00 pm on 7 June. The shell bursts are scattered over a wide area, providing an indication of the inaccuracy of the fire. This barrage drove most of the 12th Brigade to abandon their gains and move back to the Black Line (AWM J00272).

Crisis

Holmes and his brigade commanders, Glasgow and Robertson, did what they could that night to clarify the 4th Division's position once they became aware that the situation was beginning to disintegrate. This was no easy task. Even though Holmes shared his headquarters with Russell (and Glasgow and Robertson with their New Zealand counterparts), confusion reigned thanks to a series of frantic reports of counter-attacks and troops falling back in panic, most of which were completely untrue. Of the 13th Brigade units, it became clear that the 52nd Battalion was well to the north of its designated position and that, having dragged half of the 49th Battalion across with it, a gap had opened up between the two brigades. Holmes remained unaware for some hours that the 52nd had also been driven back from the Green Line by II Anzac's artillery, although he knew that these men were mixed up with troops of the 33rd Brigade who were dribbling in and being posted in platoons and companies to weak points as needed. While Glasgow knew that the 52nd's line was dangerously thin, there was an ominous silence from the 49th Battalion. At 9.00 pm Glasgow sent the 51st Battalion forward as reinforcements, despatching two companies to the 52nd and two to the 49th, the latter ordered to throw their exposed right flank, or what remained of it, back to the Black Dotted Line. He had little idea of the parlous state of the 49th Battalion which was fragmented, pinned down by heavy fire, and subjected to repeated bouts of shelling from II Anzac's guns. The 49th had suffered severely, with over 100 men killed and many more wounded. As the companies of the 51st arrived, Lieutenant Colonel Harold Paul, commanding the 49th, informed the 51st's company commander that, not only was his battalion not on its proper frontage, but he was in touch with only one of his companies. Paul's battalion was a shattered remnant of the one which had advanced from the Black Line six hours earlier. Virtually leaderless with all four company commanders killed, only two of the 49th's officers now remained in the line. When their own artillery then began falling on them late in the afternoon followed by the withdrawal of the 52nd on their left, any remaining semblance of cohesion melted away. Paul, whose isolation in his headquarters in a captured pillbox was broken only by the occasional breathless runner bearing scraps of news about the destruction of his battalion, was no longer effectively in command. When the 51st arrived shortly after 9.00 pm, it could do little more than dig in alongside the scattered parties of the 49th. Sergeant Joseph Trotman of the 49th described those hours:

> We then did the best we could by digging in, until some more of the [reinforcements] came up and helped up. The[n] the row started. He got our range + pelted us with shells + I can tell you he gave us a hot time

... He sent some H.E. over (Big Stuff) + luckily I was the only one hit. We had a muster + roll call before this + only 170 answered it so you can guess it's pretty rough.[9]

The right of the shattered 49th now rested at the northern edge of the Blauwepoortbeek with a yawning gap between its scattered platoons and the equally weakened 45th Battalion to the south. The 25th Division, confused about the identity of both Australian brigades in front of it, noted in its intelligence summary on the evening of 7 June that, 'unfortunately the 12th Australian Infantry Brigade [*referring to the 13*[th]] on the left appears to have pushed too far up North, thus leaving a considerable gap between their right flank and the 4th Australian Infantry Brigade [*referring to the 12*[th]]. In this gap and to the west were several enemy strong points and concrete block houses which offered strong resistance and could not be taken without further artillery bombardment. News: very scanty ... no reliable information as to the exact situation and position of the line held by Australian troops.'[10] Major Consett Riddell of the 12th Field Company of Engineers had men pushed forward to cut tracks and wire the captured trenches. The retreat and confusion left his men stranded on the ridge under shellfire. 'Feeling pretty sick that everything seemed to have failed and the company probably cut to pieces by waiting for hours ... found some of the infantry doubtful of their positions.'[11] Following the panicked retreat through their own barrage, the remnants of the 47th Battalion were scattered behind the Black Line, having dashed back through the New Zealand position. Some even returned to the old British front line at the foot of the ridge. Gallwey was utterly demoralised. 'We deserve to be killed for running away like this. Better that than be blown to pieces by our own guns. Our losses must be appalling ... The New Zealanders certainly held the position they had taken, but we Australians had been a miserable failure.'[12]

The situation for the 45th Battalion was, if possible, even more dire than that of the 47th. The fierce fire in the Blauwepoortbeek had cut a swathe through its two left companies and the survivors were now pinned down as bullets sprayed the ground all around and above them. Hidden among the hedges and scattered clumps of trees were nests of pillboxes containing machine-guns and concrete gun shelters for field guns which, as Bean described, 'blazed away at the 45th from 300 yards'.[13] The right companies of the 45th, hit by British artillery late in the afternoon, had either sought shelter in shell holes or had bolted back to the Black Line with the 47th. The 45th's historian summarised what had been a black day for the battalion:

View of the killing fields of the Blauwepoortbeek Valley from a German pillbox at Delporte Farm. The 45th and 49th battalions were ordered to attack down this long, open slope on 7 June and faced uncut wire, field guns and machine-guns with wide and uninterrupted fields of fire. The tower of Messines church is visible in the distance on the left with the start lines just below the crest (author photo).

... the two isolated companies, greatly reduced in strength by casualties, practically without officers or senior n.c.o.'s, and with both flanks in the air, were forced to retire to their jumping-off line. These two companies had suffered severely, as in "C" Company every officer had been killed and in "D" Company all officers had either been killed or wounded. Owing to a grave misunderstanding, when it was observed that the enemy on the left flank had been successful, our artillery put down a barrage at 7.30 p.m. right along the battalion frontage in front of the jumping off line. This cut off "A" and "B" Companies ... and they suffered heavy casualties from our own artillery with whom they were unable to communicate ... It was with bitter thoughts that they thus relinquished, through no fault of their own, the objective so gallantly captured that afternoon.[14]

One of the surviving pillboxes in the Blauwepoortbeek Valley on the site of what was Delporte Farm. The open chamber on the right sheltered a field gun (author photo).

Small parties of the 12th Brigade remained in their posts on or near the Green Line and maintained a vigorous fire, targeting Germans moving to occupy the vacant trenches on the final objective. While darkness provided some respite for the 4th Division, it also brought uncertainty as battalion commanders struggled to reorganise the remnants of their units, collect the stragglers and, most important of all, try to piece together some coherent picture of their fronts. As the light faded over Messines Ridge on 7 June the, unfortunate 4th Division, just six weeks on from its demolition at Bullecourt, teetered on the precipice of another catastrophe.

To its right, the 3rd Division's 37th Battalion and its attached company of the 40th had also been driven out by the shelling and isolated by the retirement of the 4th Division on their left. Many of the wounded had to be left behind in the scramble for safety. Story had taken what he thought was the only course open to him in pulling the 37th back to safety. Although he undoubtedly saved the lives of many of his men, it would be a decision he would live to regret. The wounded were largely abandoned. Mendoza of the 47th Battalion, wounded and separated from his now leaderless B Company and stranded in the killing zone was, like many others, unable to move without being fired on and could only hope for nightfall.[15]

· · ·

It was not until 10.45 pm, almost two hours after becoming aware of the failure of the attack due partly to his own artillery, that Godley issued an order for the guns to lengthen and fire east of the Green Line and for the 3rd and 4th divisions 'to reoccupy all ground vacated'. The major reason for this delay was the 'obscurity' which was deepened by alarmist reports and rumours that the Germans were counter-attacking or that troops had been driven from their positions on the Black Dotted Line or even the Black Line. The expectation of German counter-attacks, fully justified though it was, itself created the anxiety that any movement of German troops or increase in enemy artillery heralded them. The artillery had been primed to expect counter-attacks and trained to react quickly to changing circumstances. Of the reports of troops falling back from the main positions, Bean noted that 'most of these messages were true of some small sector or portion of the troops, but not of the front or troops in general.'[16] Although many members of the 47th Battalion had fallen back to the Black Line (and some even found their way back to the old British front line), an unknown number of men in isolated parties held out in forward positions, scattered across the broken front. Two hours after reports of the first barrage, a message from A Company called for 'bombs, ammunition and water to Owl Trench at once urgent!'[17] With most of the officers and NCOs killed or wounded, Private William Brown remained in the line and took command of the leaderless remnant of B Company. He posted his men in a widely spaced defensive line, calmed the frightened, and provided the vital rallying point for the rest. Brown's men fought off several local attacks during the afternoon, and saved the right flank from collapse.[18]

Some members of D Company had also remained in their forward positions, as had remnants of the battalion's right companies. Private Albert Bainbrigge had maintained his position in the front line throughout the barrage. When the shelling damaged his Lewis gun, he rebuilt it with parts of another, and kept firing. He later brought both guns out of the battle.[19] Citations for awards after the battle also recorded these instances of small parties of men remaining in their positions under shellfire.[20] Imlay of the 47th sent his Adjutant, Lieutenant Norm Bremner, forward at nightfall to try to sort out the confusion about B Company, lost somewhere on the right of the line. Bremner had volunteered for this very hazardous task, and found B Company at around 10.00 pm. He also stumbled across the wounded Mendoza, who informed him that Millar was missing and all other officers were either killed or wounded.[21] Bremner gathered and reorganised the leaderless company, led the men forward, and captured the objective on the Green Line, taking 80 prisoners. He then returned for Mendoza and carried him back to safety through heavy machine-gun fire and shelling. As he was carrying

Mendoza, he was attacked by five Germans. He single-handedly killed four and wounded the fifth, taking him prisoner before returning to safety. Recommended for the VC, Bremner's citation recorded that 'his prompt and gallant action altered the situation, saved the Company and imbued fresh spirit into the men'.[22]

While the scattered remnants of his front-line divisions held on, Godley remained largely unaware that the existence of independent commands, one behind the other, was the core of the problem. Plumer's determination to protect the Black Line as the main objective of the attack meant that the clumsy structure persisted long past the point where it may have been needed. In fact, it was working just as intended by the over-cautious commander of the Second Army, protecting the Black Line as the main prize and sacrificing the troops in front who were, as most in corps and army command imagined, being pushed back from the expendable Green Line by enemy counter-attacks. The problem was that the Australians were not being pushed back by German counter-attacks but by their own artillery. Barrages had been deliberately shortened by both the 25th and New Zealand divisions which remained in control of their artillery, creating havoc in the lines ahead and exacting a high cost in Australian lives. Godley's order for all artillery to fire beyond the Green Line however, would not fix the problem of the inaccurate fire of the heavy artillery which was still troublesome, nor address the issue of separate command structures occupying the same fronts. It would be a further 24 hours before II Anzac's commander would correct the error by unifying command under the forward divisions. This was not simply an oversight. Had Plumer fully committed to capturing the Green Line, it is doubtful that such a dangerous ambiguity of command would have persisted beyond the point where the 3rd and 4th divisions passed beyond the Black Line.

The order to recapture the Green Line led to a hasty conference between Holmes and Monash who patched together an equally hasty and very ambitious plan for the 3rd and 4th divisions to mount another attack on the Green Line at 3.00 am. Although neither II Anzac's diary, nor those of the 3rd or 4th Division mention any timing from Godley, the New Zealand Division's diary records that the orders to the 3rd and 4th divisions were to reoccupy the ground 'at once'.[23] With the dawning realisation at II Anzac that the second phase of the attack had fallen apart, an atmosphere of crisis descended on Godley's headquarters. While it was impractical (indeed impossible) to effect an immediate reversal of the retreat, Holmes and Monash now had the very difficult task of turning 'at once' into 'as soon as possible'. Although the first faint glow of daylight would begin soon after the 3.00 am start time, the two divisional commanders agreed that the troops would, for all intents and purposes, be mounting a night attack. Not only was an impromptu night attack a very rare event in the First World War due to the obvious difficulties it entailed, but this particular night attack was to be mounted by two divisions which had just been driven from their positions after suffering heavy casualties and having marched and fought through an entire day. The tasks of reorganising the depleted and shaken battalions and moving the reserves forward at night were themselves extremely demanding, but added to these were resupply, communication and coordination with flank units. No observation and reconnaissance was possible and, with Godley's order emanating from II Anzac just before 11.00 pm (with his divisional commanders' plans approved by Godley at 11.50 pm), the time available, once those orders had been transmitted through division, brigade and down to battalion command, was brief indeed. Godley, Holmes and Monash could only hope that the Germans were still shaken and had not been able to muster an effective defence of the Green Line. Of the far more worrying possibility — that the Germans had managed to bring fresh troops into the line — they again trusted to luck that this had not occurred.

As the reserves hurried forward to assist in the 3.00 am attack, the odds of success were not at all encouraging. For the 48th Battalion, with memories of Bullecourt still painfully fresh, the prospect of another hastily planned assault was doubly unwelcome. Lieutenant Percy Nimmo of the 48th recalled:

> Going up we heard the 45th and 47th had been driven out of their trenches, and we were in for a bad time. We reached the N.Z line at 4.30 [am] June 8th and were at once told that owing to the 45th and 47th not being able to hold Owl Trench and support, we were to go on and take it. This looked pretty rotten considering that these two battalions were full strength whilst we were only one Battn. and half strength at that.[24]

Fortunately for Nimmo and his men, it proved impossible to launch any attack. Robertson reported that his battalion commanders were 'unable to get the troops organised and into positions at that hour owing to the darkness and faulty communications'. The 47th Battalion did not receive the order to attack until minutes before the intended start time of 3.00 am and, although two companies of the 48th had arrived earlier (having been ordered up during the first crisis of the afternoon) to be placed under Imlay's command (Lieutenant Joseph Mayersbeth's company of the 48th reported to Imlay just after midnight, and another 70 men under Lieutenant Dewas Cumming arrived soon after), the task was simply beyond them.[25] The 47th's diary records that it 'was quite impossible to start at this time as Coys were still slightly disorganised and quite a good way from objective'.[26] The attack would have to wait until first light.

In the grey half-light of early dawn, the men of the 48th Battalion moved up over the ridge. Lieutenant George Mitchell, who had experienced the battles of Gallipoli and a year's hard fighting on the Western Front, was still awed by the sight:

I cannot describe the battlefield, however weakly. Giant shell craters linked up everywhere. Here and there amid the ruins were German blockhouses, usually unharmed. Outside each lay a heap of German dead, mangled and grey. Here and there amid his old wrecked trenches lay the shattered and stinking remnants of what had been German soldiers. Occasionally there lay one of our own dead.[27]

The 48th pressed on over the ridge. It is unclear whether Holmes informed Godley or Monash (or even fully knew) of the failure of the 12th Brigade's attack which had been scheduled to begin at 3.00 am. The divisional diary simply states that 'The attempt to reoccupy the Green Line during the night was only partially successful owing to the exhaustion of the troops from fighting continuously in the great heat of the previous day and from the effect of heavy enemy shelling. The difficulty of getting orders through in the dark to new headquarters was also to a large extent a contributing factor.'[28] The truth was that there was no attempt to reoccupy the Green Line and clearly no partial success.

The situation in the 3rd Division at this time was similarly confused. Major Story, keen to move his men back to their positions, sent a message to 10th Brigade Headquarters that, if the barrage would lift off the Green Line, the 37th would move forward and reoccupy the line. The battalion diary records that no answer was received from the 10th Brigade's commander, Brigadier General Walter McNicoll. McNicoll decided instead to call up the 44th Battalion to take the 37th's place and ordered it to move up and occupy the Green Line.[29] Colonel Walter Smith, in command of the 37th Battalion, later wrote that it was the Brigade Major of the 10th (Eric Connelly) who verbally informed him that the 44th Battalion would move through the 37th's positions at 3.00 am. 'Confirmation of this message' Smith wrote pointedly in his after-action report, 'has never been received.'[30] Smith further complained that he had no idea what orders the commander of the 44th had received.

The 44th moved forward and, according to its diary, the attack was 'very successful', the battalion apparently occupying the Green Line at 4.00 am with minimal losses.[31] This was incorrect. The 44th had stopped and dug in well short of the Green Line; however this mistaken belief also became the understanding of the 3rd Division which reported that the 44th began digging in on the Green

Line at 3.30 am.[32] The 44th reported that it had not connected up with the 48th Battalion which the 44th was told would be on its left flank. As the 12th Brigade had not attacked as arranged at 3.00 am (a fact of which the 44th was unaware), the 44th looked in vain to its left for support from the 12th Brigade. Unable to find the 48th on its left and believing that it was on the Green Line with both flanks in the air, the officers of the 44th then withdrew their men even further back and Captain William Rockliff of C Company decided to refuse his left flank. The mistake remained unchecked for several hours. 'From interrogation of officers' wrote Smith in the 37th's report, 'it has been ascertained that the 44th Bn. did not pass through until 3.30 a.m. & that the line taken up by them was not actually the Green Line which was previously held by this battalion, but a line some distance in rear of it.'[33] At this stage the 37th Battalion was back on the Black Line attempting to reorganise. The men had endured heavy losses (reduced to 230 rifles) and had, like the battalions of the 4th Division, been shelled from their positions on their final objective. Despite their ordeal, Story tried to inform his division that they were ready and willing to rejoin the fight, offers he claimed were met with silence from above. As difficult as the day had been for the 37th Battalion, the following hours would be remembered with far more bitterness in the years to come.

There is no doubt that the events of the afternoon and the long night of 7/8 June put the Australian divisional and brigade commanders and their headquarters under immense pressure. Likewise, the battalion commanders, some under heavy shelling in their forward positions, were also stretched to the limit. All of the assault battalions of the 3rd and 4th divisions had suffered to some extent, some severely. Since late morning, the shelling from the German batteries on the far bank of the Lys had grown in intensity and accuracy and was taking a heavy toll on the New Zealanders digging in on the ridge. Further, it was still unclear (although it was still expected) whether a strong German counter-attack was on its way. If it was, the Australians' fragile toehold on the Green Line would be swept away. Having missed the fleeting but ultimately unrealistic opportunity to reoccupy it at 3.00 am, Holmes' tired and battered division was reorganising. Monash, believing the 44th had reoccupied the Green Line, was unaware that it was still well short of it. Both generals now faced the prospect of another daylight attack against a German defensive line, fully alerted and of unknown strength.

· · ·

Holmes decided that the 4th Division's situation was so unclear that he needed to speak directly with the commanders on the spot and assess the problems for himself. He discovered at Glasgow's and Robertson's headquarters that they were as unsure as he was. Holmes then decided that, as a command group, they should talk directly with the battalion commanders in their forward headquarters on the shoulder of Messines Ridge itself. Although he took a considerable risk, as one lucky German shell could have decapitated the 4th Division's entire command structure, Holmes was, according to Bean, 'not one who would be content to allow a situation to remain vague if he could personally unravel it.'[34] In taking this decision, risky though it was, Holmes was acting on first principles, which had been re-emphasised with some vigour at the Second Army conference in May. Under the heading 'Role of Divisions in Corps Reserve and action of their Commanders' Kiggell, summarising the outcomes of that meeting wrote that:

> It is essential that the commanders of these Divisions should go forward
> and see for themselves what is the condition of affairs in order that they
> may be able to take advantage of the tactical situation. It is impossible
> for these commanders to ascertain the situation or be in the position to
> issue suitable orders rapidly if they remain at their Headquarters in dug-
> outs at a considerable distance from the scene of action merely relying on
> information received by telephone.[35]

In the midst of the 3rd Division's confusion over the reality of the 44th Battalion's situation, Bean would, famously, touch on what he believed to be Monash's major weakness as a battlefield commander as he too groped for information:

> Although the 3rd Division perhaps surpassed other Australian divisions in
> the careful carrying out of orders by subordinates, it lacked as yet their
> general high standard of personal supervision in battle by commanding
> officers. Well trained though its leaders were, some of them (as those whose
> practice was different often complained) were content to acquiesce in the
> theory, with which General Monash possibly agreed, that the commander's
> duty in time of battle was to remain strictly at his headquarters.[36]

Although Monash was not, strictly speaking, one of the reserve division commanders included in Kiggell's summary, and although the envisioned situation was one of exploitation rather than the emergency withdrawal and reoccupation they now faced, Monash had effectively become one of those reserve division commanders by virtue of the increased objective for Messines and he now commanded a division that advanced (albeit in a subsidiary role) beyond the Black Line. Kiggell's words addressed themselves directly to him, and the wisdom of such advice now became very apparent. It was certainly true, as Bean observed on more than one occasion in his narrative of Messines, that although they faced similar challenges, the headquarters of the two Australian divisions were very different in their operating methods, in the detail of their planning and even in their character.

Monash's meticulous planning had taken into account some of the contingencies and setbacks he now faced, but there was little accommodation in those plans for junior commanders to act on their initiative in the manner of Story of the 37th who had withdrawn his battalion from the hail of British artillery fire which threatened to annihilate them. The breakdown in communication merely added to both Monash's and Story's problems, and Story acted as his brother officers had all across the Green Line. Where their officers failed to act, the men took it upon themselves to escape the shellfire in any case. In the 4th Division, it was understood and rightly assumed that the men on the spot, from battalion commander down, had acted with common sense (rather than panic) and pulled their men back. In the carefully choreographed battle that Monash and his 3rd Division staff had laboured with such intensity of purpose to produce, the freedom of action that Story exercised was not to be so easily accommodated. Story had seriously blundered in neglecting to inform his attached company of the 40th Battalion that he was pulling the 37th back to the Black Line, but he was not alone that afternoon in making mistakes.

• • •

By nightfall on 7 June, Second Army Headquarters was contemplating the greatest success for British arms to that point in the war. One of the most important German strongholds on the Western Front had fallen in a few hours and the report concluded with the enormous tally of prisoners and guns captured. One brief sentence provided the only cloud in an otherwise sunny outlook: 'At 3.10 p.m. we launched an attack with fresh troops against the Oosttaverne Line which was taken with the exception of a small portion just East of Messines, where fighting is still in progress.'[37] The fighting still in progress was going badly. As the morning of 8 June dawned, the 4th Division prepared once again to assault the Green Line. The arrangements cobbled together for the aborted 3.00 am attack had been dangerously unclear, but at least it had been dark. Now the men faced the prospect of assaulting the enemy's trenches in daylight, returning past the bodies of their comrades killed in the previous day's fighting, a grim testament to the difficulty of their task.

At the northern end of the 4th Division's line, the 52nd Battalion, still mixed in with units of the 33rd Brigade and with two companies of the 51st Battalion, had been driven back to the support lines by the British shelling on the evening of 7 June. Now, alongside some members of the 33rd Brigade who had been driven out as well, they too were preparing to return to their positions on the Green Line. The confusion caused by the 52nd occupying the wrong front now almost turned fatal as Maxwell, returning from battalion headquarters where he had been vainly attempting to persuade the artillery to lengthen off the Green Line, came across a British battalion commander preparing his men to open fire on the Australians ahead, believing them to be counter-attacking Germans. Since the English would have been expecting Germans and not Australians in front of them as they advanced to the Green Line, the mistake was hardly surprising and it was only with difficulty that Maxwell persuaded them otherwise, offering to go forward on his own to meet the 'enemy'.

With the British artillery finally lifting off the Green Line in the morning, the 52nd moved forward again and engaged in bombing duels with Germans which, the battalion diary claimed, 'finished any active opposition the enemy gave us until relieved'.[38] Though still well north of its correct position, the 52nd recaptured the forward positions from which it had been shelled the night before. But it was a different story for the 49th. Although the left companies reached the Green Line, they too were nowhere near their allotted front. The battalion was now scattered across an uncertain front, the two left companies dragged away by the 52nd as it veered across the front to link up with the missing English. As the 13th Brigade diary records, it was this searching to link up with the English on the left as well as 'the formation of the ground and the machine gun fire on the right of the 49th Battalion' that created the gap in the 13th Brigade line and another between the two brigades of the 4th Division.

The 12th Brigade's right battalion was far more fortunate. With the sun rising on the morning of 8 June, and after a short artillery barrage on the vacated Green Line, Lieutenant Colonel Imlay of the 47th Battalion, in charge of both his own and the two right companies of the 48th Battalion, trusted to stealth:

> I decided to make the best of what element of perturbation remained with the Hun after the barrage had lifted and gave orders to move forward as far as possible and dig in and creep forward determinedly one by one until a definite rush could be made on the objective and lead to its final capture.[39]

The left company of the 48th under Captain Stabback, sent to support the 45th Battalion, had received no orders from the 45th's commander, Lieutenant Colonel Sydney Herring. However Stabback, watching as the men of his own battalion went forward on the right with the 47th, decided to move forward with them. The firing had died down to such an extent that the men walked fully upright in a broad line. Scouts sent forward encountered machine-guns and snipers firing in the distance on their left, but the broken lines of German trenches into and through which they climbed as they advanced provided cover. Moving carefully forward in stages, on a battlefield so unnervingly quiet that they suspected a trap, the 47th and 48th quietly reoccupied the vacant Green Line without loss. Gallwey, who was with the reorganised remnant of the 47th, described the eerily quiet advance 'as though we were moving on the parade ground … Everything was so still it seemed an ill omen and to herald the calm before the storm.'[40]

By 5.00 am Imlay's men were 180 metres short of Owl Trench (the first objective of the previous day), but with no sign of the 45th or 37th battalions on their flanks. The men of the 47th and 48th advanced the line 'inch by inch' until, by 7.00 am, they were again established in Owl Trench. By 8.30 am, Imlay's men had crept forward the last 70 metres to the Green Line (which in the 47th's sector was Owl Support Trench) and reoccupied it. 'To our intense surprise the trench was unoccupied. We had been stalking game that had long since fled … It was the easiest victory we could ever achieve.'[41] The confusion reigning in II Anzac Corps on the afternoon of 7 June had, it seemed, been matched in equal degree in the German command. The piecemeal German counter-attacks which fell on the 3rd and 4th divisions had been easily defeated and most lower echelon commanders believed their Oosttaverne Line was lost. Unaware of the full scale of the retreat that afternoon, isolated remnants of the assault battalions who remained in the line had given the Germans the impression the Australians still held the Green Line and that the line was at least still occupied if not strongly held.

It is possible also that the German High Command believed its men were still in possession of portions of the Green Line, as they were fully aware the Blauwepoortbeek Valley was strongly in German hands. This may explain the absence of any German artillery barrage on the Green Line as a whole. German troops certainly re-entered their vacant trenches. Private Idrice Beckman of the 47th Battalion was wounded in the first barrage and left in Owl Support Trench on the Green Line. He was captured by a party of Germans at around 3.00 am on 8 June.[42] The same communication problems that plagued the Australian battalions however, also blinded the Germans and it seems certain that the news that their Oosttaverne Line had effectively been abandoned was either not passed on, or not acted on. As night fell late on 7 June, the Germans needed simply to walk forward to reoccupy their lost trenches. Had they done so, the attempts by the 3rd and 4th divisions to retake the Green Line the next morning might have met with disaster. The good luck which had been so conspicuously absent for the 4th Division on 7 June now delivered it some 500 yards of the final objective unopposed and, as the sun rose to herald another brilliant and hot summer's day, the men began to dig in to defend the line so dearly won and then lost the previous day.

To the south, Monash's 44th Battalion still remained short of the Green Line and unaware that it was not where it should have been. Orders for the 37th (then reorganising on the Black Line after the retreat) to support the 44th were apparently forwarded but not received by Story who was in front-line command, despite the fact that the battalion requested precisely that support, provided the barrage was lengthened to allow it.[43] Colonel Mansbridge, commanding the 44th, was aware by late morning that the 12th Brigade on his left had not attacked as planned at 3.00 am. With the Green Line again secured on its left flank by the 48th Battalion and the survivors of the 47th (up to Owl Trench, the penultimate line before the final objective in Owl Support Trench) who were now well ahead of it with their right on Huns' Walk, the 44th was now able to move up in the clear light of midday and into the trenches from which the 37th had been driven, 'empty' wrote Bean, 'except for the crowded dead of the evening before'.[44] The brief and inadequate record contained in the 44th Battalion diary claimed incorrectly that it was on the Green Line at 4.00 am and makes no mention of the later advance. However, throughout 8 June, though well forward, the 44th was still not fully forward in the correct position.[45]

Despite Bean's criticisms, Monash had not simply sat in his headquarters on the phone. He had sent Lieutenant Colonel John Peck, the 3rd Division's GSO 2 (head of Intelligence), to ascertain the true position of the 44th and the situation on its flank. Despite reporting that it held the Green Line at 11.50 am, news had come back from the 4th Division through the New Zealand Division that the 3rd Division was not where it should be on the right, so in all likelihood, Holmes and Russell were aware before Monash that the 44th was still not in its correct position.[46] Monash, clearly frustrated by the conflicting evidence concerning the 44th's true position, sought clarification from McNicoll in a series of messages of increasing urgency. McNicoll was himself unable to find out, sending a message to Mansbridge just after 10.00 am. 'Are you on Uncanny Support? Send markings of your new line' and again at 11.40 and a third at 1.22 pm. 'Please verify your front line position. 12th Brigade definitely state they and you are digging on Owl and Uncanny Support. This would make your [previous message] inaccurate.'[47]

Since the early morning of 7 June, the RFC had maintained an almost total screen over the battlefield; however this could not continue indefinitely and four German aircraft made it through on the morning of 8 June, spotting for the German artillery on the southern bank of the Lys. These guns now began to find the range and, given their position on the south-east flank, could enfilade the trenches being dug in front of Messines and along the shoulder of the ridge which were held in strength by the New Zealanders and into the Douve Valley, now occupied by the 3rd Division. One of the first salvos of this increased and now directed fire claimed the life of Brigadier General Charles Brown, commander of the 1st New Zealand Brigade. At 12.30 pm, the 3rd New Zealand Brigade reported that Messines was being heavily shelled.[48]

This barrage was the same that fell on Monash's men in the Douve Valley. Mansbridge, in his exposed headquarters in a shell hole on the Black Line, was deeply worried that this very heavy barrage was the preparation for a German counter-attack. Given Godley's order that the artillery could not fire west of the Green Line, he feared his men might be overrun and the message from his Brigadier (McNicoll) that he would have to deal with any intrusion with his machine-guns and mortars was far from reassuring. The bombardment reached a crescendo that, according to Bean, would 'never be forgotten in the 10th Brigade' and one that threatened to wipe out the 44th's command group then trying to shelter in the open on the Black Line. Mansbridge's nerve, already strained by the ordeal of battle, now snapped under the fearful bombardment. A phone message from the 44th received by the 42nd Battalion at 3.25 and passed to the 3rd Division by phone five minutes later read: 'We are driven out of trenches. All wires cut.'[49] Such alarming news from a battalion headquarters was a bombshell, indicating in all likelihood that its command was disintegrating. This was followed by even more alarming and clearly panicked messages, untimed and written on scraps of paper and delivered by runner under his name. 'Cannot hold much longer more strength wanted to link up. Casualties heavy. Col Mansbridge'. And again: 'Cannot hold position. C.O. 44th.'[50] Such was the anxiety this caused that this message and its aftermath were reported in the corps diary. Mansbridge would later deny all responsibility for the messages, claiming they were sent without his knowledge but this seems highly unlikely. The evidence strongly suggests that Mansbridge lost his composure on the morning of 8 June under the violent shelling of the Black Line and, despite his denials, the only reasonable explanation for the messages was his breakdown.

The panicked message from the 44th Battalion on the evening of 8 June 'We are driven out of trenches. All wires cut' caused consternation at 3rd Division Headquarters. Apparently sent by the 44th's commander, Lieutenant Colonel Mansbridge, it was completely inaccurate (the 44th was holding its ground) and Mansbridge would later deny all responsibility for the message (Monash Papers).

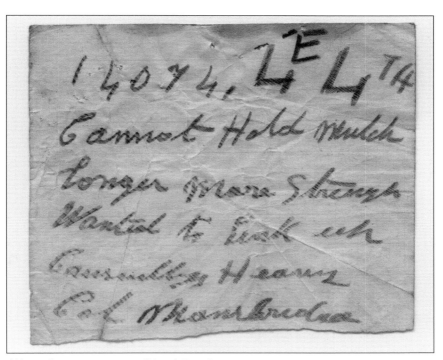

44th Battalion pigeon message 1 (Monash Papers).

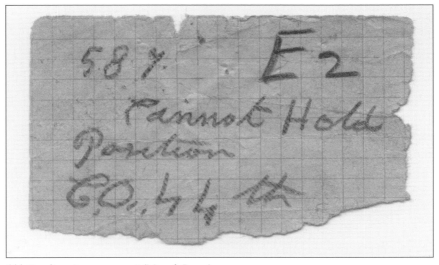

44th Battalion pigeon message 2 (Monash Papers).

Lieutenant Colonel William Mansbridge of the 44th Battalion (left). Mansbridge suffered a nervous breakdown under shellfire on the morning of 10 June. McNicoll complained to Monash that Mansbridge 'was absolutely out of touch with the doings of his battalion'. Mansbridge denied all responsibility for the panicked messages to 3rd Division Headquarters which caused so much confusion (AWM H00411).

In fact, although the battalion was still short of its correct position on the Green Line and not yet connected with the 48th on its left, the front-line report from the 44th at 6.15 pm was measured and calm. Captain

Rockliff would later claim that 'the 44th's line was at no time in danger ... It was all the time perfectly sound. The messages and rumours which got back were unfounded, and it is not clearly known where they came from.'[51] Perhaps not clearly, but although Bean sheltered Mansbridge in the *Official History*, his note that the 44th's commanding officer was 'badly shaken by the overwhelming strain of the day, and was never afterwards really fit for active service' hinted at the truth.[52] The 44th was, for a time, leaderless as Mansbridge lost control both of himself and his battalion. A further confusing message from the 38th Battalion (on the far right of the line) that the Germans were counter-attacking 'on the right of the Black Line' suggested that they had broken through the Green Line (which, in front of the 9th Brigade, was at its closest point to the Black Line and away to the right the two lines merged). Monash again appealed to Godley for permission to bring his barrage back if the Germans broke through, but this was again refused. Despite the mounting confusion caused by these messages however, Monash remained in his headquarters.

· · ·

Brigadier General Glasgow of the 13th Brigade personally sought to resolve the confusion on the far left of II Anzac's line, reposition his two battalions which had veered to the north and begin to tackle the huge difficulty of the gap in the line in the Blauwepoortbeek Valley. The chaos in the 49th Battalion was considerable and no doubt exacerbated by the terrible toll in leaders. The 49th had been shelled by its own side several times during 8 June and, at 8.45 pm, reported a very heavy enemy barrage on its front lines and again complained of British shells falling among its men.[53] The 52nd Battalion (along with companies of the 51st and 49th battalions) was still in the British 33rd Brigade's position and intermingled with the English troops, even overlapping the positions of the 57th Brigade (19th Division) on its extreme left. Glasgow proposed to bring the 52nd around the back of the remnants of the 49th Battalion, have the 33rd Brigade take over and then swing the 52nd into the gap which existed between the 45th and the 49th battalions at the head of the Blauwepoortbeek. This was easier said than done. Sorting out the confusion required a meeting between the commander of the 33rd Brigade, Glasgow, and one of the British battalion commanders followed by a joint reconnaissance of the position armed with maps.[54]

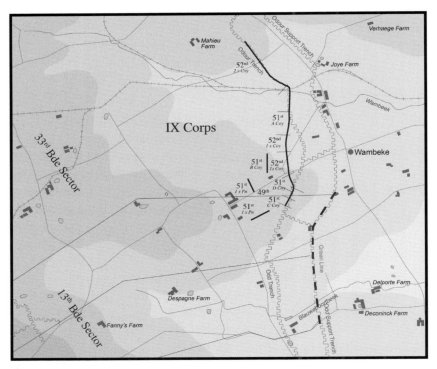

Map 16A. The 13th Brigade's positions on the evening of 7 June. Compounding errors in the 52nd Battalion saw it veer well to the north in the afternoon assault on the Green Line which, in turn, dragged the entire brigade off course and opened a wide gap across the Blauwepoortbeek Valley. This mistake effectively tore the 4th Division apart and the 12th Brigade, unsupported on its left flank was unable to reach its objective.

As the two battalions of the 33rd Brigade relieved the 52nd at dusk, the movement was noticed by the Germans opposite and, at 8.25 pm, a barrage came down. The 25th Division on the forward slope of the ridge, having received intelligence of a possible German counter-attack (which was again incorrect) at about 6.00 pm, put up a barrage in front of the Green Line. The Germans put down their own barrage at 8.30 pm which, according to the 25th Division, 'rolled backwards toward the Black line'.[55] Believing this heralded a German counter-attack, the 25th Division fired its SOS signals, to which its artillery responded, dropping shells near and behind the Green Line which mingled with the German barrage. This was yet another disastrous mix-up, catching the men of the 52nd as they were leaving the trenches, and they were now forced to run through both German and British barrages across the broken ground as fast as their legs could carry them. The 25th Division's barrage also hit the 49th which complained that 'here again our Artillery heavily shelled our front line system causing many casualties', the wounded including the 49th's Commanding Officer, Lieutenant Colonel Harold Paul.[56]

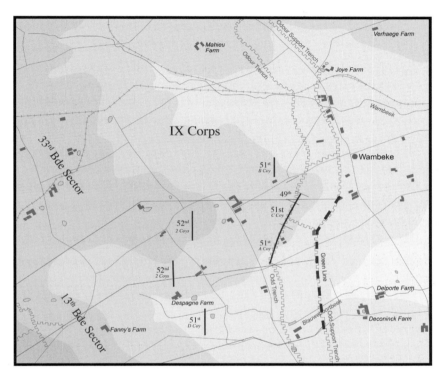

Map 16B. The 13th Brigade's positions on 8 June. Twenty-four hours later, the situation remained chaotic, with the 13th Brigade still well out of position and short of its objective despite the attempts of both Glasgow and Holmes to restore the situation. Both reserve battalions had been committed to no avail. The yawning gap in the 4th Division's line would prove a major problem in the days ahead.

Glasgow's decision to relocate the 52nd Battalion (and the attached companies of the 51st and 49th) from its positions in the 33rd Brigade sector in the evening light of 8 June was very risky and unravelled disastrously. The chaos which ensued once the movement was observed by the Germans was compounded by the 25th Division shelling which was a further breach of Godley's orders, just one of a number. Glasgow had appointed the 51st's commander, Lieutenant Colonel John Ridley, to take charge of the 52nd in place of the wounded Pope and this third change of command, unavoidable though it was, added to the disorder in the 13th

Brigade. Both the 52nd and 49th were now commanded by officers of the 51st who absorbed their own men into their new commands, two companies allocated to each. The 52nd, thus disorganised, was unable to reach its correct positions and this meant that the assault planned for the northern end of the Blauwepoortbeek that night was now impossible, and the whole unfortunate enterprise was in vain. Despite the fact that the rout had been partly caused by its own division's artillery, the 75th Brigade's narrative was highly critical of the Australians:

> At 9.00 p.m … messages were received … that Australians were running back to the Black Line where attempts were being made to rally them … The alarm was caused by the retirement of some Australian troops who ran back in considerable disorder, resisting all attempts to rally them.[57]

When the truth became known, this was later amended to read:

> At 9.00 p.m … messages were received … that Australians were moving back to the Black Line … The alarm was caused by the retirement of some Australian troops who ran back in considerable disorder.[58]

The 75th Brigade diary went on to speculate how this had occurred. 'The possible explanation of this is that an Australian relief, taking place during daylight was observed by the enemy, got shelled, some troops ran back and other troops mistaking this movement for a general retirement followed suit, finally putting up the SOS from just in front of the Black Line.' There is no evidence that the SOS was fired by Australian troops and they in turn blamed the men of the 25th for firing the SOS flares. However, it is just as likely that the Germans were responsible, again sending up their red flares which were mistaken by the British artillery for its own SOS signal. The final line in the 75th Brigade's report accused the Australians of 'firing Lewis Guns and rifles into the backs of the 11th Cheshires' following their panicked retreat.[59] Although those serious charges were later removed from the 75th Brigade's report, the blame for this debacle was still sheeted home to the luckless 52nd Battalion. But worse was to come. In a footnote, Bean recorded the story of a British officer trying to stem the retreat (as he saw it) and who was 'shot through the leg by some exasperated and reckless man of the 52nd. This crime, a grave one according to any law, military or civil, was apparently not officially reported by the officer, but word of it leaked out some time later. The officer happened to be connected with the personal staff of the Commander-in-Chief, and considerable scandal was caused by the incident.'[60]

As night fell on 8 June, II Anzac Corps Headquarters had at least identified two of the problems causing havoc with the artillery. The first was the New

Zealand and 25th divisions shortening their barrages to protect the Black Line, decisions driven by numerous reports of phantom counter-attacks and withdrawals by the Australians. The second was the red very light as the SOS signal 'a signal much used by the enemy and there is no doubt that our artillery opened frequently on seeing German lights which it was impossible to distinguish from ours.'[61] There were other contributing factors, including the increasing inaccuracy of the heavy artillery and the communication difficulties which threw a fog over the battlefield, problems Godley's order for the artillery not to fire short of the Green Line would not solve. Although the 3rd Division situation was worryingly unclear, the right of the 12th Brigade had returned to the Green Line. The attempt to move the 52nd Battalion into its correct position however, had failed completely, and any notion that the 52nd could mount an attack down the Blauwepoortbeek that night disappeared. The 13th Brigade diary devoted a mere three lines to the incident, noting with blithe imprecision that the 52nd Battalion had been 'successfully withdrawn from the 33rd Brigade area' before adding that 'owing to heavy hostile and our own artillery fire [they] were not able to successfully accomplish the task given them.'[62] As the long summer's day turned to night, the artillery fire from both sides abated. However the Blauwepoortbeek was still alive with flares and the crackle of rifle and machine-gun fire as the German defenders hung on in their pillboxes and surrounding trenches, resolute in the defence of what was now an awkward re-entrant into the 4th Division's line but one protected by strong wire and a belt of pillboxes. The 49th's diary complained that it had been shelled several times during 8 June by its own artillery and then, as it was growing dark, the Germans 'opened a very heavy barrage on our front line system as far back as Despagne Farm and then to the Black Line' which lasted 90 minutes. The intentions of both sides were very clear and, as night brought some relief to the weary troops, all knew that a desperately fierce fight lay ahead.

7

All right Sir; if it is to be taken, it will be taken.

72 Hours of Hell

All right Sir; if it is to be taken, it will be taken.

72 Hours of Hell

As the sun set on 8 June, Plumer and his staff were preparing for a visit from a grateful Commander-in-Chief keen on congratulating his victorious army in person. Although X and IX Corps had captured almost all of their objectives on 7 June, fighting still raged in the Blauwepoortbeek Valley where the Anzacs faced stubborn resistance. The German defences, shocked and overwhelmed by the initial assault, began to recover over the following days and the artillery on the far bank of the Lys began to find its range, targeting the southern flank of the Second Army. The New Zealand Division, having suffered minimal losses in capturing Messines on the morning of 7 June, was now trapped under heavy and well-directed German artillery fire. This was a largely hidden tragedy as the cost of its occupation of the ridge would be far higher than that paid in the early morning assault on 7 June. For the Australians, the final days at Messines were also marked by needless loss and the fighting began to assume the grim character of the battles of 1916 with a succession of poorly coordinated and hastily planned attacks on narrow fronts against well-armed, determined troops protected by wire and concrete.

The 4th Division's hold on the Green Line, though firming on its flanks by the afternoon of 8 June, was still dangerously fragile in the centre where the pillboxes and wire of the Blauwepoortbeek Valley barred the way. Holmes and his brigadiers, Glasgow and Robertson, worked around the clock on plans to capture the remaining portions of the Green Line. It would prove the most difficult and confused period of the battle. With the short shelling of the artillery still causing problems, the clumsy echeloned command structure on the ridge still not addressed and some units losing heavily, particularly in officers, the fighting was now bound to involve increased risk for the Australians. Hastily cobbled individual battalion and brigade-sized attacks would have to be mounted with all the hazards that these involved. Now heading into a third day with little or no sleep, tired and depleted units were called on to attack these very strong positions and it was the 4th Division once again which had the misfortune to find the bloodiest corner of the battlefield. The determined resistance in the Blauwepoortbeek showed no sign of diminishing.

The chaotic withdrawal of the 52nd Battalion on the night of 8 June under the combined German and British artillery ended any hope of an assault that night. Until Lieutenant Colonel Paul, the commander of the 49th Battalion, had been wounded by this shellfire (his place taken by Major Albert Rowe of the 51st), he and the acting commander of the 52nd (Ridley) had been working to the timetable of nightfall for the attack and planning to use the attached companies of the 51st to launch the assault. The 51st was also disorganised by the shelling, with many of its men hit, and as a result the battalion was late arriving at its jumping-off line. The 13th Brigade's order, that the two disorganised and depleted battalions 'fill the gap in the objective between the right flank of the 49th Battalion and the 12th Brigade' on the night of 8 June, was hopeful to say the least. The story of its eventual failure is barely mentioned in the battalion diaries and omitted entirely from the divisional diary. The diary of the 51st comes closest to an accurate narrative, stating that the intense barrage that fell on the men as they moved to their position of deployment inflicted heavy casualties, 'causing the troops to scatter, thus interfering with the operation which was only carried out as far as "A" and "C" Companies were concerned. "D" Company with only 30 men reached the position … but as no one came on their left they dug in just in rear. "B" Company were delayed by the shell fire and when they arrived on the jumping off mark they could not gain touch with either flank and returned to their original position'.[1] It was just as well that Glasgow had been unable to launch his attack. Had the 52nd and 51st set off that night into the Blauwepoortbeek, they would have met the same scything fire from the pillboxes that decimated the 49th and 45th battalions the previous day.

What really stymied the attempted attack on the night of 8 June was the artillery of the 25th Division which had ignored Godley's orders, issued on the evening of 7 June, that all shelling was to fall east of the Green Line. The English guns killed and wounded many men of the 52nd and 51st as they ran back, escaping German shelling which had broken out when they were observed trying to relocate from the 33rd Brigade's position. Holmes was understandably angry, the 4th Division diary recording that his brigadiers 'knew nothing' of the supposed 'retirement' of the 13th Brigade which prompted the shelling and adding that 'this readjustment had already been notified to all concerned as taking place that evening.' The Australians (and many of the English themselves) would record that some of the units of the 25th were 'jumpy' which led to the firing of SOS flares and the consequent shelling.[2] This prompted a further order from Godley at midnight on 8 June, far more imperative in tone, that barrages were not to be shortened 'under any circumstances whatever' without reference to II Anzac Headquarters. He also finally decided to deal directly with the confusion caused by independent units lined up behind one another by unifying command on each sector of the front line so that rear commanders could not shorten barrages. II Anzac also ordered the relief of the New Zealand Division which had suffered badly under the German artillery. The unfortunate New Zealanders, however, would have to wait a further 12 hours for this relief.

• • •

Monash's 9th and 10th brigades, which had carried the day in the south, were now due for a rest and, on the night of 8 June, he ordered his brigadiers to replace the front-line battalions with their reserves. With this order just issued, McNicoll then warned Monash that the 10th Brigade had suffered severely and would need to be entirely withdrawn. It had been a difficult day for the 10th Brigade commander, on the receiving end of peremptory messages from 3rd Division Headquarters concerning his brigade's exact position, and suffering the consequences of the 37th Battalion's retreat from the Green Line. McNicoll had been caught between an increasingly frustrated commander in Monash and an apparently inept and recalcitrant battalion commander in Smith.

At Monash's direction, McNicoll sent three direct messages to Smith on 8 June, directing the 37th to return to the Green Line which, Smith claimed, he passed to Story. Story received the orders but had difficulty contacting Mansbridge of the 44th to coordinate the movement. At this point Mansbridge was spiralling towards a nervous breakdown and Smith's complaint that Story was unable to secure any instructions from the 44th Battalion's commander is unsurprising.[3] Finally getting his men moving on the third attempt, Smith again complained that the 37th had received three contradictory messages from the brigade during the changeover. Smith added another complaint about McNicoll in the battalion diary: 'It was reported to me that, during the morning of 8th of June, D Coy 40th Battn. (attached) which was ahead 300 yards at the Green Line had been withdrawn from my command, no intimation whatsoever was received from Bde. HQ.'[4] There is little hint of this chaos in the 3rd Division's narrative of the 37th Battalion's role, although some sense of it can be gleaned from the statement that 'On the following night [8/9 June] the 37th Battalion again came up to relieve the 44th Battalion, and did in fact relieve it for about 10 minutes. The order for this relief was then cancelled and the 44th took over again.'[5] However the relief of the 10th Brigade by the 11th meant that the hard-pressed 9th Brigade would have to remain in the line. At 12.45 am on 9 June, the 9th's commander, Brigadier General Alexander Jobson, sent a message to the 33rd's Morshead, apologising that it would not be possible to relieve him until the following night. 'I know it will be a severe strain on you but it is not possible for me to do anything else. The 34th is now under 350 strong and the 35th about 370. The 11th relieve the 10th tonight as the latter has had heavy casualties.'[6] That relief would leave the 44th in place on the Green Line (where it supposed itself), although its actual position was still some way short of the junction at Huns' Walk with the 48th Battalion on its left. At 1.00 am on 9 June the 42nd Battalion was ordered forward to garrison the Black Line to the rear of the 44th Battalion and, in a sign that Monash was still uncertain of the position of the 44th, to 'clear up the situation between the Black and Green Lines'.[7] The 10th Brigade was in a sorry state. The 39th Battalion was hardly a battalion at all, having been shattered by the gas shelling on the morning of 7 June, and could collect only 88 men on the Black Line by 4.30 am that morning, losing more the next day. The 38th Battalion had suffered less on the march and attack and, while losing men to the increasingly accurate shellfire, had spent 7 and 8 June digging the Black Line trench. The 40th Battalion, which had been divided for the initial assault with one company attached to the 38th Battalion, sent 10 platoons forward to the Black Line. They set to work strengthening the Black Line but, by the early morning of 9 June, shelling (both from the enemy and their own guns) had reduced their numbers to a total of '70 or 80'.[8]

The 42nd, although fresh and close to full strength, was also entering a major battle for the first time. Moving through in the early morning darkness of 9 June, the men took up their positions at around 3.30 am and began digging and wiring, the battalion diary noting that 'Germans occupied the Green Line in front of us', an important detail which was omitted from the 3rd Division's diary. A huge 15-centimetre German gun was bombarding the Black Line at Schnitzel and Bethleem farms, but its fire had ceased by about 4.30 am when a solitary, low-flying German aircraft appeared at first light to spot for the artillery. It dived to within metres of the ground to strafe the men of the 42nd, firing along the trench as it went and receiving in return a fusillade of rifle and Lewis gun fire from the Australians which, apart from perforating its wings, had little noticeable effect. This aeroplane returned each dusk and dawn throughout their stay to direct the German guns. The 42nd's diarist complained that '[t]here was no interference with this by our aeroplanes'.[9] The frustration in the 42nd's report stemmed from the heavy shelling which the men endured over the next three days. Relieved by the 4th Brigade on the morning of 12 June, the 42nd had suffered over 200 casualties, an ordeal recalled with horror by Lieutenant Fisher:

> Since last writing I have had a terrible time … We had already repulsed several counter-attacks and with unceasing watch awaited what might befall … the enemy poured in a dreadful fire on us who were just behind the advancing lines. One platoon was wiped out – men blown to pieces, terrible to view, others buried and shell-shocked. To right and left, shell after shell coming over incessantly in streams, pouring upon our fragile lines, bringing death and wounds to great numbers. Men were blown up and killed all along – it is impossible to describe the scene. Morning broke to find us only 60% strength. Many were missing, probably buried. We never saw them again … The company was reduced to 58 men! … the stench from the dead was dreadful – many were in pieces and could not be identified – while the dead and unburied enemy in front of us added to the nauseous horror. We were all much shaken and gladly, very gladly, were relieved after 72 hours of hell.[10]

The 44th had remained in the line an extra day until its relief by the 43rd Battalion at 10.00 pm on the night of 10 June. By then it was clear that the 44th was still short of the Green Line on its left and two companies of the 43rd, having moved past the 44th's lines, pushed straight on a further 100 metres at 11.00 pm to attack Undulating Trench (on the Green Line), a task they completed by 12.30 am. The final section of the Green Line, a group of houses which marked the furthest eastward extent of the line on the left, remained untaken that night because both British and German artillery were falling on it. When the shelling ceased on the morning of 11 June, the Germans having withdrawn, a patrol of the 43rd scouted forward unopposed to the ruined houses where they made a gruesome discovery. 'A patrol from "A" Company found a large number of our dead belonging to 37th and 38th Battalions in these ruins. These men must have got out beyond our barrage on the first day of the battle and been unable to return.'[11] The crumpled bodies of the Australians on the Green Line were not only proof of the deadly inaccuracy of their artillery, but also vindicated Major Story's decision to withdraw his men from the area on the afternoon of 7 June, something Monash, despite his forensic inquiries after the battle, would fail to understand or forgive.

· · ·

To its left, the 4th Division was also struggling to capture the whole of the objective it had been given on 7 June. On the night of 9 June, the 12th Brigade tried to test the strength of the defences beyond the Green Line with the 47th attempting a probing advance eastwards toward Gapaard Farm, Les Quatre Rois Cabinets and Steignast Farm, only to meet strong resistance, its patrols suffering heavy casualties before being driven back to their trenches on the Green Line. Immediately to the left, the 48th and 45th battalions continued digging posts and inching towards the strongpoints in the Blauwepoortbeek Valley. This was part of a coordinating movement with the 13th Brigade which aimed to drive down from the north and link up with the 12th Brigade. Given the strength of the defences in the gap they were hoping to close, this was an exceptionally difficult task. On the afternoon of 9 June, Glasgow committed the last of his reserves to a final assault on the Green Line, ordering the 50th Battalion forward into the wide gap between the right of the 51st Battalion and the left of the 12th Brigade. Glasgow and Colonel Alfred Salisbury (commanding the 50th Battalion) decided to use stealth for the 13th Brigade's effort that night, to be launched at 10.30 pm, and dispensed with a preparatory artillery barrage, ordering the men to creep forward in silence in the darkness. The 50th could muster only 283 men for the attack, less than half its strength. A report from an English battery commander that the first objective (Odd Trench) was empty was apparently confirmed by a low-flying aircraft, but the 50th Battalion diary noted that these observations were made in daylight and it was not clear whether the Germans left it empty by day only to return in strength at nightfall. The 51st was well short of where the men reported themselves to be and the gap between the two brigades, between the right flank of the 49th Battalion and the left flank of the 45th Battalion, was also much greater than the 500 metres as calculated by the reported positions of those two battalions. The 51st believed it to be over 650 metres, but even this was well short as the actual distance was in excess of 1000 metres.[12] This error had grave implications and saw the 50th Battalion sent forward with both flanks wide open to enfilade fire and in danger of encirclement.

The 50th's attack on the night of 9 June was a calamitous failure. The men were spotted almost as soon as they crossed the start tapes and German flares illuminated them further. A German barrage crashed down behind them and started a fire which further lit up the battlefield. The machine-guns in the pillboxes opened up a deadly fusillade, supported by guns in nearby strongpoints in Deconinck and Delporte farms. The wire protecting the German positions was uncut and, now trapped between the wire and the barrage, the 50th Battalion disintegrated. The unusually honest and detailed account in the 50th's diary admitted: 'Our attack came to a standstill, some men dropping into shell holes in front of the wire, others where they came under the heavier machine gun fire scattering back to the jumping off line.'[13] One small group made it through the wire to shelter behind a concrete strongpoint only to be driven out of it by fire at daylight, suffering heavy casualties. The battalion history admitted that '[t]he absence of a barrage was very noticeable and a fair number of our boys faltered and laid in shell holes.'[14] At the southern end of the gap, the 45th (more accurately described by Bean as 'the remaining fragment' of the battalion), tried yet again to bomb northward in support of the 50th. This was always going to be an impossible task and, after a few harmless Stokes mortar shells were fired at the nearest pillbox, the men of the 45th again rose to bomb towards it when the machine-guns drove them to cover a few yards from their trench. Salisbury, believing that the 45th was bombing towards him from around 500 metres to the south, was unaware that the actual distance was almost twice that figure.

Small pillbox at Deconinck Farm in the Blauwepoortbeek Valley. This is one of a cluster of concrete strongpoints that tore the 45th Battalion apart on 7 June (author photo).

With the 13th Brigade due to be relieved by the 25th Division on the morning of 10 June, the gap in the Blauwepoortbeek had still not been closed and, as the sun rose with the 4th Division still engaged and still unsure of its exact position, the relief was postponed. Holmes and Glasgow, Bean would conclude in the *Official History*, 'were not content to hand over to the relieving brigade the task which for three nights had remained unfinished'.[15] The idea that tanks might be used to break the deadlock in the Blauwepoortbeek seems to have been considered late on the night of 7 June with II Anzac Headquarters sending word that tanks would be expected to cooperate if the attack on the Green Line was unsuccessful. B Battalion of the 2nd Brigade of the Tank Corps reported to its headquarters, 'I have told Anzac Corps that we require 6 hours notice and that we have 7 tanks that we can put into action.'[16] It was unlikely that such a suggestion found any supporters in the 4th Division, even though it may have averted some of what was to follow in the Blauwepoortbeek. Holmes' experience with the tanks at Bullecourt only six weeks earlier had been so utterly disastrous that it is unlikely the idea even came up for discussion. Even in the spring of 1918, the 48th Battalion would still look back in anger in its war diary: '… it is time these tanks were used for scrap iron for they are a mockery, delusion and a snare as far as we are concerned. It is noteworthy that on April 11th 1917, they failed us so badly also and it is to be hoped that there will be no chance of their doing so in April 1919.'[17] In any case, the six-hour turnaround time was hopeful to say the least since the Tank Corps' own post-battle estimation was 24 to 48 hours before a tank could re-enter a battle.

While the tanks which had accompanied the 45th and 47th on the afternoon of 7 June were of some assistance in silencing machine-gun nests and frightening German defenders into surrendering, they had turned around well before the infantry approached their final objective. In the morning the tanks had found the going difficult on the pulverised and occasionally waterlogged ground with many bottoming out ('bellied') and a number breaking down. Nevertheless, of the 24 tanks in action for the afternoon attack on the Green Line, 16 reached their objective and, given the firmer ground beyond the Black Line, were able to double their speed (from 10 yards a minute on heavily shelled ground to 20 yards a minute).[18] They had almost reached the limit of their endurance when they ventured beyond the Black Line and, after several hours in the cramped and hot interiors, so had their crews. Strengthening artillery fire was also a threat as were the field guns that were increasingly encountered as the extent of the advance lengthened. After five hours of operation, most were low on fuel and ammunition and those still running had to return to the safety of the old British front line.

Monash's predictions about the tanks in his brigade conferences had been very accurate. 'Tanks are very vulnerable when not in motion. As soon as the objective is captured, if a halt has to be made on the ground, tanks must seek some form of cover' (which was impossible on the exposed reverse slope of the ridge). 'Infantry must on no account wait for tanks. The machine is still imperfect.'[19] However, for the 4th Division, another improvised and adventurous experiment with the tanks was unthinkable, and would have represented a complete reversal of the pre-battle precaution that no aspect of the operation was to rely on the tanks. Despite the willingness and evident enthusiasm of the tank proponents, they would not be asked to assist by II Anzac.

Holmes personally inspected the battle front from a periscope at the 45th Battalion's barricade at dawn on 10 June, accompanied by Robertson, the Brigade Major (Joseph Lee), Captain Allen of the 45th and the artillery liaison officer. Herring remained at his battalion headquarters. Holmes, his vantage point some 40 yards from the nearest German pillbox, was able to see for himself the immense difficulty of the task. In addition to the strongly manned pillboxes, the Germans had stationed machine-guns in shell holes on the flanks, adding a further layer of defence to compensate for the limited vision and field of fire from within the blockhouses. It must also be presumed that, since he took the step of visiting the front line, he was aware, at least to some extent, of the weakened state of the 45th Battalion. Holmes ordered the artillery to bombard the blockhouses that day in preparation for a further assault once darkness fell and arranged with Glasgow for the 50th and the 52nd to again attempt an attack from the north. Following this the 45th would be relieved by the 48th Battalion. Still no-one counselled a halt.

Holmes was now determined to drive the Germans from the Blauwepoortbeek and capture the rest of the Green Line, but his division's fighting strength was rapidly diminishing. Nowhere was this more obvious than in the parlous state of the 45th Battalion. This battalion may have appeared as a functioning unit on maps at brigade and divisional headquarters but, by the evening of 10 June, it numbered less than a company under the sole surviving senior officer, Captain Allen.[20] With Herring doggedly fixed on the objective, apparently oblivious to his battalion's exhaustion and terrible losses, the 45th's tragedy played out its final, bloody act. Possession of the Blauwepoortbeek had ceased to make much sense to either side. For the Anzacs it meant closing a gap and marking a continuous line on a map. The section of the Green Line uncaptured in the Blauwepoortbeek was simply a destination point which held no great tactical value but to which all efforts were now directed to 'finish the job'. The German position in the valley was now a narrow salient, bounded on each side by high ground and rapidly becoming untenable as the flanks were pushed forward on either side. However the wider question of the wisdom of sacrificing the lives of their men in its capture was not, it seems, considered by the leadership of the 4th Division.

Lieutenant Colonel Sydney Herring who commanded the 45th Battalion at Messines. Herring's repeated, hopeless attacks on the pillboxes of the Blauwepoortbeek resulted in catastrophic losses for the 45th (AWM C04453).

Godley, had he perhaps been more inclined to make himself aware of the tactical situation in the Blauwepoortbeek, might have decided to call a halt, or at least pause the attacks, but without a direct request from Holmes, as unpalatable as that would have been, Godley was unlikely to act. No such request came and Godley remained aloof and removed where a more engaged commander might have intervened, or at the very least, questioned. Even the greatest commanders have been guilty of driving on when prudence demanded a pause, and Godley, not among their number, was doubly likely to do so. However his current preoccupation lay with his cavalry, and he busied himself with attempts to commit his small cavalry force, with little success. As Bean later wrote, 'The "Cavalry" patrols sent out last night established one post that we know of near Thatched Cottage … but no other news yet at 3rd Division. Godley altered the orders for the [Light] Horse about four times yesterday, giving them an entirely new objective the last time, after they had actually started out. This was sent through Monash by car to the C.O. who was found *en route* – but whether it ever reached the patrols is uncertain.'[21]

Men of the Anzac Mounted Corps await their call to battle. The objectives for the cavalry were completely unrealistic and the several attempts made by Godley to employ his cavalry predictably failed (AWM E00477).

At 10.00 pm on the night of 10 June, the 13th Brigade finally launched its assault on the northern flank of the gap in the Blauwepoortbeek, still in the erroneous belief that the depleted 45th, pushing up from the south, was only around 450 metres away. The stubborn resistance from the pillboxes showed no sign of slackening and every attempt by the bombers and riflemen of the 45th to surround and outflank them was defeated by sniping and machine-guns from the surrounding countryside. Attacks during daylight on 9 June had been suicidally brave and made in the hope that the Germans slept by day, but each one was met with a withering fusillade of fire and bombs. Allen had established a barricade on the northern extremity of the 45th's position in the Green Line and it was from this narrow corridor that any attack by the Australians would need to be mounted, a further difficulty.

The timing of the night attack at 10.00 pm, despite the fact that it was not completely dark, betrayed Holmes' haste. Likewise, the 13th Brigade's preparations were disrupted when its tape-laying was observed and fired on, fully alerting the Germans to the coming attack. That this was an obvious mistake was apparent to Salisbury who pointed it out with bewildered frustration in the 50th Battalion's diary.[22] The artillery bombardment during the day had at least cut some paths through the wire even if the shells, where they managed a lucky direct hit, burst harmlessly on the reinforced concrete of the pillboxes. The 13th Brigade's attack was again plagued by errors, with some members of the 50th losing their way and starting from the wrong tape line and half of the 52nd arriving late and just forming up when the attack commenced, to be subsequently caught by the defensive German shelling. The 50th made some progress on the left, but the 52nd failed, intact wire and determined German bombing barring its way. Corporal Henry Butler wrote of the death of the young Lieutenant Clyde Pearce: 'We were on our way over, and he got caught in the wire; he was killed outright - 6 or so bullets right through him … We lost a terrible lot then owing to the wire not being properly cut.'[23]

The fighting continued all night, a desperate crawling attack from shell hole to shell hole by the Australians of the 13th Brigade as they edged towards and into Odd Trench, the first objective on 7 June. The darkness above their heads was alive with the hum of bullets and the regular concussive thump of bombs and rifle grenades marked the course of fighting for shell holes and sections of trench. Flares fired from pillboxes and the strongpoints at Delporte and Deconinck farms lit up the battlefield, keeping the Australians close to the ground. As they edged closer, many of the German defenders fled and the 50th gradually prised the Germans out of the first of their lines. Despite the enormous difficulties they faced, the men of the 50th pushed on into Odd Trench and the very detailed account in the 50th Battalion diary described a bold and effective attack. 'The enemy bombed our men while getting through the wire but our bombers and the odd rifle grenadier … engaged the enemy while small parties of bayonet men worked through. When these parties charged, the remaining Germans dropped their rifles and bolted.'[24] The men of the 52nd, having failed to make any headway with their frontal assault, moved to their left into the portions of the Odd Trench captured by the 50th and combined with them to work their way south to where they believed they would soon link up with the 12th Brigade's attack. At 1.00 am the 50th sent a message to the 12th Brigade suggesting that they must by now be close to linking up. However, no-one in command was certain of the exact width of the gap between the two brigades, Salisbury's estimation of 500 yards widely at odds with Robertson who believed it to be around 1500.[25]

Detail of the reinforced concrete which made the German pillboxes safe from all but the heaviest shellfire (author photo).

213

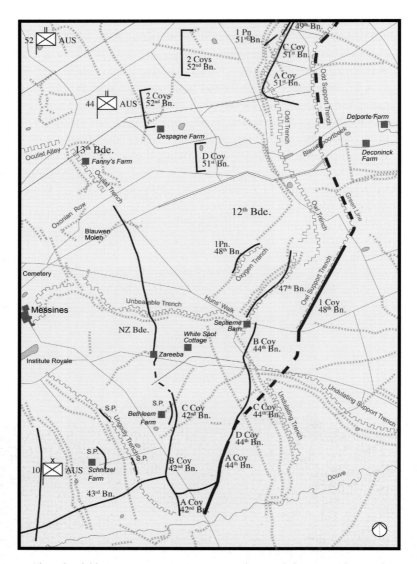

Map 17. The 3rd and 4th Division positions 8–9 June. Based on aerial observation, the map shows the results of the chaotic and failed Anzac assault on the Green Line on 7 June. Only in the southern extremity of the 3rd Division's line is the Green Line held, along with a small portion in the centre held by a company of the 48th Battalion. The yawning gap at the head of the Blauwepoortbeek Valley extends for almost a kilometre and the scattered fragments of the 13th Brigade's battalions have dug in well short of their objective. The 44th Battalion is still short of the Green Line although the men of the 44th believed they held it.

There is an air of unreality about the narrative in the 12th Brigade war diary that described the 45th Battalion's attack in the fading daylight of 10 June. 'At 19.30 p.m. two parties of 25 men each were told off from 45th Battalion to attack the enemy strongpoints.'[26] Despite the fact that they were down to last of their strength and despite a series of costly and failed attempts over the previous days to capture these strongpoints, Herring had managed to bypass Allen who had front-line command and send orders through directly by telephone to Lieutenant Thomas McIntyre, then with his platoon down to 15 men, to again attempt to storm the southernmost blockhouse which barred the way. By now, what passed for the 45th Battalion was a handful of exhausted and wounded men, long past the point where they should have been relieved. Inexplicably, the 45th was kept in the line even when the two companies of the 48th which had been attached were withdrawn on the previous night. Plainly impossible though it was, Herring's order was answered by McIntyre. 'All right Sir; if it is to be taken, it will be taken.'[27] Rising over the parapet under the glow of German flares, McIntyre and his party raced to within five yards of the pillbox before he and four others were cut down. Sergeant Alfred Stevenson was hit by an Australian grenade.

The pillbox which held up the 45th Battalion for two bloody days in Owl Trench. This was the fortress which Lieutenant Colonel Herring ordered Lieutenant McIntyre and his men to capture on 10 June, an impossible task which cost their lives (AWM E01366).

With this last gallant but futile sacrifice, the 45th was utterly spent. 'This attack was unsuccessful' noted the brigade diary, 'the officer in command being killed and the attacking party suffering considerable casualties from intense enemy machine gun fire.'[28] Bean was only obliquely critical of Herring in the *Official History*, with the observation that Captain Allen, then in charge of the 45th in the front line 'himself would not have ordered the assault', but the virtual annihilation of his battalion was the result of Herring's implacable determination to send men forward in repeated and increasingly futile assaults against the heavily defended pillboxes.[29] The battalion diary claimed, improbably, that the failure of the artillery rather than the impossibility of the task was to blame, and the strength of McIntyre's party was exaggerated three-fold to 50 men, an overstatement which cloaks this unfortunate order in an entirely undeserved veneer of reason.

• • •

On that same night, Monash's 3rd Division would attempt to push out its southernmost line to capture the trenches around La Potterie Farm. The 9th Brigade's 34th and 35th battalions had been relieved by the fresh 36th Battalion on the night of 9/10 June and the men spent the daylight of 10 June establishing themselves on the Green Line in preparation for their attack which they were due to launch at 11.00 pm. The fighting raging in the Blauwepoortbeek to the north had stirred up the German artillery which was raining down across the front of both Australian divisions. In another error which is both difficult to explain and excuse, Monash's attack on the La Potterie system and into the angle of the Lys was timed to commence a full two hours after the 4th Division's scheduled attack at 9.00 pm at a time when the retaliatory German bombardment would have eased (so Monash believed). Instead, II Anzac arranged for Holmes to attack at 10.00 pm without informing Monash and the result was that the 36th Battalion advanced into a storm of German artillery fire. Bean committed a question to his notebook at the time: '… why didn't Corps pre-arrange this?' which he was still unable to answer in 1932 when Volume IV was published.[30] Coordination was not the only problem. II Anzac's heavy artillery bombarded La Potterie from 5.00 pm until 6.00 pm, or at least it supposed it did. Their shooting was, according to Bean, 'extraordinarily erratic':

> North of the Douve shells from some of the "heavies" fell among the troops holding the captured part of the Oosttaverne Line; south of it they fell on the posts 250 yards short of that line, and even on the Black

Line, 500 yards behind the front. In the northern post of the 36th they shattered a Lewis Gun team.[31]

'And we are still living' wrote Private George Davies of the 36th Battalion as he and his comrades hung on, hoping. 'Shells burst all around us, guns roar with fearful bellowing, like the noise of a million lions roaring at the one time.'[32] Despite the confusion caused by the barrage, both the 43rd and 36th moved forward, the former relieving the 44th on the left flank and moving out to the Green Line and the 36th attacking the trenches in La Potterie. Resistance was weak, many of the Germans fleeing ahead of the creeping barrage that Lieutenant Colonel John Milne described as 'perfect'. As they did so, the 36th's Lewis guns 'did great execution' and stormed the farm buildings which were 'found strongly occupied by both Guards and Bavarians who ... proved no match for our men.'[33] The *1st Guards Reserve Infantry Regiment* which held La Potterie itself 'came out from the North evidently to offer resistance but were caught under our Lewis gun fire from the parapet of Uncertain Trench and practically annihilated.'[34] The prisoners taken in this fighting were interrogated in the morning by the 3rd Division's intelligence officers and revealed that the Germans were withdrawing to the Warneton Line, some 1200 yards further back, and that their own unit should have already retired that night but was caught by the 3rd Division's attack. The 4th Division also reported seeing the Germans abandoning their pillboxes and falling back from the Blauwepoortbeek at first light. In fact, what they witnessed was the retirement of the rearguards, the general withdrawal having taken place during the night of 10 June. The position had never really been tenable and, since the realisation that the ridge was irretrievably lost on the night of 7 June, the German commander, Crown Prince Rupprecht, had been fighting a holding battle while looking for a secure line in the rear. Fate had dealt the 4th Division another hard blow as the Blauwepoortbeek was given up without a fight. The repeated attacks on the pillboxes and wire that had cost so dearly in Australian lives had been needless.

As the morning of 11 June dawned, II Anzac Corps was now finally in control of the lines it had hoped to capture on 7 June. The fighting continued with only marginally less intensity. The 4th Brigade had moved to occupy the 4th Division's posts. Sergeant William Boyes of the 14th Battalion recalled, '... we moved forward over the country taken by the N.Z. and 3rd Division [sic] ... and occupied an old Hun trench ... and that night there was a heavy and continuous bombardment. I can remember Capt. Jacka saying to me "this is as bad as Pozières."'[35] The German shelling of Messines and the positions around the Green Line continued its dangerous pattern and patrols pushed out by both Australian divisions were still fired on by German rearguards and snipers. German aircraft were overhead in ever-increasing numbers and the shelling became more accurate and intense as a result. The New Zealand Division, which had been withdrawn on the evening of 9 June, had suffered over 5000 casualties and, late on 11 June, the 4th Brigade extended its front to the Douve River. Monash's 9th Brigade continued its digging and consolidation on the southern flank until, exhausted, it was finally relieved by the 4th New Zealand Brigade on 12 June.

That the AIF's 4th Brigade was in action at all was remarkable as it had been all but annihilated at Bullecourt six weeks earlier, less than a quarter of its number surviving the battle, and the losses had been made up by reinforcements fresh from Australia. Perhaps for that reason, Lieutenant Colonel Albert Jacka, VC, commanding the 14th Battalion and a famous figure in the AIF as the first Australian to win the VC in the war, was hesitant about taking over the advanced posts of the 52nd Battalion near Delporte and Deconinck farms. Bean's narrative of the incident in his notebook is undoubtedly influenced by his unqualified admiration for Captain Arthur Maxwell, as well as the freedom to privately entertain opinions he could later disown, but his sullying of Jacka's character is nevertheless a fascinating footnote to the story of Messines:

> When Jacka relieved [Arthur Maxwell] and he asked Jacka to take over the posts there, Jacka said they were too far from his supports and wouldn't do it. Arthur reported to Salisbury [*acting commander of the 52nd Battalion*] and Salisbury told Jacka he wouldn't accept the relief until the posts were taken over. Arthur asked Jacka to come with him to the place but Jacka stopped with the patrol part of the way out. Arthur called for volunteers and two of Jacka's men came with him to Delporte. They took Jacka then to Delporte and Arthur went right down to the road and bombed a cement place there. Jacka took over and at once reported that he had captured Delporte Farm and that he considered posts might well be pushed down to the road. For this, he and 14 Battalion are at once being given the credit. As a matter of fact, Arthur Maxwell and 52 Battalion did this ... Jacka is the sort of chap who would probably hang back while Arthur was there in order to get the credit for himself and 14 Battalion by going out later.[36]

Early on 11 June, Godley was still attempting to find some role for his cavalry and, at 10.15 am, II Anzac Mounted Regiment was ordered to have at least six patrols ready to move out. The patrols were kept in readiness all day until 4.00 pm when they were transferred to Monash's command. Major William Dunlop and the Mounted Regiment command group were given Godley's car to drive to

Monash's headquarters at Steenwerck to discuss the plan which Dunlop admitted was 'mad', requiring the cavalry to capture and hold a line of farms in advance of the 3rd Division's front line and then assault the sugar refinery on the River Lys. Five days later, Dunlop noted 'the whole of New Zealand Division were put at lesser objectives'.[37] Fortunately the plan of attack, completely detached from reality, was not attempted. That didn't stop Godley imagining that his horsemen were somewhere doing something useful. On 12 June Dunlop, who was trying to snatch some sleep, was 'disturbed all day as 2nd Anzac Corps were properly mad because we could not give them much and frequent information. The fact of the matter was that the Infantry behind our Posts would not let our runners through either way on account of drawing shell fire.'[38] With Monash's men on the Green Line hanging on under heavy shellfire and the forward troops unable to raise their heads above the shell holes and shallow trenches due to accurate sniping and machine-gun fire, the notion of men on horseback achieving anything was nonsensical. By 3.00 pm the regiment's senior officers 'departed to harangue Corps' about the impracticality of their orders and absurdity of their expectations and, as a result, were ordered to return to their billets. Dunlop recorded that, on the way back, they ran into Bean, a conversation that no doubt led the latter to commit his thoughts about the 'pure eyewash' of the idea that mounted cavalry could be of any use in the battle whatsoever.

Lieutenant Colonel Albert Jacka posing for a photograph at the Romarin terrain model. Jacka's battalion was in reserve for the attack and the posturing with the map was largely for the benefit of the camera. Bean's private criticism of the famous Australian revealed his dislike for display and self-promotion (AWM E00631).

Five days of bitter fighting had taken its toll on Godley's corps. Lieutenant Christian Nommensen of the 47th Battalion manned the trenches around Derry House, which the 25th Division had captured after some hard fighting. He was critical of the English: 'The Tommies never even take the trouble to bury their dead … Hundreds of theirs still lie on the field, with our small posts we could not find time to see to them.'[39] The 25th Division, to which those men had belonged, noted the problem in its post-operation report: 'The magnitude of the work involved in clearing the battlefield both as regards salvage and burial of the dead, does not yet seem to be realised.'[40] The report further complained that only 50 men under a burial officer had been allocated to this job, and that these men were not employed in the forward areas, so that 'the greater task of burial still devolves on working parties from the fighting troops, a task which might perhaps be more usefully assigned to others.'[41] This was another way of admitting that it was often not done at all. Nommensen, whose own body would be lost after his death at Dernancourt in 1918, was comforted by the care the Australians took to find and bury their comrades. '[I]t may have been pretty hot at times but our people would send up [men] from reserve to carry ours back.'[42]

As the Australians dug their outposts in front of their most forward trenches on the Green Line, the salvage and burial parties were scouring the abandoned battlefield to collect the bodies of their men and lay them in crumpled rows for the burials to follow. On 14 June, four days after the 45th Battalion's final assault on the pillboxes in the Blauwepoortbeek, 23-year-old Sergeant Alfred Stevenson, who had gone forward so bravely with Lieutenant McIntyre to almost certain death, was found alive, but gravely wounded, by a salvage party from the 48th Battalion. He died within hours of rescue. According to one who was with him before that fateful last assault, 'He knew before he went that he was to be killed and he left all his things behind and said what was to be done with them.'[43]

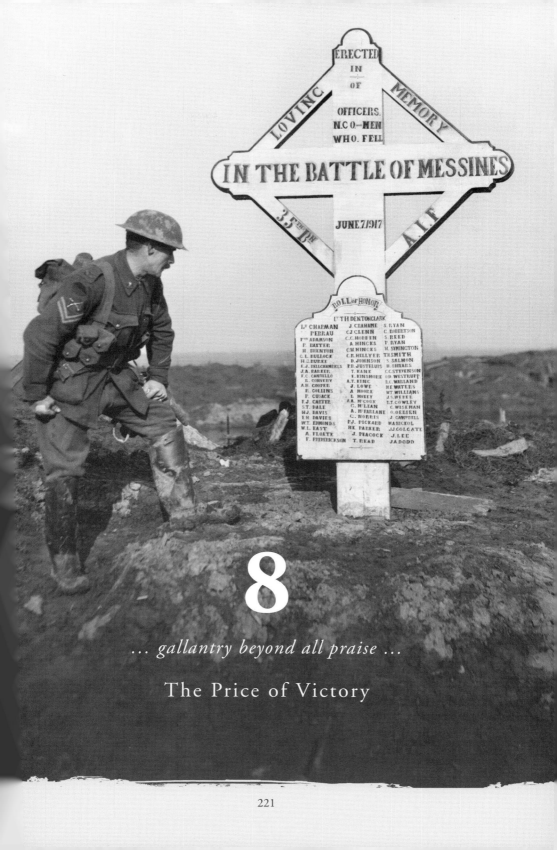

ERECTED
IN
OF
OFFICERS.
N.C.O.—MEN
WHO. FELL

LOVING MEMORY

IN THE BATTLE OF MESSINES

35TH B...   A.I.F.

JUNE 7/1917

ROLL of HONOR

I'TH DENTONCLARK

L⁺ CHAPMAN	J. CRAHAME	S. RYAN
PERRAU	C.J. CLENN	C. ROBERTSON
F⁰ᵗ ADAMSON	C.C. HODDEN	S. REED
F. BAXTER	A. HINCKS	P. RYAN
H. BUENTON	C.M. HINCKS	M. SYMINGTON
G.E. BULLOCK	C.R. HILLYER	T.R.SMITH
H.J. BURKE	D. JOHNSON	S. SALMON
F.J. BELCHAMBERS	P.D. JUSTELUIS	H. SHEARS
J.A. BARKER	T. KANE	C.C. STIVERSON
F.C. CANTELLO	K. KINSMORE	O.D. WESTRUPP
E. CONVERY	A.T. KING	E.C. WARLAND
A.H. COOPER	J. LOWE	H.E. WATERS
H. COLLINS	A. MOORE	W.T. WILLIAMS
P. CUSACK	L. MOXEY	J.S. WEBB
F.J. CARTER	A.A. M⁺COOX	R.T. COWLEY
S.T. DALE	C. M⁺LEAN	C. WISEMAN
H.J. DAVIS	A. M⁺FARLANE	O. O'BRIEN
T.H. DAVIES	C. NORRIS	J. CAMPBELL
W.T. EDMONDS	P.J. PICKARD	W.A. NICKOL
W.L. EAST	H.E. PARKER	J.J. COLGATE
A. FLOATE	J. PEACOCK	J. LEE
V. FREDRICKSON	T. READ	J.A. DODD

8

... gallantry beyond all praise ...

The Price of Victory

8

… gallantry beyond all praise …

The Price of Victory

Haig's post-battle summary, written on 9 June, clearly articulated the reasons for the success: '[G]ood staff arrangements, efficient counter battery work and the fact that the divisions who assaulted had been on the front for a long period and knew their sectors well and had ample time for training and rehearsing their parts in the assault.'[1] Unfortunately, as he wrote, the 4th Australian Division, which had not had ample time for training and rehearsing, was still engaged in a bitter struggle ahead of its lines. Haig visited the 25th Division headquarters that very day and spoke to Bainbridge and his staff. Noting in his diary that Brigadier General Douglas Baird had done well and (incorrectly) that his 75th Brigade had taken the Green Line, Haig also wrote that Baird had told Bainbridge that 'detachments of the 4th Australian Division had been wandering about in his vicinity as if they had "no leaders!"'[2] Haig responded in mitigation that the 4th Division 'was at Bullecourt and lost many officers', but Baird's wholly unjust and inaccurate statements went otherwise unchallenged. Baird was an intimate of Haig's, his former aide-de-camp (ADC), whom he referred to affectionately in his diary as 'Our Captain'. Baird had a second meeting with Haig on 11 June when he again took the opportunity to reinforce his scathing judgement of the Australians. Haig noted that Baird 'was much down upon the 4th Australian Division for their conduct on the night of the 7th and the morning of the 8th.'[3]

Baird wasn't the only staff officer of the 25th Division to complain about the Australians. Walter Guinness, Brigade Major for the 74th Brigade, wrote that the 4th Division 'did not get their final objective but spent their time in the first looking for souvenirs. Though fine men individually they have no cohesion, discipline or organisation, and are in these respects far behind the New Zealanders.'[4] The 25th was awash with ill-informed judgements and gossip about what was happening in the Australian lines in front, and the adverse and often completely inaccurate accounts in the 25th's brigade and divisional diaries merely confirmed Guinness's prejudices. His own views of Australians had been formed two years earlier at Gallipoli and nothing he had seen or heard since had improved them. Brigadier General Bethell of the 25th, who had occupied his time during the attack reading Shakespeare in his dugout, concluded the 74th Brigade's after-battle report with words of wisdom aimed directly at the Australians. 'The supreme importance of good discipline was brought out in the clearest possible light. Individual valour without discipline is entirely useless.'[5]

Private John 'Barney' Hines, the 'Souvenir King' of the 45th Battalion. A famous image of the war, it is often used to represent the larrikin and resourceful Australian. At Messines, the British of the 25th Division would complain that the Australians did not reach their objective because they spent their time 'looking for souvenirs'. The sight of Hines plying his trade behind the lines would have done little to refute the charge (AWM E00822).

It can be safely assumed that the low opinion of the Australians that Bean referred to in the 25th Division prior to the battle had sunk even lower after Messines and was certainly communicated, with some vehemence, directly to Haig himself. If, as a consequence, Haig doubted the fighting quality of the Australians however, he did not commit such doubts to his diary and the successful battles of August and September that year, in which the Australians played such a crucial role, suggested they carried little weight. Few in the command group of the 25th Division understood or wished to understand the difficulties the ill-starred 4th Division had faced over the four days of its ordeal at Messines. Plumer's decision to delay the attack on the Green Line on the afternoon of 7 June when the 4th Division had already topped the ridge had trapped the Australians in full view of the German guns and they suffered heavy casualties as a result. The difficulty the delay was intended to remedy, the late and disorganised arrival of the 33rd Brigade on II Anzac's left flank, which was left open as a result, was another blow to the 4th Division and a factor which contributed to the disruption and fracturing of the 13th Brigade's assault. Perhaps the greatest difficulty for the 4th Division was the exceptionally strong defences, numerous pillboxes and intact wire in the Blauwepoortbeek Valley, major obstacles which had not been fully identified and anticipated by either the Second Army or II Anzac Corps intelligence. These brought the advance by the 49th and 45th battalions to a bloody halt and inflicted heavy losses. The officers who bravely tried to rally their men, pinned down by machine-gun fire and blasted by field guns, were spotted and cut down by snipers while leading hopeless attacks. The precaution that officers dress as privates was a prudent one, but many, like Captain John Millar of the 47th Battalion, undid that guise by arming themselves with revolvers and carrying a lighter load.

The high casualty rate among the officers had a disastrous impact on cohesion and direction. The 49th Battalion lost all but two officers on the afternoon of 7 June and the battalion's catastrophic decapitation effectively doomed its attack from that moment. If any more ill-luck was needed to disrupt the 4th Division's assault on the Green Line, it came in the late afternoon with the shelling by its own artillery which drove back most of the troops who had successfully fought their way through and established themselves on their final objectives. The British artillery, struggling to cope with the distance and advanced lines of fire over the slope, had been erratic and deadly all afternoon, but the deluge of fire on the newly won Green Line across almost the entire front of II Anzac (and beyond to the north) was a monumental mistake which almost changed the course of the battle. Only the German failure to exploit it saved the Second Army from a serious reverse. It is clear that Godley tried repeatedly to deal with this once he became aware of it. It is also clear that he failed, but nowhere in the after-action reports is there any criticism of or serious inquiry into the short shooting.

Likewise, allowing two independent commands to operate one behind the other on the ridge, which was the direct cause of many of the artillery problems, was a grave error. Plumer's biographer, like many who have written on Messines, was inclined to forgive the General for this blunder. 'It was the one serious and avoidable error in what had been an expertly planned battle, and it was a costly one, not corrected until the 9th of June. After years of static fighting, the staffs were unpractised in rapid organisation and redeployment.'[6] This was an overly generous assessment given that it took two full days for the problem to be understood and partially remedied. Plumer, in turn, was liberal with his praise for the gunners on 7 June and just as willing to overlook their errors. In a message to his heavy artillery chief, he wrote: 'the success gained today, with comparatively little loss, is entirely due to the hard work and good shooting of the artillery.'[7] Such a glowing tribute, though certainly deserved for the gunners' contribution to the victory, smothered any tendency to question their performance at all. The chief victim of this failing was, yet again, the unfortunate 4th Division.

Most of the Australian battalions paid a heavy price at Messines. Corporal George Holliday of the 35th Battalion inspects the memorial cross erected near Ash Crater in memory of the men of the 35th killed at Messines (AWM E01649).

What is remarkable is that the problems of artillery coordination, which must be counted among the few serious failings of Messines, appear not to have been noted or addressed by an army desperately keen to absorb every lesson, no matter how minor. The pamphlet circulated after the battle by the General Staff down to the level of regiments, batteries and battalions, makes no mention of the issue despite its dealing with the minutiae of operations. Under 'Liaison (a) *Artillery and Infantry*' there is nothing to suggest anything was amiss, the pamphlet simply stating that '[t]he principle which was observed of having Senior Artillery Officers for Liaison proved good and gave the infantry confidence.'[8] The only recommendation was that liaison officers should, where possible, join their attached formation some days before the operation so that 'plans may receive the fullest discussion and co-ordination'.[9] This was despite the fact that, in II Anzac Corps, it required the personal, repeated and urgent interventions of the corps commander himself to save his men from their own side's artillery. Under 'SOS Barrage', two brief paragraphs mention only the desirability of depth and that they succeeded in destroying the half-hearted counter-attack from the Warneton Line on the afternoon of 7 June, the only serious attempt by the Germans to regain the ridge.[10] There is no doubt that the Germans were aware of the British artillery problems. A document captured from the *XV Bavarian Reserve Corps* in January 1917 noted that, in attack, '[t] he enemy's artillery does not know exactly where its own infantry is, and is therefore obliged to exercise caution.'[11]

Although Godley and his II Anzac staff, despite their frequent and unsuccessful attempts to correct the short shooting of their artillery, hardly mentioned the problems in their after-battle reports, the issue was noted by IX Corps. 'There is a tendency to place the S.O.S. Barrage too close to our own infantry … the S.O.S. Barrage should be placed at least 500 yards beyond the final objective … The old system of having F.O.O.s [forward observation officers] was tried, but owing to the dust and smoke, the observers could see nothing of the fight.'[12] While IX Corps at least acknowledged the problem, its after-battle report indicated the difficulty, and perhaps the reluctance, to deal with it and, of course, where they considered the blame really lay for any infantry casualties:

> The question of short shooting has, owing to numerous reports received during the action and the subsequent consolidation period, became a matter requiring serious attention. During the action, frequent requests were sent by both Infantry Officers and by junior Artillery Liaison Officers for the barrage to lift for the reason that it was causing casualties to our own Infantry. It should be generally understood, that the Artillery Barrage

follows a fixed program of fire and that the Infantry must conform to the movement of the Barrage ... no interference with the fixed programme of the barrage is permitted, and no rectification – should it require rectification at any particular point – is possible during that period.[13]

The remedy suggested in the IX Corps report required the impossible from men trying to survive under their own artillery fire:

If guns are shooting continually short, with reference to the main barrage, the fact should be reported in a message which should contain the following information: - Number of guns shooting short, nature of shell, location of bursts, time observed ... Such messages however as "Lift Artillery Barrage on right of ... Battalion" "Barrage falling short and causing casualties" as generally happened during the recent operation, neither time nor detail as to the extent of the short shooting, are useless as far as possible action to be taken on receipt of such messages are concerned.[14]

Having recommended the impossible, the CRA of IX Corps then virtually dismissed the complaints. 'I am confident that much short shooting which is reported is attributable to the difficulty of differentiating between enemy shell and our own.'[15] The front-line infantry commanders understandably had a different view, having seen their men blown to pieces by their own artillery. A British officer captured in July and interrogated by the Germans complained that 'We reach our objective – and then command breaks down. Artillery fire is not lifted, but kills our own people.'[16]

• • •

Similar inquiries were underway in the 3rd Division. Though thoroughly pleased with his division's part in the victory, there had been problems and Monash reported to Godley (on 15 June) that the 37th had failed to reach its objective and had fallen back from the Green Line 'without sufficient reason', a failure he attributed to Smith's 'lack of leadership, driving power and energy'. McNicoll, in his report to Monash, claimed that the 37th retreated 'because the troops on their left fell back. There is no evidence of a counter attack being made on the Brigade section.'[17] Both McNicoll and Monash failed to mention the short shelling which had virtually cleared the Green Line across II Anzac's front and which was the prime reason Story withdrew the 37th. Moreover, McNicoll claimed that he had been unable to push the 37th back to the Green

Line where it belonged. 'I sent a definite order' wrote McNicoll, '… at 8.35 a.m. on the morning of the 8th for the 37th to co-operate with the 44th Battalion in securing the Green Line. This order was not obeyed.' He went on to send a second and a third order to the same effect. 'Lieutenant-Colonel Smith … states that there was no doubt in his mind as to the meaning of my orders and yet he contented himself with repeating them from his battalion headquarters at Advanced Estaminet over the wire to Major Story at the Black Line and even after receiving a second order did not succeed in carrying it out.'[18]

Monash interviewed Smith after the battle — an interview that saw him 'mercilessly grilled and sacked'. The record of interview in Monash's files indicates that Smith was confused about the position of his battalion, unable to exercise control and unwilling to venture out of his headquarters. Monash's biographer would concede that 'doubts remain about the justice' of Smith's treatment, perhaps with good reason.[19] Monash himself had failed to have orders enacted and he too was rooted in his headquarters at the end of a phone line. It was true that Smith had not gone forward to ensure his orders were followed or discover the reason for Story's inertia, but neither had Monash. The contrast with Holmes who, facing a similar problem, had sought out his brigadiers and brought them with him onto the battlefield to talk directly with battalion commanders, could not have been starker. On 9 June Holmes went all the way forward to the 45th Battalion's front trenches to view for himself the tactical problems facing his men. Despite repeated attempts from Monash's headquarters to sort out the confusion with the 44th's dispositions and despite the fact that he sent his Chief Intelligence Officer forward to do this on his behalf, the problems with the 44th remained unresolved for three days and Monash was unable to address them.

The lack of candour over the reason for the 37th's withdrawal was also more than an oversight in Monash's report to Godley. Story hardly endeared himself to Monash by complaining in writing directly to Godley about what he considered an injustice both to himself and his men. Despite his seniority, Story would be passed over for the vacant command of the 37th (although it would eventually be his in 1918) because his performance at Messines had been, according to Monash, 'less than satisfactory'.[20] The 10-minute relief of the 44th by the 37th before the latter was unceremoniously sent to the rear dealt a demoralising, if unintended, blow to its unit pride. Added to this was Monash's unfair charge that the 37th was the only battalion which failed to achieve its objective at Messines. The men of the 37th Battalion would neither forgive nor forget Monash's treatment of them at Messines.

Monash received a similarly scathing post-battle report on Mansbridge from McNicoll which, apart from clearly suggesting that the 44th's commander had abandoned his men in a panic and fled back to a secure headquarters which he shared with the 37th's commander, also provides some insight into the chaos in command and communication which infected parts of the 3rd Division during the battle. Mansbridge, McNicoll claimed, 'was absolutely out of touch with the doings of his battalion' and he was similarly out of touch with McNicoll who 'had great trouble in having my orders carried out'.[21] Mansbridge denied every charge, claiming no knowledge of the alarming messages and maintaining that he was on the Black Line at all times except for a brief trip to Advanced Estaminet (the 37th's headquarters) to contact brigade. He conceded there were communication difficulties and that he was forced to relocate being 'shelled out of four shell holes in my endeavours to be as close as possible to my command,' adding with some justification, 'and these difficulties do not appear to be appreciated.'[22] Mansbridge was quietly moved aside later that month, as was Jobson who commanded the 9th Brigade at Messines, and whose deterioration and breakdown after the battle was embarrassingly evident at a divisional conference.

Monash's rigorous inquiries into failures following the 3rd Division's otherwise successful operation were conspicuously absent in the 4th Division, despite Holmes having far more reason to inquire. The 4th's battle had been chaotic and costly. While the lethal inaccuracy of the artillery had seen the Green Line abandoned in the 12th Brigade's sector, the 13th Brigade had largely failed to even reach it on 7 June. There was no inquiry into the yawning gap that had opened between the 12th and 13th brigades (and that between the 49th and 52nd battalions on the left) nor the numerous failed assaults of the following days and the delay in achieving the division's objectives. The narratives in the battalion and brigade diaries chart the course of those failures and the various reasons for them postulated by individual battalions, but the much larger and more important task of inquiry at the divisional level was not performed. The 4th Division's staff work, plainly inadequate at Bullecourt and under pressure with limited time to prepare, improved little at Messines.[23]

Clearly the most obvious failure was Pope's, as he had failed to communicate Holmes' vital order that the 52nd should refuse its left flank in the event of the late arrival of the 33rd Brigade. Unaware of that order, Maxwell instead took his men across to the left in search of the English. His actions radically shifted the 52nd Battalion's direction of attack, pulled the entire brigade out of position, split the division in two and opened the gap in the Blauwepoortbeek which was to cause so much difficulty over the following days. Adherence to first principles is particularly important for the inexperienced, but Maxwell, a veteran of Gallipoli and the Western Front, was hardly short of experience and must bear some responsibility for the mistake. A far more serious failing however, was that no inquiry was conducted into what had caused the problem in the first place. It was simply ignored. There could be no clearer contrast in the methods of the two Australian divisional commanders at Messines. Monash, with his engineer's mind, put the same energy and doggedness into investigating a unit's failure as he would a bridge collapse, and for the same reason. The 4th Division, battle scarred, poorly served by higher command and numbed to terrible casualties, took the chaos and inevitable errors in its stride and moved on unquestioning.

Many questions remained, however. Just why the exhausted survivors of the 45th Battalion were kept in the line to attempt again and again the most difficult task on the ridge is one of the many enduring mysteries of Messines. The unit diaries are silent on this decision, as are the battalion histories and the memoirs of the main actors. Bean's account for the *Official History* was sympathetic to the unfolding tragedy of the 45th in its portrayal of the ordeal the men faced, but he left his readers to decide who was responsible:

> The 45th had again, as ordered, launched a bomb attack, but its officers on the spot knew that the effort was hopeless. The artillery fired, but had not hit the impeding blockhouse. Even on the previous night the men had been so tired that they fell asleep as they dug the trench; a man would put in his shovel, fall asleep, and have to be shaken before he could drag it out. Captain Allen himself would not have ordered the assault. But when Colonel Herring during the afternoon telephoned to Lieutenant McIntyre, who had already led three attempts and told him that this strong point must be taken, he knew it was his death warrant.[24]

Masterly though Bean's account of the battle is, the failures of command by Herring and upwards to Robertson and Holmes passed into the *Official History* without examination or censure. It is difficult to believe that Holmes, his brigadier and, principally, the 45th's commander, were not aware both of the weakened and exhausted state of the battalion and the immense difficulty of the task they expected it to undertake. Holmes himself had personally inspected the line and seen with his own eyes the pillbox Herring ordered McIntyre to capture. Equally difficult to understand is the decision not to relieve the 45th on the night of 8 June at the latest and yet send back the two companies of the 48th which had been brought forward on the night of 7 June. While the

46th Battalion had suffered some casualties as the carrying battalion, it was still relatively fresh and strong. In a war infamous for lethal tactical miscalculations, the decision to commit the men of the 45th to attack the pillboxes of the Blauwepoortbeek, after numerous attempts had failed with heavy losses, must surely rank high among them. Bean chose to lament rather than criticise the sacrifice of the 45th Battalion. 'It had entered the battle in greater strength than any other Australian battalion' he wrote, 'and came out the weakest, having lost 16 officers and 552 men.'[25] His words were a sad coda to the story of the 45th Battalion at Messines, a tragedy somehow lost on the author of the battalion diary who, oblivious to irony, ended the narrative of the battle with wholly incongruous praise for the willingness of Herring's men to mount the repeated and ruinous attacks he ordered. 'It was gratifying to note that notwithstanding the strenuous time which the men experienced, they maintained an aggressive spirit throughout.'[26]

• • •

The British and Australian *Official Histories* had contrasting explanations for the fact that II Anzac's casualty figures were double those of the other two army corps which fought at Messines. Edmonds would attribute this to overcrowding on the ridge which was, he suggested, a consequence of the brilliant success of the morning's attack resulting in far fewer casualties than expected, and a decision to retain the assault battalions on the ridge rather than relieve them. Although higher casualties might have been expected in the initial assault, no evidence exists that the staff of either II Anzac or the Second Army were somehow unaware of the numbers manning the Black Line.[27] The New Zealand Division was given permission to withdraw one brigade (the Rifle Brigade) at 9.30 pm on the night of 7 June and the 25th Division similarly given permission to withdraw two brigades some 30 minutes later. At any rate, the vast bulk of the disproportionate casualties suffered by II Anzac Corps were incurred over the days following the initial assault, so Edmonds' claim is tenuous at best.

The retention of the New Zealand Division in greater strength than the 25th Division was a deliberate decision made in the well-founded expectation of strong German counter-attacks and maintained due to the confusion and retreats of the afternoon of 7 June. But it was a decision made against the wishes of Russell, who argued that the weight of men in trenches had little value in meeting counter-attacks. 'It is seldom, if ever that an attack is beaten off by actual hand to hand fighting in trenches. Certainly the resistance we meet ourselves on the part of the Germans, once we get to close quarters, is a matter of little concern.' Russell would 'regret very much that we were not allowed to thin out and reduce the number of men on the ridge after we had won it. Had we been allowed – as I proposed – to reduce the garrison our losses would have been considerably smaller for the same result.'[28] The caution which characterised much of the Second Army's approach to the battle again influenced a critical decision and again it cost heavily in lives. Edmonds' claim that lower than anticipated casualties created 'unforeseen congestion' (on the ridge) which 'was neither appreciated nor corrected' is an invention which has found its way into accounts of the battle ever since. It was not until 9 June that Godley considered the situation had clarified sufficiently to countenance reducing the numbers of men in the line further behind the Australian divisions.

Bean, more correctly, attributed the casualty figures to the 'comparative severity of the fighting' which, though far more accurate, still provides only part of the reason. The many errors in the artillery coordination and the rank inaccuracy of the heavy guns not only killed and wounded many Australians, it demoralised the attacking force which relied on it to support the advance. The overlapping command structures merely added to this problem, with divisions in the rear ordering artillery fire ahead of their lines which in turn fell on the Australians. That this problem was not fully understood and addressed by II Anzac staff until 9 June pointed to a significant failure in corps command. These were not the only factors. Bean hinted at problems with the 4th Division's staff work in the lead-up to the battle, contrasting the 3rd Division's highly detailed and voluminous paperwork, which he knew full well represented an intense and careful planning and remarkable efficiency, with that of the 4th Division which was 'as short as the 3rd's was long'.[29] He also knew that the 4th Division staff had blundered badly at Bullecourt, failing to inform the British 62nd Division on their left flank that they had called off their planned attack on 10 April resulting in that division attacking alone and unsupported and suffering appalling casualties as a consequence. Although Bean quite rightly pointed to the Fifth Army commander, General Hubert Gough, as the main culprit for the disaster at Bullecourt, commenting that his haste 'created an environment that made such mistakes more likely', he conceded that the 4th Division's grave oversight 'gave reason for some bitterness' in the 62nd Division.[30]

Bean went on to make two judgements in the *Official History* concerning the afternoon attack by the Australians on 7 June, one of which would obscure a costly British mistake, the other an equally costly Australian one. The first was that Plumer's decision to delay the attack on the Green Line by two hours was correct. Certainly the 33rd Brigade of the British 11th Division was hopelessly late, delayed by a combination of confused orders and a major underestimation of the distance and arduous nature of the approach march. Plumer faced a difficult choice. Any delay could give the Germans time to recover and bring up reserves. Attacking on time with part of his centre assault division not on its start tapes however, would mean that it would have little artillery protection when it finally launched its attack. It also would mean a gap in the line and leave the two brigades in the line either side with flanks 'in the air' — always a dangerous prospect. Starting on time was the bolder and riskier move, but one more in line with Haig's desire to rush the guns and certainly the one that, had it paid off, would have been rewarded handsomely. Delaying the attack was the safer, more orthodox option, the one Plumer characteristically chose and, Bean's judgement notwithstanding, the wrong one. Plumer's delay not only trapped the 12th Australian Brigade in the open under the German guns for two hours, but they also watched on helplessly as the Germans reinforced the pillboxes and trenches, many of which had been abandoned in disarray shortly before. What might have been a rapid seizure of the Green Line now became a bloody struggle to prise the Germans from their defences, pillbox by pillbox. That it had been open for exploitation in places seems clear given that the 49th Battalion's scouting party was able to push forward unmolested at the previously arranged time for the attack. The 33rd Brigade was still hours away when the attack was finally launched and the 57th Brigade, dribbling through in insignificant numbers on the left, made it with only minutes to spare. If the delay was meant to preserve attack coordination, it clearly failed.

Bean went to some trouble to discover exactly what had gone wrong with the 33rd Brigade. When he sent the drafts of his Messines chapters to Edmonds in 1932, his claim that the 6th Lincolns, when they finally arrived, were 'tired and nervy' and mixed up with the 52nd Battalion immediately caught the attention of the British Official Historian who sought out the 33rd Brigade's officers to dispute it. The Lincolns' commander, Lieutenant Colonel George Gater, responded to Edmonds: 'I have no recollection whatever of any men of the 6th Battalion being mixed up with men of another unit', a claim that was patently untrue.[31] Edmonds stood by Gater's version. 'I consider Gater a man whose word can absolutely be relied on. He joined up from Oxford – August 1914 and rose through the ranks to command a Brigade.'[32] Indeed Captain R.H. Clay of the Lincolns even responded to Edmonds with a counter-claim:

> You may remember that Colonel Mather sent a rather facetious message to Brigade H.Q. about some estaminet in the line of their advance ...

During the attack owing to the short notice and difficult nature of the ground, there was some loss of direction with the result that a part of the Australian Battalion was on our left when the objective was reached … without in any way disparaging the Australians, who had done extraordinarily well, I should say they were rather shaken by the heavy shelling which developed during the evening and practically wiped out some of their posts.[33]

What was clear however, was that the 11th Division's staff grossly underestimated the difficulties of the ground to be covered and sent the 33rd Brigade off on a meandering, elongated route with an impossible timetable. Not that such blatant mistakes were acknowledged by Lieutenant General Alexander Hamilton-Gordon in the IX Corps' report on the battle:

The capture of the Oosttaverne Line was carried out without difficulty by the 33rd Brigade attached to the 16th Division and by the 57th Brigade of the 19th Division supported by tanks from Army Reserve. The original plan had been for this operation to be carried out by the 33rd Brigade alone but the success of the attack on the Ridge itself left large divisional reserves untouched and available. The Corps commander decided therefore to strengthen the attack on the Oosttaverne Line.[34]

That this utterly fictitious account of the 33rd Brigade's role and the invented reason for the 57th Brigade's employment entered the records of the Second Army as fact in turn raises questions about the hitherto unchallenged quality of its staff work.

The second judgement by Bean, that Captain Arthur Maxwell's action in steering his company across into the absent 33rd Brigade's sector on his left saved the attack on the Green Line from 'probable failure', ignores completely the disastrous consequences of this decision for the 4th Division's cohesion. Bean was close to Maxwell and his fondness for the Tasmanian is clear in his diary. '[T]he finest officer I know - & looks it. 6ft 5, brown, fairly big in proportion, wiry as they make them.'[35] Bean went on to include anecdotes describing Maxwell's bravery and kindly character and he would be praised by the commander of the 33rd Brigade and awarded the DSO for his actions on 7 June. Though Maxwell could hardly be blamed for Pope's failure to pass on the instruction to refuse the 52nd's left flank, his decision to lead his company across to meet up with the absent 33rd Brigade pulled the 52nd away to the left, opening up a gap between its right and the left of the 49th Battalion. The decimation of the 49th Battalion, split in two by the dreadful machine-gun fire from concrete strongpoints in the

Blauwepoortbeek, in turn opened up a gap between it and the 45th Battalion on its right. Thus three Australian battalions were dangerously exposed, the 52nd and 49th each had both flanks in the air and the 45th was open on its left flank. The gap in the Blauwepoortbeek would widen to almost 1000 metres by 10 June and the confusion caused by the attempts to relocate the Australian battalions on the night of 8 June would add further unnecessary loss. The orthodox solution to the problem that confronted the commander of the 52nd was to maintain contact with the 49th Battalion on his right and to refuse his left flank, protecting his left as he edged forward. Nowhere in the battalion or brigade diaries would Maxwell's decision be applauded, nor even characterised as deliberate. It would be painted as a consequence of the very heavy fire in the Blauwepoortbeek.[36] Neither however, would it be investigated.

Official Historian Charles Bean (second from left) with Captain Arthur Maxwell (on Bean's immediate left). Bean praised Maxwell as 'the finest officer I know' and defended with high praise his decision to lead his company away from its intended position at Messines (AWM E02277).

Since the attack by the 13th Brigade on the Green Line did indeed fail, it is difficult to see how Bean could arrive at his conclusion that Maxwell 'saved' it through his actions. Bean wrote to the former commander of the 13th Brigade (and former Defence Minister), Thomas Glasgow, in 1931 seeking details of the attack, particularly the failure of the 49th Battalion and his decision to send in the 51st Battalion. Glasgow did not respond directly but phoned his former Brigade Major, Roy Morell, and the two had a discussion which led to Morell penning his recollections of the facts and passing them to Glasgow who, in apparent agreement, duly passed them to Bean. Morell's claims were extraordinary: 'I feel quite confident that the 49th Battalion got their full objective and that there was never any gap in their front line. They were able to keep touch with the 52nd Battalion on their left, but you [*referring to Glasgow*] will remember they did not at first have complete liaison with the 3rd Division and I think you, and I'm not sure whether I myself was with you, went to the 49th Battalion and they pointed out to us where the 3rd Division should have been and that they had not yet gained their objective.'[37]

Brigadier General Thomas Glasgow who commanded the 13th Brigade at Messines. Later a senator for Queensland and Minister for Defence, the much respected Glasgow referred Charles Bean's inquiries concerning the 13th Brigade's actions at Messines to his Brigade Major, Roy Morell. Although he would not put his name to the account, Glasgow assented to Morell's wildly inaccurate version which concealed the many command errors and the almost impenetrable chaos of the 13th Brigade's attack (AWM A02103).

Even allowing for the passage of time, Morell's (and presumably Glasgow's) claims were widely at odds with the truth. The 49th was well short of its objective on the right, lost touch with the 52nd Battalion and had wide gaps in its own lines thanks to the decimating fire in the Blauwepoortbeek. The 49th was also out of touch with the unit on its right which, contrary to Glasgow's and Morell's belief, was the 12th Brigade of their own division, not the 3rd Division, which was well to the south. It is true that the Germans on the left would have been, had they remained, 'in rear of the advancing [Australian] troops', but the advance those Germans might have threatened spluttered to a halt at the head of the Blauwepoortbeek in any case, and it is doubtful indeed that any Germans remained in their forward lines — even if they had, they would not have been able to direct fire at the Australians advancing down the valley given the slope of the ground. Morell praised the work of Maxwell who 'did very good work in getting through to the British on his left and it was on the supporting recommendation of a British Officer that we ultimately recommended him for the D.S.O.' He went on to make the even more extraordinary claim that the 49th 'never had any gap in their line and obtained their full objective without difficulty. I am also sure that the 52nd Battalion also obtained their objective but that there was a hiatus between their left flank and the British right.'[38] Morell denied bringing any message to Glasgow concerning the failure of the 49th and claimed that, following Pope's wounding, the 52nd's 'means of communication were disorganised', adding that Maxwell (rather than Stubbings) 'was apparently in command of the whole of the Battalion's front line.'[39]

It is easy to sympathise with Bean's predicament. Both Morell and Glasgow (who was then a senator and Deputy Leader of the Opposition) agreed to a version of the brigade's actions which could not possibly be true and was mistaken on important details. There was no mention of the confusion concerning the orders to the 52nd, fulsome praise (and a high decoration) to Maxwell for leading the battalion away from its correct position in ignorance of Holmes' and Glasgow's orders to refuse his flank, and complete denial of any problems whatsoever with the 49th Battalion. No reason was given for committing the 51st Battalion on the evening of 7 June or the 50th Battalion on 9 June, nor any mention of the obvious misplacement of the 52nd Battalion and the need to reposition it on 8 June. To his credit, Bean was explicit in his description of the 49th's failure in the *Official History*, a fact which was obvious on maps and implied in the 49th's own account in its war diary. But there would be no criticism of the senior officers in the 13th Brigade over the events of 7 June, nor of Maxwell's decision to lead his battalion away from its intended position.

• • •

Those Australians who survived Messines received recognition for their victory during a royal visit on 26 June. The Duke of Connaught, first cousin to the King, a prince in his own right with the title 'His Royal Highness' and ADC to Haig, arrived to review and congratulate the Australian divisions for their part in the victory at Messines. Unfortunately, the visit would spark an entirely new battle, this one between the two Australian divisional commanders. During the review Monash, with Holmes standing by, introduced the two most decorated and famous members of Holmes' division to the Duke. It is likely that Holmes was aware, as many in the senior ranks of the AIF were, of Monash's penchant for self-promotion and likely too that a simmering resentment boiled over as a result. Holmes, clearly angry, penned a blistering letter that very afternoon to Monash accusing him of a grave breach of protocol. 'Before I take further action in the matter I should be much obliged if you would kindly inform me under what circumstances you abruptly interposed yourself between H.R.H. the Duke of Connaught and myself on parade today when the former was inspecting representatives of my Division, and without my permission or consent, presented two of my officers Major Murray, V.C., D.S.O. and Captain Jacka V.C., M.C. to his Royal Highness. I should be glad to be furnished with an early reply.'[40] Monash replied at length, attempting to soothe Holmes and explaining that the whole matter was a misunderstanding brought about by the Duke's eagerness to meet Murray and Jacka and of Godley turning first to Monash for the introduction as they had both served under him at Gallipoli. Monash claimed he had quietly objected to Godley on Holmes' behalf. As for interposing himself, Monash claimed that 'all I did was step up on the Corps commander's request'.[41]

The breach was never healed, but it was ended. On 2 July, barely a week after receiving Monash's response, Holmes was killed by a German shell while showing the Premier of New South Wales, William Holman, the Messines battlefield from the slopes of Hill 63. The party had left its car and proceeded on foot to avoid a dangerous spot. Holman and the others were unhurt, but Holmes was hit by fragments, dying later that day. It was an area which may not have been under active German bombardment at the time, but Holmes was taking a serious risk with his visitor, something he may have been well used to, but the Parliament of New South Wales most certainly was not. Godley was aghast, not only at the death of Holmes at a particularly sensitive time, but at the obvious risk to a VIP guest in his corps. In his explanation to Senator Pearce of the loss of one of his generals and the near death of the New South Wales Premier, Godley deftly covered himself:

> I think you will like to know from me that the circumstances of [Holmes'] death were such that no blame could be attached to anyone. He asked me if he might take Mr. Holman to see the battlefield, and I expressly stipulated that he was only to take him to a hill, which was reasonably safe, and from which he could get a view of it. He carried out these instructions strictly, and the place at which he was killed was a long way behind the trenches, and the shell which killed him an absolute chance shot, fired at very long range, and a spot which has been seldom, or never, shelled since our advance.[42]

Godley was right to suggest that the risk was relatively low, but he would also have known that anywhere within 15 kilometres of the German artillery was unsafe and Hill 63 was certainly within range.[43]

In the wake of Holmes' death, Bean wrote that he felt he had never done him justice as the first successful Australian leader. This had its origin in a gentle rebuke by Brigadier General John Gellibrand that Bean's obituary of Holmes in the papers was a little underwhelming. Now more reflective in his notebook, Bean praised Holmes' modesty and disregard of jealous criticism and marvelled at his resilience at Pozières. He even put him ahead of the much-admired White (who he conceded hadn't had the chance to lead men in battle), adding that he had 'the power of command that Hobbs and Monash have not ... He set the example to his brigadiers as at Messines. He saw Monash get a division to which he himself was more entitled … but he bore no malice. Holmes did not complain … I had always discounted Holmes as being no great strategist nor especial tactician … I could see I had not done him justice and I was very remorseful. His courage was all I had grasped.'[44] Barely a fortnight after Holmes' death, Major William Locke penned a letter to Monash. An old friend and Monash's former ADC, he wrote: 'Rather a sad thing about General Holmes isn't it? Ah! Well! "Le roi est mort, vive le roi!" – apropos of which, I wonder who will step into his place; and subsequently who will get the new brigade vacancy?'[45] It is clear from Locke's jaunty tone and indelicate speculation about Holmes' successor that he didn't expect Monash to be particularly grief stricken. Holmes' replacement for the 4th Division was a Scotsman, Major General Ewen Sinclair-MacLagan, who Monash considered 'pessimistic and obstructive'.[46]

Pessimism, however, was something entirely absent from Godley's post-battle correspondence with the King's Assistant Private Secretary, Lieutenant Colonel Clive Wigram, in which he was effusive in his praise of Monash's division, the New Zealanders and the 25th Division:

> The new 3rd Australian Division was on the right of my attack and did extraordinarily well. They were heavily gassed while assembling in Ploegsteert Wood, so much so, that five strong platoons which had to cross the Douve from New Zealand territory, had only fifty left which to go over our parapet, and these fifty with their gas masks on did what we had expected of the two hundred. The New Zealanders were in the centre and took Messines brilliantly ... The 25th Division on the left had the furthest to go, and did quite excellently.[47]

Nothing pointed more to Godley's remoteness from the reality of the battle over which he had just presided than his account of the second phase. Neglecting to mention the 4th Division at all, he regaled Wigram with a wholly fictitious account of II Anzac's cavalry action:

> I had a squadron of my Corps Cavalry up closely following their Infantry Reserves, and launched them over the hill as soon as we topped the ridge. Their patrols galloped a sniper's post and took nine prisoners, captured a couple of guns, and then went on, cheered by the Infantry who were much heartened up by their appearance, and brought back some quite useful information. They materially assisted in the rout of the Bosche [sic] ...[48]

Wigram's congratulations in reply correctly framed Messines as 'one of the finest achievements in this war' before he joined Godley in his fantasy world. 'It must have been thrilling to see your Squadron of Corps Cavalry working with the Infantry.'[49] Bean was incredulous at Godley's orders to send out cavalry patrols on 12 June, noting the shelling they attracted as soon as they came into view at midday. 'Cavalry! They led their horses along Huns' Walk today and were heavily fired at. They are to put these posts beyond 9 B[riga]de today – pure eyewash.'[50] There was certainly no cheering from the infantry who, fully aware that the sight of horsemen on the ridge would draw a swift response from the German artillery on their positions, blocked the cavalry from coming through and put an end to the nonsense, saving the lives of horses and men in the process.

At least Godley had the grace to obliquely mention the 4th Division's sacrifices to the Australian Minister of Defence, Senator George Pearce, although he went on to repeat his absurd inventions concerning the contribution of the cavalry:

I am very proud to have had these two Divisions under my command in the biggest and most successful battle of the war, and there is no doubt but that their staunchness and gallantry were very material factors in our victory … I am very glad to say that my Corps Mounted Troops also had a chance and did some very useful patrol and reconnaissance work when we first topped Messines Ridge, capturing some prisoners and some guns and bringing in some most useful information. The two squadrons of the 4th Light Horse both did well, and so did Colonel Hindhaugh, who commands the Regiment.[51]

Godley noted on 15 June that prisoners and captured German guns were still dribbling in and that, overall, casualties were around half those of other battles. Most of II Anzac's casualties were due to the heavy shelling from the German guns on the Lys which enfiladed Messines, the Douve and Ploegsteert Wood 'which', Godley claimed, 'seem to be the direction in which the Germans have retired their guns'.[52] The New Zealand Division had suffered most from these guns, its casualty toll of 4978 the heaviest in the corps, while the 3rd Division lost 4122 (many of whom were gas casualties from the morning of 7 June) and the 4th a total of 2677. The 25th Division, while providing a detailed summary of what had been a great success, was keen to dispel any impression 'that the casualties sustained by this division during its attack on Messines Ridge might have been comparatively light and the losses throughout the Division almost negligible. This is not the case.' The diary listed 708 killed and over 2500 wounded and missing. 'No less than 24 Company Commanders and their successors became casualties during the attack.'[53] Even that toll did not tell the whole story. The ordeal of the 4th Division further eroded its already low morale. Godley wrote to Birdwood a month after Messines reporting that 'the crimes of desertion and absence without leave show no sign of diminishing in the 4th Australian Division' and urging again that he lobby the Australian authorities to impose the death penalty.[54] Even that may not have been sufficient deterrent. Ernest Popping of the 38th Battalion wrote home in April 1917 that he had 'never felt better or fitter in my life'; after Messines, however, the tone of his letters changed dramatically. 'I hope it is not long before I get a knock. You will hear people back home say how lucky so and so is being there all the time and not getting wounded but you take it from me a chap is far better off to get a hit and get out of it.'[55] Also on 15 June, Bean was informed by Godley that he was going to review the 3rd Division 'which meant come and report my speech'. It was not a duty Bean enjoyed, particularly as he was due to go on leave, admitting that he was 'fairly stale'. So were Godley's words which Bean wrote, 'never strikes as being the least sincere'.[56] The previous day he had addressed the 12th Brigade at La Crèche, apologising at the outset for his previous speech to Robertson's men in the aftermath of the Bullecourt disaster when he mistook them for the 13th Brigade. A simple enough error perhaps, but not one a brigade which been torn apart in a futile battle was likely to forget in a hurry. He praised their courage and the victory they had helped win but acknowledged the difficulty of their task and, with it, perhaps unwittingly, the mistakes which had killed many of their friends.

Addressing Glasgow's men, he had much the same message but directly referenced the costly fight for the Blauwepoortbeek. Describing it as 'a very awkward situation', he added '[t]his had to be taken ... You were counterattacked heavily, perhaps more heavily than we knew ... We deplore your heavy losses, but that is inevitable when a Brigade of proved valour is set such a task as you had to do. It is the result of desperate fighting against a determined and gallant enemy.'[57] Godley also put the most positive spin on the 52nd's detour to the north: 'So well and successfully was [the attack] done, that the left battalion of the Brigade went even further than was intended and took over a good bit of line on the left which was really allotted to the 9th Corps.'[58] His summary of the chaotic attacks over the next three days aimed at closing the gap created by this situation was equally affirming, but equally removed from reality, citing again the phantom counter-attacks and heaping praise on the 13th Brigade for taking a position which the Germans had abandoned. Watching Godley give much the same speech again to the 3rd Division, Bean considered they looked in fine fettle after the battle. 'The 33rd and 34th looked splendid, but the 35th looked what I believe it is – the weakest of the lot. It has a miserable poor old moaning weed of a colonel in Goddard.'[59] Bean thought the 3rd Division was 'finding its feet':

Only the CO's are a bit shy of fire in some cases and Monash is not the man to keep them up to it. In the 9th Brigade Genl Jobson, tho' a clever man does not visit his front line at all – and does not make his staff do so; only one Colonel – Morshead – who has the old 1st Division tradition – does so sufficiently ... McNicoll visits his front line as he can – and Cannan, of course, is splendid. Jackson GSO1 and Peck GSO2 go round their front in battle; & Paine, though much shocked, does so also. But Monash doesn't & it makes a great difference. It is agreed Mansbridge & I have the not the least doubt, that Jobson, ought to go.[60]

Monash also demonstrated his curious tendency to misjudge the mood of his men in his congratulatory address to the 3rd Division when he thanked them 'for their support' during the battle. 'The boys voiced indignation at the phrase about splendid support rendered to the General, arguing that it was <u>we</u> who had done the big job and that it was the General who was rather in the supporting position. He had got the bull by the teat!'[61]

The praise that Godley showered on the 4th and 3rd divisions fell on deaf ears among the senior command. The bungling by the corps commander and his staff at Messines was all too apparent to them. 'All these divisions are longing to get back under Birdwood and his staff' Bean jotted in his notebook. 'Salier of 12th Brigade told me so – Holmes of 4th Division, Leane of 48th Battalion – even Blanchard.'[62] Those commanders listened in silence as Godley described the dangers that the Second Army's plan and the last-minutes changes to it had inflicted on the Australians. 'There is nothing harder than to go through other troops to get a final objective so far in advance. It required great gallantry to go over and down a forward slope in full view of the enemy after that enemy had time to pull himself together a bit.' Their gallantry, he added was 'beyond all praise'.[63] With so many avoidable mistakes that added to those difficulties, it needed to be.

9

*It is one of those things that does not
bear thinking about ...*

That Moment of Triumph

9

It is one of those things that does not bear thinking about ...

That Moment of Triumph

By the evening of 14 June, major operations for the Battle of Messines had concluded and all of the original objectives were in British hands. Lieutenant Colonel L.E. Ward of the 36th Division's artillery wrote that Messines was 'one of the most complete successes of the war ... unstained by any form of failure.'[1] Despite the fact that Haig could have walked over the ground the Second Army had captured in a single day, this bore no relationship to the scale of the victory. With the southern bulge of the Ypres salient wiped off the map, Haig had cleared the way for the Flanders campaign to proceed. The German High Command never doubted his strategic intent in Flanders, despite Haig's attempts at deception in late June with an attack by three divisions near Lens which was meant to suggest a drive towards Lille. The German *Fourth Army* held the Flanders front and its records indicated that, as early as 9 June, it had assessed that a major British operation to clear the Belgian coast was 'certain', a conclusion also reached by Crown Prince Rupprecht on 12 June. The German *Sixth Army*, which guarded Lille, was understandably more nervous about the preparations aimed at its front, but Rupprecht's assessment of Haig's strategic intent proved correct. The stage was set for the long and ultimately disastrous Third Ypres campaign.

To the relief and surprise of the German High Command, the British would not move again until 31 July, a delay which has been much criticised for allowing momentum to lapse and providing the Germans time to recover. Although that was certainly the result, Haig could hardly be blamed. The French and Russians were simply incapable of delivering the concerted hammer blows the Chantilly plan required and the British War Committee was reluctant to unleash Haig's armies in Flanders unsupported against an enemy which it feared fully expected such an attack. Desperate for an alternative to Haig's assault against 'the strongest defences of the strongest enemy', but equally determined to maintain the pressure on the Germans somewhere, a newly formed War Policy Committee cast around for alternatives. Finding none, and with the resolve of Haig and Robertson to attack in Flanders undiminished at its meeting with them on 20 June, the War Cabinet assented to the proposed attacks in line with the original plan. But valuable time had been lost. With a timetable for the next attack on 25 July at its earliest, the government withheld its assent until 18 July, agreeing to it only if Haig adhered to the step-by-step methods, reining in any ambitions for a grand breakthrough even if that became possible. Robertson's assurance to the War Cabinet that Haig would stick to the step-by-step method was an equivocal one, claiming that he would stay within his own gun range 'until ... a real break-through occurs'.[2] Thus assured that he would stick to a step-by-step plan, but that at the same time that he might depart from that commitment if circumstances changed, the War Cabinet was apparently satisfied that it could still shut down an offensive if necessary. Robertson was instructed to assure Haig of Cabinet's full support. With ambiguity thus embedded at the outset, Haig ordered Gough's Fifth Army to commence its preliminary bombardment on 15 July, employing an even greater concentration of guns than Plumer had amassed for Messines.[3]

The rain that plagued Gough's attacks in August, and his repeated and costly narrow-fronted attacks forced a further reappraisal which saw Haig hand the Flanders operations to Plumer, who applied the Messines blueprint to the successful battles of the Third Ypres campaign — the battles of Menin Road (20 September), Polygon Wood (26 September) and Broodseinde (4 October). Harington would point to Broodseinde as 'a far better bit of work [than Messines]. We had nothing like the time for preparation, and it went like clockwork.'[4] Broodseinde, which would be the first of the German Army's 'black days', proved that successful major attacks could be mounted quickly. But there was a limit. The disastrous final phases of Third Ypres at Poelcappelle and Passchendaele suffered from entirely inadequate preparation and artillery support and, as the weather worsened, the British offensive ground to a halt in the Flanders mud. The catastrophe of Passchendaele would not only have serious consequences for the British war effort in 1918, but would haunt Haig's reputation forever. Another enduring result of Passchendaele was to render seemingly pointless the successful battles of Third Ypres and overshadow the success at Messines.

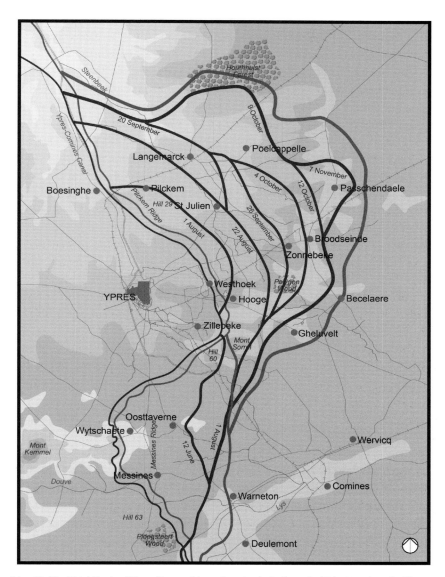

Map 18. The Third Battle of Ypres (August-November 1917). At the end of July, Haig launched his Flanders offensive. Rain in August thwarted Gough's attempts to break through and the offensive was handed to Plumer, who employed 'bite and hold' tactics based on the victory at Messines for the battles in September and October. Rain and exhaustion ended any hope of success and the offensive ended in November with the capture of Passchendaele and an enormous casualty toll. The failed Flanders campaign would be remembered as one of the most infamous military disasters in British history.

But just as A.J.P. Taylor would miss the significance of Messines in his mocking of the vast effort which had moved the line a mere two miles closer to Berlin, so too would the historians who damned Haig for Passchendaele but failed to see that the tactics and weapons systems, the improving technology in tanks, aircraft and artillery, had defeated the German defensive scheme on which their Western strategy was anchored. Haig would later claim with justification that Messines 'became a gauge of the ability of German troops to stop our advance under conditions as favourable to them as an army can ever hope for, with every advantage of ground and preparation, and with the knowledge that an attack was impending.'[5] The massive German offensive in the spring of 1918 was a tacit admission that they could not simply sit behind the now fatally vulnerable static defensive lines and, when that great effort was rebuffed and their armies exhausted, Germany's defeat was inevitable. Much would happen between June 1917 and November 1918 and the German offensive would come perilously close to forcing a result, but when it failed, the 'all arms' offensive model which harnessed the superior firepower the Allied forces now commanded, combined with the strategy of limited, progressive advances refined at Messines proved decisive. The battles of Messines and Third Ypres would not win the war, but it was clear that the deadlock was breaking.

The British press, after years of trying to put a positive spin on the bloody defeats of the previous three years, struggled to find adequate superlatives to describe Messines. *The Times* trumpeted the victory as 'England's greatest military victory' and claimed that 'not one flaw can be found in Thursday's operations which were the cleanest success ever won by British arms.'[6] The colourful exaggerations about the mine explosions were a source of amusement to the RFC's Thomas McKenny Hughes:

> Yesterday's papers arrived this morning and gave wonderfully imaginative pictures of the battle ... The description of the mine – the biggest the world had ever known – which blew Wytschaete bodily into the air, was good; also the account of how Mr. Lloyd George heard the mine go up from his "place" at Walton Heath. – most of the men slept through it here.[7]

Gallwey's home newspaper, the *Rockhampton Morning Bulletin*, well used to publishing lists of local men killed, was less enthusiastic, warning that the value of the Messines battle is that it gives an index of the cost which we are likely to pay for the conquest of Germany.'[8] The German accounts were detailed and revealing. A lengthy appreciation of the battle by the German General Headquarters, published by the *Kolnische Zeitung* in August, while not attempting to hide the fact of defeat, soothed its readers with the notion that the English had again overpaid in blood for a minor advance, adding that the fact they 'had to struggle for hours to get possession of the neighbouring heights bears witness to the courage in our troops so exalted that no words suffice to praise it.'[9] Major Moraht, writing in the *Deutsche Tageszeitung* on 4 August, was equally dismissive of the English tactics. 'Every time that he has undertaken an offensive, he has experienced the same thing. First of all there was the sudden retreat of our front, and then our new defensive method … The English giant whose tactics are still very clumsy, knows only one form of attack; massed assaults.'[10] The *Kolnische Zeitung* conceded that, although they 'accomplished miracles by way of resistance', the ordeal of the German defenders at Messines had been truly awful. 'There was no erection above ground that was not the target for a gun. The front trenches were turned into crater streaks. The plan and ambition of the English is that the elements should make themselves useful and so annihilate the enemy with iron, cold steel, fire and gas that the attack is transformed into a walk across a graveyard.'[11] The metaphor was a fitting one, particularly at Hill 60.

German pillbox overturned by a mine explosion (AWM E01320).

It suited both sides to exaggerate the impact of the mines. While they would remain the most spectacular and memorable aspect of the battle, their impact was more moral than physical. 'Owing to the fact that our trenches were thinly held there were but few victims, although the emotional effect, like that of any elemental shock, was considerable. The accompanying phenomena, the far-spread air-pressure, and the waves of heat which burned into the air spread confusion. Even the rearward troops had tales to tell of the deafening impression of the encircling explosions.'[12] Although not 'few', the number of German soldiers killed was far fewer than the figure of 10,000 which is often quoted in passing references to Messines. Total German casualties (including wounded and missing) for the period 1–10 June 1917 amounted to 19,923 with 7548 of those missing, the vast majority of the latter prisoners. Most of the mines, although undoubtedly entombing many who were sheltering in dugouts, exploded in front trench systems which were largely empty in advance of the expected attack.[13] There was one exception however.

The *204th* (*Saxonian Wurttemberg*) *Division* manned the trenches at Hill 60 and the Caterpillar on 7 June, fully expecting the attack. On these much contested heights the opposing trenches were very close and it would be one of the few spots on the ridge where the Germans held the front lines in strength. When Oliver Woodward threw the switch to blow the mines, the German trenches were crowded with men:

> At 4.00 a.m. the greatest mine explosion of the world war took place simultaneously at nineteen places. The ground trembled as in a natural earthquake, heavy concrete shelters rocked, a hurricane of hot air from the explosion swept back many kilometres, dropping fragments of wood, iron and earth and gigantic black clouds of smoke and dust spread over the country. The effect on the troops was overpowering and crushing.[14]

Ten officers and 677 men of the *204th* were killed in the mine explosions at Hill 60. Despite this calamity, the division's historian found praise for the man who had so catastrophically underestimated the threat posed by the British mines, describing Lieutenant Colonel Füsslein as 'a man of great energy', likewise praising the efforts of his miners who dug 'great defensive galleries with offensive branches' to a depth previously unknown on the Western Front. 'It was known that the enemy was also tunnelling but the aviators could nowhere discover any dumps of the dark bluish Ypres clay which would have given indication of important mining operations below the Flanders sands.' The prisoners captured by the *204th* in the days before the battle knew something was up, but could give no concrete information. 'Colonel Füsslein could hardly be blamed therefore, although at every tactical conference he declared that the mining situation was thoroughly cleared up and that his tunnelling arrangements were superior to those of the enemy.'[15] The only hint of criticism was a question which went unanswered. 'Whether he should not have tried, long before this, to get authority for a proper tunnelling organisation on a large scale, instead of contenting himself with an improvised one, cannot be discussed here.'[16]

Monash had every reason to be pleased in the aftermath of the battle. 'A great victory, thoroughly defeated the 4th Bavarian Division and the 3rd Bavarian Division (my old antagonists E. of Armentieres) – these divisions practically blotted out as far as infantry is concerned.'[17] He was less pleased with Charles Bean's report on Messines in the *Anzac Bulletin* in September of 1917, calling it 'the apotheosis of banality. Not only is the language silly tosh, but his facts are, for the most part, quite wrong.'[18] Denver Gallwey was similarly unimpressed with Bean's dispatch:

> It contrasted so much with the actual experience and shows what a cold report an official report is. From such, a stranger could glean but little of what the troops experienced and it gives one some idea of the little knowledge conveyed to the actual public, of the progress of a great battle … yet behind that report, the public will never know the daring deeds of heroism and self sacrifice on the part of those engaged in that enterprise.[19]

Fortunately, Bean had far more time and information to hand to complete his *Official History* than he had for his piece in the *Anzac Bulletin*. Published in Volume IV in 1933, Bean's two chapters on Messines are masterful, carefully documenting the twists and turns of one of the AIF's most complex and confusing, but important battles. He did much to clear the landscape for the researchers to follow, amassing a large archive of documents to supplement his own notebooks and diaries. He also sought information from British and New Zealand officers and from Edmonds who was compiling the British *Official History*. One of the most fascinating collections in the Australian War Memorial is the file of correspondence between the British Official Historian and his Australian counterpart. The exchanges occurred while both were working on their respective histories, but with Bean (with a smaller scope) to publish first. Their two approaches could hardly have been more different. Bean, with his forensic attention to detail, passionate commitment to the truth and ardent Australian nationalism, took his reader into the trenches alongside the men he admired so much. Edmonds took, of necessity, a far broader and more distant perspective, focusing on the direction of the war at the higher levels and treading a delicate and mostly uncontroversial path through the minefields of political and personal reputations. For the most part, the letters between the two historians are characterised by a polite and mutual respect. Disagreements are few, helpful suggestions many. Very occasionally Bean adds a querulous note in a margin or a question mark here or there, but in Bean's independence of mind and willingness to criticise British generals, Edmonds sensed trouble.

Winter at Messines. Tasmanians of Monash's 40th Battalion garrisoning the captured trenches to the south of the Douve River in November 1917, gas masks worn in the 'ready' position and rifles with fixed bayonets at hand in case of a surprise raid (AWM E01331).

Edmonds sent the early drafts of Bean's Messines chapters to Harington in January of 1932, and although the latter was grateful for Bean's praise, made several queries as to the fairness of judgements in respect of the 33rd Brigade in general and the 6th Lincolns in particular.[20] More criticisms would follow and, in September, Edmonds lashed out in frustration:

> We all feel that the historian of the A.I.F. could afford to be a little more generous in his allusions to British units and formations. You are now aware perhaps that the home troops regarded the Australians and Canadians as the spoiled children of G.H.Q. who were given the most rest, the pick of the fighting pitches and most of the praise ...[21]

Edmonds added that Bean's criticisms of higher (British) command were also unfair and 'outside the scope of an ordinary corps history'. Few comments could be more guaranteed to needle Bean. Mindful of the injustices dealt to the 4th Division by the English at Messines and the suffering inflicted by Gough's gamble at Bullecourt, Bean responded in kind:

> This point of view is precisely the one which raised almost all the difficulties between the Australian and British organisations during the war. If you do not recognise that the Australian official history is more than "an ordinary corps history", then you will forgive my saying that it shows me that far from having written too strongly, I must make my points even more clear in future chapters, and this I will endeavour to do.[22]

Bean would make good on that pledge. Although restrained and even handed, his willingness to criticise the decisions of higher command sets his work apart from his contemporaries as uniquely valuable for its honesty, clarity and unprecedented detail. Certainly Bean was anxious that his readers understand the true horror of war. There was no doubt that Messines, with its close-quarter fighting and brutal struggles to overcome pillboxes, had seen a hitherto unprecedented level of savagery and this presented a challenge to a historian who keenly felt the responsibility of writing truthfully a story which would be the legacy of the AIF for the ages to come. Although wary of using private soldiers' diaries, Bean would take the unusual step of mining Gallwey's account of the 47th Battalion's experience at Messines extensively to describe the second phase attack — but he had good reason to do so. With the astonishing detail that Gallwey provided, Bean was gifted with something very rare indeed — a step-by-step account of battle from an altogether unusually observant witness with almost photographic recall. Bean took the precaution of writing to Gallwey's officers to check his facts, admitting, 'The great trouble I have with dealing with accounts like Gallwey's is that while I am led to suspect that some details are inaccurate, and probably due to hearsay, I find that on other points, where I can check them, they are surprisingly accurate and honest. It is evident that the diarist has made an honest attempt to tell the exact story.'[23]

Gallwey's honesty was also troubling. Bean included the horrifying detail of the killing of the wounded gun crew in the pillbox. He wrote to Gallwey's platoon commander to check these details, and Lieutenant John Shultz confirmed that the German machine-gunners would hold out until the last minute and then attempt to surrender when the Australians were almost upon them. From this, Bean extrapolated the justification that the 'kill or be killed' frenzy of men assaulting pillboxes could not simply be turned off at will.[24] But Bean did not ask Shultz about the altogether more disturbing account of the killing of surrendering Germans that Gallwey described so graphically. That such incidents occurred is certain, as confirmed by other witnesses from the 47th Battalion.[25] Haig himself made the observation that the Australians 'took very few prisoners, being enraged at the suffering inflicted on the Australian prisoners at Bullecourt.'[26] Bean spared his readers, and the AIF, by concealing that difficult truth.

But although it is certain that such incidents took place, it is equally certain that they were not widespread given the very large haul of prisoners, nor were they confined to one section of the battlefield. The accounts by English troops of the killing of prisoners, while not as lengthy and detailed as Gallwey's, exist nevertheless.[27] A letter from an English soldier at Messines records that Germans attempting to surrender 'did the usual "Mercy Kamerad" act though I'm afraid it did not work much.'[28] In two cases at least at Messines, German prisoners took the extraordinary step of seeking formal redress from the British authorities through the Red Cross over what they considered the murder of their comrades.[29] Karl Kennel of *Bavarian Infantry Regiment No. 18*, interned at Blandford prisoner-of-war camp, filed just such a complaint over the death of his friend, Friedrich Christoffel, at the hands of the New Zealanders:

> The British attacked early that morning. Christoffel and I were together in a dugout in the front line. There was a fight and I was wounded in the dug-out by hand grenades. Christoffel and I went out of the dug-out, took off our belts and surrendered. Christoffel was next to me kneeling down with his hands raised. The British troops were aiming at Christoffel

… I let myself fall at that moment into a shell hole to escape danger. One of the Englishmen pulled the trigger and Christoffel fell back … I said to myself Christoffel is dead … I cannot say anything about the reasons, we did not defend ourselves, we begged for mercy … We saw it was useless to defend ourselves.[30]

The Foreign Office accepted that the unfortunate Christoffel had made signs of surrender but was 'accidentally' shot. The civil servant noted that 'no doubt it will be impossible to prove that it was not an accident. But why do not the [War Office] bring forward such cases themselves? There ought to be plenty of them.'[31] There were indeed plenty of similar cases, but none would be prosecuted. Surrender was a lethal lottery for troops emerging unarmed from dugouts and pillboxes and the photographs of smiling German prisoners at Messines reveal not happiness but relief at deliverance.

Some of the 7000 prisoners captured by the Second Army at Messines in their prisoner-of-war cage. Intelligence reports on the morning of the attack indicated that the Germans were 'surrendering freely' (AWM H08701).

• • •

The battle made and destroyed reputations. Viscount Plumer of Messines was a lesser light before June 1917, Haig admitting that he had resisted pressure to sack him. After his triumph, not even the mud of Passchendaele could stick to him. Edmonds conceded in a letter to Bean that 'Gough is by no means as guilty of the mistakes in the conduct of Passchendaele as was Plumer.'[32] There would be universal agreement that the Second Army's staff work was a model of efficiency and clarity, but there was a glaring contrast between the two phases of the battle, with the afternoon attack a far more chaotic and chancy undertaking with army and corps staff struggling to cope with the more flexible and dynamic landscape of exploitation. One intelligence officer would be blunt in his criticisms:

> So far as I have had anything to do with the 2nd Army Staff, who, I read, are responsible for the success of this brilliant coup, I have found their work contemptible, but perhaps one should not judge them by "Maps." Certainly many people have told me that the Staff work at the Somme and at Arras was infinitely worse.[33]

Plumer's Chief of Staff and most ardent admirer, Charles Harington, whose own reputation was stratospheric after Messines, would refuse all applause, insisting unconvincingly that 'the whole credit belongs to him and not to his staff'.[34] Both Harington and Plumer would burn their papers after the war, although the former left two books, the hagiographic *Plumer of Messines* and *Tim Harington Looks Back*, both valuable, if uncritical sources.

Godley's reputation, already poor among the Anzacs, did not improve at Messines. He would justifiably be landed with some of the responsibility for Passchendaele after his enthusiastic lobbying for the disastrous attack on 12 October and subsequent mishandling of the battle doomed not only the New Zealanders and Australians of Monash's 3rd Division, but the luckless 12th Brigade of the 4th Division yet again. Indeed 12 October would be the worst day of the war for the New Zealand Division, which suffered close to 3000 casualties with almost 900 killed. That single day at Passchendaele came close to destroying one of the finest divisions in the British Army, the fatal result of a supremely successful and self-confident unit given an impossible task. Godley, out of touch and self-deluding as a general, served out the war in various corps commands and had a distinguished and lengthy post-war life. His affection for the New Zealand forces under his command never waned, but it was never reciprocated.

Of the divisional commanders, Monash would go on to command the Australian Corps in 1918 and earn an exalted reputation, thanks to his obvious talents, his corps' astounding run of victories and his own pen in his book,

The Australian Victories in France. He even received an unexpected boost from the ex-Prime Minister, Lloyd George who, as part of his vividly written and self-justifying war memoirs mischievously suggested Monash might even have replaced Haig as Commander-in-Chief had his obvious talents not been concealed, he suggested, by a jealous, untalented and scheming clique of British generals at GHQ. Russell could justly lay claim to a superior record in command of his division and not only by virtue of the fact that he, unlike Monash, commanded a division throughout its time on the Western Front. Russell was a fearless, resilient and highly talented battlefield commander. He was also well ahead of his time in confronting and solving the enormous tactical problems of senior command in the First World War. Although Monash did not share Russell's occasional lapses of judgement in placing himself within range and sight of enemy snipers and artillery, Monash was criticised by Bean and others for his remoteness from the front line and for the poor example he set his front-line commanders by remaining in his dugout. His greatest strength was his management of battle, something that would reach full fruition in 1918, but was ridiculed by Harington as micro-management at Messines:

> 2 days before the battle Monash gave me a document about 6 inches thick laying down what every man in every section & platoon was to do. I never saw such a document – wonderful detail but not his job. He would tell you which duck board wanted repairing but never in his life ever went near a front line trench.[35]

This was untrue of course, but the mere fact of Monash handing Harington the 3rd Division's overly detailed plans when they could be of little use and certainly would not be read by the Chief of Staff, pointed clearly to his self-regard. Harington saw this as a transparent device to impress, a characteristic which was resented by many who knew Monash. Those weaknesses however, could hardly outweigh his many talents and Monash remains unarguably Australia's greatest soldier, as Russell does New Zealand's. Holmes would, of course, never have the opportunity to prove his ability in 1918 and Guy Bainbridge would go on to fight longer and harder battles with some success in 1918. Most notably he eventually mollified (if not totally won over) his petulant and ill-tempered critic Guinness, no mean feat in itself.

Four VCs were won at Messines, all awarded in II Anzac Corps. Lance Corporal Samuel Frickleton of the New Zealand Rifle Brigade was wounded and gassed before he stormed and silenced two machine-gun crews at Messines in the early morning attack on 7 June. He would not fully recover from his wounds during the war and was discharged on health grounds in 1918. After the war, Frickleton remained with the army as a captain, leaving in 1927 to try his hand at business and farming before returning in 1934 and serving as Inspector of Military Forces during the Second World War prior to his retirement in 1948. His health problems continued in later life and he died in 1971. Today a plaque in the grounds of the rebuilt Messines church records his remarkable deeds of 7 June.

Lance Corporal Samuel Frickleton, VC, of the New Zealand Rifle Brigade. Frickleton rushed machine-guns in the centre of the ruined village of Messines, clearing the way for his company to advance (nzhistory.gov.nz image).

John Carroll, 'the wild Irishman' from the 33rd Battalion who also won a VC for storming and capturing machine-guns, was wounded at Passchendaele on 12 October and returned to Australia at the end of 1917. He lost a foot in an industrial accident in 1927, remarking to a reporter from the Perth *Daily News* who came to interview him in hospital that it was 'no use crying over spilt milk'. Asked about his medal, Carroll lived up to his nickname by inventing a story that he had failed on three occasions to show up at Buckingham Palace for the award ceremony and, when he did, used the prerogative of a VC holder to call out the Palace Guard. Carroll was on his best behaviour in 1956 when he returned to Buckingham Palace for the centenary of the award in 1956. He died in 1971, but his apocryphal stories about his VC live on.

Private John Carroll, VC. Known as 'the Wild Irishman', Carroll won his VC for consistent gallantry over the three days of his 33rd Battalion's stint in the line, capturing a machine-gun and killing its crew, rushing trenches and digging out men who had been buried by a shell (AWM D00015).

William Ratcliffe of the 2nd Battalion, South Lancashire Regiment, was awarded the VC for singlehandedly capturing a machine-gun which had been bypassed and was firing on the rear of his battalion on 14 June. In a dramatic few minutes, Ratcliffe charged the gun, bayoneted the crew and brought the weapon back to his trench, firing on the retreating enemy. Ratcliffe, like Carroll, was injured after the war in an industrial accident and reduced to poverty. He was unable to afford a suit to attend the centenary celebrations in 1956, but a local tailor heard of his story and made one for him. Ratcliffe died in 1963 aged 79.

Private William Ratcliffe, VC, of the South Lancashire Regiment. His gallantry in singlehandedly silencing and capturing a bypassed German machine-gun saved the lives of many of his comrades (memorialstovalour.co.uk image).

Captain Robert Grieve, VC, was badly wounded at Messines. He left a detailed description of his company's action at Messines, but modesty prevented him from describing the deeds for which he was so highly awarded. Remarkably, it was his men who managed to push forward his recommendation as no officers in his company survived. They wrote a moving tribute to Grieve which was included in the 37th Battalion's history. He married the nurse who cared for him and returned to a business career in Australia, serving in the Volunteer Defence Corps during the Second World War. He died in 1957. Grieve's actions saved many of his men after fire from the pillbox he stormed had threatened to hold up the Victorians' attack. His VC brought great honour to his 37th Battalion and it was good news that was sorely needed. Of the 3rd Division's battalions at Messines, the 37th suffered the highest toll of casualties, but it was a battle the men would look back on with bitterness for another reason. In 1936, Norman McNicol, one of the officers who had led his platoon to the Green Line, published the history of his battalion. Of the decision to withdraw the 37th that day he wrote:

The action of Major Story and Lieut.-Colonel Smith was viewed with extreme displeasure by their superior officers, but later information has completely justified them. It should have been possible immediately in such a highly organised battle to rectify the mistake by the artillery, so that the 37th could go forward again, but the higher commanders refused to believe the artillery was in any way responsible. Instead they preferred to think that the whole blame should be placed on the 37th Battalion, whose members keenly resented the charge.[36]

Keen resentment was an understatement of their reaction to the decision in September 1918 to disband their battalion due to the recruitment crisis. Story, who despite the cloud over his name from Messines, had been appointed to command the battalion, was dismissed over a passionate but inflammatory letter appealing the decision and addressed to just about everyone above Monash's head including the Prime Minister.[37] When Monash sacked Story, the 37th mutinied and refused to disband, this last blow to their pride intolerable. Other units slated for disbandment did the same and, faced with a widening crisis, Monash wisely relented. The 37th went into the Battle of St Quentin Canal on 29 September with companies the strength of platoons. Three weeks later, only 90 men answered the roll call and the 37th Battalion finally fell on its sword on 12 October. The publication of its history in 1936 was an opportunity, as the men saw it, to set the record straight on their experiences at Messines. There would be few kind words for Monash.

• • •

On 7 June 1935 Charles Bean attended the annual reunion of the Tunnellers Old Comrades Association at the Imperial Service Club in Sydney as guest of honour. In proposing the toast to 'fallen comrades', the keynote speaker, Major James Shand, paid tribute to the tunnellers, recalling the moment Captain Oliver Woodward threw the switch to blow the Hill 60 mines at 'that crowning event that added lustre to the records of the brave and indomitable men of the Australian Imperial Force.' Bean rose to give the response and described the dramatic scenes in the build-up to the explosions. 'It was one of the most thrilling and satisfying events in the war, a day of complete victory. The Germans had been out-planned, out-dug, and out-manoeuvred.'[38]

It had been two years since publication of Volume IV of the *Official History*, which covered the battles of 1917, and Bean was still some seven years away from completing what would prove to be the most detailed, accurate and authoritative of all the histories produced by the British and Commonwealth countries after the Great War. The 12-volume *Official History of Australia in the War of 1914-18* (six of which were written by Bean) is a masterwork of military history. Uniquely, Bean wove the narratives of battalions, companies and even individuals into the larger tactical and strategic tapestry of the great battles of the war, somehow managing to hold those disparate stories together to provide the most comprehensive and coherent picture possible of the AIF's involvement and contribution. Bean shared with his readers his own intimate understanding of the men who fought that war, and his commitment to humanise its actors by adding a biographical footnote for each soldier mentioned must have seemed an almost impossible ambition at the outset, but one he achieved in what would become the great work of his life. In what was a work of almost overpowering authority which was meticulously researched, Bean maintained the tone of sober and professional objectivity that the *Official History* demanded. Rarely does the reader glimpse the compassionate and gentle soul of the man who authored it, although there were occasions when the unutterable tragedy of the events he witnessed found voice. He concluded his description of the gallant but desperately futile charges of the Light Horse at The Nek in 1915 with a battlefield strewn with the Australian dead and the pitiable sight of the unreachable, untended wounded, their suffering movements slowly ceasing over the hours as the sun rose in a brilliantly blue sky. 'Over the whole summit', Bean wrote, 'the figures lay still in the quivering heat.'[39] Likewise, his narrative of the sacrifice of the 45th Battalion at Messines in a succession of hopeless attacks on the pillboxes of the Blauwepoortbeek Valley is as desperately sad as it is compellingly unfathomable. Bean declared at the end of Volume XII that the record of the AIF in the First World War was a 'tribute to great hearted men and to their nation, a possession forever'. But it was also a requiem for the 60,000 Australian dead of that war and, great though the achievements of the AIF were, triumphalism would never find voice in his writing

For that reason, the report of his speech to the Tunnellers' reunion dinner in the *Sydney Morning Herald*, which included his praise of the tunnellers' achievements but omitted what he considered the altogether more important reality of what their bravery risked and what was sacrificed by both sides in the ultimate folly of war, touched a nerve in Bean. His letter to the newspaper was published two days later:

> Sir, - In your accurate report of the Tunnellers' Dinner last night I am correctly reported as saying that the successful explosion of the nineteen great mines on the morning of June 7, 1917 after so much struggle to lay and defend them, "was one of the most thrilling and satisfying events of the whole war." As however, this statement taken by itself might make

it appear that those present were rejoicing over an event which had a terribly tragic side to it, and not merely recalling their feelings at the time of the battle, I should be grateful if you would let me quote the sentences which followed.

Former Lieutenant John MacDiarmid Royle, of the 1st Australian Tunnelling Company, holds one of the three electrical switches used to detonate the mines under Hill 60 which obliterated the German positions on the Hill and decimated the German *204th Division* (AWM P02333.003).

These were: "The great German soldier and historian General von Kuhl, says that June 7 brought to the German army one of the worst tragedies of the war. And now after 18 years, we may, I think, send out a thought of sympathy to those for whom that day brought, and still brings, nothing but tragic grief. That moment of supreme elation for us was one which meant the instant blacking-out of thousands of young lives. That moment of our triumph tore cruel gaps in thousands of families, just as tender and loving as ours – gaps which the passage of years can never fill. It is one of those things that does not bear thinking about – and yet we must think about … It is one of those things which, when we do think about it, must make us feel profoundly thankful that the war ended in a united attempt to establish a system more worthy of our civilisation."[40]

EPILOGUE

He will live for ever in the hearts of Australia.

Epilogue

He will live for ever in the hearts of Australia.

Today the quiet fields around Messines still bear the scars of the Great War. The most obvious of those are the water-filled mine craters, much reduced in size, but still a curiosity for the determined, trench map-bearing tourist. The Spanbroekmolen crater, near Wytschaete, is the largest of those carved out on 7 June. Now fenced off and surrounded by trees, it is today a place of quiet contemplation. It was purchased in 1928 by the Christian movement Toc H, founded in 1915, and given its odd name from the military abbreviation for its headquarters in the salient at Talbot House. The crater was rededicated as the 'Peace Pool' in memory of those killed at Messines and in the hope that such bloodshed could be avoided in future — a forlorn one as the events of 1940 would show. The giant double craters of Kruisstraat in farmland some two kilometres south are equally impressive and just as peaceful. Like so many farms on these former battlefields however, there is the usual collection of rusting artillery shells next to the road awaiting collection by the Belgian military for safe disposal. Although gradually diminishing in numbers and, thankfully, in lethality, each new ploughing still draws them up a century after they fell to earth as duds.

While most of the concrete pillboxes have disappeared, Messines still has an impressive collection, some incorporated into memorials and cemeteries, like those in the old Uhlan Trench below the New Zealand memorial, and some alone and brooding in the middle of fields like ruined temples. Built to last, they survived in the post-war years because they were too difficult to remove and many have now found other uses on the farms they haunt. Private Frank Dunham of the 47th (London) Division, wandering through the captured lines at Messines after the battle, was impressed by their strength. 'I had a look round at several other German dugouts and found them all to be much stouter built than ours ... I had not seen one of our dugouts that would have withstood a direct shell hit, but most of these Jerry dugouts were still standing.'[1] A closer inspection reveals the pockmarks of bullet scoring and the tearing from direct hits by heavy shells exposing the twisted, rusting iron reinforcement beneath.

Epilogue

Although the green fields around them have long ago lost any hint of the trenches and shell holes of 1917, the scarred and broken pillboxes still provide some visual reminders of the incredible violence of the fighting here.

The remnant of one of the two giant craters at Kruisstraat (author photo).

While the French and Belgian farmers of the former Western Front have become experts at recognising the old ordnance that their ploughs unearth each planting season and, with steel plates dragged behind their tractors to protect them, equally expert at avoiding the risks, nothing could have prepared them for what happened on 17 July 1955. That evening, as a summer storm swept across the ridge, lightning hit a power pole along a road near the lonely crossroads of Le Gheer, some three kilometres south of the village of Messines. Millions of volts coursed through the earth to a rusting remnant of wire buried since 1917, travelled along a cable and supercharged the detonators connected to one of the long forgotten 'Birdcage' mines at the southern extremity of the old battle front. What happened next was testament to the skill and care of the British engineers who laid the mine — 15,500 kilograms of ammonal packed in 300 petrol tins. Meticulously waterproofed, each tin was covered with canvas coated in tar, the detonators and primers sealed in bottles and the detonator leads placed in armoured hose. Now the dormant charge wire, 40 years old but suddenly and spectacularly live again thanks to the lightning, delivered a super-abundance of electrical energy to the wires connecting the detonators which exploded within their wadding of gun-cotton, triggering a chain reaction in the petrol tins of ammonal. A giant explosion rocked the countryside for kilometres around, shattering the windows of every house within the destructive range of its shock wave and tearing open a huge crater in the field some 40 metres across and 20 metres deep. When the dust (and shock) settled, and all the villagers were accounted for, it was discovered that, apart from killing a cow and blasting out a huge crater, the sleeping mine had, very fortunately, spared the town.

A blind 18-pounder shell on the road formerly known as Huns' Walk at Messines. Shells such as these are a regular sight at farm gates along the old Western Front (author photo).

Epilogue

Six of the 25 mines placed under the Messines-Wytschaete Ridge were not fired on 7 June. One exploded during an electrical storm in 1955. Five remain there today (AWM H15258).

The Belgian government was understandably concerned, doubly so as the British had neglected to inform it of the mine's presence. Now, with the equivalent of a polite diplomatic cough, the British revealed that five more unexploded mines lay beneath Messines, the largest just below the village itself and almost twice the size of the mine which had just 'changed the geography' of Le Gheer. In reality, the failure to inform the Belgians of the presence of five abandoned mines and their 84,000 kilograms of explosive was not exactly an oversight. In Harington's correspondence with Edmonds in 1932 commenting on Bean's drafts, Harington urged caution when mentioning in the Australian *Official History* that the Birdcage mines were 'never fired':

> I do not think it is advisable to speak much about the four mines which were not fired, under the Birdcage. You may remember that after the battle of Messines I wanted to have these 4 mines blown for instructional purposes but it was not approved. Then someone in the Belgian Govt. found out that there were 4 mines under this farm, & requested us to remove them & after some correspondence we said that they would be removed at the end of the war. Nothing was done and later on the area was overrun by the Germans when they advanced in 1918 & later when they were driven back & peace came, this promise to remove was 'overlooked.'[2]

Bean agreed to what must have seemed a semantic deception and changed the wording to 'Birdcage mines never fired (which is outside my knowledge) to Birdcage mines not fired.' Edmonds responded, 'I agree – the less said about the Birdcage mines the better.'[3]

Semantics continued to play a role in the secret. The Belgians inquired after the war, asking the very specific question of whether there were any mines under Hill 63 and whether it was safe to build a village there. That question was referred to Harington who responded with the equally specific answer that there were *no* mines under Hill 63 but, as he hadn't been asked about mines under Messines and Le Gheer, apparently thought it best not to volunteer the information and to let the sleeping mines lie. His reason for suggesting a change to Bean's draft was that '… a troublesome Belgian might ask awkward questions, & demand their removal, or large compensation.'[4] Perhaps no cover-up in history has been so suddenly and spectacularly exposed. Awkward questions were indeed asked about the smoking crater at Le Gheer and equally awkward answers provided by the British government. Harington was honest on one point in his correspondence with Edmonds. It was now impossible to locate, let alone remove the mines. They remain there today, but electrical storms understandably still cause some nervousness.

The village of Messines was rebuilt in the years following the war. The Church of St Nicolas, which Corporal Adolf Hitler, serving with the *6th Bavarian Reserve Division*, famously painted as a ruin in 1915, was gradually reduced to rubble in 1917. The crypt of Queen Matilde, which served as a regimental aid post where the young Hitler was himself treated, is one of the very few surviving buildings from before the First World War. One of the casual tragedies of the fighting was the destruction of the largest brick building in Belgium, the beautiful Institute Royale de Messines, which was a boarding school and orphanage for girls. An abbey founded in 1060, it was transformed in 1776 by Empress Marie-Thérèse into a '"Hospice Royal" for the education of the daughters of pensioned military men, of small means, or of those who had died or become disabled in consequence of injuries or wounds.'[5] The school survived and prospered through political tumult and revolution, its picturesque grounds enclosed by a series of buildings of elegant eighteenth-century serenity, crowned by the basilica which rose above red roofs and dominated the skyline of the ridge. Writing of the Belgian refugees in France, Pierre Nothomb noted that '[t]he genial austerity, the sense of duty, the air of virile grace never ceased to reign among these black robed children.'[6]

Epilogue

The crater left by the explosion of one of the four 'Birdcage' mines in 1955 during an electrical storm. Villagers can be seen standing on the rim and in the pit of the crater (author photo).

At the outbreak of the war, there were 166 girls at the Institute Royale, driven out on 22 October 1914 and evacuated to Bailleul in France. A Belgian journalist wrote of returning to Messines after the battle:

> We penetrated into the town. All the havoc that I have seen on the re-conquested territory of Belgium, on the British front is as nothing compared with the spectacle of Messines … In the midst of these ruins, there lay … a gigantic 38 centimetres shell [sic]. Some visitor has placed upon it upright the shell of a British "18 pounder", as our Allies say. From a distance it looks like a small stranded submarine … The bricks have been pulverised to such an extent that in going on to the heap, one's feet sink in as when walking on sand hills. German coats lie scattered, here and there, forming patches of light grey that break the uniform shroud of sombre red. They are to be counted by the dozen. Several of them are torn to shreds. Most of them bear on the epaulettes the number 18. Almost all of them show large brown stains.[7]

An Australian officer from the 16th Battalion posing next to a dud 15-inch British shell (the 'small stranded submarine') amid the ruins of Messines. Such super-heavy shells were used to destroy concrete fortresses, although an inventory after the battle indicated that most pillboxes remained intact (AWM P11028.024.001).

'Messines will be rebuilt' predicted the authors of a small book on the Institute Royale, 'and the Royal Institution will arise from its ruins'. The village has indeed been rebuilt in its pre-war likeness, but unfortunately the Institute Royale was not rebuilt at Messines. Indeed the hope was expressed that its rebuilding would be fittingly sponsored by the nations whose armies liberated the village:

> It would indeed be a noble action and a consoling one for the families of England, Scotland, Ireland, France, Canada, Australia, New Zeeland [sic], and Belgium, whose sons have fallen on that field of honour to thus give a sort of tangible and lasting expression of their bereavement and justified pride in the reconstruction of that worthy institution of Messines, to replace, for the reception of these daughters of soldiers, that ancient and historic edifice that was ravaged and destroyed by the common enemy ... Who could fulfil with more pious solicitude the role of "Guardians of the Graves" than these girls of Messines, who have in their veins the blood of soldiers, and who have themselves suffered for the noble cause of honour and justice.[8]

Although the Institute Royale would not be rebuilt, the Peace Village opened in 2006 as a joint venture between the Irish government and the city of

Epilogue

Messines. Unfortunately, the ill fortune of the Institute followed its successor: 'Initially, the idea was that the hostel would play an active role in the peace and reconciliation process in [Northern] Ireland.' This was a bold idea which ran into difficulties immediately. 'The tricky start with the Irish partner and the City of Messines caused both to leave the sinking ship and left a huge financial crater as a result.'[9] Rescued by government funding, the Peace Village's financial situation recovered and it is now a hostel catering for the burgeoning battlefield tourism market. The war is finally repaying some of its debt to Messines.

The region is fertile ground for battlefield archaeology as well as tourism. Underneath the village, indeed honeycombing the landscape of the ridge, are numerous dugouts and tunnels, most collapsed but a few still intact. Over the years, such collapses have occasionally dropped animals, farm vehicles and even people into holes and back to a water-filled and reeking remnant of 1917. The Catacombs deep inside Hill 63 remain intact although, like most underground works of the Great War, far too unstable and dangerous to explore. The large models of the ridge and its defences which entire battalions could surround and hopefully commit to memory have long since disappeared beneath the soil. Remarkably, one was discovered in 2007, but not at Messines. In 1918, troops from the New Zealand Rifle Brigade built a terrain model of the battlefield in cement and mortar at Brocton Camp on Cannock Chase in England. Designed as a training aid, it was also a memorial to the New Zealand Division and was completed in May 1918, just in time for the first anniversary of the battle. The Messines model was fully excavated in September 2013, one of the Great War's most unusual and enlightening archaeology projects.

Many of those who fought at Messines remain there today in the war cemeteries that have become places of quiet contemplation. The carefully tended lawns and uniform headstones of the Commonwealth cemeteries are mute tribute to the sacrifice of thousands of men who fought and died at Messines and Wytschaete in June of 1917. Most of the German dead were collected and interred in nearby Langemarck military cemetery with the thousands of unknown soldiers buried in a mass grave known as the *Kameraden Grab* (Comrades Grave). Today the cemetery commemorates over 44,000 of the fallen, their graves watched over by the four solemn bronze statues of mourning soldiers. As his first symbolic act following his armies' conquest of Belgium and France in 1940, Chancellor of Germany and former corporal Adolf Hitler returned to the hallowed grounds of Langemarck cemetery to pay his respects to former comrades. Today the Great War cemeteries of Flanders also honour the memory of French, British and Belgian soldiers of the Second World War who died defending the old battlefields in 1940.

The terrain model of the Messines battlefield constructed at Cannock Chase by the New Zealand Division in 1918 was a well-known tourist attraction in the years after the war. It disappeared beneath soil and regrowth until excavated, surprisingly intact, in 2013 (image Courtesy Richard Pursehouse, Cannock Project).

Austerely beautiful and undemonstrative, the lonely white obelisk of the New Zealand Memorial sits on the crest of the forward slope of Messines Ridge, just below the village. It marks the spot of the heavily fortified Uhlan Trench system, the scene of fierce fighting on 7 June and honours over 800 men 'from the uttermost ends of the earth' who have no known grave. One of four memorials on the Western Front to the missing from the New Zealand Division, the obelisk stands behind two virtually intact and impregnable German pillboxes, mute testimony to the difficulty of their task on 7 June. Just beyond it on the narrow road that leads to the village is the Messines Ridge British Cemetery containing the graves of 1531 Australian, New Zealand and British soldiers, most of whom fell in June 1917. West Flanders today is a peaceful place, but the memory of war is everywhere in over 200 British, French, Belgian and German cemeteries from the First World War.

Walking the route of attack by II Anzac Corps on 7 June will take you to a surprising addition on the slope below Messines. The Irish Peace Tower, a monument of stone rising some 34 metres above the fields, was built in 2000 to commemorate the Good Friday Agreement which brought peace to Northern Ireland. It also commemorates the Irish who fell in the battle from the 16th (Irish) and 36th (Ulster) divisions, men from both sides of the sectarian divide whom the war united. That it is below Messines and not Wytschaete, where the Irish divisions fought so bravely, is a curious anomaly. As the historian of the Ulster divisions wrote:

> For the purist and from a battlefield perspective, the tower and park are in fact built in the wrong place. It should have been built in Wijtschate and not Mesen, since it was the New Zealanders who liberated Mesen and the Irish who liberated Wijtschate in June 1917. However, if it was left to purists, there would be no tower and park at all … every nation who took part in that terrible conflict in Flanders had a memorial to honour its dead, every nation except the Irish. Now we have one and exactly where on the battlefield the memorial is located, seems to me anyway, irrelevant.[10]

Local legend has it that the villages of Wytschaete and Messines engaged in a tug of war to attract the important monument which was to be unveiled by Queen Elizabeth II of England, Belgium's King Albert II and the Irish President, Mary McAleese, a major coup for the winning village. The battle for the Peace Tower was finally won by Messines when the Mayor persuaded one of the village's famers to donate the land. Few of its visitors today either know or care that it is in the wrong place. Its profound message on the folly of war, like the tower itself, can hardly be missed.

The Peace Tower, constructed in memory of the Irish dead at Messines and to commemorate the 1999 Good Friday Agreement which brought peace to Northern Ireland. An imposing monument, it is situated confusingly in II Anzac's position. The 16th Irish and 36th Ulster divisions attacked further north at Wytschaete (author photo).

Messines 1917

Ploegsteert Wood shelters the lonely Toronto Avenue Cemetery, the only exclusively Australian cemetery on the Western Front. A trench named by its original Canadian occupants, Toronto Avenue contains the graves of 78 men of the 3rd Division, most from the 9th Brigade who fell at Messines. The nearby cemetery of Prowse Point, close to the site of the famous Christmas Truce of 1914, holds the grave of Private Alan Mather of Inverell, whose body was found by archaeologists in August 2008 near Ultimo Crater, where so many of his 33rd Battalion comrades fell in the attack on 7 June. His identity, indecipherable from fragments of corroded identity disc, was confirmed by the modern science of DNA matching. Private Mather was buried with full military honours in 2010, 93 years after he went missing at Messines. Dr Brendan Nelson, Director of the Australian War Memorial, delivered Private Mather's eulogy. 'It is easy from the safe distance of almost a century to look back and settle for the abstract. But this man who lies before us is real. He will join these other silent witnesses to the future they have given us. Here now will lie one, "never forgotten, bearing an honoured name".'

Ultimo Crater (Trench 122 Right), the southernmost of the mine craters captured by the 33rd Battalion which defended the right flank of the 3rd Division, and the site of a remarkable discovery by battlefield archaeologists in 2008 (author photo).

Epilogue

Private Alan Mather's kit and possessions were exhumed with his body on the old Messines battlefield. Today the items he carried into battle that day are on display at the Infantry Museum at Singleton (image courtesy of the Australian Army Infantry Museum).

Portrait of Private Alan Mather of Inverell (image courtesy of Kim Blomfield).

Alan Mather was just one of the of the 11,757 Australians and New Zealanders killed and wounded at Messines. For a battle counted as one of the greatest British victories of the war, the casualty figure of around 24,000 for a few days' fighting was appallingly high. Worse was to come in the months ahead and, by the end of October, the British casualty toll for the failed Flanders campaign had risen to over 300,000. The price of victory in the First World War was indeed terrible. On 31 July 1914, just days before the outbreak of war and in the midst of an election campaign, then Opposition Leader (and soon to be Prime Minister) Andrew Fisher declared that 'should the worst happen, after everything has been done that honour will permit, Australians will stand beside the mother country to help and defend her to our last man and our last shilling.'[11] Few election promises come so close to complete fulfilment. The war drove Australia to the brink of bankruptcy in 1918 and its divisions, starved of reinforcements and stretched to the limits of endurance, were withdrawn from battle in October.

Four young officers of the 4th Australian Division's 47th Battalion on the eve of the battle of Messines. Left to right: Lieutenant Dudley Salmon and Captain John Millar with Lieutenants George Goode and William Dixon (the fifth man at the rear is unidentified). All four would die in the coming battle (AWM H03712).

Epilogue

The photograph of the four young Australian officers of the 47th Battalion taken the night before the Battle of Messines would become a poignant image of impending tragedy. None would survive the battle. Captain John Millar and Lieutenant William Dixon were killed the next day, Lieutenant George Goode died five days later from the terrible wounds he received on 7 June and Lieutenant Dudley Salmon died with five of his men on 8 June as they tried to dig themselves to safety on the Green Line. Private Denver Gallwey saw the huge German shell land among Salmon and his men, burying them in the trench. He rushed over with most of his platoon to frantically dig. 'We toiled like slaves for a quarter of an hour and one by one revealed a heap of khaki … We dug up six men and an officer, all in pieces … Not one wounded man could be found … It was a ghastly sight.' The rescue party quietly re-interred their comrades. Gallwey 'uttered a silent prayer as I closed them to view in the bottom of the trench'.[12] Salmon had been wounded the day before, but had remained with his men, one of only two surviving company commanders in the 47th. Sergeant George Thomas was one of those who responded to Red Cross requests for information on the deaths, writing at length to Vera Deakin, the founder of the Australian Red Cross Wounded and Missing Enquiry Bureau. He explained that, of all the officers and NCOs of his company, 'only Mr. Salmon and myself came out of the great fight' and that his battalion had lost very heavily. 'Well Madam, it seems a pity that so promising a young officer should be cut down … both officers and men had great faith in him as a leader he was the first over the top and the last to fall.' Thomas went on to speak of being by Salmon's side throughout the battle, helping him direct the tanks to target German machine-guns and shepherding his company through to the Green Line. Salmon's family, he thought, should be very proud of him. As he told Vera Deakin, 'Well Miss, he died a soldier and he has not got a fancy tomb stone over him but he will live for ever in the hearts of Australia.'[13]

Appendix 1

The Messines Mines

Mines		Size	Gallery	Depth
1	Hill 60	24,300 kg	354 m	30 m
2	Caterpillar	32,000 kg	427 m	33 m
3	St Eloi	43,400 kg	408 m	42 m
4	Hollandscheschur Farm 1	15,500 kg	251 m	20 m
5	Hollandscheschur Farm 2	6,800 kg	137 m	18 m
6	Hollandscheschur Farm 3	7,900 kg	244 m	18 m
7	Petit Bois 1	14,000 kg	616 m	19 m
8	Petit Bois 2	14,000 kg	631 m	23 m
9	Maedelstede Farm	43,000 kg	518 m	33 m
10	Peckham 1	39,000 kg	349 m	23 m
11	*Peckham 2*[1]	*9,100 kg*	*122 m*	*23 m*
12	Spanbroekmolen	41,000 kg	521 m	29 m
13	Kruisstraat 1[2]	14,000 kg	492 m	19 m
14	Kruisstraat 2	14,000 kg	451 m	21 m
15	Kruisstraat 3	14,000 kg	658 m	17 m
16	Kruisstraat 4	8,800 kg	492 m	19 m
17	Ontario Farm	27,000 kg	392 m	34 m
18	*La Petite Douve Farm*[3]	*23,000 kg*	*518 m*	*23 m*
19	Trench 127 Left	16,000 kg	302 m	25 m
20	Trench 127 Right	23,000 kg	405 m	26 m
21	Trench 122 Left	9,100 kg	296 m	20 m
22	Trench 122 Right	18,000 kg	241 m	25 m
23	*Birdcage 1*[4]	*9,100 kg*	*130 m*	*18 m*
24	*Birdcage 2*	*15,000 kg*	*236 m*	*18 m*
25	*Birdcage 3*[5]	*12,000 kg*	*261 m*	*20 m*
26	*Birdcage 4*	*15,000 kg*	*239 m*	*18 m*

Italics – Not blown on 7 June 1917.

Order of Battle (Infantry)
7th of June, 1917

British Second Army (General Sir Herbert Plumer)

Infantry Divisions (North-South)

X Corps (Lieutenant General Sir Thomas Morland)
23rd Division
47th (2nd London) Division
41st (Southern and Home Counties) Division
Reserve: 24th Division (second phase assault)

IX Corps (Lieutenant General Sir Alexander Hamilton-Gordon)
19th (Western) Division
16th (Irish) Division
36th (Ulster) Division
Reserve: 11th (Northern) Division (second phase assault)

II Anzac Corps (Lieutenant General Sir Alexander Godley)
25th Division
New Zealand Division
3rd Australian Division
Reserve: 4th Australian Division (second phase assault)

German Fourth Army (General Sixt von Armin)

Infantry Divisions (North-South)

Gruppe Ypern
119th Division

Gruppe Wytschaete
204th (Wurttemberg) Division

35th (Prussian) Division
2nd (East Prussian) Division
40th (Saxon) Division
3rd Bavarian Division

Gruppe Lille
4th Bavarian Division

Eingreif (Counter-attack) Divisions
7th Division
1st Guards Reserve Division
24th (Saxon) Division

II Anzac Corps (Lieutenant General Sir Alexander Godley)

3rd Australian Division (Major General John Monash)

9th Brigade (Brigadier General Walter Jobson)
33rd Battalion
34th Battalion
35th Battalion
36th Battalion

10th Brigade (Brigadier General Walter McNicoll)
37th Battalion
38th Battalion
39th Battalion
40th Battalion

11th Brigade (Brigadier General James Cannan)
41st Battalion
42nd Battalion
43rd Battalion
44th Battalion

4th Australian Division (Major General William Holmes)

12th Brigade (Brigadier General James Robertson)
45th Battalion
46th Battalion
47th Battalion
48th Battalion

13th Brigade (Brigadier General Thomas Glasgow)
49th Battalion
50th Battalion
51st Battalion
52nd Battalion

4th Brigade (Reserve) (Brigadier General Charles Brand)
13th Battalion
14th Battalion
15th Battalion
16th Battalion

Appendix 3

Intelligence

One of the most important reasons for the British success at Messines was the exceptionally high quality of the Second Army's intelligence. Second Army Intelligence produced a map showing the dispositions of every enemy unit at zero hour and updated it at 10.30 am with every enemy regiment identified and an accurate representation of every British and German unit at that moment which was then issued to all corps headquarters.

Enemy Dispositions
Second Army Front (Zero Hour and 10.30 am 7 June 1917)

Divisions in Line

195th Division (**Prussian**). Good troops. Two regiments of *Jägers*. Division arrived from Galicia end of April when they came into line: has not had much experience of hard fighting.

204th Division (**Wurttemberg**). Fair troops. Only the *120th Reserve Regiment* has had much fighting experience. Division formed June 1916 and has remained in Ypres salient since October 1916.

35th Division (**Prussian**). Moderate division. Contains some Poles. Lost heavily on the Somme. Fought near Arras in April 1917. Into line at end of May.

2nd Division (**East Prussian**). Division in Russia until February 1917 and came into line in April. Been in many successful engagements, Tannenberg etc. Has shown little spirit or enterprise on Western Front; its morale, although improved lately, is not high.

40th Division (**Saxon**). Good division when fighting on the defensive but positive in attitude like all Saxon corps. Lost on Somme estimated 70% of establishment. Has been on Messines front since November 1916.

***4th Bavarian Division* (Bavarian).** A good division. Seen considerable amount of fighting including Somme. Opposite this army front since September 1916.

Divisions in Reserve

***9th Division* (Silesian).** Not a good division. Suffered very heavily on the Somme in April. Contains number of Poles who desert regularly. Came middle of May.

***23rd Reserve Division* (Saxon).** Had good reputation early in the war but not distinguished itself since. Been engaged on the Somme and came here from Arras battle in April.

***3rd Bavarian Division* (Bavarian).** The remarks re *4th Bavarian Division* also apply to this division. Was also engaged heavily at Arras and returned at end of May.

***24th Division* (Saxon).** Sister division to the 40th Division (XIX Saxon Corps). Same remarks apply.[1]

Appendix 4

The New Platoon

SS143 *Training of Platoons for Offensive Action*, published in February 1917, harnessed the hard-won wisdom of Allied forces that had been gathered over three bloody years of fighting on the offensive. A training aid for all infantry units, it was a model of clarity and outlined the tactics platoon commanders should adopt to cope with the various German defensive schemes, specifically the new 'defence in depth' strategy which had proven so formidable in 1916. SS143 also married the new tactics with the greatly increased firepower of the platoon and the advantages conferred by the development of weapons such as the Lewis light machine-gun and the rifle grenade. SS143 emphasised flexibility, agility and manoeuvre and the importance of mutual support with platoons working together to outflank strongpoints when a neighbouring platoon was immobilised by fire from the front. The example reproduced below concerns offensive action against enemy trenches.

THE PLATOON

Taking an average strength of 36 and H.Q. 4.

(Showing 2 Platoons in 2 Waves, with the right the outer flank).

FORMATION FOR TRENCH TO TRENCH ATTACK.

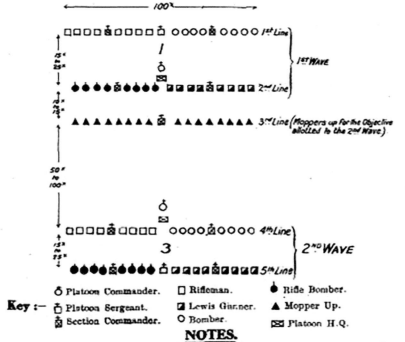

Key :—

Ŏ Platoon Commander.	☐ Rifleman.	● Rifle Bomber.
☐ Platoon Sergeant.	◪ Lewis Gunner.	▲ Mopper Up.
▨ Section Commander.	○ Bomber.	▧ Platoon H.Q.

NOTES.

Two Platoons are depicted showing the different positions of leaders in first and second waves.

The Platoon is the unit in the assault, moves in One Wave of two lines and has one definite objective.

Every man is a rifleman and a bomber, and in the assault, with the exception of the No. 1 of Lewis Gun, fixes his bayonet. Men in rifle sections must be trained either to the Lewis Gun or Rifle Bomb.

Bombing and Lewis Gun Sections are on the outer flank of Platoons.

In assembly the distance between lines and waves may conveniently be reduced to lessen the danger of rear waves being caught in enemy barrage, the distance being increased when the advance takes place.

"Moppers up" follow the second line of a wave and precede the unit for which they are to mop up. If the numbers are large they must be found from a different Company or Battalion. Small numbers are preferably found from the unit for which they are to mop up. They must carry a distinctive badge and have their own Commander. G.S.

(12605)Wt.W. 16056-9527 SPL. 44M. 3-17. H & J. Ld   O.B. No. 1919/T

Endnotes

Introduction

1. G.D. Mitchell, *Backs to the Wall*, Allen & Unwin, Crows Nest, 2007, pp. 161–62.
2. *The Queenslander*, 16 June 1917.
3. Mitchell, *Backs to the Wall*, p. 161.
4. AWM26 191/10 Battle of Messines, II Anzac Corps Intelligence, 7 to 12 June 1917, order from the *17th Bavarian Infantry Regiment*, 6 June 1917.
5. AWM38 3DRL 606/248/1, Bean Notebook.
6. Letter, Colonel Denis Bernard to Edmonds, AWM38 3DRL 7953/34 Part 1.
7. There are, in fact, more books on the exploits of the tunnellers than on the battle of Messines itself. *Crumps and Camouflets* by Damien Finlayson (Big Sky Publishing, Newport, 2010) is by some distance the finest work on the Australian tunnelling companies and a worthy contender for the finest book on tunnelling in the Great War. A recent Australian book, now a feature film, *Beneath Hill 60*, deals specifically with the story of the 1st Australian Tunnelling Company's defence of the mines at Hill 60.
8. C.E.W. Bean, *Official History of Australia in the War of 1914-18*, Vol. IV, *The AIF in France 1917*, Angus & Robertson, Sydney, 1941, p. 721.
9. A.J.P. Taylor, *The First World War*, Penguin, UK, 1963, p. 145.
10. B.H. Liddell Hart, *History of the First World War*, Pan, London, 1973, p. 326.
11. General Hermann von Kuhl, quoted in J. Edmonds, *Official History of the War*, Vol. II, *Military Operations France and Belgium 1917*, His Majesty's Stationery Office, London, 1948, p. 94.
12. David Lloyd George, *War Memoirs of David Lloyd George*, Vol. IV, Little, Brown and Company, Boston, 1933–37, pp. 2111–15.
13. J.M. Bourne, *Who's Who in World War One*, Routledge, London, 2001, pp. 234–35.
14. C.E.W. Bean, *Official History of Australia in the War of 1914-18*, Vol. II, *The Story of ANZAC*, Angus & Robertson, Sydney, 1941, p. 910.
15. Ibid.
16. IWM documents 15204, papers of Lieutenant Colonel L.E.S. Ward, DSO.

Chapter 1

1. MSS0717, O.H. Woodward, 'The Firing of the Hill 60 Mines by the First Australian Tunnelling Company', p. 92.
2. The Canadians had placed the mines in July (Hill 60) and October (the Caterpillar) of 1916 and the 1st Australian Tunnelling Company had relieved the Canadians in November. The Hill 60 mine lay at a depth of 30 metres and the Caterpillar mine at 33 metres. For an excellent overview of the Australian contribution to the mining at Messines, see Finlayson, *Crumps and Camouflets*, Chapter 6; Bean, *Official History*, Vol. IV, *The AIF in France 1917*, pp. 949–67.
3. Woodward, 'The Firing of the Hill 60 Mines by the First Australian Tunnelling Company',

Endnotes

      p. 96.

4.   This prodigious British effort, which would become the war's most famous tunnelling exploit, began in the early days of stalemate in 1915 as the brainchild of the extraordinary Lieutenant Colonel Sir John 'Empire Jack' Norton Griffiths, who conceived the idea of creating a serious of underground explosions so vast they would blow gaps in the German lines and create a monstrous, morale-sapping earthquake, 'shaking' the enemy from the ridge.

5.   W. Grant Grieve and B. Newman, *Tunnellers: The Story of the Tunnelling Companies, Royal Engineers, During the World War*, Herbert Jenkins Limited, London, 1936, p. 316.

6.   Nineteen of the 25 mines would be blown on 7 June. One (La Petit Douve Farm) was lost to German counter-mining and another (Peckham 2) to a partial mine collapse due to an inrush of wet sand. The group of four mines at the southern extremity of the line of attack (The Birdcage) was not blown for tactical reasons as the Germans had withdrawn from this part of the line. The La Petit Douve Farm and Peckham 2 mines as well as three of the four Birdcage mines still lie buried under Messines Ridge.

7.   Neville Lytton, *The Press and the General Staff*, W. Collins & Son, London, 1920, p. 97.

8.   Woodward, 'The Firing of the Hill 60 Mines by the First Australian Tunnelling Company', p. 92.

9.   Two obvious exceptions were Hill 63 (named so for its height in metres) which was in the British zone opposite Messines and the man-made Hill 60 which was created from the spoil of the Ypres–Comines Canal and which, with its location at the northern end of the Messines–Wytschaete Ridge and proximity to Ypres, explains its value.

10.   Woodward, 'The Firing of the Hill 60 Mines by the First Australian Tunnelling Company', p. 92.

11.   Mathilde was the wife of William, Duke of Normandy, and hence, from 1066, Queen of England.

12.   Bean, *Official History*, Vol. IV, *The AIF in France 1917*, p. 3.

13.   Jellicoe Memorandum to Balfour 29/10/16, British Library MS 49057.

14.   Jellicoe's intervention, which would eventually bolster the case for the Flanders campaign, was clearly not welcomed by Lloyd George who challenged his First Sea Lord in the War Committee meeting, believing him to be overstating the threat. The solution of denying the Channel ports to U-boats was not what eventually defeated the threat and was unlikely to do so in any case. The British fought the battle of the Atlantic in 1812, 1914–18 and 1940–45 and, in each case, the solution was an effective convoy system, protected by warships and backed by advances in technology to detect and capture or destroy raiders. Lloyd George had raised the issue of convoys at the War Committee meeting of November 1916, a solution dismissed by Jellicoe and the other admirals present because, they claimed, convoys presented too large a target and ships' masters lacked the skills and discipline to keep station. Since both explanations were dubious to say the least, and Jellicoe could hardly have been unaware of the Navy's previous successful convoy systems, it is difficult to believe such objections were treated seriously.

15.   PRO CAB 42/24/10: [Hankey] to Robertson, 22 November 1916; PRO CAB 42/24/13: Minutes of War Committee 20 November 1916 in French, *The Strategy of the Lloyd-George Coalition*, Oxford University Press, Oxford, 1995, pp. 50–51.

16.   Bean, *Official History*, Vol. IV, *The AIF in France 1917*, p. 546. Sir William Robertson was

the Chief of the Imperial General Staff.

17. AWM 26 185/6 G.H.Q. Royal Navy.

18. The monitors were large barges mounted with 12-inch guns which were intended to protect the left flank of the army against a German amphibious landing. Bacon rightly pointed out that they were eminently expendable as there were enough troops in France to secure the coast and they would simply rust away unused after the war. Bacon's willingness to sacrifice them all however, and his observation that 'their guns are hopelessly less than that of the large coast batteries' would not have given their crews much comfort.

19. AWM 26 185/6 G.H.Q. Royal Navy.

20. Ibid.

21. Bean, *Official History*, Vol. IV, *The AIF in France 1917*, p. 549.

22. Ibid., pp. 549–50.

23. Ibid., p. 550.

24. Ibid., p. 552.

25. Ibid., p. 556.

26. Withdrawal from the ridge was strongly counselled by Crown Prince Rupprecht's Chief of Staff (and as such, the key operational commander for *Armee Gruppe Wytschaete*), General Herman von Kuhl.

27. AWM 3DRL 7953/34 Part 1. Harington, writing in 1932, relied on his memory on this point as he (and Plumer) had destroyed their papers. Bean, although aware of Harington's observations, left his draft unchanged.

28. Harington's entry in the Second Army War Diary on 10 May referring to Haig's wish to push through on 'one day' is a clear change, so his objection on this point is unconvincing.

29. WO 95/275 Second Army War Diary 10/5/17.

30. WO 158/300 Letters, Second Army Headquarters.

31. Ibid.

32. Ibid.

33. This was the line Owl Support to Odyssey trenches. It would eventually be extended to the main German support line (the Oosttaverne Line) which would become the final objective (the Green Line).

34. WO 158/300 Letters, Second Army Headquarters.

35. Ibid.

36. AWM 3 DRL 2316/3/47, Second Army Intelligence Summary 1–15 June.

37. Bean, *Official History*, Vol. IV, *The AIF in France 1917*, p. 588.

38. Ibid.

39. Ibid.

40. AWM45 33/1 GHQ BEF Correspondence [Messines–Ypres].

41. Ibid.

42. It was not until 19 May that Plumer communicated to his corps commanders through Harington that the capture of the Oosttaverne Line would be by 'a deliberate attack' rather than the result of simply pushing out the original final objective. WO 158/300 Letters, Second Army Headquarters.

43. By 19 September, the New Zealand Division had lost 100 officers and 3000 other ranks.

Following its subsequent attacks on 25–26 September and 1 October, this had increased to a total of 7000 casualties including 1560 officers and men killed.

44.   Rawlinson quoted in H. Stewart, *The New Zealand Division 1916-1919: A Popular History Based on Records*, New Zealand Government [Intype London], London, 1920, p. 120.

45.   M. Kincaid-Smith, *The 25th Division in France and Flanders*, Harrison and Sons, London, 1918, p. 12. The attack was delivered by the 11th Cheshire, 8th South Borders, 2nd South Lancashires and 8th South Lancashires. This doomed assault was part of a series of appallingly costly and failed attempts to capture the strongpoints around Thiepval.

46.   Ibid., p. 13.

47.   Bean, *Official History*, Vol. IV, *The AIF in France 1917*, p. 579.

Chapter 2

1.   Bean, *Official History*, Vol. IV, *The AIF in France 1917*, p. 266.

2.   Ibid., p. 349.

3.   C.E.W. Bean, *Official History of Australia in the War of 1914-18*, Vol. III, *The AIF in France 1916*, Angus & Robertson, Sydney, 1941, p. 771.

4.   AWM PR 85/310, private papers of Private Denver Gallwey, 47th Battalion, p. 1789. Professor Eric Andrews' very strong comment in a note on Birdwood's correspondence with Northcliffe following Bullecourt is perhaps a modern-day equivalent of that sentiment. 'His cheerful dismissal of losses, claim to prescience, boyish description of killing Germans and comment that "Personally, I do not feel in the least war weary" can only be described as disgusting to anyone who has studied the battles.' Eric Andrews, *The Anzac Illusion*, Cambridge University Press, Cambridge, 1993, p. 238.

5.   Bean, *Official History*, Vol. IV, *The AIF in France 1917*, p. 579.

6.   WO 158/304 Second Army Administrative Operations, Battle Straggler Post: Number of men employed:
II Anzac 150 (79 Military Police)
IX Corps 44 (9 Military Police)
X Corps 42 (18 Military Police)

7.   Bean, *Official History*, Vol. IV, *The AIF in France 1917*, p. 644.

8.   Brian Bond and Simon Robbins (eds.), *Staff Officer: The Diaries of Lord Moyne, 1914-1918*, Leo Cooper, London, 1987, p. 62.

9.   Ibid., pp. 66–67.

10.   Ibid., p. 63.

11.   Bean, *Official History*, Vol. IV, *The AIF in France 1917*, p. 645.

12.   See Andrews, *The Anzac Illusion*, pp. 102–03.

13.   P. Scott, *Law and Orders: Discipline and Morale in the British Armies in France, 1917* in Peter Liddle (ed.), *Passchendaele in Perspective: The Third Battle of Ypres*, Leo Cooper, London, 1997, p. 368.

14.   See Peter Stanley, *Bad Characters: Sex, Crime, Mutiny, Murder and the Australian Imperial Force*, Allen & Unwin, Sydney, 2010.

15.   Bond (ed.), *Staff Officer*, p. 62.

16.   Lieutenant Z., 'In a Tank on Messines Ridge', *Scriber's Magazine*, Vol. 62, Jul–Dec 1917.

17.   Mitchell, *Backs to the Wall*, pp. 150–51.

18.   LHCMH Robertson: 8/1/14 Murray to Robertson 18/3/16 letter.

19.   Murray had been 'an unhappy choice' as Sir John French's Chief of Staff in 1914. Out of his depth in the role (his appointment owed more to the political feuds at the head of British command rather than military ability), he was constantly undermined by rivals, his staff and by French himself who preferred the overlooked Henry Wilson for the role. In poor health, Murray suffered a breakdown at the battle of La Cateau, was sent home and later given command of the Egyptian Expeditionary Force in January 1916. A more than capable administrator, Murray was responsible for the successful organisation of the defences of Egypt, a considerable achievement given the chaotic system he inherited and the much underestimated Turkish threat they eventually staved off. Although his letters to Robertson reveal his distrust of and contempt for Birdwood and his lack of candour when dealing with him (which Birdwood reciprocated in equal measure), Murray specifically rejected any suggestion that the Australians not proceed to France in his letter to Robertson.

20.   LHCMH Robertson: 8/1/14 Godley to Murray 24/2/16 letter.

21.   LHCMH Robertson: 8/1/14 Birdwood to Murray 25/2/16 letter.

22.   Ibid.

23.   Ibid.

24.   Christopher Pugsley, *The Anzac Experience: New Zealand, Australia and Empire in the First World War*, Reed Publishing, Auckland, 2004, p. 159.

25.   Bean, *Official History*, Vol. III, *The AIF in France 1916*, pp. 56–61.

26.   Bean, *Official History*, Vol. II, *The Story of Anzac*, p. 21.

27.   Ibid. The *Official History* is also unclear on whether Robertson even received Murray's caustic letter, claiming that the fact of its receipt 'is not known'. This may be slightly disingenuous — there is no doubt that a draft was received by Robertson and today is included in his papers and it is unlikely that Bean was unaware of this. What is uncertain is whether Murray ever formalised his letter. If he did so (which is unlikely), he ignored Birdwood's advice to make its content known to the Australian government.

28.   Ibid., p. 60.

29.   Kevin Fewster (ed.), *Bean's Gallipoli: The Diaries of Australia's Official War Correspondent*, Allen & Unwin, Sydney, 1983, p. 45.

30.   Ibid.

31.   Bean, *Official History*, Vol. IV, *The AIF in France 1917*, pp. 560–63.

32.   Edgar Rule, *Jacka's Mob*, Angus & Robertson, Sydney, 1933, p. 15.

33.   Monash finally relented in November, bringing the 3rd Division into line with the rest of the AIF. See AWM25 713/45 30/11/17.

34.   Monash letter to Lamb 27.5.17, Monash Papers NL 1884 Series 1 Correspondence, B Folder 490.

35.   Ibid.

36.   Bean, *Official History*, Vol. IV, *The AIF in France 1917*, p. 561.

37.   Ibid.

38.   Many in the 3rd Division embraced the nickname, turning it into a badge of pride. The history of the 44th Battalion by Captain Cyril Longmore took 'Eggs-a-Cook' as its title.

39.   V. Brahms, *Spirit of the Forty-Second. Narrative of the 42nd Battalion, 11th Infantry Brigade*

3rd Division, AIF 1914-18, W.R. Smith & Paterson Pty. Ltd., Brisbane, 1938.

40.   Ibid.

41.   Mitchell, *Backs to the Wall*, p. 145.

42.   References to proving the worth of the division at Messines represent a theme common to virtually all the battalion histories and are ubiquitous in the letters and diaries of the men of the 3rd in the build-up to and the aftermath of the battle.

43.   See Bean, *Official History*, Vol. IV, *The AIF in France 1917*, pp. 565–68.

44.   2 DRL/0789 Diary of Private George Davies, 36 Battalion.

45.   Ray Grover, 'Godley, Alexander John', *Dictionary of New Zealand Biography*, Te Ara, the Encyclopaedia of New Zealand, updated 1 October 2013.

46.   Mashonaland is today northern Zimbabwe.

47.   Hart Diary, 15/9/15 QEII Army Memorial Museum, Wairau, quoted in Pugsley, *The Anzac Experience*, p. 95.

48.   See Bourne, *Who's Who in World War One*, p. 107.

49.   Bond (ed.), *Staff Officer*, p. 66.

50.   WO256/19 Haig Diary.

51.   Bond (ed.), *Staff Officer*, p. 114.

52.   WO256/19 Haig Diary.

53.   Bean, *Official History*, Vol. III, *The AIF in France 1916*, p. 24. Bean mentions these factors specifically as responsible for the change in command in the case of several senior officers of the AIF (pp. 23–24) and it seems likely also that they may have been factors in Cox's case given that he was not reallocated to operational command in the British Army.

54.   WO 256/20 Haig Diary, 23 July 1917.

55.   Bean, *Official History*, Vol. III, *The AIF in France 1916*, p. 600.

56.   Bond (ed.), *Staff Officer*, p. 149.

57.   Fewster (ed.), *Bean's Gallipoli*, p. 104.

58.   Ibid., p. 200.

59.   Bean, *Official History*, Vol. II, *The Story of Anzac*, p. 589.

60.   Bond (ed.), *Staff Officer*, p. 149. Monash was 52, Guinness 37 in 1917.

61.   Geoffrey Serle, 'Monash, Sir John (1865–1931)', *Australian Dictionary of Biography*, Vol. 10, Melbourne University Press, 1986.

62.   AWM25 713/45 3rd Division Conference, 26/2/18.

63.   See Craig Deayton, *Battle Scarred: The 47th Battalion in the First World War*, Big Sky Publishing, Sydney, 2011.

64.   IWM Documents10239, Diary, Brigadier General G.N. Johnston, C.R.A. New Zealand Division.

Chapter 3

1.   AWM 26 188/1 Operations file: Second Army, Intelligence, 7 to 12 June 1917.

2.   Ibid.

3.   Soldier of the German *40th Infantry Division* quoted in J. Sheldon, *The German Army at Passchendaele*, Pen & Sword Military, Barnsley, 2007, p. 3.

4.   Ibid.

5.   Operations file: Second Army, Intelligence, 7 to 12 June 1917, AWM 26 188/1.

6.   WO 95/2245/2, 25th Division War Diary.

7.   WO 95/2215/3, 8th Battalion, the Border Regiment, War Diary.

8.   AWM41 6/47 Sister A.N. Smith.

9.   AWM27 371/32 [Medical Organisations] Messines Operations.

10.   The Catacombs remain intact (if inaccessible) today.

11.   Grieve and Newman, *The Tunnellers*, p. 239.

12.   AWM4 1/32/15, II Anzac Headquarters.

13.   Operations file: Second Army, Intelligence, 7 to 12 June 1917, AWM 26 188/1.

14.   A study of the effects of the similarly intense (though much briefer) bombardment of the Bar Lev Line in the Yom Kippur War found that confinement in concrete shelters increased the psychological stress of the artillery barrage. See R. Gal and H. Dayan, *The Psychological Effects of Intense Artillery Bombardment: The Israeli Experience in the Yom-Kippur War (1973)*, The Israeli Institute for Military Studies, Ya'Akov, 1992.

15.   AWM38 3 DRL 606/54/1, Bean Notebook.

16.   IWM Documents 10805, Captain E.G.F. Boon.

17.   Soldier of the German *4th Grenadier Regiment* quoted in Sheldon, *The German Army at Passchendaele*, p. 4.

18.   Bill Lyall, letter of 2/7/17 in K.M. Lyall, *Letters from an Anzac Gunner*, Lyall's Yarns Pty Ltd, East Kew, Victoria, 1990, p. 117.

19.   AWM PR00092 Private Alexander MacIntosh, 7th Australian Field Artillery Brigade.

20.   AWM38 3DRL 606/248/2 Lieutenant W.G. Fisher, diary 6/6/17 in Bean Notebook.

21.   AWM4 1/46/8 Part 1, 3rd Division General Staff Headquarters.

22.   AWM 26 188/1 Operations file: Second Army, Intelligence, 7 to 12 June 1917.

23.   Ian Hogg, *Allied Artillery of World War One*, Crowood Press, Ramsbury, 1998, p. 17.

24.   2nd Brigade Heavy Branch, Summary of Operations with Second Army, E2006.1792, Bovington Tank Museum.

25.   Soldier of the German *4th Grenadier Regiment* quoted in Sheldon, *The German Army at Passchendaele*, p. 4.

26.   Captain Brereton, *Under Haig in Flanders*, Blackie and Sons, London, 1917, p. 264.

27.   AWM 4 23/50/7.

28.   AWM4 1/33/13 Part 1 Intelligence II Anzac Headquarters.

29.   Ibid.

30.   Soldier of the German *1st Field Artillery Regiment*, quoted in Sheldon, *The German Army at Passchendaele*, p. 5.

31.   AWM4 1/46/7, 3rd Division General Staff Headquarters.

32.   AWM 26 188/1, Operations file: Second Army, Intelligence, 7 to 12 June 1917.

33.   AWM4 1/32/12, II Anzac War Diary.

34.   Ibid.

35.   AWM28 Recommendation for Private George Seagrott.

36.   AWM 4 23/50/4, 33rd Battalion War Diary.

37.   AWM4 1/46/7 3rd Division General Staff Headquarters.

38.   Ibid.

39.   AWM4 1/33/14 Part 1 Intelligence II Anzac Headquarters.

40.   WO 158/305 Report on Army Centre.

41.   Lieutenant Alan Archibald Leslie Downie, 40th Battalion AIF, Diary.

42.   IWM Documents12244, Private Papers of Lieutenant Thomas McKenny Hughes.

43.   Woodward, 'The Firing of the Hill 60 Mines by the First Australian Tunnelling Company', pp. 78, 80.

44.   Finlayson, *Crumps and Camouflets*, Chapter 6; Bean, *Official History*, Vol. IV, *The AIF in France 1917*, pp. 949–59. Bean cites the history of the German *204th Infantry Division* and the reports of the Second Army Controller of Mines, both recording the constant underground warfare at Hill 60.

45.   Bean, *Official History*, Vol. IV, *The AIF in France 1917*, p. 954.

46.   Ibid.

47.   Ibid.; Edmonds, Vol. II, *Military Operations in France and Belgium 1917*, p. 48.

48.   AWM 26 188/1 Operations file: Second Army, Intelligence, 7 to 12 June 1917.

49.   AWM26 186/11, 1st Australian Tunnelling Company, 20 May–6 June 1917.

50.   See Edmonds, Vol. II, *Military Operations in France and Belgium 1917*, p. 92.

51.   WO 158/487 Battle of Messines: Maps.

52.   AWM38 3DRL606/81/1, Bean Notebook.

53.   Bean, *Official History*, Vol. IV, *The AIF in France 1917*, p. 584.

54.   Hogg, *Allied Artillery of World War One*, p. 18.

55.   AWM38 3DRL606/81/1, Bean Notebook.

56.   Bean, *Official History*, Vol. IV, *The AIF in France 1917*, p. 589.

57.   2DRL/0928 Mitchell Diary.

Chapter 4

1.   Reginald Biggs, 'Reminiscences – That Other War by Private "Ashmead"', NS 2861/1/1, private papers, pp. 125–26, State Archives of Tasmania.

2.   Frank Green, *The Fortieth*, 40th Battalion Association, Hobart, 1922, p. 55.

3.   According to Biggs, the 40th Battalion route 'was divided to follow two roughly parallel routes to their "hop-over" places. The route which my crowd followed was from Regina Camp until, 400 yards west of Ploegsteert, it crossed the Messines road, then westward of Creslow farm, recrossing the road 100 yards past Hyde Park Corner, then over the slope of Hill 63 … then down the other side of the hill past Dead Cow Farm and Barossa Farm, across the Douve and in the New Zealand trenches.' Biggs, *Reminiscences*, p. 127.

4.   Green, *The Fortieth*, p. 54.

5.   Major Charles Hellar, USAR, *Chemical Warfare in World War 1- The American Experience 1917-1918*, Leavenworth Papers No. 10, Combat Studies Institute, US Command and General Staff College, Fort Leavenworth, Kansas, 1984.

6.   The Spartans used toxic smoke from burning wood, pitch and sulphur while besieging cities. See Adrienne Mayor, *Greek Fire, Poison Arrows & Scorpion Bombs: Biological and Chemical Warfare in the Ancient World*, Overlook Duckworth, Woodstock, 2003, p. 211.

7.   Hellar, *Chemical Warfare in World War 1*.

8.   IWM Sound Archive 716/8, Henry Oxley, 'Description of Rainham Gas Chambers'.

9.   Rule, *Jacka's Mob*, p. 91.
10. Hellar, *Chemical Warfare in World War 1*.
11. Ibid.
12. Despite its shortcomings, the SBR was a major advance in protection from gas attacks, replacing its often wholly ineffective predecessors. Its introduction was largely responsible for the Germans abandoning their 'cloud' gas attack (release from cylinders) and switching to gas shells (see L.F. Haber, *The Poisonous Cloud: Chemical Warfare in the First World War*, Clarendon Press, Oxford, 1986, p. 177. For obvious reasons, the SBR provided more effective protection from gas clouds for troops in static positions, the difficulties of its use for troops on the move compounded by carrying the heavy loads needed for attacks.
13. Biggs, *Reminiscences*, NS 2861 State Library of Tasmania, p. 127.
14. Ibid.
15. Those battalions were the 33rd, 34th, 35th and 36th battalions (9th Brigade) and the 37th, 38th, 39th and 40th battalions (10th Brigade).
16. Bean, *Official History*, Vol. IV, *The AIF in France 1917*, p. 592.
17. Biggs, *Reminiscences*, NS 2861 State Library of Tasmania, p. 127. Bean records that the gas was mostly lachrymatory (tear) but with phosgene and chlorine mixed in. *Official History*, Vol. IV, *The AIF in France 1917*, p. 590.
18. John Edwards, *Never a Backward Step: A History of the First 33rd Battalion, A.I.F.*, Bettong Books, Grafton, 1996, p. 40.
19. Lieutenant Alan Downie, 40th Battalion, Diary.
20. Green, *The Fortieth*, p. 59.
21. Bean, *Official History*, Vol. IV, *The AIF in France 1917*, p. 590.
22. AWM4 1/46/8 Part 1, 3rd Division General Staff, Headquarters.
23. Bean, *Official History*, Vol. IV, *The AIF in France 1917*, p. 589.
24. The first objective (Blue Line) included the German front and support trenches. The second was the Brown Line, a reserve trench system on the western edge of Messines, and the third (Yellow Line) was the village and the trenches on its eastern boundary. The final objective was the Black Line on the reverse slope of the ridge and a further position (Black Dotted Line) a series of defensive posts in advance of the main defensive line.
25. WO 256/04 Haig Diary.
26. Ibid. Haig described Russell as 'a most capable officer with considerable strength of character'.
27. David Ferguson, *The History of the Canterbury Regiment N.Z.E.F. 1914-1919*, Whitcomb and Tombs, Auckland, 1921, p. 153.
28. Ibid., p. 158.
29. Ormond Burton, *The Silent Division: New Zealanders at the Front 1914-1919*, Angus & Robertson, Sydney, 1935, p. 206.
30. William Austin, *The Official History of the New Zealand Rifle Brigade*, L.T. Watkins Ltd., Wellington, 1924, p. 198.
31. MSS0717, Oliver Woodward, 'The War Story of Oliver Holmes Woodward', p. 97.
32. Present were Major James Henry, Captain Oliver Woodward, Lieutenant John Royle, Captain James Bowry and Sergeant James Wilson.
33. AWM 26 188/1 Operations file, Second Army, Intelligence, 7 to 12 June 1917.

Endnotes

34. Woodward, 'The Firing of the Hill 60 Mines by the First Australian Tunnelling Company'.

35. AWM38 3DRL606/81/1, Bean Notebook.

36. AWM 26 186/12 Operations file, Second Army, 1st Australian Tunnelling Company, 7 to 12 June 1917.

37. IWM Documents 5, papers of J. Colinsky.

38. AWM 26 190/24 Operations file, New Zealand Division, General Staff, 7 to 12 June 1917.

39. P. Gibbs, *The War Despatches*, quoted in Ian Passingham, *Pillars of Fire*, Sutton, Phoenix Mill, 1998, p. 90.

40. The descriptions indicate the earthquake was approximately 6.0 to 6.9 on the Richter scale within a five-mile radius of the ridge.

41. AWM 2DRL/0309 Private Lancelot Smith, 10th Field Ambulance, letter.

42. Pruesser, *History Infantry Regiment 176*, quoted in Sheldon, *The German Army at Passchendaele*, p. 19.

43. German *Official History*, quoted in Passingham, *Pillars of Fire*, p. 91.

44. MLDOC 2413, State Library of New South Wales, Fuljames Diary.

45. IWM Documents 11247, Lieutenant Colonel J.B. Parks.

46. *The North Western Advocate and the Emu Bay Times* p. 5, 9 June 1917.

47. AWM MSS 1113 Appleton, Lieutenant Percy Dobson, Siege Artillery Brigade.

48. IWM Documents 3387, Major R.P. Schweder, MC.

49. Lieutenant Edward Winchester, letter, July 1918.

50. Ibid.

51. 2 DRL/0789 Diary of Private George Davies, 36 Battalion.

52. WO 95/1415/3, 3rd Battalion, the Worcestershire Regiment, War Diary.

53. Ibid.

54. H.F. Stacke, *The Worcestershire Regiment in the Great War*, Naval & Military Press Ltd., UK, 2002, p. 267.

55. IWM 9586 Arthur Stanley White, sound recording (1987).

56. WO 95/2224, 25th Division War Diary.

57. Ibid. The overwhelming factor in the success of Messines was the massive artillery advantage possessed by the Second Army. For example, supporting the 25th Division's 1200-yard front were the 25th Division Artillery, 2nd New Zealand Field Artillery Brigade, 34th Army Field Artillery Brigade, 93rd Army Field Artillery Brigade and Guards Divisional Artillery which, combined, deployed one hundred and twenty-six 18-pounders and thirty-four 4.5-inch howitzers. They were also supported by the 42nd, 49th, 16th and 11th Heavy Artillery Groups which added thirty 60-pounders, four 6-inch guns, forty 6-inch howitzers, four 8-inch howitzers, twenty 9.2-inch howitzers, four 12-inch howitzers and one 15-inch howitzer. Having destroyed a good proportion of the German guns opposite in the preliminary artillery duels and battered the defensive lines mercilessly in the two weeks leading in, the guns were now employed to pound the path ahead of the assaulting infantry.

58. 3DRL 606/248/2, AWM 38, Lieutenant W.G. Fisher, diary 7/6/17 in Bean Notebook.

59. WO 95/2245/2, 74th Brigade War Diary.

60. IWM Documents 927, Major R.J. Blackadder, 151st Siege Battery.

61. Stacke, *The Worcestershire Regiment in the Great War*, p. 267.
62. WO 95/1415/3, 3rd Battalion, the Worcestershire Regiment, War Diary.
63. WO95/2224, 25th Division War Diary.
64. Ibid.
65. WO 95/1415/3, 3rd Battalion, the Worcestershire Regiment, War Diary.
66. WO 95/2247/1, 2nd Battalion, Royal Irish Rifles, War Diary.
67. Ibid. Captain C.C. Thompson, who led the attack, was recorded as killed in action.
68. WO 95/2224, 25th Division War Diary.
69. WO 95/2246/3, 13th Battalion, the Cheshire Regiment, War Diary.
70. Ibid.
71. Bond (ed.), *Staff Officer*, p. 156.
72. WO 95/2215/3, 8th Battalion, the Border Regiment, War Diary.
73. IWM Documents12244, Lieutenant Thomas McKenny Hughes.
74. Russell had marked the Blue line (the German reserve line) as the first objective rather than the German front-line trenches which he correctly suspected would be lightly manned (if at all) and he ordered his men to simply sweep past the German front line to secure the Blue Line.
75. Austin, *The Official History of the New Zealand Rifle Brigade*, p. 201.
76. WA-77-1, 1st Canterbury Battalion War Diary.
77. WO 95/2245/2, 25th Division War Diary.
78. WA-77-1, 1st Canterbury Battalion War Diary.
79. Ferguson, *The History of the Canterbury Regiment N.Z.E.F. 1914-1919*, p. 160.
80. National Library of New Zealand OHInt-0006/11, interview with James Frederick Blakemore.
81. Lieutenant Edward Winchester, letter, July 1918.
82. Ibid.
83. The *London Gazette* (Supplement), no. 30215, p. 7906.
84. Winchester, letter, July 1918.
85. Ferguson, *The History of the Canterbury Regiment N.Z.E.F. 1914-1919*, p. 152.
86. AWM4 23/9/8, 9th Brigade AIF War Diary.
87. AWM4 23/50/8, 33rd Battalion AIF War Diary.
88. AWM4 1/46/8 Part 2, 3rd Australian Division Headquarters.
89. 1DRL /0014, Corporal Charles Akers, letter.
90. Ibid.
91. Norman Meagher, *With the Fortieth, the 40th Battalion, Australian Imperial Force Abroad*, R.J. Meagher, Hobart, 1917, p. 149.
92. AWM4 23/57/15 Part 1, 40th Battalion War Diary.
93. Bean, *Official History*, Vol. IV, *The AIF in France 1917*, p. 595.
94. MS 11651 State Library of Victoria, Private E.T. Popping, 38th Battalion, letter.
95. AWM 4 23/57/15 Part 1, 38th Battalion War Diary.
96. Ibid.
97. AWM 4 1/46/8 Part 2, 3rd Australian Division Headquarters.

98. Ibid. Only 120 of the 360 men who set out with the 39th Battalion reached the start line.
99. Ibid.
100. AWM4 23/9/8, 9th Brigade AIF War Diary.
101. Ibid.
102. AWM 4 1/46/8 Part 2, 3rd Australian Division Headquarters.
103. 1DRL/0428 Red Cross Wounded and Missing Enquiry Bureau files: Private William Bacon.
104. 1DRL/0428 Red Cross Wounded and Missing Enquiry Bureau files: Private Alan Mather.
105. AWM41 6/47 Nurse A.P. Smith.

Chapter 5

1. Denver Gallwey, 'The Silver King', three volumes, MSS 1355, p. 2111.
2. 'The Silver King' was the name of an obscure play remembered by Gallwey's parents and starring a certain Wilfred Denver whose leading performance so moved them that they christened their son 'Wilfred Denver Gallwey' in his honour. Though his lengthy memoirs are frequently quoted (particularly his account of Messines) under the name 'Wilfred Gallwey' he was known throughout his life as Denver Gallwey, a fact confirmed by his widow in an interview with the author in 2010.
3. 3DRL/2562 (A) Lieutenant Colonel Alexander Imlay, Diary.
4. AWM 38 3DRL 606/80/1, Bean Notebook.
5. Monash Papers, NL 1884 Series 1, Correspondence, B Folder, 490.
6. Bean, *Official History*, Vol. IV, *The AIF in France 1917*, p. 607.
7. AWM 38 3DRL 606/178/2, Bean Notebook.
8. AWM 4 23/13/17, 13th Brigade AIF War Diary.
9. Ibid.
10. IWM Documents 12244 McKenny Hughes, diary, entries 5–7 June.
11. Ibid.
12. Bean, *Official History*, Vol. IV, *The AIF in France 1917*, p. 609n.
13. AWM 4 23/12/16, 12th Brigade War Diary.
14. AWM4 1/46/8 General Staff, Headquarters 3rd Australian Division. It would be a full hour later than the 'practically certain' time of 9.10 am that Plumer would announce the change and later still before the news reached all the affected units.
15. AWM4 1/48/15 General Staff, Headquarters 4th Australian Division.
16. Thus 'refusing' entry to the flank.
17. Pope admitted drinking after the battle with several officers but denied being drunk. McCay's evidence was bolstered by the Brigade Major of the 14th, Major Charteris (one of those who joined Pope for a drink after the battle) whose evidence was damning. However Pope found several witnesses to attest to his sobriety, testimony he wished to present to a court martial.
18. AWM 4 23/12/16, 12th Brigade War Diary. The Blauwen Molen or 'Blue Mill' was the foundation of the now destroyed village windmill on the crest of the ridge.
19. AWM 4 23/12/16, 12th Brigade War Diary. The 'Red' Dotted Line referred to was the same 'Black' Dotted Line referred to throughout.
20. Gallwey, 'The Silver King', p. 2155.

21. AWM 4 23/12/16, 12th Brigade War Diary.

22. AWM 4 1/46/8 Part 1 General Staff, Headquarters 3rd Australian Division.

23. Edmonds, Vol. II, *Military Operations France and Belgium 1917*, p. 72.

24. The SOS (save our souls) barrage was an emergency measure which protected a position from enemy attack.

25. Bean, *Official History*, Vol. IV, *The AIF in France 1917*, p. 618.

26. Bean records that the *3rd Bavarian Division*, opposite the line shared by the 25th Division and the New Zealand Division had only two 4.1-inch guns intact and was unable to 'deal with the tempting targets offered by the columns passing over Messines. Only where the columns came within range of the 4th Bavarian Division's artillery in the south were material losses caused [i.e. in the 12th Brigade and the 3rd and New Zealand divisions].' Bean, *Official History*, Vol. IV, *The AIF in France 1917*, p. 616. This situation, along with the counter-attacks which were heaviest in the south, contributed significantly to the disproportionate casualty figures for II Anzac compared to the rest of the Second Army.

27. Mistakenly noted as the 5th Lincolns in the 52nd Battalion War Diary.

28. Bean, *Official History*, Vol. IV, *The AIF in France 1917*, p. 615.

29. WO 95/1810 33rd Infantry Brigade Headquarters.

30. Ibid. The 33rd Brigade objective was thus reduced by 600 yards to 1200 yards.

31. Via 'Vierstraat Switch' and 'Chinese Wall'. The 33rd Brigade orders do not include detailed route guides, a situation forced on it by the late decision to commit the brigade.

32. The time of receipt of the 'new zero' is recorded as 1.05 pm in the 7th Battalion War Diary, the South Staffordshire Regiment WO 95/1816. This meant that, having marched much of the night, and then endured a forced march through the heat of the morning from Vierstraat, loaded with 60 pounds in full fighting order, the men of the 33rd were still at Chinese Wall, over four kilometres from their destination. They then needed to negotiate the broken country between the old front lines, scale the ridge and organise for the attack. They were resting at Chinese Wall and didn't leave until 1.50 pm.

33. WO 95/1816, 7th Battalion, South Staffordshire Regiment, War Diary.

34. WO 95/1811/3, 33rd Infantry Brigade Headquarters War Diary.

35. Ibid.

36. The 49th Battalion diary inexplicably claims twice in its report that the battalion moved off at 'New Zero plus 90 minutes'.

37. Whether Stubbings ordered this or it was Maxwell's own decision is unclear in every record. Bean, when lauding Maxwell for this decision, clearly implied it was his.

38. The 52nd's right flank was open as was the left flank of the 49th's two left companies, the right flank of the 49th, both flanks of the 49th's two right companies and the left flank of the 45th Battalion.

39. AWM41/48/15, 4th Division Order No. 60, 4. (c) 5 June.

40. Bean, *Official History*, Vol. IV, *The AIF in France 1917*, p. 634.

41. AWM26 187/3, 36th Australian Heavy Artillery Group.

42. AWM4 23/62/16, 45th Battalion War Diary.

43. IWM Documents 15777, Lieutenant Clifford Mendoza, 47th Battalion AIF Message Book.

44. AWM 26 190/24 Operations file: New Zealand Division, General Staff, 7 to 12 June 1917.

45. AWM4 23/62/16, 45th Battalion AIF War Diary.

46. AWM28/1/204 Honours and Awards Captain A.S. Allen, DSO.

47. AWM4 23/62/16, 45th Battalion AIF War Diary.

48. Ibid.

49. AWM28/1/204 Honours and Awards Captain A.S. Allen, DSO.

50. Sapper Edward Leslie Hughes, New Zealand Engineers (Field Squadron), New Zealand Division. Private papers and recollections quoted in Passingham, *Pillars of Fire*, p. 131.

51. 1DRL/0428 Red Cross Wounded and Missing Enquiry Bureau files: Captain John Millar.

52. AWM4 23/54/12, 37th Battalion War Diary.

53. AWM 2DRL/260 Captain Robert Grieve, 'Personal Experiences at Messines'.

54. AWM26 193/23, II ANZAC Corps, Mounted Troops, 20 May to 6 June 1917.

55. AWM27/11/16, 4th Light Horse Regiment (II Anzac Corps Mounted Regiment), private diary of Major Dunlop.

56. WO 157/587 Second Army Intelligence 1–30 June 1917.

57. SS 143 *Training of Platoons for Offensive Action*, issued by the General Staff, February 1917.

58. Ibid.

59. IWM EPH 1164, *Notes on dealing with hostile machine guns in an advance.*

60. Bean, *Official History*, Vol. IV, *The AIF in France 1917*, p. 624.

61. Grieve, 'Personal Experiences at Messines'.

62. Gallwey, 'The Silver King', pp. 2165–66.

63. Ibid., p. 2167.

64. Bean's vivid description of the emotions of battle again may owe something to Gallwey's diary in which he provides a remarkable account of his own feelings as he plunged forward with his battalion and into hand-to-hand fighting. See Deayton, *Battle Scarred: The 47th Battalion in the First World War*, p. 131.

65. Gallwey, 'The Silver King', pp. 2172–73. Bean drew on Gallwey's diary almost exclusively for the narrative of the events near Huns' Walk on the afternoon of 7 June. However he omitted the graphic description of the killing of surrendering Germans while conceding that the battle had become 'a thorough melee'.

66. IWM Documents 15777, Lieutenant Clifford Mendoza, 47th Battalion AIF, Message Book.

67. WO 256/19 Haig Diary. This was a reference to Monash having circulated a document within the 3rd Division outlining the brutal treatment of the Bullecourt prisoners, something Bean noted 'had no recorded effect'. Bean, *Official History*, Vol. IV, *The AIF in France 1917*, p. 579n.

68. AWM4 23/10/8, 10th Brigade AIF War Diary.

69. For this and other accounts of the killing of German prisoners see Gallwey, 'The Silver King', pp. 2167–68 and Deayton, *Battle Scarred: The 47th Battalion in the First World War*, p. 400n.

70. AWM PR 00436 Sapper Thomas Linney, 4th Division Signalling Company, letter.

71. IWM Documents 15777, Lieutenant Clifford Mendoza, 47th Battalion AIF, Message Book.

72. 3DRL/2562 (A), Imlay papers, Messines operation.

73. WO 95/1816 7th Battalion, South Staffordshire Regiment, War Diary.

74. Stephen Royle (ed.), *From Mons to Messines and beyond …; The Great War Experiences of*

Sgt. Charles Arnold, K.A.F. Books, Studley,1985, p. 46.

75. AWM4 23/62/16, 45th Battalion AIF War Diary.

76. AWM4 23/69/15, 52nd Battalion AIF War Diary.

77. WO 95 /1811/3, 33rd Infantry Brigade Headquarters.

78. AWM4 23/13/17, 13th Brigade AIF War Diary.

79. Ibid.

80. AWM4 1/48/15, 4th Division AIF War Diary.

81. IWM Documents 12244, Lieutenant Thomas McKenny Hughes.

82. Gallwey, 'The Silver King', p. 2194.

83. Gallwey timed the artillery barrage that drove out D Company at '22:00'. Further north, the barrage that drove out C and A companies was timed at about 1730 (5.30 pm). It is possible that Gallwey was mistaken as to the time, but more probable that the barrage that hit D Company arrived later, as this company was in a more advanced position. The fact that two different artillery brigades were firing, one behind the other, and that several different SOS messages were received by various units, both New Zealand and Australian, makes this possible.

84. Gallwey, 'The Silver King', pp. 2211–12.

85. Bean, *Official History*, Vol. IV, *The AIF in France 1917*, p. 639.

86. AWM38 3DRL 606/160, Bean Notebook.

87. Gallwey, 'The Silver King', p. 2236.

88. Bean, *Official History*, Vol. IV, *The AIF in France 1917*, p. 630.

89. AWM4 23/54/12, 37th Battalion AIF War Diary.

90. Biggs, *Reminiscences*, NS 2861, State Library of Tasmania, p. 137.

91. AWM4 23/64/13, 47th Battalion AIF War Diary.

92. R.R. Freeman, *Hurcombe's Hungry Half Hundred: A Memorial History of the 50th Battalion A.I.F. 1916-1919*, Peacock Publications, Norwood, 1991, p. 111.

93. Bean, *Official History*, Vol. IV, *The AIF in France 1917*, p. 640.

94. AWM4 23/54/12, 37th Battalion AIF War Diary.

95. The history of the 37th Battalion suggests that Story communicated the orders for the 40th to withdraw along with his own battalion (see N.G. McNicol, *History of the Thirty-Seventh Battalion AIF*, Modern Printing Co., Brisbane, 1936, pp. 103–04), but the 40th Battalion diary and eyewitness accounts confirm that no orders were received by D Company of the 40th.

96. Biggs, *Reminiscences*, NS 2861, State Library of Tasmania, p. 137.

97. Ibid.

98. Bean, *Official History*, Vol. IV, *The AIF in France 1917*, p. 641.

99. IWM Documents 12244, Lieutenant Thomas McKenny Hughes. Biggs, *Reminiscences*, NS 2861 State Library of Tasmania, p. 137.

100. 100 Ibid.

Chapter 6

1. AWM4 1/32/16 Part 1, II Anzac Corps War Diary.

2. Ibid.

Endnotes

3. Certainly, as German records suggest, there were no organised counter-attacks on any major scale since the defeat of the one effort prior to the launch of II Anzac's afternoon attack. It is likely that these were local attempts to defend the Oosttaverne Line or push through to relieve or reinforce troops in pillboxes or, in the case of the 47th Battalion (described by Gallwey), to push back troops who had penetrated the Green Line.

4. AWM4 1/32/16 Part 1, II Anzac Corps War Diary.

5. AWM4 23/12/16, 12th Brigade AIF War Diary.

6. 1DRL/0428 Red Cross Files: Captain John Millar. Witness statement by Lieutenant Clifford Mendoza, 47th Battalion.

7. AWM 38 3DRL 606/81/2, Bean Notebook.

8. AWM 26 201/22, 4th Division General Staff Operations file (Messines).

9. AWM PR00511 Sergeant Joseph Trotman, 49th Battalion, letter.

10. AWM 26 190/5 Operations file: 25th Division, General Staff, 7 to 12 June 1917.

11. MS 10802 State Library of Victoria, Major Consett Carre Riddell, 12th Field Company of Engineers.

12. Gallwey, 'The Silver King', pp. 2215–16.

13. Bean, *Official History*, Vol. IV, *The AIF in France 1917*, p. 631.

14. Major J.E. Lee, DSO, MC, *The Chronicle of the 45th Battalion AIF*, Mortons, Sydney, 1919, pp. 46–47.

15. IWM Documents15777, Lieutenant Clifford Mendoza, 47th Battalion AIF Message Book.

16. Bean, *Official History*, Vol. IV, *The AIF in France 1917*, p. 643.

17. AWM 26 201/22, 4th Division General Staff Operations file (Messines). The message was timed at 1910 (7.10 pm).

18. Brown was awarded the first of his two Distinguished Conduct Medals (DCM) for his actions at Messines.

19. Bainbrigge was awarded the Military Medal (MM) for his actions. He also received the DCM while serving with the 46th Battalion at Bellenglise.

20. In the 47th Battalion, for example, Corporal William Dickson took over his platoon and kept it in the line throughout the rest of the battle, and was later awarded the DCM for his actions. Likewise, Corporal Oliver Jones took command of B Company at one point, and during 'that time he gained his objective, capturing 30 prisoners as a result'. Jones was also awarded the DCM.

21. 1DRL/0428, Captain J. Millar, Red Cross File 1770406.

22. AWM 28/1/204P1/0063: Captain N.F. Bremner. Bremner received the DSO for his actions at Messines.

23. AWM26 190/24 New Zealand Division Headquarters and Branches.

24. AWM PR00524 Lieutenant Percy Nimmo, 48th Battalion.

25. The 48th's diary does not mention the aborted attack at 3.00 am, but records the battalion moving forward at 5.30 am.

26. AWM 4 23/64/13, 47th Battalion War Diary Operation Report (Messines).

27. Mitchell, *Backs to the Wall*.

28. AWM4 1/32/16 Part 1, 4th Division AIF War Diary.

29. The 44th was temporarily with the 10th Brigade and allocated as reserve for just such a purpose.

30. AWM4 23/54/12, 37th Battalion AIF War Diary.

31. AWM4 23/6/1/9, 44th Battalion AIF War Diary.

32. AWM4 1/46/8 Part 1, 3rd Division AIF War Diary. The timing is almost certainly incorrect.

33. AWM4 23/54/12, 37th Battalion AIF War Diary.

34. Bean, *Official History*, Vol. IV, *The AIF in France 1917*, p. 654.

35. WO 158/300 Second Army Headquarters, letters.

36. Bean, *Official History*, Vol. IV, *The AIF in France 1917*, pp. 656–57.

37. AWM4 1/13/13 Second Army War Diary.

38. AWM4 23/69/15, 52nd Battalion War Diary.

39. AWM 4 23/64/13, 47th Battalion War Diary Operation Report (Messines).

40. Gallwey, 'The Silver King', p. 2238.

41. Ibid.

42. AWM 30/B10.1, prisoner of war statement: Private I. Beckman.

43. The *Official History* is the source of the claim that the 37th received orders to move forward again (Bean, *Official History*, Vol. IV, *The AIF in France 1917*, p. 649n), but no such order exists in divisional, brigade or battalion diaries and the 37th's report claims its request to return was ignored. The situation is not helped by the 3rd Division offering two versions of events — one in the divisional diary recording the narrative of the 37th (and all other battalions) and an entirely different version in the battalion war diary. The 3rd Division version makes the quite erroneous claim that 'About 3.30 a.m. (June 8th) the 44th Battalion came up to their [the 37th] relief, found them not established on the Green Line, and on completing the relief had no difficulty in making an advanced line which ran from Septieme Barn to the Messines Road about 200 yards North of the Douve Bridge.' AWM4 1/46/8 Part 1, 3rd Division AIF War Diary.

44. Bean, *Official History*, Vol. IV, *The AIF in France 1917*, p. 653.

45. AWM4 23/61/9, 44th Battalion AIF War Diary.

46. AWM26 190/24, New Zealand Division Headquarters and Branches.

47. 3DRL2316, Monash Papers.

48. AWM26 190/24, New Zealand Division Headquarters and Branches.

49. 3DRL 2316/49, Monash Papers.

50. Ibid.

51. Bean, *Official History*, Vol. IV, *The AIF in France 1917*, p. 658n.

52. Ibid., p. 659n.

53. AMM4 23/66/13, 49th Battalion War Diary.

54. Edmonds, when reviewing Bean's draft for his Messines chapter, checked with the commanding officer and others in the 33rd Brigade, none of whom could confirm that such a meeting took place. If Bean's version is correct, the 33rd was unsure of its actual position and doubtful that the 13th Brigade occupied it. The 25th Division staff were certainly aware that the 13th Brigade was too far north, so it is highly unlikely that the 33rd Brigade's officers were unsure of the location of their front lines.

55. WO 95/2249, 75th Brigade War Diary.

56. AWM4 23/66/13, 49th Battalion War Diary.

57. WO 95/2249, 75th Brigade War Diary.

58. Ibid.

59. Ibid.

60. Bean, *Official History*, Vol. IV, *The AIF in France 1917*, p. 662n. Curiously, Bean included this story even though a thorough search of the relevant records in England including courts martial documents found nothing to substantiate it.

61. AWM4 1/32/16 Part 1, General Staff, Headquarters II Anzac Corps.

62. AWM4 23/13/17, 13th Brigade War Diary.

Chapter 7

1. AWM4 23/68/4, 51st Battalion War Diary.

2. Bean was aware of the Australian view that many of the 25th Division men were 'jumpy'. Edmonds would contest this point with some determination in his post-war correspondence with the 33rd's officers, none of whom confirmed the least hint of it. Bean made only passing reference to this in the *Official History* (Vol. IV, p. 662), although there is little doubt he considered it a significant factor. The 52nd Battalion, which bore the brunt of the shelling, recorded in its diary that 'the troops in the rear were so jumpy that their steadiness was absolutely shaken'. AWM4 23/69/15, 52nd Battalion War Diary.

3. AWM4 23/54/12, 37th Battalion War Diary.

4. Ibid.

5. AWM4 1/46/8 Part 1, General Staff, Headquarters 3rd Australian Division.

6. AWM92 3DRL 2632/29 Morshead Papers: Messines (April–July).

7. AWM4 1/46/8 Part 1, 3rd Division General Staff, Headquarters.

8. Ibid.

9. Ibid.

10. Lieutenant W.G. Fisher, diary, 12/6/17 in AWM38 3DRL606/81/1, Bean Notebook.

11. AWM4 1/46/8 Part 1, 3rd Division General Staff, Headquarters.

12. The 12th Brigade diary would put the distance at 1500 yards.

13. AWM4 23/67/12, 50th Battalion War Diary.

14. Freeman, *Hurcombe's Hungry Half Hundred*, p. 108.

15. Bean, *Official History*, Vol. IV, *The AIF in France 1917*, pp. 670–71.

16. Tank Museum (Bovington) Archives E2006.1792, 2nd Brigade, 'Summary of Operations with Second Army on June 7th 1917'.

17. AWM 4 23/65/27, 48th Battalion War Diary.

18. Tank Museum (Bovington) Archives E2006.1792, 2nd Brigade, 'Summary of Operations with Second Army on June 7th 1917'.

19. AWM4 23/10/8, 10th Brigade AIF War Diary.

20. Later Major General Allen commanding the 7th Australian Division during the Second World War.

21. AWM38 3DRL606/81/1, Bean Notebook.

22. AWM4 23/67/12, 50th Battalion War Diary.

23. 1DRL/0428 Red Cross File, Lieutenant Clyde Pearce, 52nd Battalion.

24. AWM4 23/67/12, 50th Battalion War Diary.

25. AWM4 23/12/16, 12th Brigade War Diary.

26. Ibid.

27. Bean, *Official History*, Vol. IV, *The AIF in France 1917*, p. 673. Bean was moved to write of McIntyre's response to the order 'knowing this was his death warrant'.

28. AWM4 23/12/16, 12th Brigade War Diary.

29. Bean, *Official History*, Vol. IV, *The AIF in France 1917*, p. 673.

30. 3DRL606/88/1, Bean Notebook.

31. Bean, *Official History*, Vol. IV, *The AIF in France 1917*, pp. 673–74.

32. 2 DRL/0789, Diary of Private George Davies, 36th Battalion.

33. AWM423/53/8, 36th Battalion War Diary.

34. AWM4 1/46/8 Part 1, 3rd Division General Staff, Headquarters.

35. AWM 224 MSS143A Part 11, Newton Wanliss Papers (14th Battalion History).

36. AWM38 3DRL 606/161/1, Bean Notebook.

37. AWM27 111/16, II Anzac Mounted Regiment.

38. Ibid.

39. Lieutenant Christian Nommensen, letter, August, 1917.

40. WO 95/2224, 25th Division War Diary.

41. Ibid.

42. Lieutenant Christian Nommensen, letter, August, 1917.

43. 3DRL/0428 Red Cross Files: Sergeant Alfred Stevenson, statement by Private James Bowers.

Chapter 8

1. AWM45 33/1 GHQ/BEF - Correspondence Messines-Ypres.

2. WO 256/19 Haig Diary.

3. Ibid.

4. Guinness in Bond (ed.), *Staff Officer*, p. 157.

5. WO95/2245/2, 74th Brigade War Diary.

6. Geoffrey Powell, *Plumer: The Soldiers' General*, Leo Cooper, London, 1990, p. 192.

7. AWM26 192/20 'Message from 2nd ANZAC Corps to Brigadier-General (commanding) Heavy Artillery'.

8. General Staff, *Preliminary Notes on Recent Operations on the Front of the Second Army. July 1917*, p. 1.

9. Ibid.

10. Ibid., p. 5.

11. AWM 25 213/1/19, Second Army Conference.

12. WO 158/415, IX Corps Report on the Battle.

13. Ibid.

14. Ibid.

15. Ibid.

16. LHMA (Kings College): 15/2/56 1927-1967 Interrogation of a British Officer captured on 31.7.17. Letter: Dr Ernst Gottsacker to Basil Liddell Hart 15.1.62.

Endnotes

17.   NAA B2455, Service Record, Lieutenant Colonel W.J. Smith.

18.   Ibid.

19.   Geoffrey Serle, *John Monash: A Biography*, Melbourne University Press, 2002, p. 292.

20.   NAA B2455, Service Record, Lieutenant Colonel W.J. Smith.

21.   3DRL/2316 Monash Personal Files, Book 15 10/6/17-31/7/17.

22.   Ibid.

23.   For example, the 4th Division staff (under Cox) were curiously reluctant to address the serious issue of Lieutenant Colonel Raymond Leane's flagrant disobedience at Pozières. Brigadier General Duncan Glasfurd confronted Leane at the time, but was killed shortly after at Flers before he could bring the matter to a head. Leane continued to feel free to disobey orders under his new brigadier, Robertson, who allowed him to do as he pleased and it would be early 1918 before Leane was tackled by Gellibrand, sparking a nasty and prolonged power struggle between them. The most generous assessment of the 4th Division's approach to command was that it showed a willingness to devolve decisions to front-line commanders which, in Leane's case at Pozières may have been wise, but it was a policy fraught with risk. The fact that there were no inquiries into the many problems at Messines suggests the culture of trusting the commander on the spot without later inquiry into actions which departed from direct orders was an entrenched and dangerous one.

24.   Bean, *Official History*, Vol. IV, *The AIF in France 1917*, p. 673.

25.   Ibid.

26.   AWM4 23/62/16, 45th Battalion War Diary.

27.   'A great crowd of men were now on the crest and summit of the Ridge. In estimating the density of the allotted frontages, casualties had been calculated at 50 per cent. of the leading brigades for the capture of the first intermediate objective, and about 60 per cent. of the troops engaged to reach the first objective, east of Messines and Wytschaete. The actual casualties had only been a fraction of these figures, and as the unforeseen congestion was neither appreciated nor corrected, casualties began to mount rapidly.' Such appreciations may well have been made (although no mention of it can be found in the Second Army or II Anzac records), but this situation only existed for the day and early evening of 7 June when the German artillery retaliation was weak, poorly directed and sporadic.

28.   Letter, Russell to Allen 17.6.17, Allen Papers, Archives New Zealand, quoted in Pugsley, *The Anzac Experience*, p. 226.

29.   Although much of that greater volume was due to the fact that the 3rd, preparing for the battle for months, had far more time to plan than the 4th Division, a simple comparison of the volume of staff work for May, when both divisions were preparing their final plans, still shows he marked superiority of the 3rd Division's preparations.

30.   Bean, *Official History*, Vol. IV, *The AIF in France 1917*, p. 284.

31.   AWM 38 3DRL 7953/34 Bean Papers.

32.   Ibid.

33.   Ibid. No account of the 6th Lincolns' role in the Battle of Messines was included in the unit's battalion diary, nor was it included in the battalion history (by G.F. Spring). The account in *The History of the Lincolnshire Regiment* by C.R. Simpson which fails to mention any late arrival or mix-up with the 52nd Battalion is based on Clay's diary and is completely inaccurate.

34.   WO158/415, IX Corps.

35. AWM38 3DRL 606/8/1/1, Bean Notebook.

36. AWM4 23/13/17, 13th Brigade War Diary. The diary of the 52nd Battalion (AWM4 23/69/15) is inexplicably vague on this crucial point, merely stating that the two battalions 'lost touch during the advance' as a result of the non-appearance of the English, and then falsely claiming the gap 'was filled by C Company' when the objective was reached. Nowhere in the war diaries is there any explanation or justification, let alone praise, for Maxwell's actions. However he would later be awarded the DSO for this action.

37. AWM38 3DRL 606/272/1 Bean Papers.

38. Ibid.

39. Ibid.

40. NL MS 1884/1/B/491 Monash Papers.

41. Ibid.

42. 3DRL 2233, letter, Godley to Pearce 8/7/17.

43. Bean's account of Holmes' death in the *Official History* placed the White Gates where Holmes was hit 'behind Hill 63' (Vol. IV pp. 712–13) when in fact it was on the north-western slope of Hill 63, with a clear view across to Messines just two kilometres distant. On 26 July when Holmes was killed, the German gun line was between six and 10 kilometres due east of the White Gates which was well within range. The much steeper southern slope which was the 'rear' of Hill 63 was almost completely shielded from German artillery.

44. AWM38 3DRL 606/8/1/1, Bean Notebook.

45. NL MS 1884/1/14/122 Monash Papers. Locke's French phrase translates as: 'The King is dead, long live the King!'

46. Serle, *John Monash: A Biography*, p. 284.

47. Letter, Godley to Wigram, Godley Papers, Liddell Hart Military Archives 1/5-29, 1915–1918.

48. Ibid.

49. Letter, Wigram to Godley, Godley Papers, Liddell Hart Military Archives 1/5-29, 1915–1918.

50. 3DRL 606/81/1, Bean Notebook.

51. 3DRL 2233 letter, Godley to Pearce 15/6/17.

52. Ibid.

53. WO95/2224, 25th Division War Diary.

54. NL MS 1884/1/B/491, Monash Papers.

55. MS 11651 State Library of Victoria, Private E.T. Popping, 38th Battalion, letter.

56. AWM38 3DRL 606/8/1/1, Bean Notebook, June 1917.

57. AWM 38 3DRL 606/248/2, Bean Notebook.

58. Ibid.

59. AWM38 3DRL 606/8/1/1, Bean Notebook, June 1917.

60. Ibid.

61. Biggs, *Reminiscences*, NS 2861 State Library of Tasmania, p. 188.

62. Ibid.

63. AWM 38 3DRL 606/248/2, Bean Notebook.

Endnotes

Chapter 9

1. IWM Documents 15204, Papers of Lieutenant Colonel L.E.S. Ward, DSO.
2. See Bean, *Official History*, Vol. IV, *The AIF in France 1917*, p. 695.
3. One gun to every six yards of front as opposed to 1:7 at Messines.
4. AWM38 3DRL 7953/34 Part 1, Bean Papers.
5. Frank Fox, *The Battle of the Ridges*, C. Arthur Pearson, London, 1918, p. 100.
6. *The Adelaide Mail*, Saturday 9 June 1917.
7. IWM Documents 12244, Lieutenant Thomas McKenny Hughes.
8. *The Rockhampton Morning Bulletin*, Wednesday 13 June 1917.
9. AWM26 185/2 General Headquarters General Staff, Battle of Messines, 7–12 June 1917.
10. Ibid.
11. Ibid.
12. Ibid.
13. The vast inflation of the German figure for those killed by the mine explosions is a surprisingly resilient fiction. It possibly arises from a simple multiplication of the known figure of German soldiers killed in the Hill 60 explosions (almost 700) by the number of mine explosions. British intelligence was aware that most of the German troops were outside the lethal range of the mine explosions (except at Hill 60) and the fact was widely reported by the newspapers of the day. It was also recorded in the Official Histories.
14. AWM45 27/7-27/18 History of the *204th Division*.
15. Ibid.
16. Ibid.
17. 3DRL/2316 Monash Papers, Series 1.
18. Serle, *John Monash: A Biography*, p. 292.
19. Gallwey, 'The Silver King', p. 2358.
20. AWM38 3DRL 7953/34 Part 1, Bean Papers.
21. AWM38 3DRL 7953/34 Part 2, Bean Papers.
22. Ibid.
23. AWM38 3DRL 606/272/1, Bean Notebook.
24. Bean, *Official History*, Vol. IV, *The AIF in France 1917*, p. 624.
25. IWM Documents 15777, Lieutenant Clifford Mendoza, 47th Battalion AIF Message Book.
26. WO 256/19 Haig Diary.
27. A complaint was forwarded in February of 1918 to the British Foreign Office which had come via the Netherlands Foreign Minister in Berlin and then on to The Hague. Ernst Kreddig, then a prisoner at Blandford prisoner-of-war camp in Dorset, wrote of the death of his friend Karl Hasselmann at Messines. The two had joined up together in 1915, and had the misfortune to be in the front line when the British attacked on 7 June. Emerging from their dugout to surrender, Hasselmann was struck by grenade splinters on the right hip and arm and fell to the ground, rolling from side to side in agony. 'I was about to bind his wounds when we were taken prisoners', Kreddig's statement read. 'I was led away but Hasselmann who could not walk was shot by the British. His death was instantaneous.' When questioned by his gaolers at Blandford, Kreddig reversed his story. '[Hasselmann] was shot during the fighting. I did not see him die. I remember Deckoffizier Paul Schmidt

asking me to make a statement about Hasselmann's death. I did not tell Schmidt that I was going to bind up Hasselmann's wounds or that I bound them up. I told Schmidt that the British shot Hasselmann, but that was in the fight.' The sad postscript to Kreddig's quest for justice on behalf of his friend was a statement unlikely to represent his true belief. 'It was quite fair in my opinion.'

28. IWM Documents 166044, letter from an unknown soldier re the Battle of Messines.
29. FO 383/439 Prisoners of War and Aliens Department.
30. Ibid.
31. Ibid.
32. AWM38 3DRL 7953/34 Part 2.
33. IWM Documents 12244 Lieutenant Thomas McKenny Hughes.
34. AWM38 3DRL 7953/34 Part 2, Bean Papers.
35. AWM38 3DRL 7953/34 Part 1, Bean Papers.
36. McNicol, *The History of the Thirty-Seventh Battalion A.I.F.*, p. 104.
37. Story's letter was described by Bean as 'foolishly drawn'. Bean, *Official History*, Vol. VI, *The AIF in France 1918*, p. 938.
38. AWM38 3DRL 606/248/1, Bean Notebook.
39. Bean, *Official History*, Vol. II, *The Story of Anzac*, p. 633.
40. Ibid.

Epilogue

1. R.H. Haigh and P.W. Turner (eds.), *The Long Carry: The War Diary of Stretcher Bearer Frank Dunham 1916-18*, Pergamon Press, Sheffield, 1970.
2. AWM38 3DRL 7953/34 Part 1, Bean Papers.
3. Ibid.
4. Ibid.
5. Institution Royale de Messines, *Royal Institution of Messines Near Ypres for the Daughters of Belgian Officers and Non Commissioned Officers who have Died or Become Disabled in the Service of their Country*, Imprimerie Militaire Berger-Levrault, Paris-Nancy, 1918, p. 3.
6. Pierre Nothomb, *La Belgique en France. Les Refugies et Les Heros*, Bergen-Levrault, Paris, 1917; *Royal Institution of Messines*, p. 5.
7. *Royal Institution of Messines*, pp. 29–33.
8. Ibid., pp. 35–38.
9. See http://www.peacevillage.be/en/news/10-years-peace-village
10. Tom Burke, *The 16th (Irish) and 36th (Ulster) Divisions at the Battle of Wijtschate – Messines Ridge, 7 June 1917*, The Royal Dublin Fusiliers Association, Dublin, 2007, p. 263.
11. Andrews, *The Anzac Illusion*, p. 41.
12. Gallwey, 'The Silver King', pp. 2262–63.
13. 1DRL/0428 Red Cross File 2400703, Lieutenant Dudley Salmon, Statement by Sergeant George Thomas, 47th Battalion.

Appendix 1

1. Peckham 2 was lost to a collapsed gallery and an inrush of Kemmel sands.

Endnotes

2. Kruisstraat 1 and 2 were in separate chambers but are often counted together as they shared the main gallery.
3. La Petit Douve Farm was abandoned in 1916 when the Germans blew a camouflet and found the gallery.
4. The Birdcage mines were not blown for tactical reasons as the Germans had withdrawn from the area.
5. Birdcage 3 was detonated by a lightning strike in 1955.

Apendix 3
1. Source: WO 157/114.

Bibliography

Australian War Memorial Records, Canberra
AWM 4   Unit War Diaries
AWM 8   Unit Embarkation Rolls
AWM 15   Central Registry Files
AWM 16   Australian War Records Section Registry Files
AWM 21   Records of the Assistant Provost Marshal
AWM 25   Written Records 1914-1918
AWM 26   Operations Files
AWM 27   Operations Files
AWM 28   Honours and Awards
AWM 29   Casualty Lists
AWM 30   Prisoner of War Statements
AWM 38   Bean Papers
AWM 41   Official Medical History
AWM 45   Copies of British War Diaries and Other Records, 1914-18 War
AWM 92   Private Records
AWM 93   Australian War Memorial Registry Files
AWM 133   Nominal Roll of Australian Imperial Force
AWM 224   Unit Manuscript Histories
AWM 252   AWM Library Subject Classification, 1914-18 War,
AWM 255   Written Records, 1914-18 War, Second Series
1DRL/0428   Australian Red Cross Society Wounded and Missing Enquiry
               Bureau Files 1914-1918

National Archives of Australia Records, Canberra
B2455   First Australian Imperial Force Personnel Dossiers

National Library of Australia
MS1884   Monash Papers
Series 1 General Correspondence: A (Letters Received), 1879-1931
Series 1 General Correspondence: B (Outward Letters) General Copies of Outward
Letters, 1908 - 31
Series 4 Correspondence: World War I, 1915-20
Series 5 Diaries and Notebooks

Bibliography

Private Papers, Australian War Memorial, Canberra

3DRL/2422	Aitken
MSS1113	Appleton
PR00261	Barton
PR01907	Bishop
MSS1360	Brown
PR83/192	Buchanan
PR0304	Burrow
MSS0651	Colliver (et al.)
2DRL/0789	Davies
PR01020	Etherton
MSS1355	Gallwey (manuscript, 'The Silver King', three volumes)
2DRL/0785	Gallwey
PR 85/310	Gallwey
3DRL/2379	Goddard
2DRL/0260	Grieve
PR02060	Hickman
3DRL/2562 (A)	Imlay
PR90/154	Joel
1DRL/0389	Jones
PR89/063	Jungwirth
1DRL/0407	Lane
PR0092	MacIntosh
PR00229	McCaskill
2DRL/0928	Mitchell
MS108	Morse
3DRL 2632/29	Morshead
PR00524	Nimmo
PR01610	Ryan/Hood
3DRL/3835(A)	Sanders
PR88/024	Sennet
2DRL/0309	Smith
PR00511	Trotman
PR00946	Warner
MSS0717	Woodward

Private Papers, Tasmanian State Archives, Hobart

NS 2861/1/1	Biggs, Reginald

NS 1028   Meagher, Richard

Private Papers, State Library of Victoria, Melbourne
MS 11651   Poppins, Ernest T.
MS 9642   Kook, Thorvald E.
MS 10802   Riddell, Consett C.
PA 96/76   Fairey, Eric
MS TMS 155/156   King, John E.

Private Papers, State Library of New South Wales, Sydney
MLDOC 2413   Fuljames, Harris J.

National Archives of United Kingdom, Kew
AIR 1/676/2   Flying Corps
CAB 45   British Army Operations in the First World War
CAB 24   Cabinet and its Committees
FO 383/439   Prisoners of War and Aliens Department
WO 95   Unit War Diaries
WO 158   British Army Operations in the First World War
WO 153   Military Maps of the First World War
WO 157   Intelligence and Security
WO 316:   War of 1914-1918: Western Front: Photographs
WO 157   Intelligence

Imperial War Museum Records, London
EPH 1219   Preliminary Notes on Recent Operations on the Front of the Second Army.
EPH 236   The Experience Gained During the English-French Offensive in the Spring of 1917.
EPH 1191   Weekly Intelligence Summary of the Fourth German Army (12–18 July 1917)
EPH 1344   Notes on the use of Tanks and on the general principles of their employment as an adjunct to the infantry attack issued with special reference to the "Mark IV", 1917.
EPH 1164   Notes on dealing with hostile machine guns in an advance.

Bibliography

Imperial War Museum, London: Documents

12281	Brigadier T.S. Louch, MC
16044	Letter from an unknown soldier re Messines
8315	Short History of No. 6 Squadron RFC/RAF, 1914–1919
9462	Special Order of the Day, Lieutenant General Alexander Godley, June 1917
7228	Captain O.H. Woodward, CMG, MC and two bars
3521	Lieutenant Colonel Sir J. Norton Griffiths, KCB, DSO
15777	M. Hurford-Jones (Clifford Mendoza diary)
927	Major R.J. Blackadder, MC
15204	Lieutenant Colonel L.E.S. Ward, DSO, CMG
5	J. Colinsky (RFC radio operator)
2496	I.L. Bawtree
10805	Captain E.G.F. Boon, MC, FRIC
11247	Lieutenant Colonel J.B. Parks, MC
10897	H.A. Coulter
532	E. Tickle
16815	W. Howells
11666	J.M. Prower, DSO
2540	Major C.J. Saunders, MC
3387	Major R.P. Schweder, MC
3471	Lieutenant Colonel G.A. Cardew, CMG, DSO
503	L.A. Briggs
16812	W.R. Robson
11817	F.F.S. Smithwick
18453	A.R.R. Slack
16982	Captain T.C. Eckenstein, MC
2529	Miss W.M. Barnard
12244	Lieutenant T.M. Hughes

Kings College: Liddell Hart Centre for Military Archives

Godley	1/5-29 1915-1918
Godley	3/198-233 1901-1927
Liddell Hart	15/2/56 1927-1967
Montgomery-Massingberd	7/35 1917 Jun-1917 Oct
Robertson	8/1/14 1916 Mar 18

Robertson   8/5/72 1917 Aug 25
Robertson   7/6/32 1916 Apr 28

Private Papers — Other
Akers   Diary
Franks, Lieutenant Len   Memoirs
Imlay, Lieutenant Colonel Alexander   Diary
Lineham, Sergeant Claude   Letters
Nommensen, Lieutenant Christian Valentine   Letters

Books and Articles

34th Battalion A.I.F. Association, *Short History of the 34th Battalion*, Illawarra Press, Carlton, 1957.

Andrews, Eric, *The Anzac Illusion*, Cambridge University Press, Cambridge, 1993.

Asprey, Robert B., *War The German High Command at War: Hindenburg and Ludendorff Conduct World War 1*, William Morrow and Company Inc., New York, 1991.

Austin, William, *The Official History of the New Zealand Rifle Brigade*, L.T. Watkins Ltd., Wellington, 1924.

Australian Commonwealth Military Forces, *The Forty-first (Compiled by Members of the Intelligence Staff)*, n.p., 1919.

Barrie, Alexander, *War Underground: The Tunnellers of the Great War*, Tom Donovan, London, 1961.

Barton, P., Doyle, P. and Vandewalle, J., *Beneath Flanders Fields; The Tunnellers' War of 1914-18*, Spellmount, Staplehurst, 2004.

Bean, C.E.W., *Official History of Australia in the War of 1914-18*, Vol. II, *The Story of ANZAC*, Angus & Robertson, Sydney, 1941.

——, *Official History of Australia in the War of 1914-18*, Vol. III, *The AIF in France 1916*, Angus & Robertson, Sydney, 1941.

——, *Official History of Australia in the Great War of 1914-1918*, Vol. IV, *The AIF in France, 1917*, Angus & Robertson, Sydney, 1941.

Bond, Brian and Robbins, Simon (eds.), *Staff Officer: The Diaries of Lord Moyne, 1914-1918*, Leo Cooper, London, 1987.

Bourne, John and Sheffield, Gary (eds.), *Douglas Haig: War Diaries and Letters 1914-1918*, Weidenfeld & Nicolson, London, 2005.

Bourne, J. M., *Who's Who in World War One*, Routledge, London, 2001.

Brahms, Vivian, *Spirit of the Forty-Second. Narrative of the 42nd Battalion, 11th*

Bibliography

Infantry Brigade 3ʳᵈ Division, AIF 1914-18, W.R. Smith & Paterson Pty. Ltd., Brisbane, 1938.

Brereton, Captain, *Under Haig in Flanders*, Blackie and Sons, London, 1917.

Brice, Beatrix, *The Battle Book of Ypres*, John Murray, London, 1927.

Brown, Malcolm, *The Imperial War Museum Book of the Western Front*, Sidgwick and Jackson, London, 1993.

Browning, Neville, *For King and Cobbers: The History of the 51ˢᵗ Battalion A.I.F. 1916-1919*, Advance Press, Bassendean, 2007.

Burke, Tom, *The 16ᵗʰ (Irish) and 36ᵗʰ (Ulster) Divisions at the Battle of Wijtschate – Messines Ridge, 7 June 1917*, The Royal Dublin Fusiliers Association, Dublin, 2007.

Burton, Ormond, *The Silent Division: New Zealanders at the Front 1914-1919*, Angus & Robertson, Sydney, 1935.

Butler, Arthur G., *The Australian Army Medical Services in the War 1914-1918*, Australian War Memorial, Canberra, 1940.

Cammaerts, Emile, *Messines and Other Poems*, John Lane, The Bodley Head, London, 1918.

Cave, Nigel, *Passchendaele*, Leo Cooper, Pen and Sword, London, 1993.

Colliver, Eustace James and Richardson, Brian Harold, *The Forty-Third: the story and official history of the 43ʳᵈ Battalion, A.I.F.*, Rigby, Adelaide, 1920.

Corrigan, Gordon, *Mud, Blood & Poppycock*, Cassell, London, 2003.

Cowan, James, *The Maoris in the Great War: A History of the New Zealand Native Contingent and Pioneer Battalion: Gallipoli, 1915, France and Flanders, 1916-18*, Whitcombe & Tombs [for] Maori Regimental Committee, Auckland, 1926.

Cox, William, *From Western Front to Changi Gaol: The Wars of Two Friends. An Account of the War Service of the Honourable William Ellis Cox CBE, MC and Dr. Eugine Augustine (Bon) Rogers*, Artemis Publishing Consultants, Hobart, 2009.

Cranston, Fred, *Always Faithful: The History of the 49ᵗʰ Battalion*, Boolarong Publications, Brisbane, 1983.

Crawford, J. and McGibbon, I. (eds.), *New Zealand's Great War: New Zealand, the Allies & The First World War*, Exisle Publishing, Auckland, 2007.

Deayton, Craig, *Battle Scarred: The 47th Battalion in the First World War*, Big Sky Publishing, Sydney, 2011.

De Groot, Gerald J., *Douglas Haig 1861 – 1928*, Unwin Hyman, London, 1988.

Devine, William, *The Story of a Battalion* (48th Battalion), Melville and Mullen, Melbourne, 1919.

Edgar, Peter, *To Villers-Bretonneux with Brigadier-General William Glasgow DSO and the 13th Australian Infantry Brigade*, Australian Military History Publications, Loftus, NSW, 2006.

Edmonds, Brigadier General Sir James E., *Official History of the War*, Vol. II, *Military Operations France and Belgium 1917*, His Majesty's Stationery Office, London, 1948.

Edwards, John, *Never a Backward Step: A History of the First 33rd Battalion, A.I.F.*, Bettong Books, Grafton, 1996.

Evans, Eric, *So Far From Home*, Kangaroo Press, Roseville, 2002.

Evans, Martin, *The Battles of the Somme*, Weidenfeld & Nicolson, London, 1996.

Fairey, Eric, *The 38th Battalion AIF*, Cambridge Press, Bendigo, 1920.

Farrar, Martin, *News from the Front: War Correspondents on the Western Front 1914-1918*, Sutton Publishing, Phoenix Mill, 1998.

Ferguson, David, *The History of the Canterbury Regiment N.Z.E.F. 1914-1919*, Whitcomb & Tombs, Auckland, 1921.

Fewster, Kevin (ed.), *Bean's Gallipoli: The Diaries of Australia's Official War Correspondent*, Allen & Unwin, Sydney, 1983.

Finlayson, Damien, *Crumps and Camouflets: Australian Tunnelling Companies on the Western Front*, Big Sky Publishing, Newport, 2010.

Fox, Frank, *The Battle of the Ridges*, C. Arthur Pearson, London, 1918.

Freeman, R.R., *Hurcombe's Hungry Half Hundred: A Memorial History of the 50th Battalion A.I.F. 1916-1919*, Peacock Publications, Norwood, 1991.

French, David, *The Strategy of the Lloyd-George Coalition*, Oxford University Press, Oxford, 1995.

Gal, R. and Dayan, H., *The Psychological Effects of Intense Artillery Bombardment: The Israeli Experience in the Yom-Kippur War (1973)*, The Israeli Institute For Military Studies, Ya'Akov, 1992.

Gliddon, G., *VCs of the First World War: Arras & Messines 1917*, Sutton Publishing, Phoenix Mill, 1998.

Green, Andrew, *Writing the Great War: Sir James Edmonds and the Official Histories, 1915-1948*, Frank Cass, London, 2003.

Green, Frank, *The Fortieth*, 40th Battalion Association, Hobart, 1922.

Grieve, W. Grant and Newman, B, *Tunnellers: The Story of the Tunnelling Companies, Royal Engineers, During the World War*, Herbert Jenkins Limited, London, 1936.

Grover, Ray, 'Godley, Alexander John', *Dictionary of New Zealand Biography*, Te Ara, the Encyclopaedia of New Zealand, updated 1 October 2013.

Bibliography

Haber, L.F., *The Poisonous Cloud: Chemical Warfare in the First World War*, Clarendon Press, Oxford, 1986.

Haigh, R.H. and Turner, P.W. (eds.), *The Battle of Messines Ridge 7th of June 1917: A view from the British Ranks*, Department of Political Studies, Sheffield City Polytechnic, Sheffield, 1985.

—— (eds.), *The Long Carry: The War Diary of Stretcher Bearer Frank Dunham 1916-18*, Pergamon Press, Sheffield, 1970.

Harington, General Sir Charles, *Plumer of Messines*, John Murray, London, 1935.

Harris, J.P., *Douglas Haig and the First World War*, Cambridge University Press, Cambridge, 2008.

Hellar, Major Charles, USAR, *Chemical Warfare in World War 1- The American Experience 1917-1918*, Leavenworth Papers No. 10, Combat Studies Institute US Command and General Staff College, Fort Leavenworth, Kansas, 1984.

Henshaw, Trevor, *The Sky Their Battlefield*, Grub Street, London, 1995.

Hogg, Ian, *Allied Artillery of World War One*, Crowood Press, Ramsbury, 1998.

Holmes, Richard, *The Western Front*, BBC Publishing, London, 1999.

Horner, David, *The Gunners: A History of Australian Artillery*, Allen & Unwin, St. Leonards, 1995.

Institution Royale de Messines, *Royal Institution of Messines Near Ypres for the Daughters of Belgian Officers and Non Commissioned Officers who have Died or Become Disabled in the Service of their Country*, Imprimerie Militaire Berger-Levrault, Paris-Nancy, 1918.

Kincaid-Smith, M., *The 25th Division in France and Flanders*, Harrison and Sons, London, 1918.

Lee, Major J.E., DSO, MC, *The Chronicle of the 45th Battalion AIF*, Mortons, Sydney, 1919.

Liddell Hart, Basil, *History of the First World War*, Pan, London, 1973.

Liddle, Peter (ed.), *Passchendaele in Perspective: The Third Battle of Ypres*, Leo Cooper, London, 1997.

Lloyd George, David, *War Memoirs of David Lloyd George*, Little, Brown and Company, Boston, 1933–37.

Longmore, C., *"Eggs-A-Cook": The Story of the Forty-Fourth*, The Colortype Press Limited, Perth, 1921.

Lynch, E.P.F., *Somme Mud*, Will Davies (ed.), Random House, Sydney, 2006.

Lytton, Neville, *The Press and the General Staff*, W. Collins & Son, London, 1920.

MacDougall, Tony (ed.), *War Letters of General Monash*, Duffy and Snellgrove, Sydney, 2002.

Mayor, Adrienne, *Greek Fire, Poison Arrows & Scorpion Bombs: Biological and Chemical Warfare in the Ancient World*, Overlook Duckworth, Woodstock, 2003.

McNicol, N.G., *History of the Thirty-Seventh Battalion AIF*, Modern Printing Co., Brisbane, 1936.

Meagher, Norman, *With the Fortieth* (letters and writings of Lieutenant Norman Meagher, published by his parents in his memory), Hobart, 1918.

Messenger, Charles, *Call to Arms: The British Army 1914-18*, Weidenfeld & Nicholson, London, 2005.

Mitchell, George Deane, *Backs to the Wall*, Allen & Unwin, Crows Nest, 2007.

Morrow, John, *The Great War in the Air: Military Aviation from 1909 to 1921*, Smithsonian Institute Press, Washington, 1993.

Nothomb, Pierre, *La Belgique en France. Les Refugies et Les Heros*, Bergen-Levrault, Paris, 1917.

Neillands Robin, *The Great War Generals on the Western Front 1914-1918*, Robinson, London, 1999.

Oldham, Peter, *Messines Ridge*, Leo Cooper, Barnsley, 2003.

Passingham, Ian, *Pillars of Fire*, Sutton, Phoenix Mill, 1998.

Paterson, A.T., *The Thirty-Ninth*, G.W. Green & Sons Pty. Ltd., Melbourne, 1934.

Pedersen, Peter, *Monash as Military Commander*, Melbourne University Press, Melbourne, 1985.

——, *The Anzacs*, Viking (Penguin), Camberwell, 2007.

——, *Anzacs on the Western Front*, John Wiley & Sons Australia, Milton, 2012.

Piggott, Michael, *A Guide to the Personal, Family and Official Papers on C.E.W. Bean*, Australian War Memorial, Canberra, 1983.

Polanski, Ian, *We Were The 46th: the history of the 46th Battalion in the Great War of 1914-1918*, self-published, Queensland, 1999.

Powell, Geoffrey, *Plumer: The Soldiers' General*, Leo Cooper, London, 1990.

Prior, Robin and Wilson, Trevor, *Passchendaele: The Untold Story*, Yale University Press, New Haven, 2002.

——, *Command on the Western Front*, Pen & Sword Military Classics, Barnsley, 2004.

Pugsley, Christopher, *The Anzac Experience: New Zealand, Australia and Empire in the First World War*, Reed Publishing, Auckland, 2004.

Bibliography

Reid, W., *Douglas Haig: Architect of Victory*, Birlinn, Edinburgh, 2006.

Royle, Stephen (ed.), *From Mons to Messines and beyond..., The Great War Experiences of Sgt. Charles Arnold*, K.A.F. Books, Studley, 1985.

Rule, Edgar, *Jacka's Mob*, Angus & Robertson, Sydney, 1933.

Serle, Geoffrey, 'Monash, Sir John (1865–1931)', *Australian Dictionary of Biography*, Vol. 10, Melbourne University Press, 1986.

——, *John Monash: A Biography*, Melbourne University Press, 2002.

Sheffield, Gary, *Forgotten Victory*, Headline Book Publishing, London, 2001.

Sheldon, Jack, *The German Army at Passchendaele*, Pen & Sword Military, Barnsley, 2007.

Smith, Alan H., *Do Unto Others: Counter Bombardment in Australia's Military Campaigns*, Big Sky Publishing, Newport, 2011.

Stacke, H.F., *The Worcestershire Regiment in the Great War*, Naval & Military Press Ltd., UK, 2002.

Stanley, Peter, *Bad Characters: Sex, Crime, Mutiny, Murder and the Australian Imperial Force*, Allen & Unwin, Sydney, 2010.

Steel, Nigel and Hart, Peter, *Passchendaele; The Sacrificial Ground*, Cassell & Co, London, 2000.

Stewart, Colonel H., *The New Zealand Division 1916-1919: A Popular History Based on Records*, New Zealand Government (Intype London), London, 1920.

Taylor, A.J.P., *The First World War*, Penguin, UK, 1963.

Terraine, John, *The Smoke and the Fire: Myths and Anti-Myths of War 1861-1945*, Sidgwick & Jackson, London, 1980.

Turner, Alexander, *Messines 1917: The Zenith of Siege Warfare*, Osprey Publishing Ltd., Oxford, 2010.

Walker, Jonathan, *The Blood Tub*, Spellmount, Staplehurst, 1998.

Wanliss, Newton, *The History of the Fourteenth Battalion A.I.F.: being the story of the vicissitudes of an Australian unit during the Great War*, The Arrow Printery, Melbourne, 1929.

Warner, Philip, *Passchendaele*, Pen & Sword Military Classics, Barnsley, 1987.

——, *Field Marshal Earl Haig*, The Bodley Head, London, 1991.

West, Andrew A., *Haig*, Potomac Books Ltd, Washington, 2005.

Williams, John, *Anzacs, The Media and The Great War*, University of New South Wales Press, Sydney, 1999.

Wombell, Paul, *Battle: Passchendaele 1917: evidence of war's reality*, Travelling Light, London, 1981.

Newspapers
The Argus
The Courier Mail
The Examiner
The Hobart Mercury
The Rockhampton Morning Bulletin
Der Kolnische Zeitung
Der Deutsche Tageszeitung
Scriber's Magazine

Index

Index

Index

Index

Index

Messines 1917